ROMANS

J. G. VOS

Crown & Covenant

PUBLICATIONS

Pittsburgh, Pa.

© 2013

Crown & Covenant Publications

7408 Penn Avenue, Pittsburgh, PA 15208

412-241-0436

www.crownandcovenant.com

ISBN: 978-1-884527-61-6

ePub: 978-1-884527-62-3

Kindle: 978-1-884527-63-0

Library of Congress Control Number: 2012942246

Printed in the United States of America
at McNaughton & Gunn, Inc., Michigan.

Originally published in the *Blue Banner Faith and Life,* April 1951–19;
republished July 1977–March 1979.

All Scripture quotations, unless otherwise noted, are taken from the King James Version.

Typesetting by Heidi Filbert. Special thanks to the publishing interns who worked on the copyediting of this book: Rebecca Delivuk Byers and Danielle Vance.

Table of Contents

Chapter 4: The Christian Life that Follows Justification

Chapter 5: The Calling of the Gentiles and the Rejection of the Jews

Chapter 6: Practical Duties of the Christian Life

Chapter 7: Paul's Missionary Work and Plans for Further Service

Chapter 8: Conclusion of the Epistle: Personal Greetings

THE "PEOPLE'S THEOLOGIAN"

Dr. J. G. Vos was a revered Bible teacher, Reformed theologian, pastor, and missionary. He taught at Geneva College from 1954 until his retirement in 1973 and continued part-time until about 1975. For most of those years he also served as chairman of the Bible department.

Though he died 23 years ago, among older folk on campus the merest mention of his name brings warm smiles, good memories, and some funny stories. To his students he was always "Dr. Vos." To his friends he was "Jack." Both forms are shorter and handier than his full given name, Johannes Geerhardus Vos. He usually signed it simply "J. G. Vos."

J. G. Vos devoted his life to teaching the Bible and classic Reformed theology for the sanctity of the church and the salvation of the lost. An astute thinker, he often disguised his natural brilliance with an equally natural penchant for folksy humor. A number of his published essays display the incisive clarity of his scholarship. Yet unlike his father, J. G. chose not to be a scholar's scholar. Instead, he saw himself as a "people's theologian."

In a time of cultural decline for Reformed Christianity in America, J. G. worked constantly to popularize the Bible's teachings and those of classic Reformed theology. He received ministerial ordination in the Reformed Presbyterian Church of North America in 1929. He was a tall and strong 26 years old; he would serve faithfully in the RP denomination for the rest of his mortal life.

Vos talked a plain-spoken talk, a bit folksy, rather like a more godly Harry Truman. His message was usually about the plain meaning of clear biblical texts for ordinary folk to learn, to master, to love, and to obey. When biblical texts seemed to allow different interpretations, he'd give a well-studied account of the textual reasons for the divergence, and perhaps state a plain-spoken preference. Often a corny joke was served up to punctuate the point.

Occasions of non-sequitur reasoning in class invariably produced one of J. G.'s favorites: the story of the inept parachutist who jumped to a conclusion.

On more than one occasion after asking him a question in class, I'd receive a packet in the mail of relevant photocopied articles or published pamphlets, or perhaps a whole book on the subject of my question. Some of my classmates had similar "package" experiences. More often than not, J. G. would turn out to be the author of the given material. Once a package from him contained the jacket I'd mistakenly left behind in class; the return address given was "Sherlock Holmes Detective Agency." I was hoping for another book.

The "Dr." of J. G.'s name was an honorary D.D., granted for distinguished service as a professor, writer, RPCNA pastor, and Manchurian missionary.

J. G. Vos was my first professor of Bible. When I met him in 1972, the autumn of my freshman year at Geneva, his face bore several longish scars. Only much later did I learn that these wounds were inflicted by soldiers of the Japanese invasion of Manchuria, where he was a missionary for 11 years. He married Marian Milligan in China in 1931, and three out of their four children were born there. J. G. was expelled from China by the Japanese in 1941.

One of J. G. Vos's important contributions to 20th Century

Christianity is the legacy of the Reformation Translation Fellowship, which he and Dr. Charles Chao founded. This organization still serves the Chinese church by translating, publishing, and distributing a sizeable body of works in classic Reformed theology, in pastoral ministry, and in the popular study of the Scriptures. Dr. J. G. Vos continued to serve and assist RTF's work during his professorship and retirement years.

Dr. Vos earned a B.A. in history from Princeton University, class of 1925, and in 1928 a Th.B. from Princeton Theological Seminary, where his father had taught since 1894. At Princeton J. G. was elected to Phi Beta Kappa, among the most prestigious academic honors available at that time or any time in North America. Even in his old age, J. G.'s necktie would oft be adorned with his Phi Beta Kappa key.

He also held a Th.M. from Westminster Theological Seminary, class of 1937. His published thesis was entitled, *The Scottish Covenanters*. The book remains an interesting and useful historical and doctrinal study of his adopted denomination's background. It is still available from the RPCNA's Crown & Covenant Publications in Pittsburgh, Pa., where many of his works are being reprinted and sold.

During a "communion Sabbath" weekend stay in Dr. and Mrs. Vos's home in 1974, I came upon him closing his quite tattered Greek New Testament. He was nearing the completion of his 29th reading of it in its entirety. By the end of his life he had read it 42 times. He knew much of it by memory, with grammatical and exegetical precision, even down to rare participial forms. Even among scholars, not many can claim such detailed knowledge.

And yet, he chose to be a "people's theologian."

After his expulsion from China, J. G. took up a stateside pastoral call in 1942 to the Reformed Presbyterian Church of Clay Center, Kan. Four years later, convinced of the enormous need for layman's-level biblical and theological education throughout the RP denomination, he started the journal entitled *Blue Banner Faith and Life*. Among the RPs of that time, he wrote, there was "a low level of awareness of true biblical Christianity....The church seemed confused, frustrated, and unable to go ahead with a constructive program of any kind." "I decided there needed to be a very vocal but simple publication to set forth the true faith of the church," he said in a dictated letter entitled "Important Notice" sent to friends and subscribers of the *Blue Banner Faith and Life* in 1979.

The instructive content of *Blue Banner* proved to be "very vocal but simple." But for Vos, each issue of *Blue Banner Faith and Life* required massive work. He served not only as author and editor, but often as publisher and circulation director. Vos wrote most of the articles and book reviews. The earliest issues were printed on what J. G. called "my rickety mimeograph," a "home-cranked machine." The Vos family collated the copies by hand, "marching around tables" in the Hebron Church basement. Often it was Vos himself who addressed and stamped the mail-order copies.

From small beginnings and a mere 50 subscribers in 1946, J. G. Vos's *Blue Banner* grew to a subscription list of about 1,275, half of them outside the United States. He never made any money from it, and often sent it for free to students, missionaries, and to anyone else who couldn't pay the modest fees. Late in the journal's history, my student subscription joined the list of free ones.

It was during those pastoral years in rural Clay Center (1942–1954) that J. G. was able to devote significant time to his other literary calling, bringing his father's unpublished work into the light of day. After World War II this task became urgent, because his father's health was now failing.

In 1948 his son's hard work made it possible for Geerhardus Vos to see the finished copies of his own *Biblical Theology: Old and New Testaments* (Eerdmans, 1948). Geerhardus Vos died in 1949.

J. G. Vos's *Blue Banner Faith and Life* was in part responsible for the revival of confessional Reformed theology within the RPCNA. The journal survived from its 1946 mimeographed founding in Clay Center, endured through Vos's entire tenure as a professor at Geneva College, and until the last few years of his mortal life. After a severe fall in 1979 that fractured his hip, Dr. Vos decided to discontinue the 33-year-old quarterly. His family, and especially his worried wife, Marian, greeted the decision with relief. The last issue of that year, October, closed out the *Blue Banner*.

J. G. himself lasted only a little longer. Now ensconced in a wheel-chair and in care of the staff at the Reformed Presbyterian Home for the Aged, he felt himself a burden. Frustrated by his all-too-evident failing health, he couldn't think of much useful to do. He often anguished over the unknown fate of his converts and colleagues in Manchuria. In visits he would tell me that he either wanted to go out "doing something," or to be taken right away.

The Lord took J. G. Vos on June 8, 1983, at age 80. His body was buried near his son Melvin (1940–71) in the Hebron Church Cemetery, Idana, Kan.

—*Dr. Byron Curtis, associate professor of biblical studies,*
Geneva College

This article originally appeared in The Presbyterian Banner *(Australia) in August 2001.*

Chapter 1

INTRODUCTION TO THE EPISTLE

Doctrine and Practice

Lesson 1

    1) Doctrinal Section. Chapters 1–11.

    2) Practical Section. Chapters 12–16.

We can accept this division of the book for the sake of convenience. But we should realize that the doctrinal section is really very practical, and the practical section is really quite doctrinal. Perhaps a better way of division would be to say that the whole epistle is both doctrinal and practical, but that chapters 1–11 deal with the doctrine and practice of the way of salvation, while chapters 12–16 deal with the doctrine and practice of the Christian life.

We may take as the theme of the first 11 chapters "The Gospel Way of Salvation." In discussing this theme, the apostle Paul first takes up the need for salvation in chapters 1, 2, and the first 20 verses of chapter 3. The first 17 verses of chapter 1 are an introduction to the epistle. The rest of chapter 1, beginning with verse 18, sets forth the truth that humanity is hopelessly lost in sin and guilty before God. This is for

Romans 1:1–17

the purpose of laying the groundwork for his treatment of the way of salvation. We shall first consider the apostle's introduction and then see what he says about the need for salvation.

Paul Introduces Himself and His Message. 1:1–17

Paul's Epistle to the Romans was written about the year 58 A.D. from Corinth in Greece. The apostle, at the time of writing this epistle, had never been in Rome. Thus he speaks in verses 10 and 13 of his desire to visit the church at Rome and of his repeated intention of doing so—an intention which was frustrated by circumstances over which he had no control.

Note what Paul calls himself. He uses three words to describe himself. The first is "servant" (1:1)—"a servant of Jesus Christ." The Greek word *doulos* means "bondservant" or "slave."

The second term is "apostle" (1:1)—"called to be an apostle." "Apostle" means an official, accredited messenger, someone who is commissioned and sent to do something. Paul was called to be an apostle when he was "separated unto the gospel of God"—he became a messenger of the gospel.

The third term is "debtor" (1:14)—"I am debtor both to the Greeks, and to the barbarians; both to the wise, and to the unwise." He was Christ's bondservant or slave, and a debtor to his fellowmen, a debtor because he owed them the gospel message with which the Lord had entrusted him.

So much for what Paul says by way of introducing himself to a church which had never heard him preach nor seen his face. Now let us see what Paul says about his message, which he calls briefly "the gospel of God."

First, this message is no novelty, no newfangled philosophy invented by men, for it was promised long before by the prophets in the Holy Scriptures, the books of the Old Testament (1:2). What Paul preached was simply the true fruit and development of what had already been set forth long before in the Old Testament Scriptures. This shows how wrong that popular modern notion is which asserts that the New Testament gospel is something radically new and essentially different from the message of the Old Testament. The essential message of the Old Testament is identical with that of the New, the great difference between the two being that the Old Testament looks forward to a promised and coming Redeemer, while the New Testament speaks of the Redeemer who has already come and wrought His great work of redemption.

In the second place, Paul's message was a message about Jesus Christ: "Concerning his Son Jesus Christ our Lord" (1:3). Paul was not preaching salvation by character, nor salvation by good works, nor salvation by culture and education. He was not trying to "appeal to people's better nature," nor to advocate salvation by "spiritual values" and "high ideals." There were plenty of people in his day who proclaimed that type of message, but Paul was not one of them. His message was not a way of self-salvation; it was a way of salvation *by a Savior*. It was a message *about Christ*, and he tells us so at the very beginning of his epistle.

Furthermore, there is not the slightest doubt as to what Christ it was that Paul proclaimed. He did not proclaim Jesus simply as a good man, or a great teacher, or a noble example, or a martyr for his principles. No, the Christ whom Paul preached was the *divine* Christ. He was human, too, for He was "made of the seed of David according to the flesh," but that was not all; that was only His human nature. In addition to His human nature, He had another nature, His divine nature, here referred to as "the Spirit of holiness," in contrast to "the flesh." He was "declared to be the Son of God with power" according to His divine nature, by the resurrection from the dead. His rising from the dead did not *make* Him the Son of God, for He always was that, but it *declared* Him to be the Son of God. Paul did not preach the weak Christ of modern liberal theories; he preached the divine Christ of the Scriptures.

In the third place, the message Paul preached is *a universal message*. It is to be published and accepted throughout the entire world, "for obedience to the faith among all nations" (1:5). It is not for the Jews only, but for the whole world, without regard to national or racial barriers. Paul himself proposed to proclaim this message both to the Greeks and to the barbarians (1:14), to the limit of his opportunities. Obviously, the apostle Paul was a believer in foreign missions.

In the fourth place, the message Paul preached was a *powerful* message. He was not ashamed of it, for it had the power of God behind it. Unlike the doctrines and philosophies of the Greeks and the Romans, the gospel that Paul preached was not mere human speculation and theorizing; it was a message of truth and it struck home with tremendous power, the power of God unto salvation, in the case of every person who accepted the message. It was a saving, life-changing message, a message involving "the righteousness of God" (1:17). Those who accept this message obtain the righteousness of God through their faith in the Redeemer.

Paul closes this introductory section of the epistle with a quotation from the Old Testament, "The just shall live by faith." This statement of the Scripture would one day become famous as the keynote of the Protestant Reformation; indeed, it is really the keynote of the biblical doctrine of salvation. Taken originally from Habakkuk 2:4, the statement is quoted repeatedly in the New Testament (Rom. 1:17; Gal. 3:11; Heb. 10:38). The person who understands the true meaning of these words, "The just shall live by faith," understands the true meaning of the gospel of Jesus Christ, the way of salvation, and the Christian faith. As we proceed further in the study of Paul's Epistle to the Romans, we shall learn more of the meaning of this wonderful statement.

Questions:
1. How is the Epistle to the Romans commonly divided, and how many chapters are there in each of the divisions?
2. What can be said in criticism of this common way of dividing the epistle?
3. What is the theme of the first 11 chapters of Romans?
4. When was the Epistle to the Romans written?
5. Where was Paul at the time when he wrote this epistle?
6. What is the literal meaning of the word for "servant" used by Paul in speaking of himself in 1:1?

Romans 1:1–17

7. What is the meaning of the word "apostle," and when was Paul called to be an apostle?

8. What did Paul mean by calling himself a "debtor" in 1:14?

9. How does Paul guard against the idea that his gospel was something new?

10. In what respect are the Old Testament and the New Testament the same and in what respect do they differ?

11. How did Paul's gospel differ radically from the other messages of his day?

12. What do we learn from 1:3–4 concerning the Christ that Paul preached?

13. What expression in 1:3 speaks of the human nature of Christ?

14. What expression in 1:4 speaks of the divine nature of Christ?

15. What is the bearing of Christ's resurrection on His divine sonship?

16. How does 1:5 show the obligation to support foreign missions?

17. What power did Paul's message have behind it, which the philosophies of his day lacked?

18. From what place in the Old Testament is the statement "The just shall live by faith" quoted?

19. Besides Romans 1:17, where in the New Testament is this statement, "The just shall live by faith" quoted?

20. What is the importance of the statement "The just shall live by faith?"

Chapter 2

THE NEED FOR SALVATION

Humanity Is Hopelessly Lost in Sin and Guilty before God. 1:18–32

Lesson 2

In this section of Paul's Epistle to the Romans we have a very terrible, dark picture of the sinfulness of the human race placed before us. First of all, Paul tells us about God's attitude toward human sinfulness: "For the wrath of God is revealed from heaven against all ungodliness and unrighteousness of men, who hold the truth in unrighteousness" (1:18). God's righteousness is contrary to human sin. Paul lays this down as an axiom. The rest of his argument in this epistle depends upon it.

"Who *hold* the truth in unrighteousness" really means "with-hold," "restrain," or "hold down." We might translate the phrase, "Who interfere with the truth in unrighteousness." Against those who do that, "the wrath of God is revealed from heaven." We hear little about the wrath of God today. Some people even say that we should not use such an expression—that we should only speak of God's love, not of God's wrath. But the Bible speaks of God's wrath. It tells us that God's wrath is revealed from heaven against human sin.

Romans 1:18–32

First, the wrath of God is revealed from heaven in the human conscience—that still, small voice within us that tells us when we are doing what we know to be wrong. But people harden their hearts, ignore their consciences, and go on in their wicked ways. So God speaks in another way, with a louder, sterner voice, the voice of *events*. Then come wars, and rumors of wars, until men learn that the wages of sin is death. The four horsemen of the Apocalypse ride across the earth with their trail of bloodshed, famine, and pestilence. These things do not come by chance; they are the voice and judgment of God, revealing the wrath of God from heaven against man's sin.

Sin is not a figment of the imagination. Sin is a reality. God's wrath against sin is not imaginary, but terribly real. Men may try to forget it, close their minds to it, evade it, but it will follow them no matter what they do. They cannot get away from God and God's wrath against sin.

Our own day looks lightly on sin. The 19th Century almost eliminated the idea of sin from people's thinking. The same 19th Century, with its proud belief in human goodness and human progress, thought that civilization had outgrown war. But human wickedness was still the same. There were two terrible world wars in less than 30 years, and now there could be a still more terrible third world war looming on the horizon. If anyone doubts the reality of human wickedness, the present world situation ought to be enough to convince him of it.

Mankind Is Entirely without Excuse. 1:19–20

It is human nature to try to find excuses for our sins and failings. It has been so since the time of Adam and Eve. Adam tried to place the blame on Eve: "The woman whom thou gavest to be with me, she gave me of the tree, and I did eat" (Gen. 3:12). Eve tried to blame it on the devil: "The serpent beguiled me, and I did eat" (Gen. 3:13). And so on down through the ages, sinners have tried to disclaim responsibility and to take refuge in excuses and alibis. But Paul insists that sinners are "without excuse" (1:20). The human race is in a condition of ungodliness and unrighteousness, and is without excuse.

And why? Because even without the Bible, mankind had a revelation from God in the book of nature. Even without the light of Scripture, it was possible to know something about the true God. This revelation in the book of nature was universal, it was worldwide, it spoke about the true God to every human being everywhere.

The revelation of God in the book of nature included two parts. The first part is mentioned in 1:19, "because that which may be known of God *is manifest in them*." This is a revelation of God in the human heart and conscience. The second part is outside of us—the great world of nature round about us—the starry heavens, the vast, created universe. As the psalmist said, "The heavens declare the glory of God; and the firmament sheweth his handiwork" (Ps. 19:1). Just so, Paul here says that: "For the invisible things of him from the creation of the world are clearly seen, being *understood by the things that are made*, even his eternal power and Godhead; so that they are without excuse" (1:20).

Of course, the revelation of God in the book of nature is not a complete revelation. It does not tell people anything about the way of salvation; it does not tell anything about a Savior who suffered and died on the cross as the substitute for sinners; it does not tell of God's saving grace. But it does tell something about the true God. In Paul's words, it tells men of "his eternal power and Godhead." That is, it tells men that there is a God and that He is an eternal and almighty being. It tells men enough about the true God to leave them without excuse.

If there is an eternal, almighty God, a God who has created all things including the human race, then plainly it must be our duty to serve and worship Him. That much may be known simply from the book of nature, without the Bible. So the revelation of the true God in nature left the human race without excuse, because when mankind went deeper and deeper into sin, it meant that men were *sinning against the light*. Men were rejecting the light God had given them, the light of nature.

It is an axiom of human law that "ignorance of the law is no excuse." But in the case of the human race sinning against God, no person could claim ignorance of the law and the divine Law-giver. Men were sinning in spite of the law, sinning even though the law was known through God's revelation in nature.

Romans 1:18-32

Even the heathen people, in the dark regions of the world where the Bible has never penetrated, have a certain knowledge of God and the law of God from the light of nature. The law of God, as Paul tells us in chapter 2 of this epistle, is written on their own hearts.

Thus far we have considered two truths, namely, (1) that God's wrath is revealed from heaven against human sin; and (2) that mankind is entirely without excuse, because the true God has revealed Himself in nature. The rest of chapter 1 is devoted to a description of the effects of sin on the human race.

Questions:

1. What does 1:18 tell us of God's attitude toward human sin?
2. What is the meaning of the word "hold" in 1:18?
3. What is conscience, and how does it reveal God's attitude to sin?
4. When men ignore the voice of conscience, what louder voice speaks of God's attitude to sin?
5. What does the present world situation show concerning human wickedness?
6. When did sinners begin to try to find excuses for their sins?
7. Why is the human race without excuse for its sin?
8. What two parts are included in God's revelation in nature?
9. Why is God's revelation in nature not a complete revelation? What truths does it not speak of?
10. What truths concerning God may be known from His revelation in nature?
11. What does the existence of God's revelation in nature imply concerning human sinning?
12. What subject is dealt with in the rest of chapter 1, after verse 20?

The Effects of Sin in the Human Race
Lesson 3

Paul now takes up the effects of sin in the human race. First he discusses the *religious* effects of sin, and then he discusses the *moral* effects of sin.

Human sin results in false religious beliefs. False religion results in wicked life and conduct. Wicked life ends in the divine sentence of death.

Romans 1:18–32

First, then, let us look at the religious effects of sin on the human race. The revelation of God in the book of nature was terribly misused by men. Instead of leading men to revere and worship God, to glorify God, and be thankful to God, it became twisted and distorted into the heathen religions of the world.

Religion is universal in the human race. Even the atheist has a religion—he worships himself. But from where came the many religions with their numerous gods and idols? The evolutionist is ready with an easy answer. He says the heathen religions are just stages in the slow, steady evolution of religion from a crude belief in spirits to the worship of one God. It is an easy explanation, but it is not the true explanation. For the earliest and oldest religion was *monotheism*, the worship of one God. We know this not merely from the Bible, but from the facts of human religions. In China, for example, the oldest known religion was a worship of one supreme God. The numerous gods and idols worshiped by the Chinese today, in their various religions, are a later development, a corruption of their earlier worship of one God.

In Romans 1:21–23, Paul tells us the real origin of the world's heathen religious systems. They originated from perversion of God's revelation in the book of nature. God's revelation in nature was clear enough, but something terrible had happened to the human race. In Paul's words, they "became vain in their imaginations, and their foolish heart was darkened. Professing themselves to be wise, they became fools" (1:21–22).

If you look through amber-colored glasses, everything you see will be amber-colored. If you look through blue glasses, everything you see will appear blue. God's revelation in the book of nature was clear and plain, but something had happened to mankind's spiritual vision. The human race had fallen into sin, and thereafter it looked at the book of nature through colored glasses. What it saw was distorted and spoiled. "They became vain in their imaginations, and their foolish heart was darkened."

We often think of the moral effects of the fall into sin—of what the fall into sin did to people's moral sense. We realize something of the depravity and wickedness which came as the result of the sin of Adam and Eve. But we tend to forget that that is only part of the picture. It is true that the Fall corrupted our moral sense and made us wicked, but that is not all. The Fall not only made us wicked; it also made us *foolish*. It had an effect, not only on our heart and conscience, but also *on our mind, on our thinking*.

Paul is here telling us of the effects of the Fall on the human mind, of what the Fall did to man's ability to think straight. He says that the result of the Fall was that man's "foolish heart was darkened," and so on. Though regarding himself as very wise, man had become extremely foolish. He could no longer see straight nor think straight in matters of religion. He looked in his own heart, and then he looked out on the world of nature, and then he became an *idolater*. Seeing the sun, he became a sun worshiper. Seeing the stars, he began to worship them. Seeing the moon, he regarded it as a god and worshiped it. He worshiped the heavens, instead of worshiping the God who created the heavens.

Taking another look at himself, man became a man worshiper. He "changed the glory of the uncorruptible God into an image made like to corruptible man" (1:23). Man had been created in the image of God, but after the Fall he sought to reverse the order and began to make for himself gods fashioned in the image of man. The old myths of Greece and other countries show us what kind of gods man invented for himself. The gods were not only like their makers—they were sometimes even worse than their makers. There was no kind of wickedness or crime that the Greek gods and goddesses were not involved in. Decent people in ancient Greece were ashamed of the stories about their gods.

Idolatry (worshiping false gods and images) is the most degrading practice that the human race has ever engaged in. Of all the sins and evil practices of the heathen, there is none worse or more degrading than the practice of worshiping idols. The Bible says this about man-made idols: "They that make them are like unto them; so is every one that trusteth in them" (Ps. 115:8). Idolatry drags man down and down and down. He becomes a slave to falsehood, superstition, and fear; he cannot emancipate himself. Some people think that the heathen religions with their temples and rites are quaint and romantic. They

Romans 1:18–32

do not know what they are talking about. The heathen religions are unspeakably evil and terrible. God's Word gives a true estimate of them in Deuteronomy 32:32–33: "For their vine is of the vine of Sodom, and of the fields of Gomorrah: their grapes are grapes of gall, their clusters are bitter. Their wine is the poison of dragons, and the cruel venom of asps." That is a true appraisal of the false religions of the world.

But false religions are not limited to the age-old false religions of the heathen world. We have false religions in America in our own day, not to mention the other nations of the world. The outstanding false religion of today is communism. For communism, in spite of its atheistic character and its claim to be against all religion, is itself really a religion, for it claims supreme devotion of all its followers. People are even willing to die for their devotion to communism. A faith that can call forth such loyalty and such sacrifices is certainly a religion.

Many people in America are deeply concerned about the tremendous growth and expansion of communism throughout a large part of the world. But what do they have to put in its place? Those that are not Christians have nothing but another false religion to put in place of communism—the false religion of humanism, or *faith in man*. This is called by various names. Sometimes it is called "the brotherhood of man"; sometimes it is called "democracy"; sometimes it is called "progress"; sometimes it is called "service"; and sometimes it is called "the American way of life." All these, without Jesus Christ, are just false religions. Yet people put their religious faith in them.

There is only *one* true religion, and that is the religion of the Bible, the religion of Jesus Christ and Him crucified. All others are false and will be proved false in the end.

Questions:

1. What effect should God's revelation in nature have had on the human race?
2. What was the actual effect of God's revelation in nature?
3. What is the real origin of the heathen religions of the world?
4. How do evolutionists explain the heathen religions?

Romans 1:18–32

5. How do we know that this evolution explanation is false?
6. What was the oldest known form of religion in China, and what change took place in later times?
7. What was the effect of the Fall on the human mind?
8. Was the fashioning of gods in the image of man a sign of religious progress or was it a sign or religious corruption?
9. What was the character of the gods and goddesses of ancient Greece?
10. What is the effect of idolatry on the worshipper?
11. What does Psalm 115 say about idols and idolaters?
12. What does Deuteronomy 32:32–33 teach concerning the heathen religions?
13. What is the outstanding false religion of the world today?
14. Why is it correct to say that communism is a religion?
15. What is humanism, and why is it not an adequate remedy for communism?

The Moral Effects of Sin

Lesson 4

In the previous lesson we studied the religious effects of the fall into sin. We shall now consider the *moral* effects of the fall on the human race. The fact is that false religion leads to bad conduct and wicked living, and wicked living ends in destruction. Wicked living is the result of false religious beliefs.

Many people today say that beliefs do not matter very much—that what counts is whether a person lives a good life. But according to the Bible there cannot be a good life unless there is first of all a true belief. We should note that Paul first discusses the *religious* effects of sin, and then after that he discusses the *moral* effects of sin. Many people today would say that the order should be reversed; that the moral effects are more important, and come first, and the religious effects are less important and subordinate to the moral effects of sin. But it is not that way in God's Word. The apostle Paul, inspired of the Holy Spirit in writing this epistle, discusses the religious effects of sin first, and regards them as of the most basic importance; whereas he discusses

Romans 1:18–32

the moral effects of sin afterwards and regards these as the results of the religious effects of sin.

Human sin results in false religious beliefs and practices. False religion results in wicked lives. Wicked lives end in the divine sentence of death. Such, in brief, is the argument of the Apostle Paul in this first chapter of Romans.

If there is any absurd notion that is widely held in America today it is the notion that men can gather grapes of thistles—that a false belief and a good life can go together and that the one can produce the other. The truth is, of course, that moral degradation actually results from false religion. The heathen became so desperately wicked because of their worship of false gods and idols. People "changed the truth of God into a lie, and worshipped and served the creature more than the Creator" (1:25).

What was the result of this lapse into false religion? We find the answer in an awful statement which is thrice repeated in these verses:

Wherefore *God also gave them up* to uncleanness, through the lusts of their own hearts...(1:24).

For this cause God *gave them up* unto vile affections...(1:26).

And even as they did not like to retain God in their knowledge, *God gave them over* to a reprobate mind...(1:28).

Because of men's turning away from the truth to false religion, God gave them up to all kinds of moral degradation, as described in these verses.

This is still going on today. Many are concerned about the moral evils of the day; few are concerned about the false religion of the day. Many would like to reform the moral conditions who have no zeal or concern for a general return to the pure worship of the true God and the truth of the gospel of Jesus Christ and Him crucified. But the only way to get real reform of the moral conditions is by teaching and preaching the truth of God. Religious reform is the real secret of moral reform.

Romans 1:18–32

John Knox, the great Scottish Reformer, said: "Vain is it to crave reformation of manners where the religion is corrupted" (*Editor's Note*: See *Knox: On Rebellion*. This quote is found in his "Letter to the Regent of Scotland, Lady Mary, on 1556," enlarged and expanded 1558 and originally published at Geneva by J. Poullian and A. Reboul.) Knox spoke the truth as we find it in Romans 1. The real cause of the moral evils of our day—the liquor evil, the divorce evil, the crime evil, the evil of communism, and all the other moral evils—the real cause of these evils is departure from the true religion, from the true God.

We are told today that the world is hurtling toward destruction. There is indeed some reason for thinking so. But if the world is hurtling toward destruction, the reason is departure from the true religion, departure from the true God.

And what is the remedy? The remedy is the old, old story, the gospel of Jesus Christ and Him crucified, the religion of the Holy Bible, the Word of God. Do not let us deceive ourselves. Bad moral conditions are only the symptoms of the trouble; they are not the disease itself. We can never get things right by paying attention only to the bad moral conditions and trying to get people to live better moral lives. What people really need is to believe and know the truth about God. Then they will get a new heart and they will begin really to live a new life.

Questions:

1. What is the real cause of wicked living?
2. Why can there not be a good life until there is a true religious belief?
3. Why did Paul discuss the religious effects of sin first and the moral effects of sin afterwards?
4. What judicial act of God is three times mentioned in 1:24–28?
5. Why did God "give them up" to moral degradation?
6. How can real reform of bad moral conditions be attained?
7. What did John Knox say about the relation between religious reform and moral reform?
8. Are bad moral conditions the real disease of humanity, or are they only the outward symptoms of the disease?
9. What is the real remedy for humanity's sickness?

Romans 1:18–32

Both Jews and Gentiles Are Guilty before God. 2:1–3:20
Since All Are Involved in Sin, No One Has a Right to Pronounce Judgment on Others. 2:1–3
Lesson 5

Paul has shown in chapter 1 that we are all without excuse, for we have sinned against light, knowing that it was wrong. It is human nature to try to find excuses for our sins and failings, but we have no right to do so.

There is another way of trying to evade responsibility for our sins. That is by heaping judgment on the sins of others. Instead of thinking of the sins of which we personally are guilty before God, we make a specialty of denouncing the sins of others—sins in which we personally are not involved. We become loud in denouncing the wickedness of Hollywood or of Moscow. But proclaiming the wickedness of others will never cancel our own sins. We cannot escape that way. The old proverb says that "people who live in glass houses shouldn't throw stones." So far as being sinners before God is concerned, we all live in glass houses. There is not one that can claim to be sinless.

We may not have committed exactly the same kind of sins, in detail, as other persons. Yet we are sinners just the same, for we have broken the same moral law of God, we have violated the same Ten Commandments, and we have offended against the same God. So if we judge others, we cannot avoid condemning ourselves. God's Word makes this solemn pronouncement: "For thou that judgest doest the same things" (2:1).

In the ancient world, the world of the Apostle Paul, even among the pagan nations there were moralists and ethical writers who condemned the sins of men. But it was no use, for they themselves were guilty of the same sins to a greater or lesser degree. There have been many religious teachers in the various countries of the world who have taught that wickedness is wrong, but to no avail, for these very moralists and experts were themselves involved in the very sins that they condemned.

"But we are sure that the judgment of God is according to truth against them which commit such things" (2:2). God is a moral governor who will judge all according to an unchangeable standard. There is no

Romans 2:1–3:20

court in this world of which we can always be sure that the judgment of that court is according to truth. In human courts of justice there is always a possibility of error, and sometimes there exists a deplorable corruption of justice by bribery or political considerations. But the judgment of God in the court of heaven is not like that. God's judgment is incorruptible, unalterable, and always according to the strict truth of the case.

Human justice at best is only an approximation to real justice. But divine justice is total, perfect justice. For the Judge is omniscient—He knows all the facts and circumstances—and He is omnipotent—He has power to execute His sentence.

Today many people, even Christian people, have a very partial, one-sided, inadequate idea of God. This is largely the result of the common unbalanced emphasis on the biblical truth that "God is love" (1 John 4:16). It is true, of course, that God is love, but that is not all that is true about God. We have no right to say that God is love and nothing but love. God is also righteousness. He is not only a God of love but also a God of justice. He is the moral ruler of the world and will judge all His creatures by the strictest justice according to truth.

"And thinkest thou this, O man, that judgest them which do such things, and doest the same, that thou shalt escape the judgment of God?" (2:3). To the righteous judgment of God, both the common sinner and the self-righteous sinner are subject alike. It is easy to think that the common sinner will be condemned, but that we ourselves will somehow escape. We tend to think of the drunkard, the criminal, and the gangster as a sinner and forget that the highly educated university professor may be an even greater sinner in God's sight. Man looks on the outward appearance, but the Lord looks on the heart. We tend to forget that civilization, education, and culture do not give us any preferred standing with God.

The sophisticated sinners of our day think that Christianity may be all right for the type of people reached by the Salvation Army, but the educated, the enlightened, the cultured, the refined people do not need it. In fact, such sophisticated sinners are ready to condemn the sins of the common sinners, forgetting that in God's sight they, too, are guilty. To all such self-righteous sinners Paul's challenge is: "Thinkest thou, O man,...that thou shalt escape the judgment of God?"

God's Kindness Ought to Lead Men to Repentance, but Is Frustrated by the Hardness of Men's Hearts. 2:4–5

"Or despisest thou the riches of his goodness and forbearance and longsuffering; not knowing that the goodness of God leadeth thee to repentance?" (2:4). God gives many blessings to the whole human race. He makes His sun to shine on the evil and on the good and His rain to fall on the just and on the unjust. Life, health, food, clothing, shelter, etc., are all gifts of God to men—to sinful men, who have offended against God. Also by reason of God's *longsuffering*, He gives sinful man a *reprieve*—He postpones the execution of the penalty of death on human sin. This gives sinful humans a lifespan, making human life possible and permitting the continuance of the human race through the history of the world.

The intent and proper effect of this goodness of God is to lead men to repentance. God's goodness gives men both the opportunity for repentance and encouragement to repent. It ought to lead men to repent and turn from their sins to God. But does it have this effect? Alas, the hardness of the human heart frustrates this effect. As time passes, men become worse instead of better. It takes more than *natural* blessings to bring people to repentance; it takes *special divine grace* by the supernatural, almighty work of the Holy Spirit in their hearts.

Long ago God appeared to Abraham and promised him the whole land of Canaan. But God told him it would be over 400 years before his descendants would receive the land, because "the iniquity of the Amorites is not yet full" (Gen. 15:16). The Amorites were terribly wicked. Their religious worship was an abomination. But God gave these wicked people 400 years to repent. Through all that period they enjoyed the blessings of God, but they did not repent. On the contrary, they became worse than before, and finally God destroyed them at the time of Joshua.

And it is so today. Worldly success and prosperity do not bring men to repentance. Worldly prosperity leads rather to pride and vain glory, not to "a broken and a contrite heart" (Ps. 51:17).

Questions:

1. Besides trying to find excuses, what other way do sinners often try to evade responsibility for their sins?
2. Why can judging others not cancel our own sins?
3. Why could the moralists of Paul's day not accomplish anything?
4. What is the difference between human justice and divine justice?
5. Why do many people today have a one-sided view of God?
6. What is the difference between human views of sin and God's view of sin?
7. What is the attitude of the sophisticated people of our day toward Christianity?
8. What kind of blessings does God give to all mankind?
9. What is meant by saying that God's long-suffering gives sinful man a reprieve?
10. What should be the effect of God's goodness to sinful people?
11. Why do God's blessings not actually produce repentance on the part of sinners?
12. Besides natural blessings, what is required to produce repentance?
13. Why did God delay the destruction of the Amorites for 400 years?
14. What is the usual result of worldly success and prosperity?

The Principle of God's Moral Government Is to Deal with Every Person According to His Deeds. 2:6–11
Lesson 6

"But, after thy hardness and impenitent heart, treasurest up unto thyself wrath against thy day of wrath and revelation of the righteous judgment of God" (2:5). A day of judgment is coming. God's kindness and long-suffering will not last forever. Ultimately they will give place to divine judgment according to righteousness. That day will be a "day of wrath," because then the wrath of God will no longer be held back by God's longsuffering. It will burst forth and be poured out upon sinful men. We saw in 1:18 that "the wrath of God is revealed from heaven." That is going on all the time. But there will be a day of *final* outpouring of the wrath of God—the judgment day.

The principle of the divine judgment will be *desert*. God, who is absolutely righteous, will treat each person exactly as that person deserves to be treated. He "will render to every man according to his deeds" (2:6). This principle involves rewards for righteousness and penalties for sins, as explained in verses 7 to 10. Moreover, God's judgment is not only *righteous*, but also *impartial*, "For there is no respect of persons with God" (2:11). The Jew will not be favored because he is a member of the chosen people and a child of Abraham. On the contrary, divine retribution will be to "the Jew first" (2:9), because the Jew has enjoyed greater advantages than the Gentile.

This section (2:6–11) does not teach salvation by works, as some wrongly suppose. It does not deal at all with *the way of salvation*, which comes later in the epistle, but with *the principle of the divine judgment*, that is, the principle that righteousness will be rewarded with eternal life, and sin will be recompensed with tribulation and anguish. This section only lays down that principle; it does not tell us *how* a sinner can obtain righteousness. There is, of course, only one way—to believe on Jesus Christ and so obtain Christ's righteousness as a gift, reckoned or "imputed" to the sinner as if it were his own. This truth comes later on in the epistle. At the point we are now studying, Paul is simply stating the abstract principle of God's judgment of the world. He names the price of eternal life, but he does not yet tell us where the money can be obtained; that comes later on.

God's Judgment Will Take Account of the Advantages Men Have Enjoyed. 2:12–16

Those who have sinned will be condemned for their sin: "For as many as have sinned without law shall also perish without law; and as many as have sinned in the law shall be judged by the law" (2:12). Those who have sinned will be judged and condemned for their sin, whether they have known the written law of God or not. Some will be judged and condemned apart from the written law; others, by the written law.

Romans 2:1–3:20

Of course, those who believe on Christ as their Savior will not be condemned, but that is a truth that comes later in the epistle (see 8:1).

Mere hearing of God's law will not avail. The Jews placed great stress on their being *hearers* of the law. They were members of the synagogue; they heard the law of God read and expounded from Sabbath to Sabbath. They counted heavily on this hearing of the law to gain them favor with God.

Paul states that the mere hearing of the law is not enough. If we expect to be saved by the law, then we will have to do more than just hear it. We will have not only to hear it but also to *observe* it, to "do the law," that is, to obey its commandments. This means, of course, to obey them *perfectly*. "For not the hearers of the law are just before God, but the doers of the law shall be justified" (2:13). Paul is not saying that we can be justified by the works of the law. He deals with that error later. At this point he is simply emphasizing that mere hearing of the law will not get us anywhere with God. The Jews of Paul's day did not really keep the law, but they counted on God's favor because they were hearers of the law.

A writer on the life of Paul has written:

He only can be happy under a dispensation of law, who can live a lifelong lie.... But proud, downright, consistent natures cannot be put off with a lie. If they are unable to resist, they die of the lie; if they are strong, it is the lie that dies. The lie inherent in the law [as trusted in by the Jews for salvation] was the presumption that it could be fulfilled. Every one of Paul's associates understood that the commandment could not be kept, but they did not own it to themselves. The elder behaved in presence of the younger as if it could be kept; one believed it on the strength of another, and did not acknowledge the impossibility to himself. They blinded themselves to their own sin by comparing themselves with other just men, and had recourse to remote ages to Enoch and Noah and Daniel, in order to produce advocates for their souls. They hoped God would allow the good works of the saints to cover their deficiencies, and they did not forget occasionally to pray for mercy, yet, on the whole they kept up the lie and went on as if they were well (H. Weinel, *St. Paul*,

English translation, pp. 72–73; quoted in B. B. Warfield, *The Plan of Salvation*, pp. 37–38).

The Gentiles, being without the Scripture, will be judged according to the law of nature (2:14–15). Even those who never knew the Bible with its written law of God, have the law of God, that is, the law of nature, written on their heart and conscience. By this law of nature, then, they will be judged. Sin is the transgression of the law, that is, of God's law. Men will be judged according to the law they have transgressed, whether it be God's law in Scripture or God's law in nature (as in the case of the heathen).

God's judgment will be by Jesus Christ and will deal with secret matters as well as those openly known: "In the day when God shall judge the secrets of men by Jesus Christ according to my gospel" (2:16). That means the great judgment day, the last day at the end of the world, the time of Christ's second coming.

There are many sins that have been kept secret. But Christ's judgment will bring them to light in that day. When that tribunal gets under way, the secret plots and plans made behind heavily guarded doors in some of the dark places of the earth will be exposed to the daylight before the whole universe. But not only those kinds of "secrets" will be exposed; also the secret motives and thoughts of men's hearts will be judged by Jesus Christ.

Jesus Christ is both the *Savior* and the *Judge*. He is the Savior today; He will be the Judge at the last day. Those who reject or neglect Him as their Savior will discover that they cannot evade Him as their Judge.

None of us who are reading this page can lay claim to having "sinned without law." Our advantages have been of the greatest, and our responsibility before God is correspondingly greater than that of others. If the heathen are going to stand before Christ's judgment seat, how much more will we, with our Christian background and training? "Therefore be ye also ready: for in such an hour as ye think not the Son of man cometh" (Matt. 24:44).

Romans 2:1–3:20

Questions:

1. What is the judgment day called in 2:5?
2. Why will the judgment day be a "day of wrath"?
3. What is the principle of the divine judgment?
4. What verse of this section shows that God's judgment is not only righteous but also impartial?
5. Why is it incorrect to say that 2:6–11 teaches salvation by works?
6. How does this section show that God's judgment will take account of the advantages men have enjoyed?
7. Why does Paul emphasize the truth that mere hearing of the law is not enough to save us?
8. What wrong attitude toward the law was characteristic of the Jews of Paul's day?
9. On what basis will the heathen who never had the Bible be judged?
10. What will be the scope of the divine judgment according to 2:16?
11. Whom has God appointed to execute judgment?
12. What great tragedy will befall those who bypass Jesus Christ during their life on earth?

The Jews, Sinning against Boasted Light, Are Doubly Guilty before God. 2:17–24

Lesson 7

"Behold, thou art called a Jew, and resteth in the law, and makest thy boast of God, and knowest his will, and approvest the things that are more excellent, being instructed out of the law; and art confident that thou thyself art a guide of the blind, a light of them which are in darkness, an instructor of the foolish, a teacher of babes, which hast the form of knowledge and of the truth in the law" (2:17–20). Here Paul gives us in substance the boast of the Jews of his day—their proud claim that they were guides of the blind, instructors of the foolish, teachers of babes, and so forth in the things of God.

We might be inclined to think that these claims of the Jews were mere empty boasting or bragging. But they were more than that. To a very great extent, these claims were true. In that ancient pagan world, the Jews were not only beyond question the best people that could be found anywhere, but they were the *only* people that held out the light of divine truth to the heathen people surrounding them. The Jews were no longer limited to the little country of Palestine. Large numbers of them had been transplanted by various kings and rulers to Babylonia and other regions to the east. The major portion of these never returned to Palestine. Some were absorbed by heathenism in succeeding generations, but a large proportion retained their religion and Jewish identity in the lands to the east. To the west, toward Greece, Italy, etc., the Jews had gone of their own accord, chiefly for commercial reasons. In Paul's day there were Jews almost everywhere. It has been estimated that there were about one million in Egypt alone, and possibly eight million in the entire Roman Empire. Of these, only a very small fraction lived in the tiny country of Palestine.

The Jews of that day were prosperous, influential, and powerful, enjoying special privileges, their religion and their social customs being given legal protection. Even their observance of their Sabbath was sanctioned and protected by the Roman government. Everywhere the Jews had organized synagogues, which greatly strengthened their social solidarity. Some Jews held high offices under the Romans and other rulers.

By far the greatest influence of the Jew on the heathen society around him was exerted through the synagogue or what we would call the Jewish church. It is not known when the synagogue originated, but probably it was at the time of the Babylonian captivity. Wherever there were 10 Jewish families, a synagogue would be established. In these synagogues, the Scriptures were read and expounded, prayer was offered, and the Psalms were sung in praise and worship to God.

Outside of Palestine, the synagogue services would be mostly in the Greek language, for Greek was the common language of the day. We should remember that Paul's Epistle to the Romans, though written to the church in Rome, was not written in Latin but in Greek. The entire Old Testament Scriptures were available in Greek and were used by the Jews of the "Dispersion" for their synagogue services. Two features were joined to the synagogue—a school and a library. Through these, many of the surrounding heathen were influenced for good. The Jews

Romans 2:1–3:20

were strongly convinced that they had a divine mission to the people of the world. Inasmuch as they knew that in Abraham and his seed all the families of the earth would be blessed, and since they expected the coming of a Messiah, the Jews had a definite religious message. The result was that large numbers of Gentiles were converted to Judaism. Even larger were the numbers of "God-fearing" adherents, who attached themselves to the synagogue without actually becoming Jews. Cornelius was an example of such Gentiles who were attracted by the religion of the Jews.

The Jews throughout the Roman world regarded it as their special duty to enlighten the heathen religiously. In this effort, they achieved remarkable success. The Jewish historian Josephus wrote: "Many of the heathen have come over to our law; some have remained, others unable to tolerate its strictness have fallen off...Among the masses there has long been a great zeal for our mode of worship; there is no Greek nor barbarian city nor any nation in which our custom of keeping the Sabbath, fasting, the lighting of lamps and many regulations in regard to food, are not observed."

Thus we see that there was much truth in the boast of the Jews set forth by Paul in these verses (2:17–20). Paul was writing to the Christian church at Rome. There were many Jewish synagogues in Rome. Up to the time when a Christian church was established in Rome, it was certainly true that the Jews were the spiritual lighthouse of the city, as they were of the empire.

The Guilt of the Jews. 2:21–24

Great opportunities mean great responsibilities. The light that the Jews enjoyed vastly increased their responsibility before God. The fact that the boast of the Jews was not false, but true, greatly added to their obligation to live a righteous life before God. Having set forth the boast of the Jews, Paul now discusses their *guilt*. They boasted especially of the law, with which they had been entrusted by God. But what were they doing with that law?

To be sure, they were publishing it abroad and teaching it to the Gentiles around them. And, to be sure, they were making an attempt to live according to it. But now Paul looks beneath the surface. Were the Jews really keeping the law of God? Were they really keeping it as it ought to be kept, as God's righteousness requires? God's law requires perfect righteousness of man. Only a perfect obedience is really a keeping of the commandments. Were the Jews doing that?

They certainly were not. They were not keepers of the law but transgressors of the law. They were breakers of the law of God. Not in exactly the same manner as the heathen, of course; yet in the sight of the holy God, the Jews were breakers of the law. Every Jew that read Paul's words would have to admit, in the bottom of his own heart and conscience, that Paul was stating the plain truth: with all their boasting about the law, after all, each and every Jew was really a *breaker* of the law. There was not one of them that could really keep the law.

The apostle mentions various transgressions of the law, starting with the sin of stealing: "Thou that preachest a man should not steal, dost thou steal?" (2:21). Probably the reference is not to common theft, robbery, or burglary, but to dishonesty and shady financial dealings, which were legal and respectable according to human notions but dishonest in God's sight. Among those who made long prayers, there were some who also devoured widows' houses. They were very pious, very religious, and also very sharp in financial matters, taking every advantage, fair or otherwise, as long as it was technically legal. That is *stealing* in God's sight.

Then the apostle mentions adultery: "Thou that sayest a man should not commit adultery, dost thou commit adultery?" (2:22). They might be clear of the outward act of adultery and yet be adulterers as the sin was defined by Jesus. Then "sacrilege" is spoken of (2:22), the American Revised Version reading, "Dost thou rob temples?" (Compare Acts 19:37, "robbers of churches"; ARV "robbers of temples"). Possibly the meaning is that the Jews in their zeal against idolatry stole idols from the temples of the heathen.

In short, the Jew boasted of the law, yet he dishonored God by breaking the law. God's name was blasphemed among the Gentiles because of the sins of the Jews (2:23–24). Paul himself was a strict Jew, a Pharisee, and he knew what he was talking about. We might illustrate

Romans 2:1–3:20

this by a modern parallel. A professing Christian in a non-Christian country such as China or India gets drunk or becomes involved in a street brawl. As the person is known to make a Christian profession, the name of God is blasphemed by the heathen on account of his sin. Meanwhile, any number of non-Christians may become involved in like sins, and nothing special is thought of it by anyone. So with the Jews of old. Because the standard held aloft by the Jews was very high, their violation of that standard was extremely serious.

Now let us apply this to ourselves and see how we fit into this picture. Who holds aloft the torch of truth, the light of God's revelation, today? Who, but those who profess the Christian religion? Who is a teacher of babes, a guide of the blind, in the world of today, except those who call themselves Christians? Even though we may not boast of it as the ancient Jews did, it is true just the same. We are the salt of the earth, the light of the world, the city set on a hill, as our Savior said. Having such great and high privileges, how great is our responsibility before God! And how great is our sin, how much greater than other people's sin, when we act contrary to our holy religion and the commandments of God! The name of God is blasphemed every day among the modern heathen and unbelievers because of the sins of professing Christians. An unbeliever or worldly person may violate God's moral laws, and the world pays but little heed. But let a professing Christian commit some crime, or be caught in some dishonest or unethical act, and the world will never forget it. Our wonderful Christian heritage vastly increases our responsibility before God.

What are we really in God's sight? We are just poor, lost, guilty sinners needing a Savior, sinners in need of God's saving grace just the same as other people. The fact that we may be able to trace our personal or ecclesiastical ancestry to the martyr church of the Scottish Reformation does not make any difference, except to increase our guilt before God. When we are honest with our own consciences, we must admit that it is true of us as it was of the Jews of Paul's day: we are not keepers of the law but breakers of the law.

Even if we have a fine reputation among our neighbors, still we must confess that before God we are great sinners. We are not law keepers but law breakers. Our great opportunities, the light we have enjoyed, only increase our responsibility and guilt before God.

Through this section of the epistle, Paul is hammering away to drive one point home—that we are lost sinners and need a Savior. Let us admit it. We need Christ.

Questions:

1.   What claims did the Jews of Paul's day make for themselves?
2.   Were these claims warranted by the facts or were they merely conceited boasting?
3.   How many Jews may there have been in Paul's day, and where did most of them live?
4.   What was the position of the Jews in the Roman Empire? What privileges did they enjoy?
5.   What institution of the Jews greatly increased their influence in the ancient world?
6.   Why was Paul's epistle to the Romans written in Greek instead of in Latin?
7.   What did Josephus say of the success of the Jews in influencing their pagan environment?
8.   What kind of obedience does God's law require of man?
9.   When judged by God's standard of righteousness, were the Jews of Paul's day keepers of the law or breakers of the law?
10. What particular sins does Paul imply the Jews were guilty of?
11. What kind of "stealing" is probably meant in the phrase "dost thou steal" in 2:21?
12. What is the probable meaning of the phrase "commit sacrilege" in 2:22?
13. Why did the sins of the Jews specially occasion blaspheming of God's name by the Gentiles?
14. How does the teaching of 2:17–24 apply to Christians of the present day?
15. What point is Paul trying to drive home in this section of the epistle?

Romans 2:1–3:20

The Spiritual Nature of True Godliness. 2:25–29
Lesson 8

Profession without possession is of no avail in God's sight. Sacraments and rites without divine grace give us no standing with God. "For he is not a Jew, which is one outwardly..." (2:28). In like manner we may say "He is not a Christian which is one outwardly; nor is the true baptism that with water alone." He is a Christian which is one *inwardly*, and the true baptism is that of the Holy Spirit, of which baptism with water is the outward sign, the token of the reality of divine grace in the heart, which is called "the new birth"—regeneration or becoming a new creature in Christ Jesus. "If any man be in Christ, he is a new creature: old things are passed away; behold, all things are become new" (2 Cor. 5:17). There is, moreover, a test by which we can assay our religion to discern what is gold and what is mere dross. Paul gives us this test in the closing words of Romans 2, "Whose praise is not of men, but of God."

Enoch had this testimony, that he pleased God (Heb. 11:5). The true Jew, Paul says, is the one who pleases God, not the one who seeks and receives the praises of men. And the true Christian is the one who pleases God, not the one who is commended and praised by men. Samuel, after rejecting seven of Jesse's sons one after another, anointed David as the one chosen by God to be king. Samuel said to Jesse, "The Lord seeth not as man seeth; for man looketh on the outward appearance, but the Lord looketh on the heart" (1 Sam. 16:7). When we realize this truth, we will be more convinced than ever that we are guilty sinners needing a Savior. Christ is the Savior we need, the only Savior who can meet our need. "For God so loved the world, that he gave his only begotten Son, that whosoever believeth in him should not perish, but have everlasting life" (John 3:16).

The Advantages Enjoyed by the Jews. 3:1–4

This section (3:1–4) is somewhat difficult to understand, in part because the language of the King James Version of the Bible is somewhat different from that which we are accustomed to using today. While it is not the present writer's practice to quote often from modern translations of the Bible, it is sometimes advantageous to do so, because we can sometimes get help from translations of the Bible into modern English if we use them with due discernment and discrimination. The following is the translation of Romans 3:1-4 in the *Twentieth Century New Testament*:

> What is the advantage, then, of being a Jew? Or what is the good of circumcision? Great in every way. First of all, because the Jews were entrusted with God's utterances. What follows then? Some, no doubt, showed a want of faith; but will their want of faith make God break faith? Heaven forbid! God must prove true, though every man prove a liar! As Scripture says of God: "That thou mayest be pronounced righteous in what thou sayest, and gain thy cause when men would judge thee."

In the first eight verses of chapter 3, Paul takes up two objections that might be raised against his argument in chapter 2. The first objection is that if the Jews are sinners and have broken God's law as other men have, then there is no advantage in being a Jew. The objection is, in effect, that according to Paul the Jew has no advantage over the heathen, since both are breakers of God's law. Paul answers this objection in the first four verses of chapter 3.

If the Jews are sinners as other men are, then, after all, what advantage has the Jew? "Much every way," replies Paul. The advantage of the Jew is both real and great. Though both Jews and heathen were transgressors of the law and guilty in God's sight, still the Jew had great advantages over the heathen.

Then Paul proceeds to name one advantage possessed by the Jew—the chief and most important advantage: "Chiefly, because that unto them were committed the oracles of God." In other words, the Jew had a tremendous advantage because he had been entrusted with the Scriptures, the spoken and written Word of God. God had revealed Himself to the heathen in the works of nature and in the human heart and conscience; but to the Jews, to Israel, He had spoken with a much clearer voice—the voice of His Word, the Holy Scripture. Scripture was what the Jew had and the heathen lacked. Where the heathen did have it, it was only by reason of contact and association with the Jew.

Romans 2:1-3:20

Note that Paul calls Scripture "the oracles of God," that is, the *utterances* of God. With these utterances, he says, the Jew was entrusted. They were committed unto the Jew. So far as we know, every book of the Old Testament was written by Jews. According to the prevalent modern (liberal) view of the Bible, the Old Testament Scriptures were the *product* of the religious experience of the Hebrew people. As the religion of Israel developed and improved through the centuries, the best was preserved in these Old Testament books. This regards the Old Testament as the product of the religious evolution or development of the people of Israel. But Paul had no such belief. On the contrary, he held a very different view of the Old Testament. Paul knew, of course, that the Old Testament books were written by Jews. Yet he did not regard them as a product of the Jews' religious development. For Paul says that these books were *committed* to the Jews; they were entrusted with them. A person cannot be entrusted with something that he has himself produced. If a farmer has grain stored in buildings on his farm, grain that was produced on his own land by his own effort, he could not say that the grain was "committed" to him. If he were storing grain for a neighbor, that would be committed to him. But the product of a man's own activity cannot be said to be "committed" to him. The Scriptures were the oracles, the utterances, of God. They did not originate with the Jews. They came from God by the special work of the Holy Spirit. The Jews were not really their authors, in the ultimate sense, but their custodians.

The Jews, though sinners like other men, held in their hands the guide book pointing out the way of salvation from sin. This guide book contained two elements, *law* and *gospel*. The law told them that they were sinners; the gospel told them of God's remedy for sin. In the Old Testament the gospel was set forth in various ways—by promises, prophecies, and especially by the sacrifices and the lamb of the Passover feast. All these pointed forward to Christ, the Lamb of God that "taketh away the sin of the world" (John 1:29). The law said "do," meaning to live perfectly according to God's commandments. This no one could really do, not even the Jews.

But the gospel says "done," meaning that what we could never do for ourselves, God Himself has done for His people through His Son

Romans 2:1–3:20

Jesus Christ. The law proclaims the justice and righteousness of God; the gospel proclaims His mercy and love. All this is contained in the Old Testament Scriptures, which were committed to the Jews. They held in their hands the chart and compass that could point them to forgiveness, salvation, and eternal life.

But what use did the Jews make of this road map of the highway to heaven? Well, Paul admits right away that "some" failed to believe. A portion of the Jewish people failed to walk the highway of eternal life. Paul does not say how large a portion, for that has no bearing on his argument here; he only concedes that "some did not believe." From our own reading of the Old Testament, we know that this was true. Then, as now, some believed and some disbelieved. There were men like David, and there were also men like Saul. There were men like Elijah, but there were also men like Ahab. There were women like Ruth and Naomi, but also women like Jezebel. Some did not believe.

But what of it? Did that make the Old Testament a failure? Was God's program a failure? Had God's plans fallen to the ground because part of the people of Israel served the devil instead of serving God? Some people raise very similar objections today. They say that such-and-such a church member is (in their judgment) a hypocrite, and therefore Christianity is a failure. Or because of the prevalence of war and the general bad condition of international affairs, Christianity is a failure. But such objections are not new. Such talk was going on in Paul's day. Against those who held that by the failure of "some" of the people of Israel to accept God's way of salvation God's plan was a failure, Paul replies: "Shall their unbelief make the faith of God without effect?" (3:3) Or, as in the Twentieth Century New Testament, "Will their want of faith make God break faith?" And the apostle answers this question by saying, "God forbid," or, as we might say, "Far from it."

God is not a failure. The Old Testament was not a failure. Christianity is not a failure. Some people are not what they should be; some do not have real saving faith; but God keeps faith. God's plan will not fail.

As a matter of fact, there was always a goodly number of the people of Israel who believed and lived the life of faith. The apostasy of Israel, even in the darkest days of idolatry before the exile to Babylon, was

Romans 2:1–3:20

never total. Always there was a remnant left to serve God faithfully. Elijah thought he alone was left to serve God, but God revealed to him that there were 7,000 others, unknown to him, that had never bowed their knee to Baal nor worshipped his image (1 Kings 19:18).

Even today there are more Jewish Christians than we realize. Some of the most outstanding Christian leaders of the past 100 years have been converts from Israel. A Polish Jew converted to Christ was one of the first to translate the whole Bible into the Chinese language, to name but one example. It is estimated that no less than 100,000 Jews became Christians between 1800 and 1875 (Delitzsch).

Paul goes on to defend the righteousness and integrity of God. God has not failed; God can never fail. "Yea, let God be true, but every man a liar" (3:4)—"God must prove true, even though every man should prove to be a liar." Even the Jews that did not believe had their place in God's righteousness. God's perfect righteousness and justice would be manifested, by way of contrast, in judging and condemning them for their sin and their unbelief. When a person believes and is saved, that glorifies God by manifesting God's mercy and love. When a person disbelieves, continues in sin, and is finally condemned in the judgment, that also glorifies God by manifesting another side of God's character, namely, God's justice which condemns and punishes sin. So we see that the fact that some did not believe is no real objection to God's way of doing things. Even those who did not believe glorified God in spite of themselves.

Questions:

1. What is necessary, in addition to a profession of faith, in order to please God?
2. How can we test the genuineness of our religious profession?
3. What objection was raised to Paul's teaching that the Jews, like other men, were sinners?
4. What was the most important advantage possessed by the Jews?
5. What is meant by the phrase "the oracles of God"?
6. What view of the Old Testament is implied in the use of the word "committed" in 3:2?

Romans 2:1–3:20

7. What is the common "liberal" view of the Old Testament, and why is it wrong?

8. What two elements are contained in the Old Testament Scriptures?

9. How is the gospel set forth in the Old Testament?

10. What is the difference between the law and the gospel?

11. How does Paul answer the argument that some of the Jews did not believe?

12. What similar objection is often raised against Christianity today?

13. What results have been attained by missionary work among the Jews?

14. How did even the unbelieving Jews have a place in God's plan and program?

Shall We Sin to Glorify God? 3:5–8

Lesson 9

Paul now takes up the second objection that follows from what he has been saying about the first objection. He has just been telling us that God is going to be justified in His sayings even in the matter of the wicked who reject the way of salvation. In effect, as we read in verse 5, "Our unrighteousness commends the righteousness of God." That may sound like a strange thing to say, yet it is strictly true. The Bible plainly teaches that God is glorified in His righteous condemnation and punishment of sin.

Abel glorified God by a life of faith and service to God; Cain glorified God in spite of himself, because God's righteousness was displayed in the punishment of Cain for his sin.

The objection continues: If that is the way it is—if human sin glorifies God—then why should God punish the sinner? If man's sin glorifies God, then what right has God to pronounce judgment on the sinner?

Paul says, "I speak as a man." This does not mean that he is not speaking as an inspired apostle of Christ; it only means that at this particular point of his discussion, he is stating the objection from the common human point of view. To the person who does not understand the ways of God, it might seem that if human sin glorifies God, then God ought not to "take vengeance," that is, God ought not to judge and punish sin.

Romans 2:1–3:20

Of course, the objection is a very shallow, superficial one. It is true that human sin glorifies God by manifesting His justice in the punishment of sin. But for all that, God is right in punishing sin, because the *motive* of the sinner is never to glorify God, but always to follow his own lusts and desires. Cain killed Abel. In punishing Cain for this sin, God's righteousness was displayed and His justice was manifested. But Cain *deserved* to be punished. His intention had not been to glorify God, but to have his own way.

Human sin glorifies God by manifesting God's justice, but the sinner never acts with a desire to glorify God. The person who sins always intends to please himself; he never intends to please God. And God, who looks at the heart, judges according to people's character and motives, not merely according to their outward actions.

Paul rejects this objection with another "God forbid." And he adds, "For then how shall God judge the world?" That God is going to judge the world is a truth that Paul's readers already believed. This was believed by Jews as well as by Christians. Now the Judge who is going to judge the world certainly must be a just Judge. That God is absolutely just is an axiom; it does not require an argument to prove it. If God were not absolutely just and righteous, He would not be God.

But Paul takes up the same objection over again, in 3:7, "For if the truth of God hath more abounded through my lie unto his glory; why yet am I also judged as a sinner?" The Twentieth Century New Testament translates: "But, if my falsehood resounds to the glory of God, by making his truthfulness more apparent, why am I, like others, still condemned as a sinner?"

If I tell a lie, and this falsehood of mine glorifies God by making His truthfulness more apparent by way of contrast, then why should God treat me as a sinner? Why not tell ten lies, and glorify God ten times as much? Or why not tell a thousand lies, and glorify God a thousand times as much? Or why not tell nothing but lies, all the time, for the more lies we tell, the more God is glorified? So ran the objection. There were some that went even further than that. They slandered Paul and his fellow Christians and claimed that Paul actually taught that we should do evil that good may come.

Romans 2:1–3:20

Of course, we may never do evil that good may come. We may not commit one little sin or tell one little lie, that good may come. Sin is what God hates, and we may not do what God hates in order to please God! Certainly not!

God has the power to turn evil into good. Joseph's brothers sold him to be a slave in Egypt. That was evil, a sin. They meant it for evil, but God turned it to good. By it, the whole land of Egypt and many people in neighboring countries were saved from starvation during the seven years of famine. But still, it was *wrong* for Joseph's brothers to sell him as a slave, and they deserved to be punished for doing it.

It is a vicious slander against Christianity to allege that it teaches the devilish doctrine of "Let us do evil that good may come." That is the doctrine, not of God, but of Satan. Satan has always been suggesting this to people. He started by suggesting it to Eve long ago: "Do evil that good may come." He told Eve that great good would come from disobeying the command of God. God had forbidden Adam and Eve to eat of the fruit of the tree of the knowledge of good and evil. It was therefore wrong to eat the fruit of that tree; it involved the sin of disobedience to God.

But Satan came and said, "Your eyes shall be opened, and ye shall be as gods, knowing good and evil" (Gen. 3:5). In effect he said, "Go ahead and eat the fruit, and you will accomplish a splendid, wonderful result. A great deal of good will come out of it. Why not do a little evil for the sake of so much good?"

There have always been plenty of people working for Satan who suggest the same thing—that it is sometimes right to tell a lie or that it is right to break one of the Ten Commandments, if you do it for a good purpose. People were no doubt saying to Paul, and about Paul, "If human sin results in glorifying God, why, then, we might just as well go ahead and sin. The more the better. Do evil that good may come; the more evil we do, the more good will come." Thus they slandered Paul and represented him as a preacher of Satan's gospel.

How does Paul answer these slanders? He does not stoop to argue with them. He just says about them, "Whose damnation is just" (3:8). People who talk like that deserve to be condemned. Those who do

Romans 2:1–3:20

evil that good may come deserve to be condemned; those who slander Christianity by saying that it teaches such a doctrine deserve to be condemned.

When someone suggests compromise with evil for the sake of some good purpose, remember what this verse says about those who try to do evil that good may come. Their damnation is just. We may not commit one little sin or tell one little lie to keep the whole world from going to pieces.

God is glorified even by wicked people. They glorify God in spite of themselves, without intending to glorify God. God is glorified in punishing their wickedness. But such people bring eternal ruin and loss upon themselves. God is glorified, but they are the losers, forever and ever, because of their own sin.

How much better to glorify God by obedience and righteousness! Especially by accepting and believing on Jesus Christ as our Savior and following Him through the days and years of our lives in this world! How much better to glorify God by embracing His offers of grace and mercy and by becoming His children!

Questions:

1. What is meant by saying that our unrighteousness commends the righteousness of God?
2. What was the difference between the way God was glorified by Abel and the way He was glorified by Cain?
3. What objection to his teaching does Paul mention in 3:5?
4. What is the meaning of Paul's statement, "I speak as a man," in 3:5?
5. Why was God just in punishing Cain, even though Cain's sin resulted in glorifying God?
6. Why is it true that the person who sins never does so with the intention of pleasing or glorifying God?
7. How does Paul answer the objection mentioned in 3:5?
8. Why is it always wrong to do evil that good may come?
9. Show from the history of Joseph that God has the power to turn evil to good in the end.
10. Why were Joseph's brothers deserving of punishment?

Romans 2:1–3:20

11. What is the real source of the doctrine "Let us do evil that good
    may come"?

12. When was this doctrine first introduced into the world, by whom,
    and with what result?

13. What does Paul say about those who advocate doing evil that good
    may come?

14. What is the best and only safe way of glorifying God?

Summary of Argument: Both Jews and Gentiles Are Guilty before God. 3:9–18

Lesson 10

The Jew had great advantages, but these did not enable him to
stand on his own feet before God. Like the Gentile, he too was a
guilty sinner in God's judgment. Paul sums it all up in 3:9. You are
under sin. Humanity as a race is lost in sin and guilty before God.
The Jew, in spite of his advantages, is not an exception. Having stated
this conclusion of his argument, Paul next supports it by a number
of texts quoted from the Old Testament. There are some half dozen
of these given one after another, all with the same teaching, namely,
the universal sinfulness and wickedness of the human race. Most of
these Old Testament texts are quoted from the book of Psalms. One
is from Isaiah. Thus Paul shows that he was not preaching anything
strange or new. It agreed perfectly with the Old Testament. The Jew
could not claim to be sinless, for his own Scriptures emphasized the
universal sinfulness of the human race.

Since all humanity is guilty and lost in sin, the question must be
faced: What is the remedy for this state of affairs? Paul proceeds to
this, but first he carefully tells us of something which is *not* the remedy,
by rejecting what may be called *the old delusion*.

The Old Delusion Rejected. 3:19–20

The "old delusion" is the ancient, popular, ingrained error that man
can somehow save himself. It is properly called "salvation by works,"
but in our day it is more likely to be labeled "salvation by character,"
"character building," or perhaps "the religion of the Golden Rule."

Romans 2:1–3:20

Paul rejects this idea that sinful man can save himself by living a good life, reforming, changing his habits, or "turning over a new leaf." Salvation by human works, which Paul calls "the works of the law," is forever impossible. "Therefore by the deeds of the law there shall no flesh be justified in his sight: for by the law is the knowledge of sin" (3:20).

There is no more serious religious fallacy than this old delusion. It is an age-old error, yet ever new, ever recurring, never dying. It is Satan's most effective snare for keeping millions of people from Christ. "Be good and you will go to heaven"; "live a good life"; or "be religious; go to church, and you will be saved." Obviously such a program is not Christianity, for it is common to all the heathen religions of the world. There is not a false religion or heathen cult in the world that does not teach that man can save himself by good works or a good life.

God's holy law cuts off such expectations at the root. Why? Because God's law cannot be satisfied with a *partial, imperfect obedience*. God's law demands *moral perfection*—to love the Lord our God with all our heart, with all our soul, with all our mind, and with all our strength, and to love our neighbor as ourselves. That is moral perfection. Falling short of that is sin. Hence the law of God not only cannot save us; it reduces us to an admission of our guilt before God: "Now we know that what things soever the law saith, it saith to them who are under the law: that every mouth may be stopped, and all the world may become guilty before God" (3:19). The law, and works performed in obedience to the law, cannot save us. They cannot justify us before God. The law is for diagnosis, not for cure. "By the law is the knowledge of sin" (3:20). The law of God is a mirror, showing us ourselves as we really are in God's sight. It reveals that we are deathly sick of an incurable disease—the disease of sin. For the remedy we must go to God, who alone has the power to work miracles and to accomplish impossible things.

God's law is, to the sinner, not good advice, but an indictment. It declares him guilty, it convicts him of sin.

Romans 2:1–3:20

Application to Ourselves.

In applying these truths to ourselves, we may ask ourselves three questions, namely:

(1) Do we rebel in our hearts against the statements of 3:10–18? Do we feel that we cannot be as bad as that? If we do, then it is our *feelings* against the testimony of God's word. We are fighting against God. It is only God's grace that has kept any of us from being in full detail as wicked as the description given in these verses. Our nature and our sinful heart are exactly as described in 3:10–18; only God in His mercy has held the outward expression of our sin partly in check. We need the Holy Spirit in our hearts, and then we can read these verses over and say "Amen" to them verse by verse.

(2) Have we finished with the old delusion of self-salvation? A drowning man must quit struggling before he can be rescued. We must stop trying to save ourselves before we can receive salvation from Christ. We might as well try to swim across the Atlantic Ocean as try to save ourselves from sin and gain eternal life by our own works or character. Jesus said, "Come unto me, all ye that labour and are heavy laden, and I will give you rest" (Matt. 11:28). That means, first and foremost, rest from the futile struggle of trying to save ourselves by our own actions and efforts. We are to stop trying to save ourselves and to rest in Christ's salvation.

(3) Have we learned the great lesson of the law of God? "By the law is the knowledge of sin" (3:20). If we have learned this great lesson we will realize that the law has a *personal* meaning for us individually. We can read over the Ten Commandments and ask ourselves after each one, How do I plead, guilty or not guilty? If we have learned the great lesson of the law of God, we will plead guilty after every commandment. We will realize and confess that there is not one of them that we have not broken in word, thought, and deed. We will realize that our only hope is to throw ourselves on the mercy of the court—that is, on God's mercy. When a person gets to that point, he soon finds out what it is to experience God's salvation. For if we have really learned the great lesson of the law of God, we will go to Christ and trust Him as our Savior. If the law of God has done us any real good, it will drive us to Christ.

Questions:

1. What conclusion of his argument does Paul state in 3:9?
2. Why does Paul cite several texts from the Old Testament in support of this conclusion?
3. What is the truth set forth in all these Old Testament texts?
4. What is "the old delusion" that Paul rejects in 3:19–20?
5. What are some of the names by which this old delusion is called in our own day?
6. How is this old delusion used by Satan?
7. How can it be shown that this old delusion is not Christianity?
8. How does God's law cut the root of all schemes of self-salvation?
9. What kind of obedience is demanded by the law of God?
10. If the law cannot save, what is its function in relation to the sinner?
11. If our hearts rebel against the teaching of 3:10–18, what does this indicate as to our spiritual state?
12. What is the meaning of Jesus' invitation in Matthew 11:28?
13. What is the great lesson of the law of God for sinners?
14. If we have really learned the great lesson of the law of God, what will we do next?

Romans 2:1–3:20

Chapter 3

GOD'S WAY OF JUSTIFYING SINNERS

Justification by Faith Defined and Expounded. 3:21–31
Lesson 11

The apostle has already shown that we are all sinners needing salvation. The Jews and the Gentiles are alike in this respect. People may differ in the kinds of sin they are involved in, and in the degree of their sin, but not in the *fact* of their being sinners against God. All are lost sinners; all need salvation.

Paul has also pointed out the great mistake of supposing that we can somehow save ourselves by being good or by doing good. It is no use. All attempts to save ourselves by a good life—"the deeds of the law"—are bound to result in dismal failure, because we cannot obey God's law perfectly. The law cannot save us; it can only convince us that we are sinners. Paul sums it all up in 3:20, "Therefore by the deeds of the law there shall no flesh be justified in his sight: for by the law is the knowledge of sin." These words are a stone wall against which all schemes of self-salvation must inevitably crash.

Having exposed the hopelessness of self-salvation, Paul now proceeds to explain God's way of salvation for lost sinners. He calls it "justification" or "being justified."

Romans 3:21–31

Justification Introduced. 3:21–23

We can never attain or achieve righteousness by our own efforts. But there is *another kind of righteousness*, which Paul begins to explain in verse 21. He calls it "the righteousness of God." That is by way of contrast; it is the righteousness that we get from God not from ourselves. When a person thinks himself pretty good, we say that such a person is "self-righteous." Now the "righteousness of God" is the opposite of "self-righteousness." The self-righteous person tries to be righteous by his own efforts. But the person who has the righteousness of God gets it as a gift from God.

Paul goes on to say that this righteousness of God is "without the law." People try to be self-righteous by strenuous efforts to obey the law of God. They think that the harder they try, the more righteous they will be. Self-righteousness is "with the law." It is an attempt to attain righteousness by law observance. But the righteousness of God is "without the law." No matter how lawless or wicked a person has been, he can still receive the righteousness of God. And no matter how hard a person has tried to obey the laws of God, he cannot contribute the least bit to the righteousness of God. We get it, perfect and entire, as a *gift of God*, quite apart from any efforts of our own at keeping God's law.

Paul adds that this righteousness of God is "witnessed by the law and the prophets." That is, this righteousness of God that he is speaking of is not a novelty, not a strange, new doctrine; it is something described and illustrated in the Old Testament Scriptures. Not so fully as in the New Testament, of course, but still the essence of the truth was there in the Old Testament.

In introducing the righteousness of God, Paul tells one more thing about it. It is "by faith"—by faith in Jesus Christ—to all believers. All need it; it is available to all; all who really want it can have it, not by struggling and working, but by believing on Christ as their Savior.

Justification Defined: Its Meaning Stated. 3:24

It is very clear that the words "justify" and "justification" in Paul's writings have a *legal* meaning. Justification is explained by Paul as a judicial sentence.

Romans 3:21–31

The word "justify" means literally "to pronounce or declare righteous." It means more than "pardon," more than "forgive," even more than "acquit." If a person is accused of some crime and tried in a court of justice, and finally the jury brings in a verdict of acquittal, the members of the jury will say, "Not guilty." In other words, that the accused person is not a bad citizen, because he has not broken the law by committing the crime of which he was accused. But "justification" means more than that. When God *justifies* a person, He does more than pardon that person, more than forgive that person's sins, more than pronounce that person "not guilty." When God justifies a person, He not only pronounces that person "not guilty," but He goes on and pronounces that person "positively righteous."

Suppose a mother is going out for the afternoon and leaves two children alone in the house for a couple of hours. Before leaving, she says, "Don't play with the dishes; don't play with the water; and don't touch the sugar bowl." If the children are careful to leave all those things alone, they will be "not guilty" of disobeying their mother. But suppose they want to please their mother very much, so while she is out they pick up all the toys and playthings from all over the house and carefully put them where they belong, and then get rags and dust all the furniture in the living room. Now when the mother returns she can pronounce them not only "not guilty" but also "positively righteous."

Someone has said that "Justified means just-as-if-I'd." Of course, this is not the derivation of the word. But it may help us to grasp the meaning of the term. If I am justified, it is just-as-if-I'd never done anything wrong, and it is just-as-if-I'd always done everything that is good and right. Because I am a sinner, I have not only done many things that I ought not to have done, but have also neglected the things that I ought to have done. But when I am justified, it is just-as-if-I'd always done everything that it was my duty to do. God not only forgives my sins, and declares me "not guilty," but He goes further than that and says that it is just-as-if-I'd always done all kinds of good things, just-as-if-I'd always lived a perfect life, a life of perfect righteousness.

Romans 3:21–31

To live a perfect life (which, of course, is impossible for us sinners to do) means to love God supremely, with all our heart and soul and mind and strength, and to love our fellow man as ourselves. Of course we have fallen far, far short of that ideal. But when we are justified, God Himself declares that it is *just as if* we had always lived a perfect life.

Questions:

1. What verse in Romans 3 is a stone wall against which all schemes of self-salvation must crash?
2. After explaining that we cannot attain righteousness by our own efforts, what other kind of righteousness does Paul speak of?
3. What is the opposite of "the righteousness of God"?
4. What is meant by saying that the righteousness of God is "without the law"?
5. What statement of Paul shows that the truth of the righteousness of God is not a novelty?
6. What is the literal meaning of the word "justify"?
7. Why is it true that justification means more than pardon, forgiveness, or acquittal?
8. What is meant by saying "justified means just-as-if-I'd"?
9. In addition to declaring a person "not guilty," what further declaration does God make in justifying a person?
10. What is involved in living a perfect life?
11. How can a sinner be credited with the righteousness of a perfect life?

Justification Is Free.

Lesson 12

In defining justification, Paul goes on to tell us three facts about it. Firstly, justification is *free*. "Being justified freely" (3:24). When something is free, we get it without paying for it or working for it; we get it for nothing. The most important thing in life can be had for nothing, as a free gift, without money and without price.

The most important thing in life is a legal standing with God. By nature, as sinners, we are outlaws and rebels against God. We need a

Romans 3:21–31

legal standing with God that will make us citizens of His kingdom and thus open the way for the other blessings that only God can give us.

Suppose a man comes to the United States from some foreign country by hiding on a ship as a stowaway. When the ship reaches the shores of America, this stowaway watches for his chance, evades the immigration officers, and sneaks into this country like a thief. He is in America, but he has no legal standing in this country. All around him he sees opportunities; he would like to get a job and improve his condition, but he cannot because he has no legal standing in the country. As soon as he applies for a position of any importance, he will be investigated, and it will be discovered that he entered this country illegally. Before he can take advantage of the opportunities of America, he must have a legal standing in the country. The U. S. government does not bestow a legal standing as a free gift on people who have entered the country illegally. There is only one way such a person can get the legal standing he needs: He must give himself up to the officers of the law, be deported back to his native country, wait his turn for immigration papers, and come to the United States all over again as a legal immigrant.

Our greatest need is for a legal standing with God, for God to pronounce us righteous. And He does it freely, as a gift. It is not something that we deserve; it is not something that we can ever earn or achieve; it is just a free *gift*.

Justification Is by Grace.

Secondly, Paul adds that we are justified "by His grace" (3:24). This means that justification is not only a free gift, but a free gift to the unworthy—and not only to the unworthy, but to those who have offended against God and deserve to be punished. Before God, we are not merely undeserving; we are actually ill-deserving. As the *Westminster Shorter Catechism* says, we deserve God's wrath and curse (Q. 84). God takes sinners who deserve His wrath and curse and declares that they are righteous persons, that it is just as if they had always lived a perfect life! That is the meaning of *grace*.

Suppose a beggar comes to your door and asks for something to eat. You give him a sandwich and a cup of coffee. That is a gift, it is free, because he has not earned it. But now suppose that this same person has broken into your house, stolen some of your property, and taken your automobile and wrecked it. Later he is arrested by the police, and you are given an opportunity to bring legal charges against him and also to sue him for civil damages. Instead of that, you refuse to press any charges, you give the man a new suit of clothes and $100 in cash, and you find a job for him so that he can become a respectable member of the community. That would be not merely a gift, but a gift of grace; it would be favor given not merely to the undeserving, but to the ill-deserving.

God's gift of justification is like that, only we have offended against God far more seriously than the burglar mentioned above has offended against the property owner. We have offended so seriously against God that we actually deserve to die and go to hell forever. Yet God not only does not condemn us to hell; He actually declares that we are as righteous as if we had always done all the good He had a right to expect of us; and He makes us citizens of His kingdom and bestows all blessings, temporal and eternal, upon us. That is *grace*.

Justification Is through Christ's Redemption.

Thirdly, in defining justification, Paul states that it is "through the redemption that is in Christ Jesus" (3:24). At the creation, God said, "Let there be light," and immediately "there was light" (Gen. 1:3), just like that, just by a word of divine creative power. God could make light come out of darkness that way, but even God could not forgive sinners that way. Even God could not just say "let there be forgiveness," "let there be salvation," "let there be justification," and have all those things come to pass just by speaking a word of divine power.

God is almighty, but the Bible teaches us there is one thing that God cannot do. It teaches us that God cannot deny Himself (2 Tim. 2:13). Again the Bible says that God cannot tell a lie (Tit. 1:2; Heb. 6:18). Why cannot God tell a lie? He cannot tell a lie because to tell a lie would be to deny Himself. It would be contrary to His holy nature to tell a lie. God could not tell a lie any more than He could create a square circle or a five sided triangle. It would be contrary to His nature to do so. He cannot deny Himself. God is almighty, but He cannot justify sinners by simply speaking a word of divine power, like saying "Let there be light." For that would be to deny Himself. It would be a contradiction of His absolute justice.

If God were to justify sinners by simply saying, "Let them be justified," then God's justice, which demands that sin be punished, would be denied. No, God does not and cannot justify sinners by simply speaking a word of power. It is not as simple as that. He saves sinners by a plan of salvation, and the central fact of that plan is "the redemption that is in Christ Jesus" (3:24).

God is an honest God. Sinners are not smuggled to heaven by trickery. We believe in an honest God. Because God is absolutely honest, the penalty of the sinner's sin had to be borne, if not by the sinner personally, then by a divinely-provided substitute. Jesus Christ is that divinely-provided substitute, the Lamb of God who takes away the sins of the world.

Jesus Christ suffered and died on the cross to save us from our sins. Salvation is free to us, but look what it cost God to make it free! It cost the sacrifice, the sufferings and death of His beloved Son, Jesus Christ our Redeemer, to make salvation free to sinners. Truly, salvation is a purchased gift. It was purchased at an infinitely costly price, so that it could be bestowed on you and me as a free gift, without money and without price. And that purchase price was the sacrifice on Calvary of the Son of God!

Questions:

1. What is meant by the statement that we are justified freely?
2. What is our great need as sinners?
3. What is the meaning of God's grace, and how does it go beyond a mere gift?
4. What is the difference between being undeserving and being ill-deserving?
5. How seriously have we as sinners offended against God?
6. How did God make light at the Creation?
7. According to the Bible, what is there that God cannot do?

Romans 3:21-31

8. Why can God not tell a lie?

9. Why can God not justify sinners by simply speaking a word of divine power?

10. What is the central fact of God's plan of salvation?

11. What is meant by saying that God is an honest God, and what is the relation of this to the salvation of sinners?

12. What do we mean by calling salvation "a purchased gift"? In what sense is salvation a gift and in what sense is it purchased?

The Ground of Justification. 3:25

Lesson 13

"Christ Jesus: Whom God hath set forth to be a propitiation through faith in his blood, to declare his righteousness for the remission of sins that are past, through the forbearance of God" (3:24–25). The wages of sin is death (6:23), but as far as God's law is concerned, the Christian has already suffered that penalty. He has already been put to death, not in his own person, but in the person of his substitute, Jesus Christ.

Paul tells us that Jesus Christ was set forth to be "a propitiation through faith in his blood." *Propitiation* means "a sacrifice to cancel sin" so that God could justify sinners and still be righteous. The just claims of the law have already been satisfied by Christ on behalf of His people. In Him was no sin; on Him were our sins (Isa. 53:6).

"In his blood." Bloodshed stands for *death*. It was not just the life or the teachings or the example of Christ, but the death of Christ that laid the foundation for our salvation. It was by His death, bearing the penalty of sin in our stead.

Scripture says that we are justified "by faith" and "through faith," but it never says that we are justified "on account of faith." Faith is not the ground of our justification, though without faith we cannot be justified. Nor is the ground of our justification any kind of human merit, such as good works, repentance, or sorrow for sin.

The real ground of our justification is the finished work of Jesus Christ as our substitute—His blood and righteousness. This is shown by Romans 3:25, and also by many other Scripture texts, such as 1 Peter 2:24, "Who his own self bare our sins in his own body on the tree, that

Romans 3:21–31

we, being dead to sins, should live unto righteousness: by whose stripes ye were healed." Also Romans 6:23, "For the wages of sin is death; but the gift of God is eternal life through Jesus Christ our Lord."

The Means of Justification. 3:25

We are justified "by" or "through" faith, but not "on account of" faith. This is very clear from the usage of the Greek New Testament. Faith is not the ground or cause of our justification; it is just the connecting link between us and Christ.

We should realize that faith is a channel, not a force. There is a great deal of unscriptural and very foolish talk about the power of faith. People talk about faith as if it were a force comparable to electricity or atomic energy. We are told that faith has more power than dynamite and so forth. This is extremely false and foolish. The truth is that faith itself has no power at all. It is not a force; it is a channel that connects us to the source of power. An electric wire is not a force; it is the channel of connection with the dynamo (or generator) that is the real source of the power. The electric energy comes from the dynamo, not from the wire, but the wire has to be there as the channel for the energy to flow through.

Faith as a connecting link or means of contact with Christ is illustrated by Christ's miracles during the days of His flesh. The power to work the miracles was in Christ alone. Yet He would often ask whether the person believed or not; and sometimes He would specify some action to be performed that would serve as a token or evidence of faith: to go and wash in the Pool of Siloam or to roll away the stone from the door of the tomb of Lazarus, for example. These actions in themselves had no power to perform any mighty work, but they manifested the *faith* that connected these persons with Christ who had all the power that was needed.

There is today no end of vague talk about faith. Some say that "we must have faith in the things we believe in" (a roundabout way of saying nothing at all); some say that we must have faith in our fellow men; while others say that we must have faith in ourselves. But in the Bible we are commanded to have faith *in Christ*. Faith in ourselves will not save us; faith in our fellow men will not save us; the only faith that can save us is faith in Christ as our Savior.

The Aim of Justification. 3:26

"To declare, I say, at this time his righteousness: that he might be just, and the justifier of him which believeth in Jesus" (3:26).

The aim of justification is to manifest God's glory in the salvation of human beings. Justification brings no credit whatever to us; all of the glory goes to God, who is the source and author of it. It declares, or brings out plainly, two things about God's character: His love, and His justice.

For God merely to forgive sin would be unrighteous; it would be a contradiction to His justice, for He cannot clear the guilty. God's love leads Him to forgive and justify sinful man, but His justice demands that sinners be condemned and punished. How can this problem be solved? Only by the cross of Jesus Christ, who suffered the penalty that justice demanded, so that we can receive forgiveness as the gift of God's love.

So it appears how God can both be righteous and also justify sinners; how he can be just and, at the same time, be the justifier of him that believes in Jesus. This is very different from the easy-going modern idea that God is too kind and loving to punish anyone for sin. According to the Bible, sin was such a serious matter and such a terrible contradiction of God's character that the only way God could justify sinful human beings was for God's own Son, Jesus Christ, to bear the penalty of the broken law in the sinner's stead.

The Effect of Justification. 3:27–31

"Where is boasting then? It is excluded. By what law? or works? Nay: but by the law of faith. Therefore we conclude that a man is justified by faith without the deeds of the law" (3:27–28).

The effect of God's way of justification is, in a word, to humble man and exalt God, which is exactly the opposite of the popular religion of the present day. "Boasting" or self-righteousness is excluded, Paul affirms, because what we receive in justification is simply a free gift to which we had no claim. If we could earn our salvation by living a good life, then we might have something to be proud about, to boast about. It is not so.

The popular religion of today approaches God saying, "Something in my hand I bring"—good works, social service, a good character, etc. But the true Christian approaches God saying, "Nothing in my hand I bring." If we bring nothing, then we have nothing to boast about. The lie of self-righteousness is cut off at the root.

Another effect of justification is that it establishes the law: "Do we then make void the law through faith? God forbid: yea, we establish the law" (3:31). Some of Paul's Jewish opponents would accuse him of "making void" (nullifying) the authority of the law of God by his doctrine of salvation by free grace through faith. Paul repudiates the criticism. The doctrine of justification by faith does not in any way cancel or even minimize the claims of the law of God. For the justification of sinners is not accomplished by any evasion or bypassing of the law. God does not somehow relax the demands of His law and agree to take sinners into heaven on lower terms than an absolute and perfect obedience. On the contrary, God demands perfect obedience, and no one will ever get into heaven by any other way. By God's plan of salvation that perfect obedience is rendered, not by the sinner personally, but by the divinely-provided substitute, the Lord Jesus Christ. The law required that the death penalty be paid for sin: "The wages of sin is death" (6:23). But the penalty, in full, was paid on Calvary. The claims of the law were not disregarded or bypassed; they were satisfied to the full. Hence God's way of justification actually establishes the law. It provides for the salvation of sinners while maintaining the absolute sanctity of the law of God.

Today many people have no real sense of guilt before God. This is the problem with the modern Church. It is not that we do not have good enough methods or that we have too little evangelism, but that the sense of guilt has been thoroughly undermined and subverted by modern thought, which is today percolating clear through to the grass-roots level of our culture. Christ did not come to call the righteous, but sinners to repentance. The church that attempts to call the righteous to repentance is engaging in an impossible task. Human self-righteousness must be cut off at the root and sinners humbled before God.

The doctrine of justification is the heart of the Bible, the center of Christianity, and the very core of the gospel. In essence it is taught in the Old Testament, but it is set forth more fully and more clearly in the New Testament, especially in Paul's Epistles to the Romans and Galatians. This great truth was known by the early Church but was gradually lost and forgotten. For about a thousand years, it was practically unknown. At the Reformation, beginning with Martin Luther (1517), it was recovered and preached with power. The result was the greatest revival the world has ever known.

Today the truth of justification is all but forgotten again. Many church members and professing Christians have never even heard of it. But we have received it as a torch of divine truth from those who knew and believed it before us. It is ours to hold high, not only for the present, but for transmission to the future. It is the bulwark of our Christian faith and the rock of our liberties. "If the Son therefore shall make you free, ye shall be free indeed" (John 8:36). There is no freedom like the freedom from the guilt and condemnation of sin.

Questions:

1. What is the wages of sin, and how has the Christian already suffered that penalty?
2. What is the meaning of the term "propitiation"?
3. Why is the phrase "in his blood" added to "propitiation"?
4. What is the difference between being justified "by" or "through" faith and being justified "on account of" faith?
5. What is the real grounds of our justification?
6. Why is faith not the grounds of our justification?
7. What is meant by saying that faith is a channel not a force?
8. How is the truth that faith is a channel not a force illustrated by Christ's miracles?
9. What is the only kind of faith that can save us?
10. What is the aim of justification?
11. What two facts about God's character does justification bring out?

Romans 3:21–31

12. What is the effect of justification with reference to human pride?

13. Why does justification by faith exclude human boasting?

14. What is the effect of justification with reference to the claims of the law of God?

15. How does justification establish the law?

16. Why is it that many people today have no sense of guilt before God?

17. Why are all church programs and endeavors futile unless people are brought to a sense of guilt before God?

18. What Reformer was prominent in reviving the doctrine of justification by faith after it had been forgotten for centuries?

19. What is the importance of the doctrine of justification in the Bible?

20. In what books of the Bible is the doctrine of justification most clearly and fully set forth?

21. What is the present status of the doctrine of justification?

22. What is our duty with respect to the doctrine of justification?

Justification by Faith Illustrated from the Life of Abraham. 4:1–25

Lesson 14

In chapters 1–3 of this epistle, Paul has established the universal need for salvation and has defined and expounded God's way of justifying sinners. We come now, in chapter 4, to an illustration of the truth of justification by faith taken from the life of the patriarch Abraham.

The Old Testament Teaches that Abraham Was Justified by Faith. 4:1–3

If Abraham had been justified by works, he would have had something to glory about. If his standing with God was a matter of performance, achievement, character, or works, then he would have had something to be proud of. But Paul immediately says, "but not before God." That is to say that Abraham did *not* have anything to glory of before God. For the Scripture said plainly, "Abraham believed God, and it was counted unto him for righteousness" (4:3, quoted from

Romans 4:1–25

Gen. 15:6). Therefore, it is plain that the Old Testament teaches that Abraham's standing with God was not obtained by *doing* something but by *believing* something; it was by faith, not by works.

Therefore Abraham Was Not Justified by Works. 4:4–8

In teaching that Abraham was justified by faith, the Old Testament at the same time teaches that he was not justified by works, for these two principles, grace and works, exclude each other. It is a case of "either...or," not of "both...and." In verses 4–8, Paul brings out this antithesis between faith and works and supports it by the statements of David in Psalm 32.

First of all, *grace* is contrasted with *debt*. If a person is justified by works, then his salvation is not a matter of grace but of debt. In that case, salvation is not a gift but a payment; not God giving us a gift but God paying us a debt; not something that comes to us from the free mercy and love of God but something that comes from God's honesty in meeting His obligations.

But, according to the Bible, salvation is not like that. It is not a matter of God paying debts; it is a matter of God's grace. Therefore it comes "to him that worketh not, but believeth on him that justifieth the ungodly" (4:5). Salvation is not a debt that God pays to good people; it is a free gift that He gives to bad people, to "the ungodly." To such bad people who believe God counts their faith for righteousness. Thus verse 5 proves that, according to the Bible, faith is not a work in the sense of having any merit or deserving any reward. Some people say that God no longer requires of people today the perfect obedience that He originally required of Adam. It is impossible for us sinners to obey God's law perfectly, so God has graciously condescended to lower His requirements and now requires of us only faith, or believing, and our act of believing is a substitute for the perfect works of righteousness that we cannot render. According to this idea, God is like a creditor who cannot collect the full amount of a debt from a debtor, so he says, "Since this man obviously cannot pay the full amount of his debt, I will be satisfied with a token payment of one dollar, and when that one dollar is paid, I will just regard the whole debt as paid and close the account." So, some people say, "We cannot perfectly obey the Ten Commandments, but we can believe. That, at least is a work within our power to perform, and God is willing to accept our act of believing as a token payment and close the account."

The interpretation we have just been mentioning is, of course, entirely wrong. God has never lowered His requirements of the human race. He still requires a perfect righteousness, a perfect obedience to His law, and no one will ever receive eternal life on lower terms. What God has done is not to lower His requirements, but to accept the perfect obedience of a substitute, Jesus Christ, instead of the sinner's personal obedience. God's plan of salvation involves not a lowering of God's requirements, but a substitution of the person who complies with the requirements.

That believing is not regarded as a work, and is not accepted by God as a token obedience to His requirements, is proved by the first part of verse 5, which directly contrasts "working" and "believing"— "But to him that worketh not, but believeth..." That is, salvation is not a matter of working, but a matter of believing; not a matter of doing something, but a matter of receiving something. Therefore, believing is not a token form of working. Believing is the opposite of working; it is the negation of working. Believing is not an activity at all, but it is a receptivity.

In verses 6–8, this truth is confirmed from the words of David, quoted from Psalm 32:1–2. David describes the blessedness of the saved man. He says that this man's iniquities are forgiven, his sins are covered, and the Lord will not impute sin to him. Therefore, says Paul, David is describing the blessedness of the man to whom God imputes righteousness without works. Here "imputeth" (4:6) is contrasted with the idea of ill works. God imputes righteousness without works. Righteousness, therefore, does not come by our earning it or deserving it, but by God imputing it to us when we have not earned it and do not deserve it.

This word "impute," and the corresponding noun "imputation," is one of the great terms of the Scriptures. We cannot understand the gospel without understanding the meaning of "impute" and

Romans 4:1–25

"imputation." To impute means to reckon or to place something to
the credit or debit of someone. When God imputes sin to a person
(4:8), He holds or regards that person guilty of sin. When God imputes
righteousness to a person, He regards that person as righteous, and He
reckons righteousness to the credit of that person. Paul is telling us that
righteousness comes, not by our earning it, but by God imputing it to us.

We have seen, in 4:4–8, grace contrasted with debt, faith contrasted
with works, and imputation contrasted with earning. Salvation comes
to a person by grace, by faith, by imputation; it does not come to a
person as payment of a debt nor by works nor by earning it.

Questions:

1. What truths has Paul established in the first three chapters of the
    epistle?
2. What is the subject of chapter 4?
3. What text of the Old Testament proves that Abraham was justified
    by faith?
4. Why could not Abraham have been justified by both faith and
    works?
5. What is the difference between giving a gift and paying a debt?
6. Is salvation given to good people or to bad people? What phrase
    in 4:5 proves this?
7. What wrong interpretation of 4:5 has been advocated by some?
8. What is wrong with the idea that "believing" is accepted by God
    as a token payment of the obedience that we owe to His law?
9. How does 4:5 prove that believing is not a token form of working
    and does not involve any merit?
10. Instead of lowering His requirement of a perfect righteousness,
    what has God done to make it possible for sinners to receive eternal
    life?
11. What is meant by saying, "Believing is not an activity at all, but it
    is a receptivity"?
12. From what Psalm does Paul quote in 4:7–8?
13. What is the meaning of the words "impute" and "imputation"?
14. What contrast is set forth in 4:6?

Romans 4:1–25

Abraham Was Justified Apart from Sacraments. 4:9–12
Lesson 15

In verses 9–12, Paul proceeds to show that Abraham was justified apart from sacraments. He carefully shows that Abraham was pronounced righteous by God (Gen. 15:6) *before* he received the rite of circumcision (Gen. 17:26). Therefore he was not justified because of circumcision. He received justification first and circumcision afterwards. Therefore, justification does not depend on circumcision.

The rite of circumcision was the seal of the covenant relationship in Old Testament times (Gen. 17:11). It was the Old Testament counterpart of the sacrament of baptism. Just as Abraham was justified apart from circumcision, so we today are justified apart from baptism and apart from the Lord's supper.

Many people today are not clear on this point. There are formalists who count heavily on their careful observance of baptism and the Lord's supper to give them a standing with God. In the case of some people, this becomes a form of salvation by works very much like that of the Pharisees of Paul's day. It is easy to see that they look upon their baptism with a complacent feeling and regard their regular attendance upon the Lord's supper as entitling them to some credit with God.

But the Bible is against them. Sacraments are appointed in God's Word. They are a real means of grace, and it is our duty to observe them conscientiously. But they do not constitute a form of "works," and they do not bring about our being pronounced righteous by God.

Abraham was justified prior to his circumcision. This establishes the principle. Sacraments are our duty, but they cannot contribute anything to our justification. We are justified apart from sacraments by faith.

Abraham Was Justified Apart from Law. 4:13–16

Here a new contrast is added. Paul contrasts "the law" with "the righteousness of faith" (4:13). He tells us that God's promise to Abraham was not "through the law" but "through the righteousness of faith."

The effect of added and particularized law is to increase transgression. Therefore it cannot be the means of Abraham or his seed becoming heir of the world (4:14–15). God made to Abraham *an absolute promise* "that he should be the heir of the world" (4:13). Now if Abraham was justified by the law, then this absolute promise of God must have fallen to the ground. "Because the law worketh wrath: for where no law is, there is no transgression" (4:15). Consider, for example, the income tax law. If there were no income tax law, then there would be no violations of the income tax law. The more comprehensive and particularized the law is made, the more occasions for violations there will be. The more law, the more transgression of law. This is especially true in the case of God's absolute, perfect, holy law. Since it is true that "the law worketh wrath," the law cannot be the source of Abraham's justification. And, as a matter of fact, the law was not the source of his justification. Actually, he was justified apart from the law, as a matter of free grace or promise.

Since it was a matter, not of law, but of promise, it was also "of faith" and "by grace" (4:16). The same thing is true today. Justification is not obtained by carefully obeying God's commandments; it is in fulfilment of God's promise, a matter of faith by grace. We receive it just as Abraham did, not by works, not by sacraments, not by law-obedience, but through faith, by God's grace or gift.

The Nature of Abraham's Faith. 4:17–22

We are next given a summary of the nature of Abraham's faith. First of all, it was faith in God, that is, of course, in the living and true God. It is not just faith that saves people, not just faith as a psychological trait or attitude, but faith in the living and true God. In the Bible, faith is never considered in the abstract apart from its object. Always it is considered as faith *in* something or someone. It is the object of faith that makes all the difference. Abraham did not merely believe; he believed God. That was why his faith had such wonderful consequences.

Then Abraham's faith was faith in God's supernatural working: "God, who quickeneth the dead, and calleth those things which be not as though they were" (4:17). Abraham was not a pantheist like the modernists and liberals of the present day, who think of God as caught and meshed in the laws of the universe so that He is limited by natural laws.

Romans 4:1–25

Abraham believed in a supernatural God, a God who can and does work miracles, a God in whose hands the universe with its laws is absolutely obedient, a God who can act directly, apart from natural laws, if He chooses to do so. He is a God that gives life to the dead—something contrary to nature. There is no life in death, but God, being almighty, can give life to the dead. He is a supernatural, miracle-working God. (Compare with Hebrews 11:17–19.)

Also, Abraham's faith was a faith that believed in spite of apparent impossibility (4:19–20). According to human experience, it was impossible for Isaac to be born to Abraham and Sarah in their old age. But this was what God had promised, and though humanly it would be regarded as impossible, Abraham believed the promise. "He staggered not at the promise of God through unbelief; but was strong in faith, giving glory to God" (4:20).

His faith was not founded in probability, but on the reliability of God, regardless of appearances or probabilities (4:21). He was fully persuaded that God was able to perform what He had promised, even though the promise concerned something that human experience would regard as impossible. It was this faith that "was imputed to him for righteousness," that is, it was this faith in the almighty, miracle-working God that resulted in God's accounting Abraham righteous.

We Are Justified in the Same Way that Abraham Was. 4:23–25

The principle is the same in Abraham's case as in our own. He believed on the strength of a promise concerning future redemption; we believe on the promise already fulfilled, on a Savior who has already come and accomplished our redemption: Jesus Christ "who was delivered for our offenses, and was raised again for our justification" (4:25). In both cases justification is by faith, and this faith in both cases is faith in the almighty, miracle-working God.

Questions:
1. How can it be shown from the book of Genesis that Abraham was justified apart from sacraments?
2. What is the true place of sacraments in a person's salvation?

Romans 4:1–25

3. What do we call those who place their trust in their observance of the sacraments?

4. What promise did God make to Abraham? Was this an absolute promise or a conditional one?

5. If Abraham had been justified by law, what would have happened to God's promise?

6. What truth about God's law is taught in 4:15?

7. What is the true place of obeying God's law in a person's Christian life?

8. What is meant by saying that in the Bible faith is never considered in the abstract?

9. What is pantheism, and what is wrong with its idea of God?

10. What false system of the present day is largely dominated by a pantheistic idea of God?

11. How was Abraham's faith different from that of a pantheist?

12. What is God's relation to the natural laws of the universe?

13. What was the character of Abraham's faith concerning the promised birth of Isaac?

14. In what respect is the Christian's faith the same as Abraham's faith?

15. In what respect is the Christian's faith different from Abraham's faith?

The Results of a Legal Standing before God. 5:1–11
Lesson 16

In Chapters 1–4, Paul has, first, discussed the *need* for justification or a legal standing before God; second, revealed the *meaning* of justification; third, illustrated the *truth* of justification from the life of Abraham, showing that Abraham was justified by faith, not by sacraments or law observance. Beginning with chapter 5, the apostle moves on to consider the *fruits* of justification, or what we may call the results of a legal standing before God.

Peace with God. 5:1

Scripture speaks of two kinds of peace: (1) the peace of God, which passes all understanding; (2) peace with God. We must have peace *with* God before we can enjoy the peace *of* God.

Romans 5:1–11

Verse 1 tells us that the person who has been justified by faith has peace with God through our Lord Jesus Christ. This assumes that formerly we were at war with God. If we had never been at war with God, we could not talk about obtaining peace with God.

If someone were to tell us that next week a treaty of peace would be made between Canada and the United States, we would rightly reply: "Why? Canada and the United States are not at war with each other; they are at peace with each other and have been for more than 100 years." But if someone speaks of making a peace treaty between Germany and the United States, that makes sense, because a few years ago Germany and the United States were at war with each other, and no final peace treaty has yet been made between them. (*Editor's Note:* The Treaty on the Final Settlement with Respect to Germany was negotiated and finalized on Sept. 12, 1990 and officially ended World War II.)

Before sinful human beings can have peace with God, the cause of the enmity between them must be taken away. No war, even in human affairs, is really settled until the cause has been dealt with and corrected. A peace that leaves the old cause of friction the same as it was before is not a peace but only an armistice.

In the case between God and ourselves, the cause of the enmity was sin. It was sin that separated God from the human race. That sin has been taken care of by the atonement of our Savior Jesus Christ. The cause of the enmity has been taken away. So the justified person has, first of all, peace with God.

Peace with God is the necessary preparation for all the later steps of the Christian life. Nothing can be right with us or our life as long as we are at war with God, our Maker. So the apostle first of all mentions peace with God as the result of justification.

Joy in Anticipation of Future Glory. 5:2

We "rejoice in hope of the glory of God" (5:2). This word *rejoice* means, literally, "triumph." It is the joy that accompanies a great victory. We triumph in *hope* of the glory of God. Glory is what is reserved for the life of eternity. We get it in heaven and especially after the resurrection of the body at the end of the world. When we shall rise with changed

and immortal bodies to live forever, we shall receive the highest glory
and blessedness. Since glory is something reserved for the future, and
we cannot have it right away, we look forward to it with hope—with
anticipation of enjoying it.

We are looking forward to a day when the present conflict in
Korea will come to an end, and the men in the armed forces can come
home to their families again and enjoy life in their own country. (*Editor's Note:* The Korean War lasted from June 25, 1950 to July 27, 1953.
President Harry Truman authorized the United States Armed Forces
to assist non-Communist South Korea on June 27, 1950.) That is hope
concerning matters of this present earthly life. But as Christians we
look forward to the time when we shall inherit the glory of God, the
fullness of eternal life that is reserved for us in heaven.

Triumph Even in Present Troubles. 5:3–5

We are not in the state of glory now; on the contrary, we are in
a life that is replete with trouble, suffering, and woe. Yet these verses
state that we can triumph even in our present troubles—our "tribulations." This triumph comes by reason of the progress of our Christian
growth. Look at the ascending ladder of Christian growth which is
here placed before us.

(A) Tribulation. This is unavoidable for a Christian in this present
world, as our Savior said: "In the world ye shall have tribulation;
but be of good cheer; I have overcome the world" (John 16:33).

(B) Patience, or endurance, by tribulation successfully endured
by going through it and learning that we can maintain our
Christian faith and testimony in spite of tribulation.

(C) Experience, or more accurately approval; that is, God's approval of us and our own consciousness of His approval of us.

(D) New and reliable hope, which will not disappoint us as a fading
mirage—a hope that "maketh not ashamed."

(E) God's love shed abroad in our hearts. This does not mean our
love for God; it means God's love for us. The Bible tells us,
"he careth for you" (1 Pet. 5:7).

Romans 5:1–11

The consciousness of God's love is made to fill our hearts by the operation of the Holy Spirit within us. The present consciousness of God's favor is a proof that our Christian hope will not disappoint us and will not make us ashamed.

Parenthesis. 5:6–8

Here the apostle pauses in his argument to speak of the wonder of God's love for us. It is a love for helpless enemies (compare 5:10), which is unparalleled in human relationships. Men might be willing to die for a really good man, but certainly not for a merely righteous man. Note that Paul does not speak of merely risking life, but of actually dying for another. But God's love is bestowed on the sinful and rebellious. God's grace does not find men fit to be loved; it makes them fit to be loved.

Salvation from the Wrath of God. 5:9

"The wrath of God is revealed from heaven against all ungodliness and unrighteousness of men" (1:18). But so far as the Christian is concerned, God's wrath is a fire that has already burnt itself out. It cannot touch him.

Christ in His sufferings and death in Gethsemane and on Calvary absorbed it all, every bit of the wrath of God. None was left to fall upon us. He drank the bitter cup to the last drop. There may be sufferings, tribulations, and afflictions appointed for us, but they will not be bitter by reason of the wrath of God mixed with them. The Christian must pass through death and must also stand before the judgment seat of Christ, but neither death nor the judgment is a messenger of divine wrath to the Christian. That wrath has already been exhausted on Calvary; that wrath has been completely extracted from God's dealings with the Christian.

The one place that is really safe in a raging prairie fire is a large patch that has already been thoroughly burned over. The flames cannot come there to destroy. The Christian is "in Christ," in whom the flames of God's wrath against sin have already consumed to the limit. It is a safe refuge from the wrath of God.

Romans 5:1–11

Salvation with Life. 5:10

Since Christ suffered and died to cancel our debt to God's righteous law, it is certain that He will not forsake us, but that the power of His risen life will be exerted to save us to the very end. "I am come that they might have it more abundantly" (John 10:10). Christ is a living Savior, not only from the awful guilt of sin but also from its enslaving power. Jesus died for us, rose again for us, and now He lives to help us.

Salvation Super Abundant. 5:11

Through Christ we have received the "atonement" or reconciliation. Having named the different results of being justified, Paul says again, "We also joy in God through our Lord Jesus Christ." We are saved "in a triumphant manner and frame of mind." Think of Paul and Silas singing praises to God at midnight in the jail at Philippi. God has provided enough and to spare for our salvation. God never does anything by halves, in a partial or incomplete way. So our salvation is full and free, suited to the depth and breadth of our need. We are great sinners, it is true; but let us never forget Christ is a great Savior. "Where sin abounded, grace did much more abound" (5:20).

Questions:

1. What new subject is taken up in Chapter 5?
2. Of what two kinds of peace does the Bible speak?
3. Which must come first, the peace of God or peace with God?
4   Why is it necessary for us to obtain peace with God?
5. What was the cause of the enmity between God and ourselves?
6. What is the place of peace with God in the Christian life?
7. When shall Christians receive the highest glory and blessedness?
8. Why is glory a matter of hope?
9. What steps of Christian growth are mentioned in 5:3–5?
10. What is the love that is shed abroad in for us?
11. What is the special wonder of God's love?
12. Why can the wrath of God not touch the Christian?
13. What is the meaning of "we shall be saved by his life" (5:10)?
14. What is the meaning of "the atonement" (5:11)?

In Bringing Men Eternal Life, Christ Succeeds where Adam Failed. 5:12–21

Lesson 17

We might call this section, 5:12–21, "The Covenant of Works Fulfilled in the Covenant of Grace." It is the great New Testament interpretation of the Covenant of Works and its relation to the saving work of Christ.

The historical characters of Adam and Eve and their fall into sin is assumed in these verses. The apostle's argument depends on it. Any view of the book of Genesis that interprets the story of Adam and Eve and their fall into sin otherwise than literally, makes utter nonsense of Paul's argument in the verses that are before us. If the story of Adam and Eve is a mere myth or allegory, as many claim today, then what the apostle says in Romans 5:12–21 is just foolishness. It depends on the fact there was a real Adam and a real Eve, who lived at a particular time and place, and on a particular day fell into sin.

A popular news magazine made the following statement: "Anthropologists no longer look for a definite single place where the human race first appeared on earth. They know that man's ancestors were numerous, varied and widely distributed before they were fully human." ("Cultural Eden," *TIME*, Nov. 12, 1945, p. 50).

In spite of this unbelief of the scientists, it is perfectly clear that both Paul and Jesus Christ taught that Adam was the first man and that he was a single, definite, historical person who lived at a particular time and place—an individual person, the first ancestor and head of the human race.

Summary of the Covenant of Works in the Garden of Eden.

In order to understand Romans 5:12–21, we must have in mind the Covenant of Works, the first covenant God made with the human race. The Covenant of Works was an arrangement made by God and imposed on the human race to bridge the infinite distance between the Creator and His creatures. God took the initiative and approached mankind, so that men could enjoy religious communion with God—could worship, glorify and enjoy God. The creature himself could never have bridged that gap. If God had not taken the initiative and approached mankind, we would have been forever separated by an infinite distance from God.

The Covenant of Works was a temporary probation or test appointed by God, by which, if successfully withstood, Adam and all his posterity would have been confirmed in their original condition of righteousness, so that it would have become forever impossible for mankind to fall into sin. The particular test involved in the probation was a command not to eat the fruit of a particular tree, called the tree of the knowledge of good and evil. This command was intentionally arbitrary to make it a sheer test of obedience to the revealed will of God apart from all reasons of suitability or considerations of human prudence.

The reward for obedience to the will of God was to be life; that is, of course, eternal life, which was symbolized in the garden of Eden by the tree of life that grew in the midst of the garden. If Adam and Eve had gone through the period of probation without disobeying God, the time would have come, sooner or later (we do not know when), when they would have been given the right to eat the fruit of the tree of life. That would have meant that the possibility of sin and death was forever abolished, not only for Adam and Eve personally, but for the entire human race through all the centuries and millennia of human history. There would never have been any such thing as sin or death in the human race.

Thus Adam and Eve had something that we do not have today, namely, an opportunity to earn eternal life by *doing* something, that is, by their works.

The penalty for disobedience was death. This meant, of course, not merely physical death, the death of the body, but total death, that is, eternal death, which the Bible calls "the second death."

In this Covenant of Works, Adam acted not merely as an individual man but as a head or representative of the human race. We might express the matter by saying that Adam acted not merely in a private capacity but also in an official capacity. He acted not merely for himself but for other people also—in fact, for the whole human race.

Romans 5:12–21

The covenant was made with Adam as representing all future generations of men from the garden of Eden to the end of the world. If Adam had remained faithful and obedient to God, all future generations would have been born sinless and would automatically have received eternal life.

On the other hand, when Adam fell into sin, as we know he did, the result was that all human generations to the end of time would be born into this world with a sinful nature and guilty before God because of Adam's first sin.

Although some people object violently to this doctrine, there is no denying that the Word of God teaches it, especially the fifth chapter of the Epistle to the Romans. It is our purpose to expound the Word of God, not to tone it down or apologize for its statements.

The Results of Adam's Breaking the Covenant of Works.

In 5:12 we are informed that "sin entered into the world." This is not only a truth of the Bible, but also something that can be observed around us on every side and within our own hearts and lives. The fact and the universality of sin are obvious everywhere.

The origin of sin in the universe is a mystery. The Bible does not try to explain it to us. What made Satan, a holy angel, change his character and begin to sin against God, we simply do not know. We do know that sin originated outside the human race; it began, not with men, but with the devil. From the devil, it was imported into the human race and entered into the world through one individual human being, namely, Adam.

Sin having entered the world, death also entered the world as the necessary consequence of sin. Both sin and death became universal, coextensive with the human race: "and so death passed upon all men, for that all have sinned" (5:12).

The universality of sin is sometimes questioned or denied, but no one can deny the universality of death. Wherever there are human beings, there you find death. Mankind hungers and thirsts for life. The thirst for life is the strongest of all human impulses. Men will cling to life when all else is gone. They will struggle and strive to live just a few more days or a few more minutes. Yet in spite of this insatiable thirst for life, death overtakes every human being. How can this strange fact be explained?

The evolutionist who regards the present average condition of men as normal cannot explain the fact of death in the face of the hunger for life. But the Bible explains it: "And so death passed upon all men, for that all have sinned" (5:12). The explanation of the thirst for life lies in the nature of mankind, created by God not to die but to eat the fruit of the tree of life and live forever. That deep longing, that powerful impulse toward life, comes down to us today from Adam and Eve who were created to eat the fruit of the tree of life and never die but live forever.

Questions:

1. What is the subject of 5:12–21?
2. What difference does it make whether we believe that Adam and Eve were historical characters and the Fall a historical event?
3. If the story of Adam and Eve is a myth or allegory, what is the effect of this on the apostle Paul's argument in Romans 5:12–21?
4. What is the prevalent theory of scientists concerning the first man?
5. What was the purpose of the Covenant of Works?
6. Why was it necessary that the initiative in bridging the gap be taken by God?
7. What probation or test was involved in the Covenant of Works?
8. What would have been the outcome if Adam had not disobeyed God?
9. What was the reward for obedience in the Covenant of Works?
10. What was the penalty for disobedience in the Covenant of Works?
11. What is the meaning of death as the penalty of sin?
12. What can be said about the origin of sin in the universe?
13. What is the strongest of all human impulses? How is it contradicted by universal human experience?
14. Why can evolutionists not explain the universality of death in the face of the universal hunger for life?
15. How does the Bible explain this mysterious contradiction?
16. What is the source of our powerful hunger for life?

Romans 5:12–21

Death Reigned over Men from Adam to Moses. 5:13–14
Lesson 18

The apostle Paul proves the fact that Adam's transgression affected all his posterity by a reference to the period between Adam and Moses, a period of at least 3,000 years. We should realize that the period from Adam to Moses was at least as long as the period from Moses to the present day.

Sin by definition is "the transgression of the law" (1 John 3:4). The law was formally given in the days of Moses. Adam died because he disobeyed a specific command of God—the command not to eat the fruit of the tree of the knowledge of good and evil. Clearly Adam was a lawbreaker, a transgressor. But what about the people during the long period from Adam to Moses, 3,000 years or more?

Of course during that long period people had the law of God written on their heart and conscience. But the apostle in these verses is not speaking of the law of nature written on all men's hearts. He is speaking about the Ten Commandments, the specially revealed moral law of God. Between Adam and Moses, men did not have that specially revealed moral law of God. Thus they could not be *transgressors* in the full, exact sense of the word. They could not be transgressors as the Jews were after the Ten Commandments were given. They were not exactly transgressors. But were they sinners?

Yes, they must have been sinners, because, Paul tells us, death reigned over them. He says that death reigned from Adam to Moses, even over them that had not sinned after the similitude of Adam's transgression—that is to say, even over those who had not sinned in the same way as Adam sinned, even over those who had not transgressed a positive, specific, specially revealed command of God, as Adam had. Even they were sinners, as is evident from the fact that they all died. Death reigned over them. If they had not been sinners they would not and could not have died, for death is the wages of sin. Thus Adam's transgression resulted in the wreck and ruin of the human race.

Note Paul's clear statements. By Adam's fall, many were made sinners (5:19). By Adam's fall, sin and death reigned over the human

Romans 5:12–21

race (5:17, 21). By Adam's fall, the whole human race was brought under divine judgment unto condemnation (5:16).

Adam and Christ Compared.

Adam was, first of all, our natural head and ancestor. Secondly, he was our federal head or representative in the Covenant of Works. Thirdly, Adam was a "figure" or type of Christ (5:14).

"For as by one man's disobedience many were made sinners, so by the obedience of one shall many be made righteous" (5:19). Note the exact parallel between Adam and Christ. This is why Christ is sometimes called "the second Adam." Just as Adam's fall made us sinners, so Christ's obedience makes us righteous.

Adam brought us into condemnation; that is, he brought us under the condemning judgment of God (5:18). But Christ brings us just the opposite, namely, "justification of life"; that is, justification which results in eternal life.

God never abandoned or abrogated the Covenant of Works. When Adam broke it, it became impossible for sinful human beings to attain eternal life by the Covenant of Works. But God did not discard the Covenant of Works. He simply held it in suspense until the proper time, called in the Bible "the fullness of time," when the second Adam, that is, Jesus Christ, should appear to accomplish what the first Adam had failed to accomplish, namely, to win eternal life for men by perfect obedience to God.

Jesus Christ, the second Adam, by fulfilling the Covenant of Works, made it possible for God to save sinners by a different covenant—the Covenant of Grace. In other words, the Covenant of Works was fulfilled in Christ and thus made a part of a new covenant, the Covenant of Grace, by which sinners are saved.

We should always remember that we are saved, not merely by the sufferings and death of Jesus for us, but also by His perfect life of obedience to God that is reckoned to our account. Both in His life and in His death Jesus rendered a perfect obedience to God as our representative.

Romans 5:12–21

Adam and Christ Contrasted.

Note verse 18, where the phrase "came upon all men" occurs twice. Adam's fall made all men sinners, with only one exception (Jesus Christ, who was born with a sinless human nature). Verse 18 seems to tell us that Christ's obedience makes all men righteous just as Adam's fall made all men sinners. Yet we know from the Bible as well as from experience that not all, but only some, are saved by Christ and receive eternal life. What can be the explanation of the apostle's statement?

It is evident that the "all men" in the first part of verse 18 does not cover exactly the same ground as the "all men" in the second part of the verse. For the bond of connection is different in the two cases. We are connected with Adam by the bond of nature, whereas we are connected with Christ by the bond of faith. Everybody in the world is descended from Adam. In the Covenant of Works he represented all humanity. So judgment and condemnation come upon all men because all men are connected with Adam by the bond of nature. (Of course, the fact that Adam was the ancestor or natural head of the human race was the basis for God constituting him the federal head or representative of all mankind in the Covenant of Works. It was Adam, not Seth or Noah, that was made the representative of all mankind, precisely because it was Adam that was the natural head or ancestor of all mankind.)

But we are not connected to Christ that way. Even though Christ is called "the second Adam," we are not literally His posterity; we are not physically descended from Him. Christ is not the ancestor of the human race as Adam was. The bond of connection between us and Christ is not a natural, but a spiritual bond of faith. Not everybody, but only those who believe, receive justification and eternal life from Christ.

All who are connected with Adam receive condemnation and death from Adam, and since all people are connected with him, this includes everyone. All who are connected with Christ receive justification and eternal life from Him. But since not all, but only some, are connected with Christ by faith, this includes only a part of the human race, namely, those who believe on Christ as their Savior.

Romans 5:12–21

There is also another contrast between Adam and Christ. It is the contrast between a debt and a gift. God owes us judgment and condemnation, but He does not owe us salvation and eternal life. We deserve what we receive from Adam; God would not be just if He did not lay it on us. But we do not deserve what we receive from Christ. God gives salvation to us, not as a matter of debt, but as a free gift.

Note verse 15, where Paul contrasts the offense of Adam with the free gift of Christ. Again in verses 16, 17, and 18 we find this same contrast repeated, with great emphasis laid on the fact that we receive salvation from Christ not as something we are entitled to, but as a *gift of grace*, that is, an undeserved gift. God owes us judgment, but He gives us salvation.

There is still another contrast between Adam and Christ. That concerns the abundance of sin compared with the superabundance of God's grace, as we see in verse 20: "Moreover...where sin abounded, grace did much more abound." God's grace is wider and fuller than man's sin; God's provision is richer than our greatest need.

This may help us to find a partial answer to the question, Why did God permit sin to enter the world? At least we can say that God permitted sin to enter the world because He planned to provide grace and salvation far more rich and abundant than the sin that was allowed to enter. "Grace did much more abound." This does not mean, of course, that everybody is going to be saved, but it does mean that God's salvation is more than enough to meet our every need.

Are You Still under Condemnation?

Adam failed; Christ succeeded. There has thus been provided a perfect, completed plan of salvation. "Whosoever will, let him come." May we accept and receive Christ as our Savior and so make sure that this abounding grace shall be ours.

If we have not received Christ, the second Adam, we are still under the curse and condemnation of the covenant broken by the first Adam. A woman in a local business establishment said to the writer of these notes: "God is kind and loving, and no one should be afraid of God." The writer replied to her: "You should get your ideas of God from the

Bible, not from your own mind. The Bible teaches that God is just and holy and will by no means clear the guilty. If any person is not a Christian he certainly ought to be afraid of God."

If anyone is under the broken Covenant of Works, he ought to be afraid of God. Only when we are sure we are under the Covenant of Grace can we really feel safe and secure.

Questions:

1. Why does Paul speak of the period from Adam to Moses?
2. How long was the period of time between Adam and Moses?
3. Why were the people between Adam and Moses not transgressors in the full sense of the term?
4. How do we know that the people from Adam to Moses were sinners?
5. What two relationships exist between Adam and ourselves?
6. What is the relation of the Covenant of Works to the Covenant of Grace? Was the Covenant of Works abolished when Adam sinned?
7. Does 5:18, "the free gift came upon all men unto justification of life," mean that everybody will be saved?
8. What is the difference between "all men" in the first part of verse 18 and "all men" in the second part of the verse?
9. Wherein does our bond of connection with Adam differ from our bond of connection with Christ?
10. How does our relation to Adam and Christ involve the contrast between a debt and a gift?
11. Which abounds more, human sin or divine grace?
12. Does 5:20 mean that everyone will be saved? If not, what is the meaning of the second part of this verse?
13. Of what great mystery can 5:20 help us to find a partial solution?
14. Who is still under the condemnation of the broken Covenant of Works?
15. Who should be afraid of God and why?
16. When are we warranted in feeling safe and secure?

Chapter 4

THE CHRISTIAN LIFE WHICH FOLLOWS JUSTIFICATION

Objections to the Doctrine of Justification Answered. 6:1–23

Lesson 19

At this point in the epistle, Paul passes from the subject of justification by faith to the consideration of the theme of sanctification, or the moral and spiritual consequences of a legal standing with God. What difference will the fact that a person is justified by faith make in that person's character and daily life?

Paul introduces this new subject by stating and answering two objections to the doctrine of justification by faith as a free gift of God. The first objection is referred to in verse 1 and the second in verse 15.

First Objection Stated and Answered. 6:1–13

An objection to the truth of justification by faith is suggested in verse 1, "What shall we say then? Shall we continue in sin, that grace may abound?" The objection suggested is that the doctrine of free justification implies that a person may continue living in sin in order that grace may abound.

No doubt Paul's opponents were actually making this slanderous charge against the apostle's teaching. Indeed, there has been no time from the apostles to the present day when the same objection has not been raised by opponents of the doctrine of free justification.

Paul has shown that we are justified simply as a free gift of God, just by receiving righteousness imputed to us as a free gift, by an act of faith, that is, of *pure receptivity*, entirely apart from our own character, merits, conduct, good deeds, and so forth. As stated in 3:28, "Therefore we conclude that a man is justified by faith without the deeds of the law."

The opponents of free justification object to this idea. They say, "Well, if a man is justified as a free gift, if he doesn't have to do anything toward earning or deserving his own salvation, then why can a person not accept justification as a free gift, and then go right ahead and live a sinful life? If God is glorified in forgiving my sins and saving me just as a free gift, then the more sins I commit, the more sins God can forgive, and the more sins God forgives, the more He will be glorified! Then justification is just like a blanket permission to go ahead and commit sins, for no matter how many or how wicked the sins we commit, we can always get them forgiven by God as a free gift, to His name's honor and glory. If we are justified just as a free gift of God, then what incentive is there to live a good life? If I am saved anyway, why should I make any effort to live a good life? Why not just continue in sin, that grace may abound?"

So ran the objection. Since opponents were making this slanderous charge, the apostle at this point undertakes to answer it. First of all he denies the charge flatly: "God forbid!" or as we might say today, "Certainly not! Far from it." Then he explains the reasons why we may not continue in sin that grace may abound. We shall consider these point by point.

The Implications of Our Baptism. 6:2-10

As represented by his baptism, the Christian is dead to sin but alive to God. The Christian has, of course, been baptized in obedience to Christ's command. Was this baptism a mere empty formality, or did it mean something? Doubtless, it meant something very important. What did our baptism mean?

Primarily, of course, baptism means the washing away of our sins by the precious blood of Christ and the cleansing of our hearts by the Holy Spirit. But baptism means more than that. It also means *union with Christ*. We are baptized "in," or more correctly "into," the name of Christ. But in what particular way are we united with Christ?

Certainly baptism means union with Christ in respect to His death and His resurrection, for it is especially by those two historical facts that our redemption was accomplished. But Christ's death was connected with sin—not His own sin, of course, for He had none, but the sins of His people, which were laid on Him by the Father. Verse 10 informs us that "in that he died, he died unto sin once." Death is the wages of sin. Death is always connected with sin. If there had been no sin, there would not have been any death either. Christ "died unto sin"; that is, by His death He finished off His connection with the matter of sin. Verse 10 adds: "But in that he liveth, he liveth unto God." Christ finished His connection with sin, once for all, when He died on the cross. Now He lives a new life, a life not connected with sin but devoted to God.

If the Christian is really united with Christ, as represented by his baptism, and if that really means anything, then it must involve the parallel facts in our own experience, namely, death unto sin and life unto God. We have been baptized into the name of Christ. That sacrament is full of meaning, and it certainly means union with Christ in the matter of death unto sin and life unto God.

So Paul, answering the objectors, exclaims: "God forbid! How shall we, that are dead to sin, live any longer therein?" (6:2). As represented or implied by baptism, the Christian is united with Christ in the matter of His death and shall also be united with Him in the matter of His resurrection (6:5). This will take place fully, of course, at the last day, the resurrection day, when Christ shall come again in glory. But in a spiritual way it also takes place here and now by a day-to-day life of holiness.

Questions:

1. What is the subject of Romans 6–8?

Romans 6:1–23

2. What new doctrine is introduced at the beginning of chapter 6?
3. What was the first objection urged against the doctrine of justification by faith?
4. According to the objectors, what must be the effect of the doctrine of free justification?
5. How does Paul start to answer this first objection?
6. What is the primary meaning of the sacrament of baptism?
7. In addition to this primary meaning, what truth is implied by baptism?
8. What kind of union with Christ is implied by baptism?
9. What is the meaning of the statement: "In that he died, he died unto sin once: but in that he liveth, he liveth unto God" (2:10)?
10. What does this truth about Christ imply concerning the life of the Christian?

Justification Is Not an Isolated Fact.
Lesson 20

The objection that was urged against Paul's doctrine of justification by faith assumes that justification takes place alone, as an isolated fact, in a vacuum, as if justification—just that alone and nothing more—constituted the sum total of the Christian life.

The objectors really saw only one part of the picture. They reasoned as if God would take a sinner, justify that sinner as a free gift, forgive his sins and pronounce him righteous in His sight. Then God would just leave off and never do anything more for the person—as if God would simply justify a person and let it go at that. This was the partial, incomplete view of the matter that was at the bottom of the objection. If the objectors had seen the rest of the picture, they could never have raised such an objection against the apostle's doctrine.

Of course, God does not act in any such way as that. There is no such thing as a Christian who is merely justified and nothing more. Justification does not take place alone all by itself as an isolated fact. It is a link in the chain of salvation. It is always accompanied by the other links in the chain of salvation, including adoption, sanctification, and so forth.

Romans 6:1–23

In particular, justification is always accompanied by regeneration or new birth, by which a person "dead in trespasses and sins" is given "a new heart" or a new nature so that that person becomes "a new creature" in Christ Jesus (John 3:3; 2 Cor. 5:17). Justification is always accompanied by the new birth, to which Paul alludes here by mentioning "newness of life" (6:4), and saying that we should "walk in newness of life." Of course, we have to receive "newness of life" before we can "walk" in it, and receiving newness of life is simply new birth or regeneration by the Holy Spirit.

God does not merely justify people and then drop the matter. God goes on and completes His work. What God begins, He carries on to completion. When God justifies a person, He also regenerates that person, gives that person "newness of life," a new nature, a new heart.

How then can any real Christian talk about continuing in sin that grace may abound? It was the objectors to Paul's doctrine that talked that way. But they did not speak the language of Zion. They spoke, rather, like the inhabitants of Sodom and Egypt. If they were really Christians, they would have spoken in a very different way. No real Christian will ever talk about continuing in sin that grace may abound.

The Christian is indeed dead to sin but alive to God by virtue of his union with Christ, which was effected by the regenerating work of the Holy Spirit and was implied by his baptism.

That the Christian is dead to sin but alive to God is not an exhortation or a pious wish but a statement of fact. It is true of every real Christian—of everyone who sincerely believes on Jesus Christ as his Savior. He may be an inconsistent Christian, he may be a weak and faltering Christian, but if he truly believes on Christ as his Savior then it is true of him that he is dead to sin but alive to God. Such is the fact of the matter.

What Difference Will it Make in Our Daily Life? 6:11-13

What are we going to do about it? We are dead to sin and alive to God. What difference is that going to make in our daily manner of living?

Since we are united to Christ in His death and resurrection, it follows that we must live accordingly of our own voluntary decision and purpose. How are we going to regard our life in this mortal body, here and now, in this present world in which we are living? As Paul has already shown, first of all, we may not continue in sin that grace may abound. On the contrary, we are to "reckon" or regard ourselves as dead to sin and alive to God through Jesus Christ our Lord (6:11). Therefore we are not to let sin reign over us while we are still in this mortal body (6:12). This does not mean that we can live a perfect or sinless life here below, for we cannot. But we are not to submit to the dictatorship of sin. We are not to let sin "reign" over us as a tyrannical dictator or oppressor.

Remember God's warning to Cain, in Genesis 4:7 (ARV): "It thou doest not well, sin croucheth at the door; and unto thee shall be its desire; but do thou rule over it."

"Let not sin therefore reign in your mortal body, that ye should obey it in the lusts thereof" (6:12). Sin will remain in us as a principle as long as we continue in this mortal body here in this life on earth. But we are not to let it work itself out to the full in our conduct by obeying its impulses. On the contrary, as those that are alive from the dead—we who once were "dead in trespasses and sins"—we are to place ourselves and all our faculties not at the disposal of sin but at the disposal of God as "instruments of righteousness unto God" (6:12).

Summary of Answer to the First Objection

"For sin shall not have dominion over you, for ye are not under the law, but under grace?" (6:14). While people are still under the law as a condemning power, sin has dominion over them. Wicked, worldly people are not free men; they are slaves to sin. Sin is their cruel, harsh master, and they obey that master day by day. What sin demands, they do all the time.

But if the Son of God shall make us free, then we shall be free indeed. We are free, first of all, from the condemning power of the law of God: "There is no condemnation to them that are in Christ Jesus" (8:1). But that is not all. We are freed also from the bondage, the slavery of sin. Remember the introduction to the Ten Commandments: "I am the Lord thy God, which have brought thee out of the land of Egypt, out of the house of bondage" (Ex. 20:2). Sin is an enslaving power. We need not merely to be forgiven because of our guilt, but to be emancipated because of the enslaving power of sin. Christ brings us not only forgiveness but also freedom, emancipation.

True, we still fall into sin. Our lives are still marked by sins and transgressions, omissions and shortcomings, failures and offences against God. We still have to repent and seek forgiveness and cleansing day by day. But one thing we are not, if we are Christians—we are not slaves, not in bondage, to sin. "Sin shall not have dominion over you" (6:14). Paul does not say, "Don't let sin have dominion over you." He says, "Sin *shall not* have dominion over you." It is not an exhortation, but a statement of fact, a promise of God. If anyone is really a slave to sin, with sin reigning over him as a harsh, cruel dictator, then that person still needs to be set free by the Son of God.

So we see that the truth of justification by faith not only does not lead to a careless, sinful life but actually has just the opposite result: It leads to a holy life, devoted to God's service.

Questions:
1. What mistaken idea did the objectors have of justification?
2. Besides justification, what are some of the links in the chain of salvation?
3. What great spiritual change always accompanies justification?
4. What is meant by "newness of life" (6:4)?
5. In speaking as they did, what did the objectors to Paul's doctrine show about their own Christian experience or lack of Christian experience?
6. What does our union with Christ in His death and resurrection imply concerning our own daily life?
7. Does Paul's statement in 6:12 imply that we can live a sinless life here and now?
8. If we cannot live a sinless life here and now, then what is the meaning of Paul's statement in 6:12?
9. What is the difference between committing sin and letting sin reign in our mortal body that we should obey it in the lusts thereof?
10. Why do we need emancipation?

Romans 6:1–23

11.   Who can emancipate us from the enslaving power of sin?

12.   Is the statement of 6:14 an exhortation or a statement of fact?

13.   Instead of leading to a sinful life, what is really the result of the doctrine of justification by faith?

Second Objection Stated and Answered. 6:14–23
Lesson 21

In this sixth chapter of Romans, Paul takes up sanctification, or the moral and spiritual results of a legal standing with God. He does this by stating and answering two objections to the doctrine of justification by faith as a free gift of God. The first objection is referred to in 6:1: "Shall we continue in sin, that grace may abound?" Having disposed of this objection, the apostle takes up the second objection in verse 15. "What then? Shall we sin, because we are not under the law, but under grace?"

Think just what this question means. The Christian is no longer under the law of God as a condemning power. The power of the law to condemn him to eternal death has been taken away. There is no condemnation to them that are in Christ Jesus. The Christian has been forever delivered from liability to God's wrath and the curse of the law. He is not under the law, but under grace. The Christian seeks to do what is right and to avoid what is wrong, not because of a motive of fear—fear of hell—but because of love and thankfulness to God. He has a desire to please God. The Christian is no longer an enemy, no longer an alien. He has become a citizen of God's kingdom, and a member of God's household and family. The privileges of the household are his. He is not under the condemnation of the law; he is under grace. He has been received into God's loving favor.

Now, does this mean that since the Christian needs no longer fear the eternal punishment of hell, it will be all right for him to go ahead and live a wicked life? He is no longer on the road to hell; he is not afraid of that anymore, so he might as well enjoy himself by committing sins if he feels like it. He might as well go ahead and sin, since he is no longer under the law but under grace.

So ran the second objection. In essence, it was a claim that Paul's doctrine of justification would lead to a wicked life. It was a claim that people would impose on God, that they would take advantage of God's mercy and make it an excuse for living a life of wicked immorality.

Suppose a child is caught in some city crowd trying to steal a purse with money in it from a strange man. Since he was caught in the act, he can be dealt with by the authorities. Perhaps his case will come up in court, and he will be sent to a reform school or some other kind of institution.

But the gentleman whose pocket was picked is a kindhearted, generous man who feels sorry for the poor boy who tried to steal his wallet. So he goes to see the judge and arranges to have the lad paroled in his custody. Later he discovers that the boy has no parents and no home. He is filled with compassion for the unfortunate child and takes him into his own home. He even goes to court and arranges to adopt the lad as his own son.

This child is not afraid of the law now. He is under grace. He knows that the man, who has been so kind to him and has done so much for him, will not turn him over to the police to be sent to a reformatory. Now, what will be the effect on the boy? Will he say, "I am through with stealing. From now on I will try to go straight and lead an honest life?" Or will he say, "Now is my chance. This man has been so kind to me. He will never treat me badly or unkindly. I will just take advantage of him. Since I need not fear any punishment, I will see how much of his money and property I can steal!"

The objection urged against Paul's doctrine of justification as a free gift of God was like that. It was based on the assumption that the Christian will be only too ready to take advantage of God's kindness, to live a life of sin and "get away with it," because the fear of punishment has been removed once and for all.

Let us see how Paul answers this objection. First of all, he flatly denies the charge: "God forbid!" "Certainly not; for from it." Then he gives reasons to prove his point. Let us examine them.

We Serve either Sin or Righteousness. 6:16

"Know ye not, that to whom ye yield yourselves servants to obey, his servants ye are to whom ye obey; whether of sin unto death, or of obedience unto righteousness?" (6:16).

Romans 6:1–23

Nobody can be neutral in the great conflict between right and wrong, between righteousness and sin. During the first and second world wars, some nations succeeded, though with great difficulty, in remaining neutral. But no person can remain neutral in the battle between sin and righteousness. Everyone is on one side or the other. If he obeys the dictates and impulses of sin, he is on the side of sin, if he obeys the commands and principles of righteousness, he is on the side of righteousness.

There is no real middle ground between the two. Every one of us, every day of our lives, is either serving sin or serving righteousness. There is no other alternative.

Our Allegiance Has Already Been Decided. 6:17–18

Once we did not know God. We were not Christians. At that time, we were in bondage to sin. We were servants—slaves—of sin. Sin had dominion over us in those days. Sin had a total dominion over us. We were not just slightly under its influence, but we were totally enslaved to it, under its power. At that time, before we received salvation, our allegiance was to sin—a total allegiance to sin.

But a change came. God's special grace came into our lives. We were saved. It came, not by our own efforts or goodness, but as a free gift of God's love. Just by receiving it, we were justified and declared to be eternally righteous in God's sight. We became heirs of God and joint heirs with Christ.

By receiving Christ and His salvation, we proclaimed our allegiance and loyalty to Him. We "obeyed from the heart that form of doctrine which was delivered" to us (6:17). We received Christ to be our Savior, and we promised to serve and obey Him. We promised it, and we meant it from the bottom of our hearts. That is, if we were really converted to Christ, we meant it from the bottom of our hearts. Our professions, our covenant vows to God were sincere. Therefore, our allegiance is now to the total service of righteousness, just as formerly it was to the total service of sin.

In other words, this great gift of justification does not stand by itself. It is always accompanied by regeneration by which God gives us a new heart, making us new creatures in Christ Jesus so that we have new motives, new desires, and live in a new way, which Paul calls "newness of life." And justification is also always accompanied by a change of allegiance of the person who is justified. It is accompanied or followed by *consecration*, a pledging of our loyalty and allegiance to God, to seek His kingdom and His righteousness in all our life.

This Change of Allegiance Is a Reality. 6:19

"I speak after the manner of men because of the infirmity of your flesh: for as ye have yielded your members servants to uncleanness and to iniquity unto iniquity; even so now yield your members servants to righteousness unto holiness" (6:19). This change of allegiance is not a mere formality or empty promise, not just a matter of words, but a reality. It involves a sincere honest purpose to carry out its implications in our lives day by day—to yield our members servants to righteousness unto holiness.

You see, the objection we have been considering—that people will commit sin because they are not under the law but under grace—is, like the first objection, purely theoretical. No real Christian ever talked that way. No person with a bit of love of God in his heart would say such a thing. No person with an atom of real Christian experience would tolerate any such proposal. What! Practice sin, commit sin, just because I am no longer afraid of going to hell? Far from it! I pledged my whole allegiance to Jesus Christ when I received Him as my Savior. I meant what I said. I may fall into some sin through weakness or temptation—in fact I do constantly—but I do not propose to take advantage of God's mercy by deliberately sinning just because I am not under law but under grace. My very soul rebels against such a thought!

Non-Christian Experience Contrasted with Christian Experience. 6:20–22

"Those things whereof ye are now ashamed" (6:21). Here is a contrast between *then* and *now*. Then, our whole inclination and desire was to practice what we now know to be sin, violation of the moral law of

God. We were not ashamed of it, not at all. It came naturally to us. But now, as we think back on the way we once lived and remember how we dishonored God's name and resisted His grace, we are filled with self-reproach for our wickedness.

A person's life always bears fruit, which may be either good or bad. What fruit did we have from our former life of sin and iniquity, before we knew Christ as our Savior? Did we get any real, abiding satisfaction out of those things that we are now ashamed of? Did they give us any real contentment or peace of heart and mind?

No. We know very well, now that we are Christians, what kind of fruit those things produce. Just death. That is, in the end. "The end of those things is death" (6:21). No doubt they seemed pleasant enough to us for a time, but it could not last. In the end they bring bitterness and death. If it had not been for the special grace and salvation of God overtaking us, they would have produced the fruit of death to the limit—eternal death, the second death.

Such was non-Christian experience, the experience of a sinner in his sin, without Christ. What a contrast is the experience of a Christian, which we find stated in verse 22. Set free from the bondage and slavery of sin and transferred to the service of God, a person's life moves in a different direction. The tendency is different and the fruit is different. The fruit is holiness and the end is everlasting life.

What did we get out of a life of sin? What is the outcome of a Christian life? That is the contrast of these verses.

Summary: Wages of Sin or Gift of God—Which? 6:23

Here is the gospel of Christ set forth in 20 words in verse 23. All will be paid the wages of sin except those who accept and receive the free gift of God in Christ. If we are still under our old employer, the slave driver sin, he will pay us our wages in the coin of his realm in the end. The final payment will be eternal death. But if our relationship and allegiance has changed from sin to God—really and truly changed—then our destiny is eternal life. The very thought of sinning because we are not under law but under grace will be repulsive to us.

Romans 6:1–23

Questions:

1. What is the second objection to justification by faith that Paul undertakes to answer?
2. What is meant by saying that the Christian is not under the law but under grace?
3. Why does the Christian seek to do what is right and avoid what is wrong?
4. What wrong idea of the Christian life is taken for granted by the second objection?
5. Why is it not possible to remain neutral in the conflict between sin and righteousness?
6. What was our allegiance before we became Christians?
7. What change of allegiance is involved in becoming a Christian?
8. What is the reaction of a real Christian to the idea of committing sin because he is not under the law but under grace?
9. What is the moral and religious experience of a non-Christian?
10. How is the moral and religious experience of a Christian different from that of a non-Christian?
11. Why is "death" spoken of as "wages," whereas "eternal life" is spoken of as a "gift"?
12. What is the full meaning of the word "death" in 6:23?

The Continual Conflict of the Christian Life. 7:1–25
Lesson 22

This portion of the epistle, as we have noted, deals with the subject of sanctification. In chapter 6, the apostle disposed of two objections to the doctrine of justification by faith by answering the questions: (1) Shall we continue in sin that grace may abound? (2) Shall we continue in sin because we are not under the law but under grace? He has answered "no" to both questions and given his reasons. We now come to the more specific discussion of the subject of sanctification, or the cultivation of a holy character.

We Are Made Holy, First, by Release from the Curse of the Law. 7:1–6

Release from the curse of the law is necessary before we can even begin to be holy or to live the good life. In human law it is an accepted principle that the law has claims on a person as long as that person lives. But when a person dies, the claims of the law are at an end.

Paul lays down this principle in Romans 7:1, not referring specially to the law of God, but to laws in general. The principle is that *death terminates the claims of the law on a person*. A dead man cannot be sued for damages, nor indicted by the grand jury, nor sentenced to suffer any penalty, nor fined any sum of money. The law's claims have been terminated by death.

Next Paul uses an illustration taken from the law of marriage. Death terminates the bond of marriage, so that the woman whose husband is dead is free to marry another man (7:2–3). This is applied to the Christian by a figure of speech. Before we believed on Christ as our Savior, we were under the curse and condemnation of God's law. We were "married" to the law; therefore we were not free. But when we believed on Christ as our Savior, who was crucified, dead, and buried for us, it is just as if we, too, had been crucified, dead, and buried. Our union with Christ means that we are reckoned as dead to our old life, and dead to the curse and condemnation of God's law. So, in verse 4, Paul tells us "Ye also are become dead to the law by the body of Christ"—that is, by the crucified body of Christ, by Christ's death on the cross—"that ye should be married to another, even to him who is raised from the dead, that we should bring forth fruit unto God." According to this figure of speech, before we accepted Christ as our Savior, we were "married" or united to the law; but since we have received Christ we are "married" or joined to Christ.

Back in those days when we were "married" to the law, what was our life like? We read it in verse 5: "For when we were in the flesh"— that is, before we were Christians—"the motions of sins, which were by the law, did work in our members to bring forth fruit unto death." "To bring forth fruit unto death" means a sinful life, resulting finally in death—the death of the body and also that more awful death called "the second death," the eternal death of the lost in hell.

The person who is under the condemnation of the law of God is walking the downgrade of that highway: sin, death, hell. No one who is walking on that highway can live a holy life. No one on that highway can ever live a truly good life in God's sight. No one on that highway can even do one single deed that is truly good in God's sight. It is all only sin and evil.

What is the first thing necessary if we are to live a good life, to be holy, to be sanctified, and to be made like Christ in our heart and life? The first thing necessary is to get into a right relationship to God, to get free from the condemnation and curse of God's law, to get past being a slave in bondage and to become a free man in Christ.

Now look at verse 6: "But now we are delivered from the law, that being dead wherein we were held; that we should serve in newness of spirit, and not in the oldness of the letter." "Newness of spirit" means a new life, a life under the control and influence of the Holy Spirit. That is what is before us as Christians. That is what will mean a real life of holiness and goodness.

"Not in the oldness of the letter." Paul here contrasts "the spirit" with "the letter." Now "the letter" means precisely the law that was written in letters on two tablets of stone; in other words, the Ten Commandments. "Newness of spirit," on the other hand, means new life that we receive from the Holy Spirit through regeneration or new birth. Release from "the oldness of the letter" is needed before we can even begin to make any progress in a life of holiness. That law of God, those Ten Commandments, pronounces an awful doom: "Cursed is every one that continueth not in all things which are written in the book of the law to do them" (Gal. 3:10). From that curse we must be released before we can really begin to live a good life.

We may recall the incident in Bunyan's *Pilgrim's Progress*, where Christian is trying to get rid of the heavy burden on his back that is weighing him down so cruelly. He is on the right track, but he has not yet been released from the burden. He becomes discouraged. Then someone meets him who tells him that there is a better way, a real shortcut, to get rid of the burden. There is a man called Mr. Legality who is said to be an expert on burdens and how to deal with them. He lives at the foot of a mountain called Mount Sinai. If Christian will only turn aside and find Mr. Legality, he will show him how to get rid of his burden, for, it is said, he has already helped many with the same problem.

Romans 7:1–25

Christian proves rather gullible and starts out to follow this bad advice. But before he gets to Mr. Legality's house he is nearly frightened to death, because the whole mountain trembles, quakes, and rumbles, and there are flashes of lightning and roars of thunder coming out of it and great bursts of smoke rising up as from an active volcano. The appearance is so terrifying that Christian is nearly petrified with fear. He never does get all the way to Mr. Legality's house because a better guide named Evangelist meets him and directs him along a better way, toward the cross of Christ, where he is really released from his intolerable burden of sin.

Mount Sinai, of course, stands for the law of God. Mr. Legality stands for the person who advocates seeking salvation by a strict, careful observance of the moral law, the Ten Commandments. Mr. Legality is a spiritually blind man, so he doesn't know any better. But Christian, whose conscience has been awakened, cannot endure such a thing. The more he thinks of the law of God, the more terrible it seems. The more he ponders it, the more he realizes that he can never, never save himself that way. That law cannot save him; it can only condemn him to everlasting doom. He is terrified. Only when he gets to the cross of Calvary and believes on Christ as his Savior is he really set free from that doom of the law, so that he can really begin to live a good life.

Questions:
1. What is the first thing necessary for a person to live a holy life?
2. What principle, concerning the claims of law on a person is set forth in 7:1?
3. By what event is the bond of marriage terminated?
4. To what is a person "married" before he believes on Christ?
5. How does it come about that this "marriage" is terminated?
6. To whom is the true Christian "married"?
7. What is the inevitable result of being "married" to God's law?
8. What does Paul mean by the expression "the oldness of the letter"?
9. What is meant by "newness of spirit" and how do we get it?
10. In Bunyan's *Pilgrim's Progress*, what is meant by the heavy burden on Christian's back?

Romans 7:1-25

11. How would Mr. Legality deal with that burden?
12. Why did Christian, in the end, not adopt Mr. Legality's method?
13. How did Christian really get rid of the burden?
14. Why is release from the condemnation of God's law necessary before we can really live a good life?

The Law of God Shows Us We Cannot Make Ourselves Holy. 7:7–14

Lesson 23

Here Paul tells us a bit about his own personal experience. The law of God, he tells us, finally convinced him that he was a sinner. "I had not known sin, but by the law: for I had not known lust, except the law had said, Thou shalt not covet" (7:7). Think of Saul the Pharisee, the strict, conscientious, scrupulous observer of all the details of the law of God, both the moral law and the ceremonial law. If we had asked Saul the Pharisee, "Are you a poor, lost, guilty sinner?" what would he have replied? Beyond question, he would have said, "No; I am a righteous Pharisee, for I have observed the law blamelessly." Yes, he thought he had. He tells us, "I was alive without the law once" (7:9). That represents Paul's former opinion of himself. We might paraphrase it this way: "There was a time when I thought I was all right; there was a time when I thought I had lived a perfect life in my own strength."

But something happened. "But when the commandment came, sin revived, and I died" (7:9b). There came a time when light—spiritual light from God—dawned in his soul. He came to understand the true meaning of God's law, the Ten Commandments. When he came to understand the true meaning of God's law, then he came to see himself as he really was. His bubble burst. His illusions about himself faded out. "When the commandment came, sin revived, and I died." That is to say: "When I came to a real understanding of God's law, I realized myself a hopeless victim and slave of sin—guilty before God and spiritually helpless."

The result was that Saul the Pharisee became Paul the Christian. It was the tenth and last commandment—"Thou shalt not covet"—that brought him to conviction of sin, to the end of his own resources, at last. Paul tells us that this commandment "slew" him, or rather that "sin, taking occasion by the commandment, deceived me, and by it slew me" (7:11).

The law, Paul tells us, is holy, just, and good (7:12), but it cannot make a sinful human being holy, just, and good. Far from it. It works on that sinful human being and shows his sin in its true colors, "that sin...might become exceeding sinful" (7:13). The law cannot make us holy. On the contrary, it makes us realize that we are exceedingly sinful. For the law of God is spiritual, but we sinners are not spiritual. We are just the opposite of spiritual; we are carnal, "sold under sin" (7:14).

Every Christian Faces a Battle in His Own Life. 7:15–25

This section is one of the classic passages of Scripture on the experience of a Christian. If we really know Christ and His salvation, we will find our own portrait and history in verses 15–25. We will see our own souls here as in a mirror.

Sin means war, conflict, battles, enmity, and division. Sin means separation. It separated Adam and Eve from God; then it separated Abel from Cain. God said to the serpent, "I will put enmity between thee and the woman, and between thy seed and her seed" (Gen. 3:15). That is the age-long warfare between Christ and Satan, the Church and the world.

The world is a place of warfare and battles today because of sin. If there had been no sin, there would have been no war and no suffering. When sin entered the human race it came as a divisive element, an element of extreme anarchy and disorder. The result is never ceasing conflicts, kingdom against kingdom, race against race, class against class.

But there is another kind of conflict which has come because sin entered the world—the internal conflict, the conflict in the Christian's soul. The person who is not a Christian has never experienced this battle in his soul. He enjoys peace because his conscience is asleep and does not bother him. He just placidly drifts downstream, doing whatever is popular and customary, and he seems to get along very well. He has no battles being fought in his soul. He drifts peacefully along, and finally, he goes to hell.

The Christian is very different. His soul is a battlefield day by day. Two forces are contending in his soul, back and forth. It is a fight to the death, a desperate struggle, from the day a person believes in Christ to the very end of his life here on earth. This desperate battle is described in the verses we are considering. Let us see what they tell us about it.

There are two forces which are enemies of each other. One of them Paul calls "the inward man" (7:22). He says, "I delight in the law of God after the inward man." For "the inward man," we might say, is "my inmost self." My inmost self (if I am a Christian) really delights in God's law and wants to follow the way of holiness. This "inward man" is called in the next verse (23) "the law of my mind." Over against the "inward man" or the "law of the mind," there is a contrary power, called in verse 20, "sin that dwelleth in me," and in verse 23, "the law of sin which is in my members."

In the Epistle to the Galatians, Paul spoke of this same conflict and called it a battle between "the flesh" and "the Spirit": "The flesh lusteth against the Spirit, and the Spirit against the flesh" (Gal. 5:17). Our old sinful nature that we received from Adam, Paul calls "the flesh" or "the law of sin in our members." The new, holy nature that we receive from the Holy Spirit by being born again, Paul calls "the inward man" or "the law of the mind."

We have a sinful nature, but when we are born again we receive a new nature. But the old nature is not entirely removed. It remains in our personality. So a conflict is inevitable, a lifelong battle between the new nature and the old. They cannot mix, and they cannot tolerate one another, any more than oil and water can be mixed. As long as these two natures are at war in our personality, there will be no real peace but continual conflict.

Someone may say, "But did not Christ promise us peace? Does not God's Word speak of peace that passeth all understanding?" Yes, peace with God, but not peace with evil, not peace with sin, not peace with our old sinful nature. So Paul describes the battle. The new nature, "the inward man," he identifies with his real personality. The other nature, the old sinful nature, is an alien force in his life.

Because of this battle in his soul, the Christian frequently does things which, in his deepest soul, he really hates. He hates them, and he knows he hates them, yet he does them, "For what I would, that do I not; but what I hate, that do I" (7:15); "For the good that I would I do not: but the evil which I would not, that I do. Now if I do that I would not, it is no more I that do it, but sin that dwelleth in me" (7:19–20). My inmost self, my new nature received from regeneration by the Holy Spirit, seeks holiness and strives for holiness in my life and conduct. But there is the old nature pulling and tugging the other way all the time. The result is inevitable: continual warfare, "the law of sin in my members" carrying on warfare against the law of the mind, the new nature. This conflict is so real and so desperate a struggle that Paul cries out: "O wretched man that I am! who shall deliver me from the body of this death?" (7:24). Who shall deliver me from this embattled state of affairs that continues while I live in the body in this present life?

If anyone thinks that verse 24 is foreign to Christian experience, he has not yet really come to grips with the evil in his own soul. He has not yet really made contact with the enemy. "O wretched man that I am!" Conflict always means suffering, discomfort, and misery. Because the Christian must always go through this never-ceasing battle with sin, he can never enjoy perfect peace, perfect rest, and perfect happiness during this present life. There are some lighthearted people who claim that they have perfect peace and perfect happiness here and now. Their experience is much shallower than Paul's. They have not really faced the full power of the enemy.

But the cry of verse 24 is not a cry of despair. It is not even a cry of discouragement. For it is followed immediately by a note of thanksgiving and praise: "I thank God through Jesus Christ our Lord" (7:25). He is the One that will give deliverance from this conflict in His own appointed time.

So Paul sums it up: "So then with the mind"—the new nature, the real personality of a Christian—"I myself serve the law of God; but with the flesh"— the old nature —"I serve the law of sin" (7:25b).

Romans 7:1–25

The Battle, by the Holy Spirit's Power, Ends in Victory

There is one practical application that we should certainly consider in this connection. The conflict in our souls is nothing to be discouraged about. Some people have a wrong idea of the Christian life. They expect everything to be peace and joy—"a bed of roses." When they find a battle going on day after day in their soul, they think that maybe they are not really saved after all. They become terribly discouraged.

But we should not be discouraged. The battle in our souls is a good sign. It is a sign of life. If we were not saved Christians, there would be no battle. If we did not have a new nature from God, there would be no battle. Because we are spiritually alive, there is a continual battle in our souls. God has put enmity there between the old nature and the new nature. This conflict is the experience of all God's true children. It is not something exceptional that you and I have to face alone. All of us have this same ordeal to pass through.

It is a battle that is sure to end in victory. Our Lord Jesus Christ is going to give us the victory in the end. All armies expect to lose some battles at times, but what counts is to win the war. So if we lose sometimes in the battle with sin, we must not let the devil throw us into a fit of discouragement and despair. He will if he can, but we must not let him do it. Remember, victory is sure.

Questions:

1.   What does Paul mean by saying "I was alive without the law once"?
2.   What does he mean by saying, "When the commandment came, sin revived, and I died"?
3.   What particular commandment brought Paul to conviction of sin?
4.   What does the apostle mean by saying, "Sin, taking occasion by the commandment, deceived me, and by it slew me"?
5.   What is the real cause of conflict in the world?
6.   Who put enmity between the seed of the woman and the seed of the serpent?
7.   What divisions have been caused by sin?
8.   Why does the person who is not a Christian enjoy internal peace?

Romans 7:1–25

9. What terms does Paul use to designate the Christian's new nature?
10. What terms does he use to designate the sinful nature?
11. What kind of peace did Christ promise His disciples?
12. Why does the Christian often do what he really hates?
13. Is 7:24 foreign to Christian experience? What can be said of the experience of those who claim that it is?
14. How does Paul sum up the Christian's internal conflict (7:25)?
15. Why is the battle in our souls a good sign?
16. Why should we not become discouraged because of our spiritual conflict?
17. Why is final victory in the battle against sin a certainty?

The Outcome of the Conflict, Here and Hereafter. 8:1–25

The Outcome of the Conflict in the Present Life. 8:1–17
Lesson 24

Even during this present life on earth, the new nature or "law of the mind" in the Christian, by the power of the indwelling Holy Spirit of God, gains control over the old nature or "the flesh." This control is not absolute nor complete, but it is real and considerable. Let us note what the apostle tells us about it.

The Christian is Freed from the Dominating Power of Sin. 8:1–4

By believing on Jesus Christ as his Savior, the Christian has, of course, been freed from the condemnation of sin, as we are told in 8:1: "There is therefore now no condemnation to them which are in Christ Jesus." Sin can no longer condemn the Christian and doom him to eternal punishment in hell. That power of sin to condemn has been canceled by the atonement of Christ. The Christian is freed from the condemnation of sin, but that is not all he is freed from. He is also delivered from the dominating power of sin by the even mightier power of the Holy Spirit, as we read in verses 2–4.

The Holy Spirit of God lives in the heart of every Christian. The Holy Spirit is divine, He is God, He is one of the Persons of the Holy Trinity. Being divine, the Holy Spirit is almighty. Sin is a tremendous

Romans 8:1–25

power, we know, but the Holy Spirit can cope with it, for He is almighty; His power is infinite.

The law could never save us either from the condemnation of sin or from the power of sin. But God sent His own Son, to become a human being (that is, "in the likeness of sinful flesh" [8:3]), to accomplish our redemption from both the condemnation and the power of sin. "That the righteousness of the law might be fulfilled in us, who walk not after the flesh, but after the Spirit" (8:4). The law could not save us, because we cannot really keep its precepts. We break God's commandments daily in thought, word, and deed. So God sent His Son. When our Savior was here on earth, He promised to send the Holy Spirit, the third person of the divine Trinity, to carry on His work in the hearts of His people.

The Holy Spirit gives us the power to live a good life. The good that the law demands, we could never attain of ourselves. We could never live that kind of a good life except by believing on Christ and receiving the power of the Holy Spirit. This is what is meant by the expression, "Who walk not after the flesh but after the Spirit" (8:4). Note that the word "Spirit" is printed in the Bible in this verse with a capital "S." It means "the Holy Spirit of God." Those who "walk after the flesh"—ordinary human beings with only their original sinful nature—can never really live a good life. But Christians can, for they have a new power that ordinary people do not have. They do not walk after the flesh, according to their old sinful nature; they "walk after the Spirit," that is, they walk as influenced and led by the Spirit of God.

The Wicked Person Cannot Please God, for He Is Radically Different from the Christian, Being a Stranger to the Holy Spirit. 8:5–8

There are two radically different kinds of people in this world, namely Christians and non-Christians. Different names are used in the Bible to describe these two kinds of people, such as "the righteous" and "the wicked"; those born again and those not born again; "the people of God" and "the world"; and as we read here in Romans 8, "they that are after the flesh" and "they that are after the Spirit" (8:5).

"They that are after the flesh" is a description of the class of people whom we call non-Christians. In another epistle Paul calls them "the natural man" (1 Cor. 2:14). These people who "are after the flesh" are dominated by their sinful nature, which they received from Adam. That sinful nature is all they have. Consequently, they are controlled by it and act according to its impulses. As Paul tells us, they "mind the things of the flesh."

The apostle gives us a contrast between these two classes of people. The non-Christian minds "the things of the flesh"—his thoughts and actions are the working out of his sinful nature. But the Christian is not like that. On the contrary, he "minds the things of the Spirit"—his thoughts and actions, to a greater or less extent, are the working out of the Holy Spirit in his heart and life.

"For to be carnally minded is death" (8:6). To follow the thoughts and impulses of the original sinful nature, as the non-Christian continually does, ends in death. Remember that this means not merely physical death but eternal death, the second death, eternal separation from God and from all that is good and pure and holy, in hell. That is the final outcome of the sinful nature, "the mind of the flesh."

The carnal or fleshly mind, the sinful nature, is at enmity against God. It is at war with God. It "is not subject to the law of God, neither indeed can be" (8:7). That is why we must be born again—because our old sinful nature is so wicked and corrupt that it cannot be repaired or reformed; it must be supplanted by a new, holy nature in which the Spirit of God can dwell and work.

Since the non-Christian's whole nature is at war with God, it is obvious that such a person cannot please God. No matter what he does or tries to do, he can never do anything that is really pleasing to God. "So then they that are in the flesh cannot please God" (8:8).

It is necessary at this point to guard against an extremely common error in interpretation of Paul's epistles, the error which holds that "the flesh" means the human body and that "they that are in the flesh" means people who habitually commit certain sins in which the body is prominently involved. It is really very clear that in Paul's epistles "the flesh" cannot be identical with "the body." "They that are in the flesh cannot please God" (8:8). If "the flesh" and "the body" are identical, then this text means, "They that are in the body cannot please God."

Romans 8:1–25

But Christians, during this present life, are in the body just as truly as non-Christians are. Therefore "the flesh" cannot mean simply "the body." If we will turn to Galatians 5:19–21, we will find a list of "the works of the flesh." In this list there are 17 different sins. Of this list of 17 sins, 11 are either exclusively or predominantly sins of the mind (idolatry, witchcraft, hatred, variance, emulations, wrath, strife, seditions, heresies, envyings, murders). Only six are sins in which the body plays a prominent part (adultery, fornication, uncleanness, lasciviousness, drunkenness, revellings). Thus almost two-thirds of Paul's list of "the works of the flesh" are predominantly sins of the mind. This proves conclusively that "the flesh" is not identical with "the body," and, moreover, that in the expression, "the flesh," the emphasis is not on what are sometimes called "gross" or "fleshly" sins.

The careless and non biblical use of "the flesh" as if it meant simply "the body" on the part of many Bible teachers who ought to know better is misleading and deplorable. We should realize that while it is true that sin has affected all parts of the human personality, nevertheless the seat of sin, according to the Bible, is not in *the body* but in what the Bible calls *the heart*, that is, the inmost personality whence are the issues of life. See Matthew 12:34–35 and Mark 7:14–23, and note the teaching of Jesus on this subject. "For from within, out of the heart of men, proceed evil thoughts, adulteries, fornications, murders, thefts, covetousness, wickedness, deceit, lasciviousness, an evil eye, blasphemy, pride, foolishness: all these evil things come from within, and defile the man" (Mark 7:21–23). The notion that the human body with its blood, bones, nerves, glands, and organs, is the seat and source of sin seems to be rather common, but it is definitely not biblical. Sin is a spiritual evil, and its seat and source cannot be in material objects or organisms. It resides in man's "heart" or deepest personality, which of course is spiritual, not material. From that "heart" it radiates outward and affects all elements of the personality and all a person's life and conduct.

The non-Christian can never do anything really pleasing to God. For one thing, the non-Christian never does anything with the right motive, namely, to glorify God. His motives may be selfish, or they

Romans 8:1–25

may be altruistic; he may live for self, or he may live for others (for society), but he never lives for God. So he cannot please God.

Very different is the Christian, the person who believes on Christ as his Savior. He is "after the Spirit"; that is, in addition to his old sinful nature, he has received a new, holy nature, in which the Holy Spirit of God dwells. Being "after the Spirit," the Christian "minds the things "Spirit." His thoughts, words, and actions are more and more the product of the working of the Holy Spirit in his life. The result of this kind of life is not "death," but just the opposite, namely, life and peace (8:6b). "Life," of course, does not mean merely the life of the body, here and now; it means eternal life, life more abundant.

Questions:

1. Why did God send His Son in the likeness of sinful flesh?
2. What is meant by the expression "in the likeness of sinful flesh"?
3. Why is the word "Spirit" capitalized in Romans 8:1–4?
4. What is meant by "they that are after the flesh"?
5. What is meant by "they that are after the Spirit"?
6. What is the final outcome of "the mind of the flesh"?
7. Why must we be born again?
8. How can it be proved that in Paul's epistles "the flesh" does not mean "the body"?
9. Where is the real seat of sin in the human personality?
10. Why can the non-Christian never really please god?
11. Why does the Christian "mind the things of the Spirit"?
12. What is the outcome of being "after the Spirit?"

Every Christian Possesses the Holy Spirit. 8:9
Lesson 25

"But ye are not in the flesh, but in the Spirit, if so be that the Spirit of God dwell in you. Now if any man have not the Spirit of Christ, he is none of his" (8:9). We might paraphrase this verse thusly: "Now if the Spirit of God is living in your heart, then you are born again and have a new nature, and are a different kind of person from the non-Christian who has only his old sinful nature. And if anyone does *not* have the Holy Spirit, which Christ promised to send, living in his heart, then that person is not a Christian at all and does not really belong to Christ." If anyone does not have the Holy Spirit in him, he is none of Christ's; he is not a Christian at all.

There are some sects that teach that we must first believe on Christ for salvation, and then, at some later time by a second act of faith, we must accept and receive the Holy Spirit. They teach that there are two classes of Christians: (1) those that are only justified, but do not have the Holy Spirit, or "the second blessing"; (2) those that, in addition to being justified, have also received the Holy Spirit, or "the second blessing." But Paul did not teach any such doctrine. He did not recognize two classes of Christians, those with the Holy Spirit and those without the Holy Spirit. According to Paul, there is no such thing as a Christian without the Holy Spirit. Every Christian receives the Holy Spirit when he is regenerated or born again and becomes a new creature in Christ Jesus. The idea that there are some Christians, who truly believe on Christ as their Savior from sin, who yet have not received the Holy Spirit, is contrary to what the Bible says.

The Holy Spirit Will Complete His Work in Every Christian. 8:10–13

"And if Christ be in you, the body is dead because of sin; but the Spirit is life because of righteousness" (8:10). If a person is a Christian, his old nature is no longer supreme in his life. It is kept under control by the Spirit of God. But the new nature is very much alive; it is the real life of the person.

Someday the Holy Spirit, who now dwells in us, will "quicken" our mortal bodies. This word, *quicken*, means "give life to." The Holy Spirit, who raised Christ from the dead, will also give life to our mortal bodies. At the last day, when Christ comes again to the world, we shall rise from the dead with new life, immortality. The resurrection of the body will be the completion of the Holy Spirit's work in us. He has come to live in our hearts, to keep our old nature under control, and to give power to our new nature. This work of the Holy Spirit

Romans 8:1–25

in us never stops, though of course it may suffer some setbacks from time to time. It continues until our death, when we enter the state of glory, and shall be instantly made perfect in holiness.

But that is not the end of the Holy Spirit's work in the Christian. He still has one great work to do—the raising of our human, mortal bodies at the resurrection. That mighty work of supernatural power will be the climax, the completion of the Holy Spirit's work in us. Such is our destiny and our hope. Since such wonderful things are in store for us, what kind of life ought we to live here and now?

Paul tells us, in verses 12 and 13: "Therefore, brethren, we are debtors, not to the flesh, to live after the flesh. For if ye live after the flesh, ye shall die: but if ye through the Spirit do mortify the deeds of the body, ye shall live." We are debtors. We owe a debt. But we don't owe any debts to our old sinful nature. Some people make some payments in that direction sometimes, but really the Christian owes no debts to his old nature. He is not a debtor to the flesh, to live after the flesh. Rather, the Christian's obligation is just the opposite: through the Holy Spirit to mortify or deaden the deeds of the old sinful nature.

(Note: In 8:10, 13, Paul uses the term "the body" not at all implying that the human body itself is the seat or source of sin [which we have already shown to be an unbiblical error], but as a figurative designation for the sinful nature that remains in the Christian.)

Justification Is also Followed by Adoption. 8:14–17

Verses 14 and 15 tell of the grace of adoption, which accompanies justification and the gift of the Holy Spirit. Those who have the Spirit of God in their hearts, are also the *sons* or *children* of God. Once we were not the children of God, because we were alienated from Him, far away from Him, in our sin. But we have been adopted into the family of God and have received the Spirit of adoption, enabling us to cry "Abba, Father," that is, to experience the fact that God is our Father and we are His children. This is a personal experience in the Christian's life: "The Spirit itself beareth witness with our spirit, that we are the children of God" (8:16). This position of sonship carries with it a joint-heirship with Christ, to suffer with Him now and to be glorified with Him later (8:17).

Questions:

1. If anyone does not have the Holy Spirit living in him, what does that prove concerning that person?
2. What does Romans 8:9 show concerning the doctrine that there are two classes of Christians, those with and those without the Holy Spirit?
3. What is the meaning of the statement: "And if Christ be in you, the body is dead because of sin but the Spirit is life because of righteousness"?
4. What is the meaning of the word "quicken"?
5. What act of the Holy Spirit will constitute the completion of the work of redemption in the Christian?
6. What effect should the thought of his future destiny have on the Christian's daily life here and now?
7. To what is the Christian a debtor, and to what is he not a debtor?
8. What is the significance of the term "the body" in 8:10, 13?
9. What is meant by adoption?
10. What is the result of the Spirit of adoption living in a Christian?

The Outcome of the Conflict in the Future Life. 8:18–25
The Crown Contrasted with the Cross. 8:18
Lesson 26

Present sufferings are real, certainly, but they are insignificant in comparison with the future glory that awaits us. The word "glory" is often used in a careless and trivial sense in the present day. We say that we enjoyed a glorious picnic or that a chocolate cake was simply glorious. This is part of the inflated condition of our speech, by which it has deviated far from the gold standard of meaning. In the Bible the word "glory" usually has a specific meaning, and in many of its occurrences it refers to the future destiny of the Christian at and after the resurrection day. Psalm 84 tells us, "The Lord will give grace and glory." We receive grace now, but glory chiefly in the life to come. One of the old Covenanters of Scotland said, "Grace is young glory," a very true statement. If we are included in God's saving grace today, the day will come when we shall participate in glory. Christ's kingdom now is a kingdom of grace; in eternity, it will be a kingdom of glory.

All Nature Yearns for the Dawn of Glory. 8:19–23

The non-human creation awaits the dawn of glory. Here the word "creature" should really be translated "creation": "For the earnest expectation of the creation waiteth for the manifestation of the sons of God" (8:19). The world of nature is to be released from "vanity" (8:20–21). The word here translated *vanity* means "futility" or "frustration." The world of nature, in bondage to destructive forces because of human sin, is to be restored to its normal and rightful condition, and nature itself longs and yearns for this release. "For the [creation] was made subject to vanity, not willingly, but by reason of him who hath subjected the same in hope" (8:20). Vanity, or futility or frustration, is the present condition of the world of nature because of subjection to the law of decay—the destructive forces that resulted from man's sin. We look out upon the world of nature and everywhere we see the forces of destruction, dissolution, and death. The giant Redwood or Sequoia trees of California sometimes reach an age of 2,000 years or more, but even these great trees, the oldest living organisms on earth today, finally die and decay.

Geologists have discovered that in the arctic regions where it is so cold that hardly anything will grow, buried in the ground are the fossil remains of tropical plants and trees such as palms. The inference is plain: that frigid region once had a mild and balmy climate. Something has happened to the world of nature. Paul tells us what it is. The creation has been subjected to futility. It has been enslaved to the law of death and decay. It has been placed in bondage to destructive forces.

God saw everything that He had created, and it was "very good" (Gen. 1:31). It was not of its own impulses or desires that the world of nature became enslaved to evil and sinister forces. If left to its original tendencies and impulses, nature would have gone on in a beautiful, lovely harmony. But something happened. Mankind, the human race, for whom the natural world was created as an environment to develop his personality in, fell away from God into sin and apostasy. Man, the king and crown of creation, debased himself by sinning against God. He alienated himself from God and became an enemy of the living, holy God.

What was the result? We know that the result for the human race was that both sin and death became universal (Rom. 5:12). What about the world of nature below man? Nature was placed under a curse, not for its own sake, but on account of man's sin (Gen. 3:17–19). "Cursed is the ground for thy sake." It was subjected to futility, not willingly, but because of God's will and purpose. "By reason of him who hath subjected the same in hope" (8:20). That is, it was God's will to place the natural world in bondage to destructive forces because of man's sin for a certain period of time. The natural world was not merely subjected to futility, but subjected in hope—that is, subjected for a definite duration of time with the hope or prospect of deliverance from that state of affairs when that period of time should have passed.

Man's sin has subjected nature to futility, and man's redemption will lift nature out of futility again. Over and over again the Bible teaches this same lesson. It speaks of a new heaven and a new earth with no more sea, the first heaven and the first earth having passed away. Peter speaks of the "times of restitution of all things" (Acts 3:21). *Restitution* means restoration to original, normal condition again. Note also the statements of Isaiah 11:6–9; 65:25.

The present sin-cursed world is in a state of groaning and travailing in pain (8:22). This is true both of the realm of nature and of the human race. In the Christian, the longing for release from this law of decay is intensified and assumes a conscious, definite form, that is, longing for and expectation of the resurrection of the body (8:23). What the Christian longs for is not merely immortality, or a life after death, but, specifically, the resurrection of the body, here called "the redemption of our body." All lesser hopes will fail fully to satisfy our hearts. The resurrection at Christ's second coming is our real hope. It will really satisfy.

Romans 8:1–25

Ourselves, as Christians, though we already possess the first-bestowed portion of the Holy Spirit, still long for something better and more complete: our total redemption, when even our human body shall be delivered from corruption and death and endowed with fullness of life and immortality.

"Waiting for the adoption" (8:23). We have already, as Christians, received the grace of adoption, being received into the family of God. But there is one element still reserved for the future, the final element of our adoption and redemption, and that is "the redemption of our body," the resurrection at the last day. Jesus said of those who shall rise in glory, that they "are the children of God, being the children of the resurrection" (Luke 20:36). This verse shows that there is a sense in which the resurrection of the body is the completion of God's act of adoption and that we shall be "the children of God" in the life of the resurrection in an even fuller and more wonderful sense than we are His children today.

On this we should set our hope, and refuse to be dazzled by any of the illusory false hopes cherished by worldly and unenlightened people today. Nothing short of the resurrection of the body is going to make this world anything else than a state of groaning and travailing in pain (8:22–23). The Bible warrants no hope of a state of perfect bliss and peace and joy and happiness before the resurrection. Paul—rather, the Holy Spirit speaking through Paul—does not say, "waiting for the building of the kingdom throughout the world"; he says, "waiting for the adoption, to wit, the redemption of our body" (8:23).

Questions:

1. How are the words "glory" and "glorious" often misused today?
2. What is a common meaning of "glory" in the Bible?
3. What is meant by saying "grace is young glory?"
4. What is the meaning of "vanity" in Romans 8:20?
5. How does the present condition of the world of nature compare with its original condition as created by God?
6. Why was the world of nature subjected to "vanity"?
7. What truth is implied by the words "in hope" in the phrase "subjected...in hope" in 8:20?

Romans 8:1–25

8. When will the realm of nature be restored to its normal condition?

9. In what specific way does the Christian long for release from the law of corruption and decay?

10. What is the connection between adoption and the resurrection?

11. What is the real object of the Christian's highest hope?

12. What will be the condition of the realm of nature prior to the resurrection?

The State of Glory Is the Substance and Object of Our Christian Hope. 8:24–25

Lesson 27

The object of our Christian hope is not merely immortality or personal survival after the death of the body, but specifically the resurrection of the body, which is called "the redemption of our body" in 8:23b.

"For we are saved by hope" (8:24). If we received all that God has for us here and now, obviously there would be nothing left to hope for. But God has set a portion of our redemption aside and said to us, "You cannot have this part now, but you shall receive it in the future."

By faith we trust Jesus Christ for our salvation here and now. That is faith. By hope we look forward with confidence and eager anticipation to the portion of our inheritance that God has set apart and reserved for the future. What should be our attitude toward that future portion?

(1) We should realize that it is something which "we see not"; we cannot attain it now, nor at any time during the present life; it is reserved for the future, for eternity.

(2) We should "hope" for it, that is, look forward to it with longing and eager anticipation of possessing and enjoying it in that glorious life of the eternal future.

(3) We should "with patience wait for it," not being impatient under present burdens and sufferings, realizing that our portion now is to glorify God by bearing the cross He has appointed for us, and recognizing that in God's own appointed time, we shall receive the crown of eternal glory.

This passage emphasizes the eschatological character of real Christianity. It is preeminently occupied with the things which are

Romans 8:1–25

eternal. It does not neglect the present life, but it places the chief emphasis and weight always upon the life eternal. Life here and now is not the main thing—it is only a preparation for eternity. This attitude, which permeates the New Testament through and through, is utterly foreign to the dominant spirit of the 20th Century. We live in a dominant atmosphere of "this-worldliness," in which even expounders of the Christian faith often seem to be more interested in the things that are temporal than in the things that are eternal. But every true Christian will adhere to the New Testament in its predominant emphasis on the life of eternity.

The resurrection of the body will be the completion of our redemption and our introduction to the full glory of eternity. Note the wonderful expression of this truth in the *Westminster Larger Catechism*, Question 90:

> At the day of judgment, the righteous, being caught up to Christ in the clouds, shall be set on his right hand, and there openly acknowledged and acquitted, shall join with him in the judging of reprobate angels and men, and shall be received into heaven, where they shall be fully and for ever freed from all sin and misery; filled with inconceivable joys, made perfectly holy and happy both in body and soul, in the company of innumerable saints and holy angels, but especially in the immediate vision and fruition of God the Father, of our Lord Jesus Christ, and of the Holy Spirit, to all eternity. And this is the perfect and full communion, which the members of the invisible Church shall enjoy with Christ in glory, at the resurrection and day of judgment.

All lesser hopes will disappoint and fail us. Even if attained, they cannot satisfy our souls. The resurrection, the redemption of our body, is our real and ultimate hope. It will come at the last day, at Christ's second coming. Meantime, we must "with patience wait for it." Hope comes to the help of faith, and increases faith for the conflict we are engaged in here and now. For our victory over sin, over our old nature, is necessarily incomplete and imperfect in the present life. But there is always that Christian hope before us—the thought of our sure destiny,

Romans 8:1-25

absolute perfection, moral, intellectual, and physical, to encourage us. The afflictions of this present time are indeed not worthy to be compared with the glory that shall be revealed in us.

Questions:

1. What is the resurrection called in 8:23?
2. What part of our redemption is reserved for the future?
3. What is meant by the statement, "we are saved by hope"?
4. What is the difference between faith and hope?
5. What should be a Christian's attitude toward that portion of his redemption that is reserved for the future?
6. How are we to glorify God during this present life?
7. What characteristic of Christianity is shown by 8:24-25?
8. How is this characteristic contradicted by the dominant spirit of the 20th Century?
9. What is the sure destiny of every true Christian?
10. What effect does hope have on our faith?

The Christian's Reasons for Encouragement during this Present Life. 8:26-39

The Experience of the Help of the Holy Spirit. 8:26-27
Lesson 28

"Likewise the Spirit also helpeth our infirmities"—our weaknesses (8:26). There is a special help for our weakness from the Holy Spirit. The apostle cites just one example of such special help, chosen from the various things he might have mentioned. That is the help of the Holy Spirit in the matter of prayer.

"For we know not what we should pray for as we ought" (8:26). There are two things about prayer that we do not know of ourselves—what to pray for and how to pray for it. We can make some progress in learning them, of course, but never in this life will we acquire this knowledge completely and perfectly. Always we shall need the special help of the Holy Spirit in the matter of prayer.

We know that we should pray for things in accordance with God's will, yet often we pray, ignorantly, for things that are not really in accordance with God's will. The Holy Spirit comes to our help, making intercession for us with groanings that cannot be uttered. Jesus Christ our Savior is making intercession for us in heaven at the right hand of God the Father. But this intercession of the Holy Spirit is something different. It is not in heaven, but here on this earth, in our hearts and minds. The Holy Spirit dwells and has His abode in the heart of every Christian, as we saw from verse 9, "If any man have not the Spirit of Christ, he is none of his." It is the Holy Spirit that stirs up in our hearts the desire to pray and that enables us to pray aright.

But our prayers that we put into definite words are often foolish and childish prayers, and not really in accordance with the will of God. As the heavens are higher than the earth, so are His thoughts higher than our thoughts and His ways higher than our ways. His judgments are a great deep, but underneath the definite spoken prayers that we form into definite words, there arise within our hearts desires and yearnings and longings that we cannot express in words. These are the work of the Holy Spirit, making intercession in us "with groanings which cannot be uttered" (8:26).

"The Spirit of God in us, knowing our wants better than we know them ourselves, pleads in our prayers, raising us to higher and holier desires than we can express in words, which can only find utterance in sighings and aspirations" (Henry Alford, *The New Testament for English Readers*, p. 913).

"The Spirit dwells in the believer as a principle of life. In our consciousness there is no difference between our own actings and those of' the Spirit. There is, however...a joint agency of the divine and human in all holy exercises, and more especially in those emotions, desires and aspirations which we are unable to clothe in words" (Charles Hodge. *A Commentary on the Epistle to the Romans*, p. 279).

The Greek word translated "infirmities" includes both the idea of weakness and of suffering. The word *helpeth* means, in the Greek, "to take hold of anything with another," to share a burden or task and thus to render effective aid. Thus, we see that the help of the Holy Spirit in prayer is not a mere teaching or persuasion, but an actual help by the exercise of divine power that shares our task and thus helps our weakness.

Romans 8:26–39

"And he that searcheth the hearts knoweth what is the mind of the Spirit, because he maketh intercession for the saints according to the will of God" (8:27). The Father notes not merely our own childish and often foolish prayers, but also the unexpressed desires and yearnings of our hearts which arise within us from the Holy Spirit making intercession in us. This intercession, which, as far as we are concerned, is merely "groanings which cannot be uttered," the Father understands, because it is an intercession completely in accordance with His holy will. This intercession meets with the approval of God. It is therefore certain to be accepted and answered. The realization of this should be a great comfort to every Christian.

The Certainty that Providence Is Friendly to Us. 8:28

"God's works of providence are, his most holy, wise, and powerful preserving and governing all his creatures, and all their actions" (*Westminster Shorter Catechism*, Q. 11). God's providence is all-inclusive. It takes in all that ever comes to pass. All things are under God's control; all works together as parts of a great plan devised by God in eternity. From the evaporation of a dewdrop to the motion of the forty billion stars in the Milky Way, from the fall of a sparrow to the rise of an empire, from the splitting of an atom in a laboratory to the melting of the elements with fervent heat at last (2 Pet. 3:10)—every fact, every event, is completely under the providential control of God to whom there are no surprises and no frustrations, who is sovereign over all, "who worketh all things after the counsel of his own will" (Eph. 1:11).

This great plan neither functions by blind chance nor by mere natural laws and mechanical forces. Beneath and beyond all laws and all forces is the mind and will of a person—the Infinite Person, Almighty God, our Father in heaven. This person, infinite, eternal, and unchangeable in His being, wisdom, power, holiness, justice, goodness, and truth, absolutely controls all that ever comes to pass. Verse 28 tells us that this stupendous, divine plan is so constituted that "all things work together for good to them that love God, to them who are the called according to his purpose."

All things work together for good, not to everybody, but to people included in a certain class, namely, those who love God, who are the called according to His purpose. This verse is often misused by being incompletely quoted and wrongly applied. Even worldly people sometimes say, "All things work together for good." Christian preachers sometimes give a terribly wrong impression by preaching on this text and failing to make it clear that the truth stated is limited to Christians. Thus, people who do not love God and who are not the called according to His purpose get the idea that they can continue in their miserable, self-centered, God-ignoring life and somehow all things will work together for good.

As a matter of fact, all things work together for evil to those who do not love God and are not the called according to His purpose. Even God's good gifts and blessings in the realm of nature turn into curses in the end to those who are not God's children. Finally, they will spend eternity in hell, where nothing works together for good to anyone. But to the Christian it is true that all things work together for good.

"Called according to his purpose" is also misunderstood. In this and similar verses, the verb "called" does not mean merely "invited." It is "called according to his purpose." That purpose is an unbreakable, unchangeable purpose of grace to God's elect. The person who is called according to that purpose is *effectually* called. This is an invitation that brings about a favorable response. Those thus called are actually made partakers of salvation in accordance with God's purpose of grace. (See *The Shorter Catechism*, Question 31, for a definition of "effectual calling"; and the texts listed under that question for Scripture proof of this doctrine.)

"All things work together for good," of course does not mean "all things turn out the way we want them to," nor "all things work together for what we think is good." It means our real and permanent good as purposed by God, and as we shall see and realize ourselves when we look back at our life on earth from the glory of heaven.

I'll bless the Hand that guided,

I'll bless the Heart that planned,

When throned where glory dwelleth,

In Immanuel's Land.

—"The Sands of Time Are Sinking," by Anne Cousin (from Samuel
       Rutherford's Letters) in *The Christian Treasury*, 1857.

Romans 8:26–39

Worldly people, poets, and philosophers wonder and speculate as to whether the universe is friendly or hostile to man. They can wonder and theorize and discover facts that seem to be on both sides of the question. But the Christian knows the real answer—the universe is friendly to the person who is a friend of the universe's God, and the whole universe is an enemy with the person who is an enemy of the universe's God.

Only the Christian can have the conviction that all things work together for good. It comes by faith in God's all-inclusive providence, faith that behind nature there is a personal God infinite in both power and love. The worldly person does not have that faith, so he can never enjoy the confidence that the Christian enjoys.

Question:

1. Why do we need the special help of the Holy Spirit in prayer?
2. What is the meaning of "groanings which cannot be uttered"?
3. Why is the Spirit's intercession sure of acceptance and answer?
4. What are God's works of providence?
5. What is behind the laws and forces of the universe?
6. For whom do all things work together for good?
7. How is 8:28 often misused?
8. What is the meaning of "called according to his purpose"?
9. When will we understand how all things worked together for our good?
10. Why can worldly people not decide whether the universe is friendly or hostile?

The Assurance that God's Work of Saving Grace Will Be Completed. 8:29–30
Lesson 29

"For whom he did foreknow, he also did predestinate to be conformed to the image of his Son, that he might be the firstborn among many brethren. Moreover whom he did predestinate, them he also called: and whom he called, them he also justified: and whom he justified, them he also glorified" (8:29–30).

Romans 8:26–39

Here, for the Christian's encouragement during the difficulties of the present life, he is clearly assured that God's work of saving grace in him will certainly be completed, even to his final glorification. What God has begun shall be carried through to completion. Those whom God foreknew, predestinated, etc., shall certainly receive eternal glory.

Many people have misinterpreted this passage in an effort to eliminate from it the idea that God, from all eternity, has decided who shall be saved. This passage, in its proper meaning, teaches very clearly and forcefully the doctrine of sovereign election on God's part—that ultimately the determining factor in an individual's salvation is not that person's own decision but God's choice. Man's decision in time is subordinate to God's choice in eternity.

The word *foreknow* may mean to know something beforehand, to possess advance information about something. The term *foreknowledge* is used in this sense in Acts 2:23. But in verse 29 the word "foreknew" cannot have this meaning, for this verse does not speak of all human beings, but of a certain class only, namely Christians. God "foreknew" everything about every human being that ever lived or ever will live, if the term "foreknew" in this verse means "to know something beforehand" or "to possess advance information about something." Since God foreknew all human beings, in the sense of knowing about them beforehand, and since verse 29 obviously speaks not of all human beings but of a special class, the term cannot here be used in the sense of knowing beforehand about them.

Those who object to the doctrine of sovereign election, therefore, have to add something to the verse in order to obtain a meaning that will suit the idea of "foreknew" as "knowing something beforehand." Accordingly, they say that the verse means: "For those persons concerning whom he foreknew that they would (of their own free will) repent and believe on Christ, he also did predestinate to be conformed to the image of his Son," etc. This interpretation makes man's free will the determining factor in his salvation and reduces God's predestination to a rubberstamp ratification of what He knew beforehand that certain persons would decide to do. In other words, the work of salvation is divided between God and man, and the deciding factor is taken out of the hands of God and placed in the hands of man. It is this doctrine that leads some prominent evangelists to say such things as: "God wants to save you, but His hands are tied; He can only wait for you to make your own decision"; "God has done all He can; He is helpless until you make your own decision." This teaching exalts sinful man and his powers by degrading God and taking the eternal issues of life out of His hands.

The interpretation we have just been discussing is, however, quite unwarranted. God's election or predestination is not a rubberstamp act. God's eternal predestination is not subordinate to, or contingent upon, any act of man during this present life or at any time. God's foreknowledge (knowing about everything beforehand) depends upon his predestination, by which He has, from all eternity, foreordained whatsoever comes to pass. God knows what will happen next year precisely because God has, from all eternity, *decreed* all that will happen next year down to the smallest detail. God is, of course, omniscient, that is, He knows everything. As He knows everything, He also knows His own plans and decrees. Therefore His foreknowledge is based on His eternal foreordination. Note Acts 2:23, where the betrayal of Jesus Christ is stated to have been done "by the determinate counsel and foreknowledge of God." Note that God's determinate counsel is mentioned first, and His foreknowledge afterwards. God knew beforehand that Jesus would be delivered up, because He had decreed from eternity that this would be done.

The unsound interpretation that we have been discussing is really a denial, or at least an evasion, of the doctrine of predestination that is so clearly taught in the Bible. It has been called, not unfairly, the doctrine that "God elects those that elect themselves." The truth is, of course, that those whom God has (from eternity) chosen, will in time repent and believe. Note Acts 13:48: "And as many as were ordained to eternal life believed." That is the order that God has established.

Having now disposed of a very common (and very old) unsound interpretation of verse 29, let us now consider what this verse really does mean. The words *foreknow* and *foreknowledge* in the Bible do not always mean "to know something beforehand." They also have a different meaning, namely, to love with a special love, to set one's affection upon in a special way, to prefer as the object of special affection. We shall show from the Bible that this is true. God said to the children of Israel: "You only have I known of all the families of the earth: therefore I will punish you for all your iniquities" (Amos 3:2). Certainly God knows all the people of the world, and all about all of them, yet to Israel He said, "You only have I known." Clearly "known" here means "loved," "regarded as object of special favor." To the five foolish virgins in the parable, the bridegroom (Christ) said, "Verily I say unto you, I know you not" (Matt. 25:12). He knew all about them, but He did not know them as His own. At the judgment day, many will claim to belong to Christ and to have cast out devils in His name, but He will reply to them, "I never knew you: depart from me, ye that work iniquity" (Matt. 7:23). In these texts, again, we see the terms "know" and "knew" used in the sense of "love" and "regard as object of favor."

Similarly, in verse 29, "foreknew" means "loved beforehand" (from eternity), "regarded (from eternity) as object of special favor." The Greek word for "foreknew" is the same as the word for "knew" in Matthew 7:23, with the prefix "pro," meaning "before" or "antecedently." So we see that our text teaches that God, from all eternity, set His love, His special affection, upon certain persons, who were thus singled out from the mass of the human race. He did this for His own reasons. We cannot say what those reasons were, only we know that they did not concern any foreseen good character, good works, repentance, faith, or other acts of the persons concerned.

Next, we are told that those whom God "foreknew" (loved specially from eternity), He also did predestinate to be conformed to the image of His Son. This means that those who are the objects of God's special love are to be changed until they are like unto Christ, God's Son. "We are to be like our Savior in moral character, in our present sufferings and in future glory" (Charles Hodge, *A Commentary on the Epistle to the Romans*, p. 285). God did not choose us because He saw that we would someday become like His Son; on the contrary, we will someday be like

His Son because He has chosen us. He has predestinated His people to be conformed to the image of His Son.

"That he might be the firstborn among many brethren" (8:29). Here we see that the plan of salvation is designed to further the glory of God. It is not intended simply or primarily for the welfare of human beings. We are predestinated to be conformed to the image of God's Son, so that the Son may be glorified and exalted in having many brethren in heaven redeemed by Him.

Questions:

1. In what way is 8:29–30 intended to encourage the Christian during this present life?
2. What prejudice lies behind the many attempts to misinterpret 8:29?
3. Why can the term "foreknew" in 8:29 not have the meaning of "knowing about something beforehand"?
4. What idea has to be added to 8:29 to make the verse give a sensible meaning if "foreknew" is taken in the sense of "knowing about something beforehand"?
5. What unscriptural statements are made by some prominent evangelists concerning God's power to save sinners?
6. What is meant by reducing God's predestination to a rubberstamp ratification of the acts of men?
7. Is God's predestination dependent on His foreknowledge of what will happen anyway, or is His foreknowledge dependent on what He has decreed?
8. What is wrong with the statement, "God elects those that elect themselves"?
9. What is the meaning of the word "known" in Amos 3:2?
10. Why did the Bridegroom say to the five foolish virgins, "I know you not"?
11. What is the meaning of being conformed to the image of God's Son?
12. What is the great design of God's plan of salvation, as illustrated by 8:29?

Romans 8:26–39

Lesson 30

"Moreover, whom he did predestinate, them he also called: and whom he called, them he also justified: and whom he justified, them he also glorified" (8:30). Here we have a chain of acts of God: foreknew, predestinated, called, justified, glorified. It is a chain that starts in the eternity that is past, before the creation of the universe, when God foreknew (set His love upon) and predestinated certain particular persons, thus electing or choosing them from out of the mass of the human race. (For a very clear proof of election before the creation of the universe, see Ephesians 1:4.) It is a chain that reaches through this present life and on into the future eternity. Those whom God foreknew in the eternity before the creation, shall certainly be glorified in the eternity after the judgment day.

"Whom he did predestinate, them he also called" (8:30). The word *called* here does not merely mean "invited"; it does not merely mean the external call of the gospel that a person hears with his ears. The meaning may be seen from 1 Corinthians 1:23–24, 26: "But we preach Christ crucified, unto the Jews a stumbling block, and unto the Greeks foolishness; but unto them which are called, both Jews and Greeks, Christ the power of God, and the wisdom of God...For ye see your calling, brethren, how that not many wise men after the flesh, not many mighty, not many noble, are called." Note also 1 Corinthians 1:2, "Them that are sanctified in Christ Jesus, called to be saints." This is what is known as "effectual calling," an inward work of the Holy Spirit in the hearts and minds of God's elect. (For a definition of "effectual calling," see *The Shorter Catechism*, Q. 31; *Larger Catechism*, Q. 67; *Westminster Confession of Faith*, Chapter 10.) Clearly in Romans 8:30 the word *called* is used in the sense of effectual calling, a powerful inward work of the Holy Spirit, by which the persons "called" are brought into union with Christ. For the meaning of the term *justified*, the student is referred to lessons 11–13, where the matter is fully expounded.

The word *glorified*, of course, means the completion of the work of redemption in the Christian by his bodily resurrection at the last day and his inheritance thereupon of the eternal kingdom of glory. For a summary see Romans 8:16–23 and *The Larger Catechism*, Questions 87 and 90.

Romans 8:26–39

We should understand that this chain of divine acts that we are considering is an unbreakable chain. It contains no open links that might permit part of the chain to drop off and be lost. Everything is fast, solid, and secure. The very grammar of the sentence, in English as in the original Greek, shows that this is an unbreakable chain. "For whom he did foreknow, he also did predestinate." The number predestinated is identical with the number foreknown. He did not predestinate part, but all, of those whom He foreknew. And so on through verses 29 and 30. "Whom he did predestinate, them he also called"—not part, but all, of those predestinated are called. "Whom he called, them he also justified"—not part, but all, of those called are justified. "And whom he justified, them he also glorified"—not part, but all, of those justified are to be glorified. With mathematical exactitude and certainty, every individual human being that was foreknown by God from eternity (singled out as the object of His special affection) will be glorified in the eternity that is future. The language of these verses leaves no room for any of those originally foreknown to drop out anywhere in the long process. When the glory of eternity dawns at the resurrection day, all those foreknown back in eternity will be present and accounted for. There will be none listed as missing. God is almighty; He completes what He plans.

> Whatsoever the Lord pleased, that did he in heaven, and in earth, in the seas, and all deep places (Ps. 135:6).

> The counsel of the Lord standeth for ever, the thoughts of his heart to all generations (Ps. 33:11).

> There are many devices in a man's heart; nevertheless the counsel of the Lord, that shall stand (Prov. 19:21).

We sometimes begin work that we are not able to finish, but God does not. What God begins He carries on to completion, for His power is infinite. If we are conscious of the work of God's saving grace in our hearts now, think what this means with respect to our eternal destiny! What God begins, He carries through to perfection, to completion.

Romans 8:26–39

He does not start a work and then abandon it. If we are really partakers of God's salvation now, then we may enjoy assurance that having been called and justified, we shall certainly be glorified. If we have received the first part, we shall receive the last part, too. "The Lord will perfect that which concerneth me: thy mercy, O Lord, endureth forever: forsake not the works of thine own hands" (Ps. 138:8). "Being confident of this very thing, that he which hath begun a good work in you will perform it until the day of Jesus Christ" (Phil. 1:6).

Questions:

1. Why can the divine acts mentioned in 8:29–30 be likened to the links of a chain?
2. Where does this chain start and where does it end?
3. What verse in the Epistle to the Ephesians affords clear proof of the doctrine of election before the creation?
4. How do we know that the word *called* in 8:30 means more than merely "invited"?
5. How is "effectual calling" defined in the *Shorter Catechism*?
6. Why is the chain of salvation in 8:29–30 an unbreakable chain?
7. Give some verses from other parts of the Bible to prove the sovereignty and almighty power of God.
8. Give some Bible texts that prove that God will carry His saving grace in His children through to completion.
9. If we have truly experienced the saving grace of God in our lives, what assurance are we warranted in enjoying?
10. What comfort should we derive from the fact that every link in the chain of 8:29–30 is an act of God, not an act of ourselves?

The Realization that Almighty God Is for Us. 8:31–39
Lesson 31

"What shall we then say to these things? If God be for us, who can be against us? He that spared not his own Son, but delivered him up for us all, how shall he not with him also freely give us all things?" (8:31–32).

God has given us the greatest gift of all—the gift of His own Son, so all lesser gifts and benefits must necessarily be included. Those who receive God's lesser gifts, and natural blessings, do not always receive the greatest gift. But those who have already received the greatest gift—Christ—really have a title deed to all the rest. Everything is included with Christ.

Christ is the firstborn among many brethren. God's children are Christ's brethren, hence they are members of God's family. Therefore they have an inheritance of everything along with Christ—they are heirs of God and joint heirs with Christ, as we saw in verse 17. This does not mean that we have possession of everything to enjoy here and now, but that we are assured of this possession for the life of eternity.

Christ is called God's *own* Son in contrast to Christians, who are God's *adopted* sons. Christ, God's own Son, was delivered up to suffering and death for us all, that is, for all of us Christians, for all of God's elect. "For us all" means not for our benefit in general, but as a substitute to suffer and die in our place. Here we see that the sufferings and death of Christ, His sacrifice, were part of the plan and purpose of God.

"How shall he not also with him freely give us all things?" (8:32). As the gift of Christ includes all other gifts, it must also include the gift of the Holy Spirit to apply Christ's redemption to us, working faith in us, and so uniting us to Christ in our effectual calling. "The believer is assured of salvation, not merely because he is assured of his own constancy, but simply because he is assured of the immutability of the divine love, and he is assured of its immutability because he is assured of its greatness. Infinite love cannot change. A love which spared not the eternal Son of God, but freely gave him up, cannot fail of its object" (Charles Hodge, *A Commentary on the Epistle to the Romans*, p. 288).

"[Christ] has not been sent to us void of blessings or empty, but filled with all celestial treasures, so that they who possess him may not want for anything necessary for their perfect felicity" (John Calvin, *Commentary on Romans,* pp. 322–323).

Everything that is necessary for salvation and eternal life is included in God's gift of His Son. This includes not only all that God has done *for* His people, but also all that He, by the Holy Spirit, does *in* His people. We should realize that our own repentance, our own faith, our own praying, our own love to God are all gifts of God to us just as truly as

Jesus Christ is God's gift to us. Of ourselves we would not repent, we would not believe, we would not love God. "For I know that in me (that is, in my flesh), dwelleth no good thing" (7:18). It is God the Holy Spirit that gives us these gifts enabling and helping us to repent, believe, etc. Of ourselves alone we would never do any of these things. This gift of the Holy Spirit is part of the "all things" that are freely given to those to whom God has already given His own Son.

We can see, then, the crude error of all those who try to separate between receiving Christ and receiving the Holy Spirit, as if a person could be a Christian and have Christ without having the Holy Spirit. The redemptive work of Christ and the applying work of the Holy Spirit cannot be separated or divorced in this way. There is an organic bond between them. To those for whom God's own Son was delivered up, all things (including the Holy Spirit) are given. The Holy Spirit brings these particular persons to repentance, faith in Christ, and all other saving graces. It is all linked together. It is all wrapped in one and the same package.

Questions:

1. What is the greatest of all God's gifts to men?
2. What is included together with this greatest of all gifts?
3. Does 8:32 mean that Christians shall receive all things to enjoy during this present life? What is its real meaning?
4. Why is Christ called God's *own* Son? What contrast is implied in this expression?
5. What is meant by the statement that Christ was delivered up for us all?
6. What benefits does the gift of the Holy Spirit bring to God's elect?
7. Why is it wrong to try to separate between receiving Christ and receiving the Holy Spirit?
8. Why would we, if left to ourselves, never repent or believe on Christ?

Lesson 32

"Who shall lay any thing to the charge of God's elect? It is God that justifieth. Who is he that condemneth? It is Christ that died, yea

Romans 8:26–39

rather, that is risen again, who is even at the right hand of God, who also maketh intercession for us" (8:33–34).

God has justified the Christian; who then can condemn him? When a person is justified, it is declared that all claims of justice in his case are fully satisfied. There is no tribunal that can reverse the judgment of the supreme court of the universe, the judgment throne of God Himself.

> To justify, is to declare the claims of justice satisfied. If God, the supreme judge, makes this declaration, it must be true, and it must stop every mouth. No rational creature, no enlightened conscience, can call for the punishment of those whom God justifies. If justice is not satisfied, there can be no justification, no peace of conscience, no security either for salvation or for the moral government of God. The Bible knows nothing of mere pardon. There can be no pardon except on the ground of satisfaction of justice. It is by declaring a man just, (that is, that justice in relation to him is satisfied) that he is freed from the penalty of the law, and restored to the favor of God (Charles Hodge, *A Commentary on the Epistle to the Romans*, p. 289).

"Who is he that condemneth?" This means that no one can condemn the Christian, whom God has justified, or pronounced righteous. The apostle next presents four strong reasons why no one can condemn the Christian, namely, (1) Christ's death, (2) Christ's resurrection, (3) Christ's exaltation at the right hand of the Father, and (4) Christ's heavenly ministry of intercession for His people.

Note that Paul makes no mention of any works of the Christian among the reasons why no one can condemn him. He does not say that the believer's earnestness, faithfulness, zeal, love, good deeds, religious worship, etc., keep him from ever being condemned. These are not even mentioned. What keeps the Christian from condemnation is not his own character, works, or faithfulness, but the four great redemptive facts about Christ that are listed in verse 34.

Incidentally, this verse proves that Christ's death on the cross was not a mere manifestation of the love of God, as people so often hold today, but a true sacrifice for the satisfaction of divine justice. For if Christ died merely to reveal to men the love of God, how could His death keep the Christian from ever being condemned? It is because His death was a sacrifice, a satisfaction of the demands of divine justice, a bearing of the wrath and curse of God in our stead that it keeps us from condemnation. Nothing can bring a person under condemnation except guilt. Guilt comes only from sin, and all the sin of the Christian—past, present, and future sin—was laid on the Lord Jesus Christ and its penalty fully borne by Him on Calvary, so that all claims of divine justice were fully satisfied. He who would condemn a Christian must find a sin that Christ did not bear the penalty of on the cross. There are no such sins of Christians; Christ bore them all; all were laid upon Him.

"Who is even at the right hand of God" (8:34). This refers to Christ's exaltation in heaven, where He as mediatorial king rules over the entire universe (Ps. 110:1; Eph. 1:20; Rev. 3:21; Heb. 1:3; 1 Cor. 15:24–28). All authority is given by the Father to the risen Christ, both in heaven and on earth (Matt. 28:18). The Lord Jesus Christ, the God-man, is on the supreme throne of the universe, all except God the Father being made subject unto Him. It is this Christ who undertakes to save His people from their sins, not only now, but eternally.

"Who also maketh intercession for us" (8:34). This means that Christ is our advocate in heaven. When we fall into sin, Christ is there to plead our cause, showing that His own precious blood was shed to atone for that very sin. Think about what this means for the security and encouragement of the Christian. We should realize, of course, that when the Bible speaks of Christ sitting at the right hand of God, pleading our cause, etc., this involves the use of figurative language. God is a pure spirit and does not have a body with hands. Charles Hodge puts it this way: "Of course this language is figurative; the meaning is, that Christ continues since his resurrection and exaltation to secure for his people the benefits of his death, everything comes through him, and for his sake" (*A Commentary on the Epistle to the Romans*, p. 290).

Questions:

1. When a person is justified, what does this mean concerning the claims of justice against him?

Romans 8:26–39

2. What is the meaning of Hodge's statement, "The Bible knows nothing of mere pardon"? Why is this very important?

3. Why can no one reverse God's sentence of justification of a person?

4. What four strong reasons does Paul give why no one can condemn a Christian?

5. What kind of acts are strikingly absent from Paul's list of strong reasons why a Christian cannot be condemned?

6. What does 8:34 prove concerning the meaning and purpose of Christ's death on the cross?

7. Why can sins committed by a Christian not bring him into condemnation?

8. What kind of sin would have to be found to bring a real Christian under condemnation? Why can such sin not be found?

9. Give some Bible texts that speak of Christ's exaltation to supreme power in heaven.

10. How does Christ's exaltation in heaven affect the Christian's security?

11. What is the meaning of Christ's heavenly intercession for us?

Nothing Can Separate Us from the Love of God Which Is in Christ Jesus Our Lord. 8:35–39.

Lesson 33

"Who shall separate us from the love of Christ?" (8:35). Quite evidently, it is Christ's love for us, not our love for Him, that is spoken of here. Paul is trying to encourage Christians, to impart confidence to them. To speak of their love for Christ would not serve his purpose in this passage. It would not in any way encourage them; rather, they would feel discouraged because their love of Christ is so often weak and inconsistent. But Christ's love for us is another matter. In His love, there is no weakness, no inconstancy, no intermission. It can never change. Those for whom He suffered and died and rose again, He will love forever. That very fact guarantees that they will remain in union with Him forever, for His love is a love that accomplishes its purpose.

The great difficulty with many Christians is that they cannot persuade themselves that Christ (or God) loves them; and the reason why they cannot feel confident of the love of God, is, that they know they do

Romans 8:26–39

not deserve his love, on the contrary, that they are in the highest degree unlovely. How can the infinitely pure God love those who are defiled with sin, who are proud, selfish, discontented, ungrateful, disobedient? This, indeed, is hard to believe. But it is the very thing we are required to believe, not only as the condition of peace and hope, but as the condition of salvation. If our hope of God's mercy and love is founded on our own goodness or attractiveness, it is a false hope. We must believe that his love is gratuitous, mysterious, without any known or conceivable cause, certainly without the cause of loveliness in its object; that it is, in short, what it is so often declared to be in the Bible, analogous to the love of a parent for his child. A father's or mother's love is independent of the attractiveness of its object, and often in spite of its deformity (Charles Hodge, *A Commentary on the Epistle to the Romans*, p. 290–1).

The apostle mentions 16 things, none of which can separate a Christian from the love of God in Christ: tribulation, distress, persecution, famine, nakedness, peril, sword, death, life, angels, principalities, powers, things present, things to come, height, and depth. Then to this already long list he adds a broad, inclusive expression: "nor any other creature." Think how safe a Christian really is! Nothing, absolutely nothing, can separate him from the love of Christ.

Yet in spite of all that the apostle has said, there are those who hold that a Christian can fall away from God's grace and perish in hell. They hold that a Christian may be a saved person today, but at some future time, he may backslide and perish, losing his salvation. Such people freely admit that tribulation, distress, persecution, famine, etc., cannot separate a Christian from the love of Christ. They say that nothing outside of the Christian himself can do it. But they add, a Christian can fall away from Christ of his own free will and so perish forever.

What superficial thinking such an idea discloses! Among the things mentioned by Paul that cannot separate a Christian from Christ are "things present" and "things to come." Surely a Christian's free will comes under these categories. His free will today is a "thing present," and his free will in the future is a "thing to come." Therefore it cannot

Romans 8:26–39

separate him from Christ. Again, the apostle says, "Nor any other creature." Is human free will a creature, or not? Is it a created thing, or not? If not created, it must be divine, for of all that exists, only God is not a creature. So if our human free will is not divine—if we are men and not God—then it is a creature. Then it falls into Paul's category of "any other creature"—it cannot separate a Christian from the love of God that is in Christ Jesus our Lord. The Christian is not only saved but also safe, eternally safe.

Those who hold the Arminian view of human free will regard the human will as creatively original. They believe that man's choices and decisions are independent of the foreordination of God, so that man is the absolute, ultimate source of all his own decisions. Thus the human will is regarded as not subject to the foreordination and providence of God. This position virtually, though not explicitly, denies that the human will is a creature. But Arminianism is certainly false. The truth is that the human personality, including the human will, is a creature of God, and all its functioning has been foreordained by God and is under God's providential control. The Bible definitely teaches this—that the free decisions of the human will are in every case foreordained and controlled by God. A few Bible texts may be cited as evidence:

> The king's heart is in the hand of the Lord, as the rivers of water: he turneth it whithersoever he will (Prov. 21:1).

> For of a truth against thy holy child Jesus, whom thou hast anointed, both Herod, and Pontius Pilate, with the Gentiles, and the people of Israel, were gathered together, for to do whatsoever thy hand and thy counsel determined before to be done (Acts 4:27–28).

> Notwithstanding, they [Eli's sons] hearkened not unto the voice of their father, because the Lord would slay them (1 Sam. 2:25).

> So now it was not you that sent me hither, but God...But as for you, ye thought evil against me; but God meant it unto good, to bring to pass, as it is this day, to save much people alive (Gen. 45:8; 50:20).

Romans 8:26–39

The human mind and will are not "creative" in the real sense; they can originate nothing. Every thought in a human mind was first in the mind of God and foreordained by God from eternity. Every decision of a human will was first in the mind of God and foreordained by God from eternity. Man ultimately creates or originates nothing; God is the only Creator, the only real originator. Man may invent a complicated machine such as an automobile engine, but it was all in the mind of God and in the purpose of God before the idea ever occurred to the human inventor. Man through his life, decisions, and actions, merely reproduces in the world the eternal thoughts and purposes of God. Neither man's thinking nor his will are ever truly independent.

We have turned aside a little from our study of Romans to say something about the Arminian notion of free will because of the conviction that the Arminian notion of man's freedom and independence is not only false but also religiously injurious. It is contrary to the true relationship between creature and Creator. It undermines the basis of a truly religious relationship between man and God. It regards man as the ultimate determiner of his own life and destiny. In a word, the Arminian view attributes to man what the Bible attributes to the Lord God, and, in doing so, detracts from the glory and majesty of God and provides man with a false ground of glorying and self-confidence.

We realize, of course, that multitudes of Arminians are saved Christians. But this is in spite of their Arminian views, not because of them. It is because they hold their Arminian views inconsistently, not following them through to their final logical conclusion. For example, Arminians who believe that human will is absolutely free nevertheless pray to God for the conversion of sinners. The same evangelist will say, "God's hands are tied. He cannot save people until they make their own decision," and then he will offer earnest prayer that God will bring people to repentance and faith in Christ. We rejoice in the Christian faith and testimony of our Arminian brethren, but, at the same time, we must insist that it is because of a happy inconsistency that they can be Christians.

Romans 8:26–39

Questions:

1. What is the difference between our love for Christ and Christ's love for us?

2. Why is it difficult for us to believe that the holy God really loves us?

3. How many things does Paul mention that cannot separate a Christian from the love of Christ?

4. At the conclusion of this list of things that cannot separate us from the love of Christ, what inclusive expression is added?

5. What is the doctrine of "falling away from grace" that is held by some Christians?

6. According to the doctrine of "falling away from grace," what is there that can separate a Christian from the love of Christ?

7. How can it be shown that human free will cannot separate a Christian from the love of Christ?

8. What is the Arminian view of human free will?

9. According to the Arminian view, what is the relationship between human decisions and God's eternal foreordination?

10. Show from the Bible, both the Old Testament and the New, that the free decisions of the human will are foreordained by God.

11. Why is it wrong to say that the human mind and will are "creative" in the real sense?

12. How should Arminianism be appraised from the religious point of view?

13. How is it that multitudes of Arminians, holding the views they do, can still be devout Christians?

14. What inconsistency is often noted in the actions of Arminian evangelists?

15. What is meant by saying that Arminianism divides the work of salvation between God and man and places the deciding factor in the hands of man?

Romans 8:26–39

Chapter 5

THE CALLING OF THE GENTILES AND THE REJECTION OF THE JEWS

God's Rejection of the Jews and Calling of the Gentiles Not Inconsistent with His Promises. 9:1–24

Paul Expresses His Love and Concern for His Jewish Brethren. 9:1–5
Lesson 34

Paul's discussion of the plan of salvation, in the strict sense, closes with the end of chapter 8. He now proceeds to discuss the question of God's calling of the Gentiles and His rejection of the Jews. As this was a subject that was bound to be very painful and embarrassing to the Jewish readers of his epistle, he approaches it cautiously and tactfully, so as to give as little offense as possible. "Fidelity does not require that we should make the truth as offensive as possible. On the contrary, we are bound to endeavor, as Paul did, to allay all opposing or inimical feelings in the minds of those whom we address, and to allow the truth, unimpeded by the exhibition of anything offensive on our part, to do its work upon the heart and conscience" (Charles Hodge, *A Commentary on the Epistle to the Romans*, p. 303).

Accordingly, Paul protests earnestly that he is deeply concerned for the welfare and salvation of his Jewish brethren, his kinsmen according to the flesh. "I say the truth in Christ, I lie not, my conscience also bearing me witness in the Holy Ghost" (9:1)—a very earnest, solemn and emphatic way of introducing a statement.

"I have great heaviness and continual sorrow in my heart" (9:2). The Jews had rejected their Messiah, Jesus Christ. Their special blessings, standing, and privileges were to be taken away. They would be left forlorn and hopeless in this world. As Paul thinks of this situation, he is filled with sorrow and is burdened with heaviness.

"For I could wish that myself were accursed from Christ for my brethren, my kinsmen according to the flesh" (9:3). This verse has been greatly misunderstood by those who say it teaches the idea that a person should be willing to be damned for the glory of God. The Chinese Bible (Kuoyu Union Version) wrongly translates the verse so as to make it mean: "For I am even willing that myself should be accursed, separated from Christ, for my brethren, my kinsmen according to the flesh." But we should note that Paul does not say "for I wish" or "for I do wish," but "for I could wish," which is a very different idea. He merely says that if such a thing were proper, or if it were possible, he would be willing to make such a sacrifice for the salvation of his Jewish kinsmen. Of course it was not proper, nor was it possible. As Charles Hodge points out, "There seems to be a contradiction involved in the very terms of the wish. Can one love God so much as to wish to hate him? Can he be so good as to desire to be bad? We must be willing to give up houses and lands, parents and brethren, and our life also, for Christ and his kingdom, but we are never required to give up holiness for his sake, for this would be a contradiction" (*A Commentary on the Epistle to the Romans,* p. 302).

Paul's meaning in verse 3 evidently is, then, that he *could* wish himself separated from Christ for his brethren's sake, if it were not wrong to wish for such a thing and if the thing wished for were not itself impossible.

Next, in verses 4 and 5, Paul briefly sums up the privileges enjoyed by the children of Israel. He mentions eight particulars, as follows: (1) the adoption, (2) the glory, (3) the covenants, (4) the giving of the law, (5) the service of God, (6) the promises, (7) the descent from the fathers, (8) the human parentage of Christ.

Romans 9:1–24

"To whom pertaineth the adoption." The adoption mentioned here cannot be identical with that mentioned in chapter 8, for that 6 adoption is a part of the Christian's experience of salvation. What is spoken of here in chapter 9 is an adoption to external privileges and standing, because Paul is not talking about Christians and their experience of salvation, but about the natural or national Israel. The children of Israel were chosen from among the nations of the world to receive special privileges and blessings from God. Note the statements of the Old Testament on this subject, such as Exodus 4:22, Deuteronomy 14:1, and Jeremiah 31:9. Israel's external, national adoption and sonship was a type that prefigured the Christian's personal spiritual adoption and sonship. During the period from Moses to Christ, the children of Israel enjoyed a special standing with special privileges, and so they were nationally God's children even though many of them—sometimes most of them—were personally strangers to God's saving grace.

"And the glory." What glory does the apostle refer to here? Probably he is referring to the *Shekinah*, the supernatural cloud of glory that appeared in the Holy of Holies of the tabernacle and temple above the ark 7 of the covenant symbolically to represent the presence of God among His covenant people in the place where the sacrifices were offered with the shedding of blood to atone for sin. (See Ex. 40:34; 29:43; Lev. 16:2; 1 Kings 8:11; 2 Chron. 5:14; Hag. 2:7.) No other nation possessed any such evidence of the living God dwelling in their midst. It was a special privilege of Israel.

"And the covenants." There is only one Covenant of Grace, and the entire history of Israel from Abraham to Christ is subordinate to that one Covenant of Grace. But here we read of "the covenants" in the plural. What does this mean? Obviously it cannot mean "the Covenant of Works and the Covenant of Grace," for the Covenant of Works was broken and superseded by the Covenant of Grace ages before Abraham was born. By "the covenants" Paul no doubt refers to the various times when God entered into covenant with Abraham, Isaac, Jacob, and the 8 children of Israel, thereby confirming to them special privileges connected with the one Covenant of Grace. While the real spiritual blessing of these covenants (forgiveness of sin and eternal salvation) was given only to a part of the children of Israel, not to all, still there were many blessings and privileges that came to the nation as a whole by reason of their covenant standing.

"The giving of the law." It was the possession of the specially revealed law of God that singled out the children of Israel especially from all other nations of the world. "Did ever people hear the voice of God speaking out of the midst of the fire, as thou hast heard, and live?...Out of heaven he made thee to hear his voice, that he might instruct thee: and upon earth he shewed thee his great fire; and thou heardest his words out of the midst of the fire" (Deut. 4:33, 36). The other nations had their myths and legends, their philosophers and their religious teachers; but Israel had heard the living voice of God, Israel had divine special revelation, and Israel had the infallible written Scripture, the very word of God.

"And the service of God." This expression evidently means the whole ritual service, everything connected with the priesthood, the sacrifices, the tabernacle, and the temple. While other nations worshipped in blind ignorance, bowing down to dumb idols or expressing homage to some "unknown God," Israel had divinely appointed ordinances of divine service, ordinances that themselves were revelatory of God's plan of redemption through Christ.

"And the promises." Undoubtedly the reference here is to the Messianic promises of the Old Testament, the promises of the coming of a Redeemer, of His person and work, of His kingdom and glory. The Messianic promises, beginning with Genesis 3:15, became more and more definite and particular as time passed. First it is only "the seed of the woman," then "the seed of Abraham," then it is to be "one of the tribe of Judah," then "the Son of David." God made it clear that the promises of a Redeemer were linked with the children of Israel.

"Whose are the fathers." This refers, of course, to the great patriarchs, Abraham, Isaac, and Jacob from whom it pleased God to raise up the nation of Israel. The Jews of Paul's day regarded it as a great honor and blessing to be descended from Abraham, Isaac, and Jacob. Indeed it was, but they should not have rested upon descent from Abraham for their salvation, as many of them seem to have done.

Romans 9:1–24

Questions:

1. What division of the Epistle to the Romans is closed by the end of chapter 8?
2. What new subject is introduced with the beginning of chapter 9?
3. What would be the attitude of many Jewish readers of the epistle to the new subject Paul is about to discuss?
4. In view of this attitude on the part of Jewish readers, what special precaution does Paul take in introducing the subject?
5. Does 9:3 mean that Paul was really willing to be accursed from Christ? If not, what is the meaning of his statement?
6. What is the meaning of "the adoption" mentioned in 9:4, and how does it differ from the kind of adoption discussed in 8:14–17?
7. What is the probable meaning of "the glory" in 9:4?
8. What are "the covenants" of 9:4, and what was their connection with the Covenant of Grace?
9. How did "the giving of the law" distinguish the children of Israel from all other nations of ancient times?
10. What is included in the expression "the service of God" in 9:4?
11. What kind of promises were specially given to the children of Israel?
12. What Old Testament characters are meant by "the fathers" in 9:5?

Lesson 35

"And of whom as concerning the flesh Christ came, who is over all, God blessed for ever. Amen" (9:5b).

Here we have presented the crowning honor and glory granted by God to the Jewish people, namely that the Redeemer, the Lord Jesus Christ, was, as to His human nature, born of them. The "seed of the woman" predicted from of old was at last born of the descendants of Abraham, of the tribe of Judah, and of the royal family of David. But this human descent, important as it was (as shown by the carefully recorded genealogies in Matthew and Luke), was only one aspect of the matter, so the apostle carefully qualifies his statement. He carefully says that it was "as concerning the flesh" that Christ was descended from the children of Israel, for in another sense He was not of human descent

Romans 9:1–24

at all, but the eternally begotten Son of the Father. "As concerning the flesh" means simply "as to His human nature." The word "flesh" here does not have any sinful implication; it is merely a term to designate that which is human.

"Who is over all, God blessed for ever. Amen." This is one of the great Bible texts that prove the doctrine of the deity of Jesus Christ. This text teaches the deity of our Lord so clearly and conclusively that various attempts have been made to translate the Greek so as to avoid this doctrine. The American Revised Version (1901) gives in the text a translation similar to that of the King James Version, but in the margin it gives as an alternative translation the following: "He who is over all, God, be blessed forever." This takes the statement as applying to God the Father, not to Jesus Christ. The Revised Standard Version (1946) translates: "God who is over all be blessed forever." Various other modern translations give a similar reading, eliminating completely the idea of the Deity of Christ from the text. It may be safely be affirmed that these modern translations of the verse are motivated by doctrinal prejudice (desire to get rid of the idea of the deity of Jesus Christ), not by the rules and usages of Greek grammar. Charles Hodge says: "There is but one interpretation of this important passage which can, with the least regard to the rules of construction, be maintained." He then sets forth the accepted interpretation that is in harmony with the verse as translated in the King James Version (*A Commentary on the Epistle to the Romans*). Henry Alford in his *Greek Testament* translates the expression: "who is God over all, blessed forever," and adds that this translation is "not only that most agreeable to the usage of the Apostle, but the only one admissible by the rules of grammar and arrangement. It also admirably suits the context: for, having enumerated the historic advantages of the Jewish people, he concludes by stating one which ranks far higher than all—that from them sprung, according to the flesh, He who is God over all, blessed forever" (p. 920).

It is obvious that verse 5 embodies a contrast. The apostle has mentioned that Christ, so far as His human nature is concerned, was descended from the children of Israel. But the mention thus of His human nature ("as concerning the flesh") implies that there is more than

His human nature, that He has also another nature that is higher than human, His divine nature. So there is a contrast between our Lord's human nature and His divine nature. As to His human nature, He is descended from Israel; but as to His divine nature, He is the one who is over all, He is God, He is blessed forever.

What honor and glory is here ascribed to our Lord Jesus Christ! He is said to be the One who is *God over all*. The fact that God is over all is the fact of His sovereignty; all that exists, except God Himself, is the product of God's work of creation over which God rules in supreme power and dominion. In Romans 9:5, this absolute sovereignty is ascribed to Jesus Christ.

In the theological world of the present day, the expressions "the divinity of Christ" and "the deity of Christ" are like money that has gone off the gold standard. These phrases are used constantly as pious camouflage by men who do not for one moment really believe that Jesus Christ is God. These men talk glibly about Christ's "divinity" and His "deity" and thereby deceive many a simple Christian who is not aware of the inflation of theological coinage today. But if sufficiently pressed they may explain what they mean by the "deity" or "divinity" of Christ, and then it becomes evident that they do not mean by these terms what the Christian church through its history has meant by them.

Thus one man will say, "By affirming Christ's divinity I mean that he is perfectly human; his perfect manhood shows him to be more divine than any other human being." Another will say, "By saying that Christ is divine, I mean that he is the first man who ever dared to be divine." Still another will say: "When I call Christ divine, I do not mean that he is really God, but that he possesses the value of God to us." These are just a few examples of this theological double-talk, here considerably condensed for the sake of brevity. The men who use language in this way are dishonest. They are unethical. Language is the currency of thought just as money is the currency of commerce. The man who uses language in other than its commonly accepted meaning, and does not define his terms, is a chiseler and should be regarded with contempt. Lewis Carroll's character, Humpty Dumpty, in *Through the Looking Glass* said, "When I use a word, it means just what I choose it to mean, neither more nor

Romans 9:1–24

less." Many theological scholars, regarded by some as "authorities," use words very much after the fashion of Humpty Dumpty.

Some of these modernists will say right out, without hesitation, that "Jesus is God." This sounds like a real confession of the truth, but it means practically nothing. For the meaning of the statement "Jesus is God" depends entirely on what the person making the statement means by "God." Many modernists have a pantheistic idea of God, that is, they regard God as just "the soul of the universe," "the integral wholeness of things," or some similar concept. They think of God as an aspect of the universe or as the intelligence or moving power of the universe, but they do not think of God as the Creator who exists independently of His creation. When such men say that they believe that "Jesus is God," this is not because they have a high view of Jesus but because they have an extremely low view of God.   *10*

In the Bible there is no double-talk. And there is no double-talk in the great historic creeds and confessions of the Christian Church. The Bible and the creeds of the Church speak an honest, gold standard language; their statements are to be taken at face value. In the text before us, the Bible tells us, plainly and simply, the stupendous truth that Jesus Christ is none other than God over all and blessed forever. It was this person, whom we know as the Lord Jesus Christ, that created the *11* starry heavens and the earth (John 1:3). The vast Milky Way with its 200–400 billion stars was created by Him and is sustained in existence by Him from moment to moment. The Andromeda Nebula, affirmed by competent astronomers to be some 2.54 million light years distant from this earth, is held in the hollow of His hand. To Him a thousand years are as one day and one day as a thousand years. He is the infinite Christ. And yet He became flesh, and dwelt among us. He was wrapped in swaddling clothes and laid in a manger. He experienced hunger, thirst, and weariness; He was crucified, dead, and buried, and continued under the power of death for a time. But through all this earthly career, in "the days of his flesh," He never ceased for one moment to be God over all, blessed forever. He emptied Himself of the glory and joy of heaven that He might experience the humiliation and bitterness of earth, but He never emptied Himself of His deity. Always He was God over all, blessed forever. As Paul exclaimed in another epistle, "Great is the mystery of godliness: God was manifest in the flesh" (1 Tim. 3:16). *) 2*

Questions:

1. What was the greatest honor granted by God to the Jewish people?
2. What is the meaning of the expression "as concerning the flesh" in 9:5?
3. Why do some scholars object to the way 9:5 is translated in the King James Version?
4. How does the Revised Standard Version (1946) translate the latter part of verse 5?
5. What did Charles Hodge say concerning the interpretation of 9:5?
6. What contrast is involved in 9:5?
7. What words in verse 5 set forth the sovereignty of God?
8. How are the terms "divinity of Christ" and "deity of Christ" misused in the present day?
9. Why is it dishonest to use language other than in its commonly accepted meaning?
10. Why does the statement "Jesus is God" sometimes not mean what these words properly mean?
11. What divine act is ascribed to Christ in John 1:3?
12. What truth caused Paul to exclaim "great is the mystery of godliness"?

God Is Absolutely Sovereign in Bestowing His Favors on Men. 9:6–24

Lesson 36

Having expressed his love and concern for his Jewish brethren in verses 15, Paul now takes up the subject of God's rejection of the Jews and His calling of the Gentiles. In Romans 9:6–8, the apostle shows that the promises of God were not made to the Jews as such, as natural descendants of Abraham, but to a smaller group called "the children of the promise" who "are counted for the seed" (9:8).

If God's rejection of the Jews and calling of the Gentiles involved the breaking of any of God's promises, then it would be "as though

the word of God hath taken none effect" (9:6), that is, it would be as
though the word of God had been canceled or nullified. But Paul says
that it is not as though the word of God had been canceled. This means
that God's rejection of the Jews and calling of the Gentiles must be
regarded as perfectly consistent with all of God's promises and with
everything in the Old Testament Scriptures.

But to any zealous Jew such an act on God's part would certainly
seem to be inconsistent with God's promises and His past actions toward
the Jews. So Paul undertakes to explain the apparent inconsistency. He
explains that the word Israel is used in two different senses: "For they
are not all Israel, which are of Israel" (9:6). We might paraphrase this,
"For not all the people of Israel are genuine Israelites." There is an
Israel in the external sense, the nation of Israel, the natural posterity
of Abraham, Isaac, and Jacob. This external Israel includes people who
truly know God and people who do not truly know God. It includes
true believers such as Samuel and David, and it also includes wicked
men such as Saul and Ahab. In this external sense, Saul and Ahab were
Israelites just as truly as Samuel and David were.

Within this inclusive external Israel, there is an inner core of real
children of God, true believers, saved persons. This inner core is the
real Israel. It is the Israel that has real significance in God's plan. It is
the Israel with which God is truly in covenant. It is the Israel to whom
the promises were made. It is the vital Israel within the larger body of
the external Israel.

It is a very common and harmful error of the present day to hold
that the gracious promises of God were made to the inclusive, external
nation of Israel, to the natural posterity of Abraham as such. This false
notion leads to various other harmful errors concerning the future of
the Jewish nation, the return of the Jews to Palestine, and other related
matters. The truth is that the gracious promises of God were made to
the spiritual, believing core, the Israel within Israel, "the children of
the promise" that "are counted for the seed" (9:8). Only those in that
inner, genuine core had any claim on the promises of God.

To make this plain, Paul continues: "Neither, because they are the
seed of Abraham, are they all children: but, in Isaac shall thy seed be

called. That is, they which are the children of the flesh, these are not the children of God: but the children of the promise are counted for the seed" (9:7–8).

Let us paraphrase this as follows: "Nor are all the people of the nation of Israel to be regarded as children of God just because they are descended from Abraham; for God said to Abraham, 'In Isaac shall thy seed be called.' That is to say, those that are mere natural descendants of Abraham, as Ishmael was, are not counted as the children of God, but the children to whom God's promise really belongs, are regarded and treated as the real seed of Abraham."

We should realize that the Jews, or the children of Israel, were only a part of the descendants of Abraham. Abraham also had a numerous posterity through Ishmael and through the sons of Keturah (Gen. 25:1–18). If mere physical descent is what counts, we will have to admit that Abraham's blood flows in the veins of the Arabs as well as those of the Jews. Nowhere in the Bible is mere physical descent from Abraham made the key to the gracious promises and blessings of God. The promises are made and the blessings given to the group that is truly in covenant with God, not to the inclusive, external nation of Israel.

God made this clear to Abraham when He said to him, "In Isaac shall thy seed be called" (Gen. 21:12). Abraham thought that Ishmael might be the promised "seed," and he said to God, "O that Ishmael might live before thee!" (Gen. 17:18). But God had other plans, and He replied to Abraham,

> Sarah thy wife shall bear thee a son indeed; and thou shalt call his name Isaac: and I will establish my covenant with him for an everlasting covenant, and with his seed after him. And as for Ishmael, I have heard thee: Behold, I have blessed him, and will make him fruitful, and will multiply him exceedingly; twelve princes shall he beget, and I will make him a great nation. *But my covenant will I establish with Isaac*, which Sarah shall bear unto thee at this set time in the next year (Gen. 17:19–21).

Prosperity and worldly success are promised to Ishmael and his descendants, "but my covenant will I establish with Isaac." Then when Ishmael and Hagar were finally cast out, God said to Abraham, "In

Romans 9:1–24

Isaac shall thy seed be called" (Gen. 21:12). Thus it was made clear to
Abraham, during his own lifetime, that the gracious promises of God
and the covenant relationship were not to be given to *all* of his posterity, but only the part chosen by God with whom His covenant would
be established and who would be counted as his "seed."

Questions:

1. Did God's rejection of the Jews and calling of the Gentiles involve
   the breaking of any of God's promises?
2. How would the zealous Jews of Paul's day regard the doctrine of
   God's rejecting the Jews and calling the Gentiles?
3. In what two senses is the word "Israel" used in 9:6?
4. What were the characteristics of the smaller "Israel" in contrast
   to those of the larger "Israel"?
5. What harmful error concerning the promises of God to Israel is
   very common today?
6. Why did God say to Abraham, "In Isaac shall thy seed be called"?
7. How can it be shown that mere physical descent from Abraham
   was never the key to the gracious promises and blessings of God?
8. What idea did Abraham have concerning Ishmael?
9. What promises did God make concerning Ishmael, and what different promise did He make concerning Isaac?
10. What people besides the Jews are descended from Abraham?

Lesson 37

> For this is the word of promise, At this time will I come, and Sarah
> shall have a son. And not only this; but when Rebecca also had con-
> ceived by one, even by our father Isaac; (for the children being not
> yet born, neither having done any good or evil, that the purpose of
> God according to election might stand, not of works, but of him that
> calleth;) It was said unto her, The elder shall serve the younger. As it
> is written, Jacob have I loved, but Esau have I hated (9:9-13).

God's sovereignty in bestowing His favors on men is exemplified,
first, in the birth of Isaac, the divinely-chosen heir to the promise, in

Romans 9:1-24

spite of Abraham's own ideas about Ishmael (Gen. 17:18). According to man's viewpoint, Ishmael might have been a good choice, but God in His sovereignty rejected Ishmael and chose Isaac (Gen. 17:21).

By God's "sovereignty" we mean God's absolute, unchallengeable supremacy, by reason of which He deals with all His creatures as He Himself sees fit, being responsible to no one but Himself. *The Westminster Confession of Faith* summarizes God's sovereignty as follows: "God...is the alone fountain of all being, of whom, through whom, and to whom are all things; and hath most sovereign dominion over them, to do by them, for them, or upon them whatsoever Himself pleaseth...To Him is due from angels and men, and every other creature, whatsoever worship, service or obedience He is pleased to require of them" (II.2). There is an expression used many times in the Bible, and also in the *Westminster Confession* and *Catechisms*, to describe the operation of God's sovereignty: "It pleased the Lord." When we read that "it pleased the Lord" or "it pleased God" to do this, or to do that, we are to understand that we are face to face with God's sovereignty, with an act of God that proceeds from His own choice. We may mention a few instances of this expression.

It pleased the Lord to bruise him (Isa. 53:10).

But our God is in the heavens: he hath done whatsoever he hath pleased? (Ps. 115:3).

Thou, O Lord, hast done as it pleased thee"(Jonah 1:14).

It pleased God by the foolishness of preaching to save them that believe (1 Cor. 1:21).

But when it pleased God...to reveal his Son in me (Gal. 1:15–16).

From the *Confession of Faith*:

Therefore it pleased the Lord...to reveal Himself (I.1).

The rest of mankind God was pleased, according to the unsearchable counsel of His own will, whereby He extendeth or withholdeth mercy, as He pleaseth, for the glory of His sovereign power over His creatures, to pass by (III.7).

Man by his fall having made himself incapable of life by that covenant, the Lord was pleased to make a second, commonly called the covenant of grace (VII.3).

It pleased God, in His eternal purpose, to choose and ordain the Lord Jesus, His only begotten Son, to be the Mediator between God and man (VIII.1).

We cannot understand the Bible without accepting the truth of the sovereignty of God, and especially we cannot grasp the teaching of Paul's Epistle to the Romans without knowing and accepting this doctrine. God's sovereign acts and choices cannot be explained by human reason, and they cannot be justified by maxims of human conduct. There is no person higher than God, to whom God must give an account of His deeds. He is supreme, He is sovereign, He is responsible only to Himself and not to created beings.

Next, God's sovereignty in bestowing His favors on men is proved by the history of Jacob and Esau. Contrary to all human custom and propriety, God said of Jacob and Esau, "The elder shall serve the younger." According to human custom, especially in eastern lands, the elder brother takes precedence over the younger. The elder is the head of the family whom the younger must obey. But God in His sovereignty can and does reverse this natural and customary order saying, "The elder shall serve the younger."

Moreover, this statement was made by God before Jacob and Esau were born, prior to all action of their own, whether good or evil, as Paul tells us, precisely in order that it might be clear that the decision proceeded from God's sovereignty and not from the conduct of Jacob and Esau themselves. The choice was announced prior to the birth of Jacob and Esau, "that the purpose of God according to election might stand, not of works, but of Him that calleth" (9:11).

Romans 9:1–24

If the choice had been announced by God after Jacob and Esau had been born and grown up, it might appear to be based on the good or bad conduct of one or the other of them. But Paul tells us that this purpose of God was *according to election*—it was a sovereign choice of God; and it was *not of works*—not based on the moral character or conduct of Jacob or Esau. He adds, *"but of Him that calleth"*—that is, this choice proceeded from the pure sovereignty of God, to which we human beings can assign no reasons and for which we can give no explanations. Before Jacob or Esau were born, God chose the former and rejected the latter.

We may note here, in passing, that the Arminian notion that God's election is based upon His foresight of men's repentance and faith, is disproved by the passage before us. The Arminian idea is that God, from eternity, saw and knew beforehand what persons would repent and believe, and He predestinated or elected unto eternal life those persons whom He foresaw would (of their own free will) repent and believe. According to this idea, God elects people before they are born, but it is still on account of those persons' own actions (repentance and faith) that God chooses them. It has been not unfairly said, that according to Arminianism, God from eternity elected those whom He foresaw would elect themselves; or that God from eternity chose those whom He foresaw would someday choose Him. But the Apostle Paul cites the choice of Jacob and rejection of Esau before they were born as evidence that this divine choice was not of works: "that the purpose of God according to election might stand, not of works, but of him that calleth." Evidently Paul did not hold the Arminian view of election, for it never occurred to him to suppose that God might have chosen Jacob, before the latter's birth, because of foreseen repentance, faith, and good works, etc. As a matter of fact, the whole Arminian construction of election based on foreseen acts of men simply cannot be fitted in with Paul's argument in Romans 9:10–13.

All non-Christians, as well as many Christians, object violently to the doctrine of sovereign election that is taught in this passage. The purpose of the present series of lessons is not to apologize for the teachings of Scripture, but to expound them. The doctrine of

Romans 9:1–24

sovereign election is there in the inspired text, and not only in this chapter, not only in the Epistle to the Romans, but throughout the whole Word of God, both Old Testament and New. We may not /1 like it, but it is there, and we cannot eliminate it. If we object to this doctrine, our quarrel is with God the Holy Spirit, the author of Holy Scripture.

Verse 13 is quoted from Malachi 1:2–3. "As it is written, Jacob have I loved, but Esau have I hated."

> This passage, as well as the one quoted in verse 12...relates to the descendants of Jacob and Esau, and to the individuals themselves; the favor shown to the posterity of the one, and withheld from that of the other, being founded on the distinction originally made between the two brothers. The meaning therefore is, that God preferred the one to the other, or chose one instead of the other. As this is the idea meant to be expressed, it is evident that in this case the word hate means to love less, to regard and treat with less favor /2 (Charles Hodge, *A Commentary on the Epistle to the Romans*, p. 312).

This usage of "love" and "hate" is well known in the Bible, as shown by Matthew 6:24, Luke 14:26, John 12:25, and other places.

The apostle has shown that God is perfectly sovereign in His bestowal of His favors on men. He does not have to conform to any human pattern or principle, He does not have to explain or justify /3 His choices to us. This is proved by the history of Jacob and Esau.

Questions:

1. How was God's sovereignty exemplified in His choice of Isaac in preference to Ishmael?
2. What do we mean by God's "sovereignty"?
3. What expression is often used in the Bible and in the Westminster *Confession of Faith* to describe the operation of God's sovereignty?
4. Give some instances of the use of this expression in the Bible and in the *Confession of Faith*.
5. Why is God responsible only to Himself for His decisions and acts?

Romans 9:1–24

6. What statement to Rebekah concerning her sons proves the sovereignty of God?

7. What is the importance of the fact that this statement was made before Jacob and Esau were born?

8. How does Paul describe God's purpose of election in 9:11?

9. What does 9:10–13 show concerning the Arminian teaching that God from eternity elected persons because He foresaw that they would repent and believe?

10. Did God choose Jacob because Jacob was going to become a godly man, or did Jacob eventually become a godly man because God had chosen him?

11. Why do many people object violently to the doctrine of sovereign election?

12. What is the meaning of the statement "Jacob have I loved, but Esau have I hated"?

13. What is the bearing of this discussion of Jacob and Esau on the matter of God rejecting the Jews and calling the Gentiles?

Lesson 38

Having set forth the doctrine of God's absolute sovereignty and having shown that it is true from the history of Jacob and Esau, Paul proceeds to deal with two objections that people might raise against this doctrine. These objections, on the surface, seem plausible, and therefore they require to be evaluated and answered.

He takes up the first objection in 9:14–18 and the second one in 9:19–24.

The first objection is that the doctrine of God's absolute sovereignty in His bestowal of favors on men represents God as being unjust. "What shall we say then: is there unrighteousness with God?" (9:14). The objection is, in essence, that if God in His sovereignty gives His favor to one person and withholds it from another person, He is unjust or unfair. Behind this objection lies the assumption that in order to be fair or just, God must treat all persons exactly alike. That is to say, behind the objection lies the notion that God owes something to people—that what God gives to one, every other can claim as a right.

Romans 9:1–24

Following his usual method, Paul first emphatically denies the point of the objection. He says, "God forbid." Then, having denied it, he proceeds to state his reasons. First he quotes the Old Testament Scripture (Ex. 33:19) to show that God, in His Word, expressly claims this absolute sovereignty: "I will have mercy on whom I will have mercy, and I will have compassion on whom I will have compassion." Those were God's own words to Moses; from them there is no appeal. This sovereignty which God so plainly claims for Himself cannot be subordinated to human ideas of fairness or justice. So Paul draws the inference, "So then it is not of him that willeth, nor of him that runneth, but of God that showeth mercy" (9:16). A person's election, his salvation, his receiving the gracious favor of God, does not ultimately depend on his own will or decision ("not of him that willeth"), nor upon his own conduct, works, or actions ("nor of him that runneth"), but upon the free and sovereign grace of God ("but of God that showeth mercy").

Next, Paul illustrates this truth from the history of Pharaoh: "For the Scripture saith unto Pharaoh, even for this same purpose have I raised thee up, that I might show my power in thee, and that my name might be declared throughout all the earth" (9:17). This is quoted from Exodus 9:16. Charles Hodge comments on this,

> It is not the design of Pharaoh's creation that is here asserted; but the end for which God determined his appearance and position in the history of the world. Nor does the apostle refer Pharaoh's wickedness to God as its author, but his appearance at that period, the form in which the evil of his heart developed itself, and the circumstances attending its manifestation, were all determined by the providence of God, and ordered for the promotion of his infinitely wise and benevolent purposes (*A Commentary on the Epistle to the Romans*, p. 314–5).

That is to say, God raised Pharaoh up, and determined the events of his career, not for Pharaoh's own benefit, but for a wider purpose of God—a purpose that involved the destruction of Pharaoh in order that the glory of God might be magnified. It was not that Pharaoh was

Romans 9:1–24

worse than other Egyptians, nor that he was by nature any worse than Moses or Aaron, but that God might be glorified. God was glorified by Pharaoh's destruction as truly as He was glorified by the salvation of Moses or Aaron. 7

"The ground, therefore, on which Pharaoh was made an object of the divine justice, or the reason why the law was in his case allowed to take its course, is not to be sought in any peculiarity of his character or conduct in comparison with those of others, but in the sovereign pleasure of God" (Charles Hodge, *A Commentary on the Epistle to the Romans*, p. 315). God might have chosen to save Pharaoh and give him eternal life; actually, He chose to bring Pharaoh under judgment unto destruction. The one choice was as proper for God as the other.

"Therefore hath he mercy on whom he will have mercy, and whom he will he hardeneth" (9:18). This statement forms the conclusion, not only to the preceding verse, but to the entire passage consisting of verses 14–17. Paul sums it all up by an unqualified affirmation of the sovereignty of God in bestowing His gracious favor upon men. God has mercy on those on whom He chooses to have mercy; He withholds mercy from those whom He chooses to withhold mercy. Those from whom He chooses to withhold mercy are inevitably hardened in their sins. 8

To return to the question, "Is there unrighteousness with God?" (9:14)—does the doctrine of God's sovereignty imply that God is unjust or unfair? We have already remarked that behind the objection there lies an assumption that God is somehow under obligation to treat all persons exactly alike, to give to all what He gives to any. But this idea that God must distribute His favors with absolute equality, like a ration board issuing coupons to purchase commodities during war time, is not founded upon the Bible, but upon sinful human prejudices. 9

Justice means to give every person what that person *deserves*. 10 God would be unjust if He were to punish those who deserve to be rewarded. He would be unjust if He were to reject persons who deserve to be elected, if He were to treat the righteous as if they were wicked. Such action on God's part would certainly be unjust, it would certainly be unfair.

Romans 9:1–24

But that is not the real situation at all. The whole human race has fallen away from God and is sunk in sin. Of all this mass of human beings, there is none that deserves anything from God except His wrath and curse, judgment unto condemnation, punishment in hell. That is what all mankind alike deserves. If God were to condemn and punish all mankind alike, it would not be unjust, it would only be what men deserve, it would be strictly in accordance with justice.

Still, out of the mass of fallen humanity God, in His sovereignty, has elected *some*—not all, but some—to eternal life. This is not because they deserve it, but because of the free mercy and love of God granted to the elect. Now the objector comes and says, "God is unjust. If He saves any, He must save all; He has no right to give salvation as a free gift to some and leave others to perish in their own sins."

Where does the objector get this idea that "God has no right" to give to some what He withholds from others? Even men do not act on such a principle. If we give a dime or a quarter to a hungry man to buy some food, are we unfair if we do not give the same amount to every hungry man in the world? Why is God obligated to do for all what He does for some? Neither from Scripture nor from reason can such a claim be vindicated. This objection comes from Satan, the father of lies, who wants men to impugn the justice of God.

Certainly the Bible represents God as treating men unequally, in giving mercy to some while withholding it from others. But this is not injustice, for God owes nothing to any human being, and He never punishes any person except as that person himself deserves.

Questions:

1. What objection to the doctrine of God's sovereignty does Paul take up in 9:14–18?
2. What assumption lies behind this objection in the minds of the objectors?
3. What does Paul first say in reply to this objection?
4. What statement of God does Paul quote from Exodus, and what is the bearing of this statement on the objection being faced?
5. What is the meaning of the statement of 9:16?

Romans 9:1–24

6. How is God's sovereignty illustrated in the history of Pharaoh?

7. Why was Pharaoh judged and punished for sin when Moses was saved and given eternal life?

8. What happens in a person's life and character when God's saving mercy is withheld from that person?

9. Does God have to issue His gracious favors with absolute equality like a ration board issuing coupons?

10. What is the meaning of justice?

11. What kind of action on God's part would really be unjust?

12. Why would it not be unjust for God to condemn and punish the entire human race without electing and saving any?

13. What is the real source of the idea that "God has no right" to withhold from some what He gives to others?

Lesson 39

Paul has already disposed of one objection to the doctrine of God's sovereignty in bestowing gracious favors upon men, namely the objection that this doctrine represents God as being unjust or unrighteous. This objection was answered in 9:14–18. The apostle now takes up the second objection to the doctrine. This objection is, essentially, the claim that the doctrine of God's sovereignty destroys human responsibility. The claim is that if God is sovereign in bestowing salvation on men, then men are not themselves responsible for their sinful condition and their sinful actions.

"Thou wilt say then unto me, why doth he yet find fault? For who hath resisted his will?" (9:19). If God has decreed from all eternity, by His mere good pleasure, to redeem part of the human race from their sins while passing by the rest and leaving them to perish in their sins, then—so ran the objection—why does God hold men responsible for their sinful condition and life? Everything is foreordained by God from all eternity; nobody can possibly thwart or successfully resist this eternal decree of God; men fulfill the divine decree in spite of themselves; so why should God hold them responsible? Does not the doctrine of divine sovereignty reduce men to mere puppets manipulated by strings, to mere machines with no real freedom of their own? Such was the thinking involved in the objection "Why doth he yet find fault? For who hath resisted his will?"

If Paul had held the Arminian theology that is so common and so popular today, he could have answered this second objection very easily. He would only have needed to say, "God's eternal decree of election is based on His foresight of men's future actions. God from eternity foresaw who would repent and believe and who would not. All God's decree of election means is that He has decided to choose those whom He foresaw would of their own accord repent and believe. Therefore this doctrine does not destroy human responsibility at all. It is man and not God that really decides the great question of salvation." If Paul had had the Arminian scheme in mind, we should certainly expect him to answer the objection by some such statement as the above. But he did nothing of the kind. Instead of explaining God's sovereign election away, saying it is really only a following-up of man's own decision, Paul answers the objection in a very different way.

He does not tone down the divine sovereignty nor try to explain it away. Nor does he undertake to reason with the objector on the basis of human logic or philosophy. Instead, Paul rules the objection out of court by citing the Creator/creature relationship. "Nay but, O man, who art thou that repliest against God? Shall the thing formed say to him that formed it, why hast thou made me thus?" (9:20).

The man who argues against the divine sovereignty on the ground that it destroys human responsibility forgets that he is a creature and God is the Creator. This man holds that he cannot be responsible for his acts if God has foreordained whatsoever comes to pass. He sets up an antithesis between God's sovereignty and man's responsibility, and says that either God is sovereign, or man is responsible—one or the other, but not both. Then he proceeds to deny God's sovereignty in order to hold on to man's responsibility.

This man who forgets that he is a creature and God is the Creator thinks that he cannot be responsible for his acts unless he is the ultimate, absolute originator of them—unless his acts are outside of the great eternal plan of God. In other words, he holds that man cannot be responsible as long as God is really God.

Romans 9:1–24

The truth is, of course, that all that comes to pass has been foreordained by God from all eternity, yet man is a free agent and is therefore morally responsible for the state of his heart and for his thoughts, words, and deeds. This involves a paradox that human reason cannot solve—an apparent contradiction. How God can be sovereign and man can be free (and responsible) is, we repeat, a paradox that human reason cannot solve. We are not intended to try to solve it by human reason. This paradox will be a stumbling block only to the person who insists on exalting human reason above the divine revelation in the Bible. There is not the slightest question as to the fact that the Bible teaches both God's sovereignty and man's freedom (and responsibility). If we give up either of these truths, we only land in far greater problems and difficulties. The only safe course, and the only right course, is to take what the Bible tells us and leave the insoluble mystery to God. We should beware of any teacher who claims that he can solve this paradox. It has been recognized for centuries that it cannot be solved; it is one of the secret things that belong to the Lord our God. We should firmly hold on to both the truth of God's sovereignty and that of man's responsibility, and reverently refuse to attempt to cut the knot by human reason.

As Paul points out, a recognition of the Creator/creature relationship should keep us from raising such an objection as that of verse 19. The person who is willing for God really to be God will not raise it. The person who has the slightest notion of the infinite greatness of the Creator and the absolute dependence of the creature will not raise it. The person who has any truly religious reverence for God as his Creator and sustainer, the one in whom he lives and moves and has his being, will not raise such an objection. He will humbly acknowledge that God has foreordained all that comes to pass, and that man is still free and responsible. God has foreordained man's acts without thereby destroying man's freedom.

God is the potter, and man is the clay. God has so created and fashioned man that man's actions are free—he is responsible for them—and yet they are foreordained by God from eternity. Those who object to this are not willing to be the clay in God's hands; they want to dictate to the divine potter. For the clay is dependent, but the

Romans 9:1–24

potter is independent. If man were independent, as God alone really
is, his free actions could not have been foreordained. But precisely
because man as a creature is dependent upon God, the independent
Creator and ruler of all, man's actions are free even though they are 10
foreordained. God created man that way. He fashioned man to be that
kind of a creature. God fashioned man as a being whose actions are
to be foreordained and yet free. God fashioned man as a dependent
being, to think God's thoughts after Him and to live out in human
history the plan that God had made in eternity. God did not create
man to be an independent being, the absolute originator of his own
ideas and acts.

Man is not only a creature of God and therefore dependent on
God; he is also a *sinful* creature of God and therefore has no claim))
on the love and mercy of God. God has the perfect right to elect
some sinful human beings to eternal life, while passing by others and
punishing them for their sin. This involves no injustice. It gives no
one any ground for complaint. The reprobate are punished for their
sins; that is only what they deserve. The elect are saved from their
sins; that is the free mercy of God, which He gives to whom He will.

Paul next calls our attention to something else that the objector
has forgotten, namely that the punishment of wicked men, no less than
the salvation of the elect, serves to manifest the glory of God. This
is brought out in verses 22–24. God, in much longsuffering, endures
the "vessels of wrath fitted to destruction," because He is "willing to
show his wrath" and "to make his power known." "The punishment
of the wicked is not an arbitrary act, having no object but to make
them miserable; it is designed to manifest the displeasure of God
against sin, and to make known his true character. On the other hand,
the salvation of the righteous is designed to display the riches of his
grace. Both in the punishment of the one class and the salvation of
the other, most important and benevolent ends are to be answered"
(Charles Hodge, *A Commentary on the Epistle to the Romans*, p. 319).

Our own age, with its unbalanced and unbiblical overemphasis
on the love of God, has all but forgotten that the punishment of the
wicked glorifies God as truly as does the salvation of the elect. The

punishment of the wicked manifests God's justice, as the salvation of *12*
the elect manifests His mercy. Today we have all but forgotten that
there really are people whom the Holy Spirit speaking in Scripture
calls "vessels of wrath fitted to destruction." Yet this is a truth of God's
Word beyond a doubt.

If we had a truly biblical viewpoint and emphasis, we would marvel,
not that some human beings are eternally lost, but that any are saved.
That is the real wonder. The early Church, as portrayed in the New
Testament, was not scandalized by the idea that some human beings are
vessels of wrath fitted to destruction. That was quite obvious. But the
early Church was filled with a great wonder and amazement at the good
news that God had provided salvation at all for sinful human beings.

Paul points out, then (9:22–24) that God is glorified both in the
destruction of the wicked and in the salvation of the elect. He adds
that the elect, who shall be saved, are "not of the Jews only, but also
of the Gentiles"—something that seems obvious to us today, but that
was a new and difficult truth in Jewish and Jewish/Christian circles at
the time he was writing this epistle.

Questions:

1. What is the second objection to the doctrine of divine sovereignty
    that Paul takes up?
2. If Paul had held the Arminian theology, how could he easily have
    answered this second objection?
3. How does Paul first deal with the objection that God's sovereignty
    rules out man's responsibility?
4. What is the meaning of the term "paradox"?
5. What great paradox is involved in man's relation to his Creator?
6. What will be the result if we deny either God's sovereignty or man's
    freedom?
7. To what kind of people will this paradox be a stumbling block?
8. What should be our attitude toward this great paradox of divine
    sovereignty and human freedom?
9. What truth is implied in the fact that God is the potter and man
    is the clay?

Romans 9:1–24

10. What is involved in the truth that God fashioned man as a dependent being?

11. Why is it not unjust or wrong for God to elect some to eternal life while passing by others and leaving them to perish in their sin?

12. In what ways does the destruction of wicked men manifest God's glory?

The Jews Rejected because of Their Unbelief, as Predicted in the Old Testament Scriptures. 9:25-33
Lesson 40

In 9:1-24, Paul has shown that God's rejection of the Jews and His calling of the Gentiles is not inconsistent with His promises, and he has set forth with emphasis the truth that God is absolutely sovereign in bestowing His gracious favor upon men. God is accountable to no one but Himself, and He has always acted in absolute consistency with Himself—with His own nature, Word, and promises.

Next, the apostle undertakes to show that the Jews were rejected for their unbelief, as predicted in the Old Testament Scriptures. First, he quotes from the prophet Hosea, "I will call them my people, which were not my people, and her beloved, which was not beloved... And it shall come to pass, that in the place where it was said unto them, ye are not my people; there shall they be called the children of the living God" (Rom. 9:25-26; see Hos. 2:23, 1:10). The name "Osee" in Romans 9:25 is of course merely a Greek form of the Old Testament "Hosea." It will be noted that Paul's quotation of Hosea differs somewhat from the wording in the Authorized Version of the Old Testament. This is not a serious difficulty, for Paul's version is a legitimate translation of the Hebrew original, as in the Hebrew the same word can mean both "have mercy on" and "love." Moreover, the Holy Spirit is the real author of both the prophecy of Hosea and the Epistle to the Romans, and when an author is quoting from his own earlier writings, absolute literal identity is not required. An author has some liberty in quoting his own words that would be improper in quoting the words of another.

Romans 9:25-33

A more serious problem concerns the fact that in Hosea the promise concerns the ten tribes of the northern kingdom of Israel, whereas Paul (and also Peter in 1 Peter 2:10) applies it to the Gentiles. Because Hosea was writing about the ten tribes, some scholars have supposed that Paul in Romans 9:25 had a restoration of the Jews in mind. This interpretation is untenable, however, because it cannot be made to fit the context in Romans 9, where the subject is very plainly the rejection of the Jews and the calling of the Gentiles. The most probable solution of the difficulty is that in Hosea's time the ten tribes were in a heathenish condition, being deeply involved in idolatry, and therefore from the religious point of view they were practically on a par with the Gentile nations. Hence what Hosea said of the Gentile–like ten tribes, Paul could properly apply to the Gentiles in general—the time would come when those who were not God's people would be called His people, and when she who was not beloved, would be called beloved.

In considering verses 25 and 26, we should realize how utterly contrary these verses are to the common popular notion of "the universal brotherhood of man." In the world, there are two classes of people, those who are God's people and those who are not God's people; those who are beloved with God's redemptive love and those who are not so beloved. The one class is in a covenant relationship with God: they know God as their own God, so God is their God, and they are God's people. The other class is strangers and foreigners, aliens from God, at enmity with God, far away from any religious communion or covenant bond with God. By the gracious calling of God, those who were not His people may become His people. What we should note is that this comes to pass only by the gracious calling of God. It is not true that all mankind are God's children (in the religious and ethical sense) by nature. By nature they are the children of wrath. By the special, saving grace of God alone do they become children of God, His people, beloved. We should keep this truth clearly in mind in a day when the liberal dogma of "the universal brotherhood of man" seems to be regarded as an unquestionable truth by many of the leading religious teachers of our day.

The Old Testament, then, predicted the calling and salvation of Gentiles. While this seems quite obvious to us today, we must

Romans 9:25–33

remember that it was a strange and difficult teaching to those who
had been brought up in the tenets of Pharisaic Judaism, as many of
Paul's original readers had been. If the rejection of the Jews and the
calling of the Gentiles had not been regarded as an extremely difficult
doctrine, certainly the apostle would not have labored so long and
elaborately to prove the point.

Next, the apostle quotes from the prophecy of Isaiah (10:22–23;
1:9), to prove from the Old Testament Scriptures that the Jews as a
nation were not to be saved, but only a remnant or inner core of the
external nation of Israel. It will be observed that Paul's quotation
varies somewhat from Isaiah 10:22–23 as it appears in the Authorized
Version. The apostle's version is more like the Septuagint (the Greek
translation of the Old Testament) than like the Hebrew original, although the general meaning is identical. Here again it must be borne
in mind that this is a case of the divine author, the Holy Spirit, quoting
His own previous writings. It is not, therefore, inconsistent with the
doctrine of the verbal inspiration of Scripture!

The point is evidently that, according to Isaiah's prophecy, it is
not the virtual body of Israel, in number as the sand of the sea, that
is to receive salvation, but only a small fraction of this whole body,
namely, a "remnant." This plainly implies, then, the divine purpose
of rejection of the Jews as a nation. Verse 28, quoting from Isaiah,
predicts the divine work of judgment that is threatened against the
apostate mass of the Jews.

Verse 29 is from Isaiah 1:9. Where Paul has "a seed," Isaiah has
"a very small remnant." The word "seed" is taken by Paul from the
Greek version of the Old Testament, and its meaning in this context
is precisely the same as that of "a very small remnant"—the seed
reserved for sowing the future crop, which is a very small fraction of
the total harvest of the previous year. It was only the grace of God
that prevented Israel from becoming completely like Sodom and
Gomorrah. The great majority became thus apostate and heathenish.
But God preserved a "seed," a "very small remnant" of saved, spiritual
persons, to maintain the continuity of the covenant people. How
mistaken it is then to hold that the gracious promises of God were

Romans 9:25–33

given to Israel after the flesh, to the Jews as Jews, as those physically descended from Abraham!

Questions:

1. What does Paul undertake to show in 9:25–33?
2. From what Old Testament prophet does the apostle first quote?
3. How can we explain the fact that Romans 9:25 differs from Hosea 2:23 as found in the Authorized Version?
4. Who is the real author of both Old Testament and New Testament?
5. What liberty may an author properly take in quoting from his own previous writings?
6. Concerning whom was Hosea speaking in Hosea 2:23?
7. How can it be explained that Paul applies Hosea 2:23 to the calling of the Gentiles?
8. What is the bearing of Rom. 9:25–26 on the liberal notion of "the universal brotherhood of man"?
9. Why does Paul argue at such length to prove the rejection of the Jews and the calling of Gentiles?
10. What Old Testament prophet is next quoted by Paul?
11. What does Isaiah 10:22–23 show concerning the salvation of the Jews?
12. Why is the meaning of "seed" the same as that of "a very small remnant"?
13. How was the continuity of God's covenant people maintained in the face of general apostasy?

Lesson 41

From the human point of view, it would have seemed very improbable to the Jews that the Gentiles would receive salvation. But that which was contrary to human probability actually took place. The Gentiles, who were deeply sunk in sin and very far from God, received righteousness and salvation through faith in Jesus Christ, while the Jews, who considered themselves specialists in achieving righteousness, failed to attain it. This is Paul's argument in 9:30–31. The Gentiles "followed not after righteousness"—it was not a serious concern to them as it was to the Pharisaic Jews. Yet, through the saving grace of God, they actually attained to "the righteousness which is of faith"; that is to say, they came to believe on Jesus Christ as their Savior and were justified, or pronounced righteous before God, by the perfect righteousness of Christ being imputed to them.

It was the paradox and tragedy of Israel that those who were intensely concerned about righteousness and who prided themselves on the attainment and possession of righteousness failed of the righteousness that can meet the requirements of God's holy law. They "followed after the law of righteousness"—they made a business of seeking righteousness. There is some difficulty as to precisely what is meant by "the law of righteousness." Calvin interprets the expression as meaning the law that they thought would result in their attaining righteousness or being justified (*Commentary on Romans*, p. 378).

The reason why the Jews failed to attain righteousness is stated in verse 32. It was "Because they sought it not by faith, but as it were by the works of the law." That is, they refused to accept the only way of justification that meets the need of sinners, and they attempted to attain righteousness on the basis of works, as Adam and Eve might have done before the Fall. Just as Cain attempted to stand before God on the basis of his own works or character, so the Jews of Paul's day attempted to stand before God on the basis of their own works or character. Just as Cain was unwilling to approach God by faith, confessing himself a sinner and placing his trust simply in the slain lamb of the sacrifice (as Abel did), so the Jews of Paul's day were unwilling—perversely and stubbornly unwilling—to approach God by faith, confessing themselves sinners and placing their trust simply in the shed blood of Jesus Christ, the Lamb of God that takes away the sin of the world. Thus their rejection by God was their own fault; no one but themselves was to blame for it. Those who are saved are saved solely because of the sovereign grace of God. But those who are rejected and condemned are rejected and condemned because of their own sin.

"As it were by the works of the law" (9:32). The phrase "as it were" here means that they supposed that righteousness could be attached by the works of the law. Actually, it is impossible for sinners to obtain righteousness by their own personal works of law observance (3:20), but the Jews were self-deceived and so went on with their vain quest for righteousness with zeal and earnestness.

"For they stumbled at that stumbling stone" (9:32). "That stumbling stone" of course, is Jesus Christ, the Messiah. The Jews stumbled in accepting Jesus Christ as the Messiah. They were not willing to confess themselves sinners and accept salvation according to God's plan and on God's terms.

That Christ would be "a stumbling stone" was revealed in the Old Testament Scriptures. Paul here refers to Isaiah 28:16 and 8:14. The apostle has evidently combined parts of these two texts of Isaiah into a single statement in Romans 9:33. Being inspired by the same Holy Spirit who was the real author of the prophecy of Isaiah, it was of course entirely proper for Paul to do this. As already explained in the previous lesson, in every case where the New Testament quotes the Old, we really have a case of the author (God the Holy Spirit) quoting from His own previous writings; consequently a freedom is proper that would be out of place in one human author quoting the writings of another, apart from divine inspiration.

Isaiah 28 is a prophecy directed against those who trusted in others than God, seeking an alliance with Egypt as protection against the danger of Assyrian aggression. In other words, it is directed against those who placed their confidence in man and in human methods and power rather than in the power of God. To such persons, the message of God was that He would "lay in Zion for a foundation a stone, a tried stone, a precious corner stone, a sure foundation" (Isa. 28:16). This is a prophecy of the coming of Jesus Christ, the Messiah. Israel could not be destroyed by enemies until the promised Messiah had come. Therefore they need not fear the power of Assyria; they should place their trust in the promises of God, in the coming Messiah and His work of redemption, rather than in worldly alliances and methods.

Isaiah 8:14 urges the people of Judah not to fear the alliance between Syria and Ephraim. "Say ye not, a confederacy, to all them to whom this people shall say, a confederacy; neither fear ye their fear, nor be afraid. Sanctify the Lord of hosts himself; and let him be your fear, and let him be your dread. And he shall be for a sanctuary; but for a stone of stumbling and for a rock of offense to both the houses of Israel, for a gin and for a snare to the inhabitants of Jerusalem" (Isa. 8:12–14). God thus announced that He would be a sanctuary or refuge to one class of persons, but a rock of offense to another class of persons. Some would put their trust in Him, while others would stubbornly refuse to put their trust in Him. The Apostle Paul properly uses this text as applying to people's attitude toward Jesus Christ. He, as the Son of God, would be accepted by some, but proudly rejected by others.

> "The whole spirit, opinions, and expectations of the Jews were adverse to the person, character, and doctrines of the Redeemer. He was, therefore, to them a stumblingblock, as he was to others foolishness. They could not recognize him as their fondly anticipated Messiah, nor consent to enter the kingdom of heaven on the terms which he prescribed. In them, therefore, were fulfilled the ancient prophecies, which spoke of their rejection of Christ, and consequent excision from the people of God" (Charles Hodge, *A Commentary on the Epistle to the Romans*, p. 331).

Questions:

1. What seemed very improbable to the Jews from their human point of view?
2. What is meant by the statement that the Gentiles "followed not after righteousness"?
3. How did the Gentiles attain to righteousness?
4. What was the great paradox and tragedy of Israel?
5. Why did the Jews fail to attain righteousness?
6. How did Cain attempt to approach God?
7. How was Abel's approach to God different?
8. In what way were the Jews of Paul's day similar to Cain?
9. On what ground are some people rejected and condemned by God?
10. What is the stumbling stone at which the Jews stumbled?
11. How does Isaiah 28:16 apply to Paul's argument?
12. What is the bearing of Isaiah 8:14 on Paul's argument?

Romans 9:25–33

The Simplicity and Adequacy of the Gospel Way of Salvation. 10:1–10

Lesson 42

In the closing verses of chapter 9, Paul explained how Israel came to miss salvation, and how the Gentiles came to receive it. The Jews attempted to substitute a wrong, counterfeit, impossible way of obtaining righteousness. They were sincere and intensely earnest, but completely wrong. Before his conversion to Jesus Christ, Paul himself had been of their persuasion. Sincerity and zeal are not enough to save us. We must also be in the pathway of truth. Why do so many sincere and earnest people reject the gospel of Christ today? They reject it because, like the Jews of old, their minds are already prejudiced in favor of false notions of their own. *1*

In the opening verses of chapter 10, Paul expresses his affectionate desire for the salvation of the people of Israel. It was his heart's *2* desire and prayer to God that they might be saved (10:1). As the truth *3* that the apostle was teaching was most distasteful to Jewish readers, he takes special pains to assure them of his affection and real desire for their welfare. "We here see with what solicitude the holy man obviated offences" (John Calvin, *Commentary on Romans*, p. 381). We, too, should seek to avoid giving offense as far as possible without sacrificing loyalty to the truth. Bearing witness to divine truth does not imply that we must make the truth seem as distasteful as possible. On the contrary, we should make every effort to remove difficulties and occasions of offense. If people insist on contradicting the truth of God, that is their responsibility, but we should see to it that we present the truth in as acceptable and winsome a manner as possible, *3* lest our spirit of anger or impatience or hostility turn men away from the truth we proclaim.

"For I bear them record that they have a zeal of God, but not according to knowledge" (10:2). Having a zeal of God was good: it was commendable, as far as it went. However, the Jews' zeal of God was *3 4* really worthless because it was "not according to knowledge." Their zeal was directed to a wrong object, and therefore it was a sinful and ineffective zeal. The word for *knowledge* here is the very strong Greek

term *epignosis*, meaning "moral knowledge," "correct knowledge and 5
appreciation" (Charles Hodge, *A Commentary on the Epistle to the Romans*,
p. 334). The ordinary Greek term for knowledge is *gnosis*, which
means simply "knowledge," "information"; whereas *epignosis* means
right knowledge, a morally discerning knowledge. Their knowledge
was "neither enlightened nor wise; neither right as to its objects, nor
correct in its character" (Charles Hodge, *A Commentary on the Epistle
to the Romans*, p. 334). The Jews were very zealous for their inherited
traditions and for the establishment of their own legal righteousness,
and at the same time, naturally, they were very proud and censorious.
Their zeal, so far as it was a zeal for God, was better than indifference,
which explains why the apostle could commend it with reservations.

"For they being ignorant of God's righteousness, and going about
to establish their own righteousness, have not submitted themselves
unto the righteousness of God" (10:3). In spite of all their earnest zeal,
the Jews were completely wrong about the most important question,
namely, how can a sinful man be justified by the holy God? To this 6
vitally important question they gave the wrong answer that man can ⌐
be justified by God on the basis of his own personal observance of
the law of God. This error was not a mere innocent mistake; it was an
error that involved deep moral guilt on their part. For their notion of
justification implied wrong views of God, of the requirements of God's
law, and of their own moral and spiritual condition. They had much too
low an idea of the character of God, they had much too low an idea of
the requirements of God's law, and they had much too high an idea of 8
themselves and their own powers and attainments. To be wrong about
such matters as these is not only the result of sin, but also is itself great
sin. Those who were wrong at these crucial points were spiritually blind
men, and it was no advantage to them that they were perhaps in the
right on many other matters—minor matters.

Here "their own righteousness" is contrasted with "the righteousness of God." The former expression clearly means the righteousness
that they attempted to establish by their own actions. There is some
difficulty as to the exact meaning of the phrase "the righteousness of
God" in this passage. As it is contrasted with "their own righteousness,"

Romans 10:1–10

the meaning is probably "the righteousness of which God is the source *q* or the righteousness which is received from God."

Not realizing that there is a "righteousness of God" available to sinners by faith in the Redeemer, the Jews went busily about attempting to establish their own righteousness by a careful, laborious life of obedience to all the precepts of the law of God. Knowing nothing of the availability of salvation as a gift of grace, they continued in their vain, impossible effort to attain righteousness by their own good lives. *10*

We should realize that this error was not peculiar to the Jews of Paul's time. It is characteristic of sinners of every time and place. The human heart, in its sinful pride and stubbornness, naturally tends to attempt to establish its own righteousness by good works. This is the explanation of the tremendous popularity of what is today called "the religion of the Golden Rule." Prominent men are quoted as saying, "the golden rule is all the religion I need," and similar statements. As there is no gospel, no Christ, and no salvation in the golden rule, such men are saying that they need no gospel, no Christ, and no salvation. Their religion, though differing greatly in outward form, is essentially the same as that of the Pharisees of old. They regard religion as a matter of human works and character, no more and no less. It is the old theology of Cain, still alive in the world today. Though it is still the same old error, it goes by different names today. Some of the common ones are as follows: salvation by character, high ideals, spiritual values, service, the Jesus way of life, the Christian way of life, character building, character education, being true to one's own better nature, seeking the higher *17* things of life, brotherhood, religious emphasis, and social service. All of these, if not founded upon the shed blood of Jesus Christ and the imputation of Christ's righteousness to the sinner (and they usually are not), are only forms of the false religion of human works or merit and are essentially identical with the efforts of the Pharisaic Jews to establish "their own righteousness" while they remained ignorant of the righteousness of God.

"Have not submitted themselves unto the righteousness of God" (10:3). This expression ("have not submitted themselves") indicates a sinful stubbornness, a guilty unbelief. It implies an unwillingness to *12*

Romans 10:1–10

know, accept, and yield to the plan of salvation revealed by God in the gospel of Jesus Christ. So also at the present day, those who reject or bypass the gospel of the Lord Jesus Christ and seek to substitute for it their own miserable makeshifts such as "character building," are not only unfortunately mistaken, they are involved in guilty unbelief. This is not mitigated by the fact that they may seem to be very earnest, very pious, very religious, and to be doing a lot of good in human society.

Questions:

1. Why do sincere and earnest people reject the gospel of Christ today?
2. What desire does Paul express in 10:1?
3. What lesson can we learn from Paul's statement in 10:1?
4. Why was the Jews' zeal of God really worthless?
5. What is the meaning of the Greek word translated "knowledge" in 10:2?
6. Concerning what vitally important question were the Jews completely wrong?
7. What was wrong with their idea of God's character and of the requirements of God's law?
8. What was wrong with their idea of their own powers and attainments?
9. What is meant by the expression "the righteousness of God"?
10. What error is characteristic of sinners of every time and place?
11. What are some of the popular terms used today to designate the religion of salvation by human works?
12. What is implied by the expression "have not submitted themselves" in 10:3?

Lesson 43

"For Christ is the end of the law for righteousness to every one that believeth" (10:4). The heart of the gospel is the person and work of Jesus Christ, our Savior. Salvation comes not by our own keeping of the law, but by Christ's work for us. He contains within Himself all that the law demands for our justification.

Romans 10:1–10

Though the general meaning of this verse is perfectly clear, there is some difficulty concerning the precise meaning of the expression "end of the law." It may mean (1) "Christ is the one toward whom the law, in all its parts and elements, pointed and to whom it leads the sinner" (compare Gal. 3:24); (2) "Christ is the One who fulfills and completes all the requirements of the law, and who satisfies all the demands of the law"; or (3) "Christ is the One who terminates the law, who puts an end to the law, abolished the law, transfers the believer from the Covenant of Works to the Covenant of Grace." Charles Hodge (*A Commentary on the Epistle to the Romans*, p. 335) states that the first meaning is adopted by Calvin and most of the commentators; that the second is Scriptural in doctrine, but is not consistent with the meaning of the Greek word for "end" (*telos*, which does not properly mean "completion" or "fulfillment," for which the Greek word would be not *telos* but *pleroma*); and that the third meaning is the correct one.

The doctrine is clearly taught in Scripture, that those who are out of Christ are under the law, subject to its demands and exposed to its penalty. His coming and work have put an end to its authority, we are no longer under the law, but under grace (Rom. 6:14); we are no longer under the system which says, "Do this, and live"; but under that which says, "Believe, and thou shalt be saved." This abrogation of the law, however, is not by setting it aside, but by fulfilling its demands. It is because Christ is the fulfiller of the law, that he is the end of it. It is the latter truth that the apostle here asserts (Charles Hodge, *A Commentary on the Epistle to the Romans*, p. 336).

The meaning, then, we take to be: "Christ has put an end to the law as a requirement for righteousness before God, by fulfilling its demands and satisfying its penalty." So far as being counted righteous before God is concerned, the believer is finished with the law. He has been transferred from the Covenant of Works to the Covenant of Grace. No longer is he under the penalty of the broken Covenant of Works; no longer need he continue the desperate and futile attempt to attain righteousness of obedience to the law of God. Just as a person who is naturalized as a citizen of the United States of America is finished with the claims of his former country, so the Christian, so far as obtaining righteousness is concerned, is finished with the requirements of the law.

This may be illustrated as follows: a person who is burdened with a heavy load of debt finds himself unable to pay it off. He would like to get free, and he tries hard to do so, but finds that it is all he can do just to pay the interest on the debt, let alone paying anything on the principal. It takes all his efforts to pay the interest from time to time; in fact, he cannot even do that, so that, instead of getting out of debt, he gets deeper and deeper in debt all the time. Then a wealthy friend steps in and magnanimously pays off the entire debt for him, all in one lump sum. Then he is finished with trying to wipe out his obligations by paying small installments that do not even take care of the interest on his debt. He is finished with that, because the principal has been paid off for him by another. Similarly the Christian is finished with the law, so far as being justified before God is concerned; Christ has paid off the obligation for him, once for all.

In considering the interpretation of Romans 10:4, two errors must be carefully avoided. The first of these errors is the idea that the people of Israel from Moses to Christ lived under a system of justification by works of the law. Such is not the meaning of the apostle nor of Charles Hodge in his comments upon this verse. Some modern dispensationalists, however, have held (though usually inconsistently) that Israel from Moses to Christ lived under a system of justification by works—that from Abraham to Moses, salvation was by "promise"; from Moses to Christ by "law"; and after Christ by "grace." This doctrine involves a serious misunderstanding of the Old Testament. The Pharisaic system of Judaism, of course, taught salvation by works, as Judaism still does today. But this is nowhere taught in the Old Testament. Judaism is one thing; the religion revealed in the Old Testament is another. The former is legalistic; the latter is gracious.

The Covenant of Works as an actual way of obtaining eternal life began and ended in the garden of Eden. When Adam sinned, the Covenant of Works came to an end as an actual way by which human beings could obtain eternal life. But all sinners who have not come under the provisions of the Covenant of Grace are still under the curse and penalty

Romans 10:1–10

of the broken Covenant of Works. Such persons try to gain eternal life
by their own works—a vain and futile attempt, to be sure, but still the
attempt is continually being made. Paul, in Galatians 5:3, informs all
who attempt to gain eternal life that way that they are debtors to keep
the whole law of God. That is, God's law requires perfect obedience
and absolute moral perfection, and those who attempt to gain eternal
life by law observance are in the position of undertaking to render
this—a manifest impossibility.

Actually, the religion of the Old Testament is gracious through
and through. It is not a covenant of works, but the old dispensation
of the Covenant of Grace. Through the sacrifices, provision was made
for salvation by grace through faith in the promised Redeemer. When
Paul says that Christ is the end of the law for righteousness to every
one that believes, he does not mean that before the time of Christ
the Jews obtained or could have obtained righteousness by the law. He
only means that they attempted to obtain righteousness by the law,
and that for every one that believes, Christ puts a stop to the futile
attempt. What the sinner could never really do, Christ has done for
him, once and for all. The law always says "Do!" but the gospel of
Christ says "Done!"

The second error that must be avoided is the teaching that the
Christian believer is no longer under the law in any sense whatever.
There are those who teach that since Christ is the end of the law to
every one that believes, the Christian is no longer under any obligation to obey the law of God. Those who teach this include both the
ceremonial law and the moral law. Even the Ten Commandments, they
claim, are no longer binding upon the Christian, because he is not under law, but under grace. The writer of these studies has noted the sad
results of this kind of teaching on the foreign mission field. "We are
not under law but under grace" becomes the ready excuse for serious
lapses from moral rectitude.

It must be pointed out that while the believer is delivered from
the law as a supposed way of obtaining righteousness, and although
the believer has been delivered from the penalty and curse of the law
(Gal. 3:13), this does not mean that the Christian is no longer under the

Romans 10:1–10

moral law of God as the rule of his life. The moral law is an expression of
the character of God and hence is eternal and unchangeable. It cannot
be repelled; no rational creature can ever, to all eternity, be exempted
from the duty of obeying it. Paul himself specifically disclaimed being
exempt from the law in this sense (1 Cor. 9:21). The Christian is saved
unto a life of righteousness (1 Peter 2:24). But what is a life of righteousness? How is the Christian to know what is righteous and what is not,
what is right and what is wrong in his daily life? By the moral law of
God, which is summarized in the Ten Commandments and expanded
in the whole Bible. Day by day, the Christian is to strive after a life that
is in harmony with the moral law of God, not in order to obtain eternal
life, but because he has already obtained eternal life and now desires to
thank and please God. The moral law tells the Christian what is right
(pleasing to God) and what is wrong (displeasing to God). In this sense
the Christian remains under the law.

Questions:

1. What three possible meanings have been suggested for the phrase
   "the end of the law"?
2. Which of these possible meanings is probably the correct one?
3. How has Christ put an end to the law for the believer?
4. How may the truth that Christ has put an end to the law for the
   believer be illustrated?
5. What error concerning the period from Moses to Christ is held
   by some modern dispensationalists?
6. What is the difference between Judaism and the religion of the
   Old Testament?
7. When did the Covenant of Works end as an actual way of obtaining eternal life?
8. In what respect are unsaved sinners still under the Covenant of
   Works?
9. How can it be shown that the religion of the Old Testament was
   gracious?
10. In what respect is the Christian believer still under the moral
    law?

Romans 10:1–10

11. What did Paul state in 1 Corinthians 9:21 concerning his own relation to the law?

12. Why should a Christian try to obey the law of God?

13. Why can the moral law never be canceled or repealed?

14. What text in Peter's first epistle teaches that the Christian is saved unto a life of righteousness?

Lesson 44

"For Moses describeth the righteousness which is of the law, 'That the man which doeth those things shall live by them'" (10:5). This verse quotes from Leviticus 18:5. The meaning is that the law requires perfect obedience, and only by rendering such perfect obedience can anyone obtain righteousness by the law. Neither Paul nor Moses meant that it was ever, since the Fall, actually possible for men to render perfect obedience and so obtain righteousness and eternal life. Paul (and Moses) merely set forth the principle of righteousness by works; there had been a time (in Eden before the Fall) when men could actually obtain righteousness and life in accordance with that principle; but in the time of Paul (as in the time of Moses) that was no longer an actual possibility, because man had fallen into sin and had become corrupt in heart and life. Though righteousness by works was no longer an actual possibility, the principle of it could still be cited, for the purpose of contrast with the principle of righteousness by the grace of God in Jesus Christ.

The life mentioned in verse 5 "is a life which includes the whole man, soul and body, and the whole course of his existence, in this world and in that which is to come" (Charles Hodge, *A Commentary on the Epistle to the Romans*, p. 337). This is the life that was symbolized by the tree of life in the garden of Eden, of which man was deprived after his fall into sin (Gen. 3:22–24). Since that sad day, man's only way of obtaining righteousness and eternal life has been through the Mediator, the Lord Jesus Christ.

"But the righteousness which is of faith speaketh on this wise, Say not in thine heart, 'Who shall ascend into heaven?' (that is, to bring Christ down from above) Or, 'Who shall descend into the deep?' (that is, to bring up Christ again from the dead)" (10:6–7). Paul has just been implying (10:5) that it is impossible for man to attain righteousness by rendering a perfect obedience to the law of God. The law as set forth by Moses calls for performance that sinful man cannot render. Hence the attainment of righteousness by that method is impossible.

Paul proceeds to show that the gospel way of salvation does not involve any such impossibilities. It does not make righteousness and life depend upon conditions that are utterly beyond the power of sinful man to meet. We do not have to climb to heaven to obtain righteousness, nor do we have to descend to the abyss to get it— both of which are utterly beyond human power. Paul is alluding here to the language used by Moses in Deuteronomy 30:10–14. In that passage, to bring something down from heaven or to go over the sea to bring something from beyond the sea are represented as impossible tasks, beyond human power of accomplishment. In contrast to these impossible tasks, what God set before the people of Israel was within the capacity of those enabled by divine grace: "But the word is very nigh unto thee, in thy mouth, and in thy heart, that thou mayest do it" (Deut. 30:14). What is spoken of is, of course, not merely the moral law (which no sinner can perfectly fulfill), but the whole system given to Israel through Moses, including its sacrifices, types, symbols, ordinances, priesthood, and prophecies by which the way of salvation through a Redeemer was placed before the minds of the people. This was the system of salvation by grace. By accenting and living in this system, the Israelite professed his faith and was a recipient of salvation.

Clearly "to ascend into heaven," "to go beyond the sea," "to descend into the deep" (or the abyss, the bottomless deep) were proverbial expressions used to designate something regarded as utterly impossible. Various parallels from other parts of the Scriptures can be cited (Ps. 139:6; Prov. 24:7; Amos 9:2; Ps. 139:8–9). Paul changes Moses' expression "who shall go over the sea for us?" to "Who shall descend into the deep?" The Greek word for "deep" is the word from which our English word "abyss" is derived. Its proper meaning is "bottomless." In the New Testament, except for Romans 10:7, this word always means the place of lost souls and fallen angels (Luke 8:31; Rev. 17:8; 20:1). Probably Paul changed Moses' expression about going over the sea to one about descending into the abyss, because the latter is more suitable for referring to Christ's resurrection from the dead.

Paul's purpose in the present passage is to show the simplicity and adequacy of God's way of salvation. Accordingly, he first refutes the notion that it requires impossible achievements of men. It does not require men to render absolute perfect obedience to God's law as the condition of righteousness and life—something that is, in reality, as impossible as climbing to heaven or descending to the abyss. We do not have to try to save ourselves; we have a Savior. We do not have to attempt to provide a Savior for ourselves by bringing Him down from heaven to earth or by bringing him up from the realm of death; all this has already been done for us by God. Salvation is now offered to men in the gospel of Christ.

Questions:

1. What is the meaning of Leviticus 18:5, "The man which doeth those things shall live by them"?
2. Why does Leviticus 18:5 not mean that sinful man can actually obtain righteousness by his own works?
3. When did the principle of righteousness by works operate as an actual way by which man could obtain eternal life?
4. What is the meaning of the life referred to in 10:5?
5. What was represented by the tree of life in the garden of Eden?
6. Why were Adam and Eve debarred from access to the tree of life?
7. What expressions does Paul use to serve as examples of something impossible for man to accomplish?
8. What is the meaning of Deuteronomy 30:10–14?
9. What is the meaning of the Greek word "deep" in 10:7?
10. What place does this word almost always designate in the New Testament?
11. What has God done for sinners that they could never do for themselves?

Lesson 45

"But what saith it? 'The word is nigh thee, even in thy mouth, and in thy heart': that is, the word of faith, which we preach" (10:8). The gospel way of salvation is not something inaccessible, beyond human reach, too far, too high, or too low to be taken hold of; it does not require us to perform impossible feats before we can be saved. On the contrary, what the gospel way of salvation asks of a person is something near at hand, within reach, and easy to take hold of. "'The word is nigh thee, even in they mouth, and in thy heart': that is, the word of faith, which we preach." The person who really wants salvation is not baffled and frustrated by impossible demands; the person who really hungers and thirsts for righteousness is not mocked by being told to do some great thing. As Naaman the Syrian finally learned, what is required is not grand achievements, but a simple, childlike, obedient faith in the Word of God (see 2 Kings 5).

"That if thou shalt confess with thy mouth the Lord Jesus, and shalt believe in thine heart that God hath raised him from the dead, thou shalt be saved. For with the heart man believeth unto righteousness; and with the mouth confession is made unto salvation" (10:9–10). Here Paul presents to us what the gospel way of salvation requires of men: confession and faith. With the mouth we are to confess the Lord Jesus (or, more precisely, "that Jesus is Lord"); with the heart we are to believe that God has raised Him from the dead.

Faith comes before confession (or profession) in a person's experience, but confession is here mentioned first because it is the outward evidence of faith.

The thing to be confessed is that Jesus Christ is Lord. That is, we must openly recognize his authority to the full extent in which he is Lord; acknowledge that he is exalted above all principality and powers, that angels are made subject to him, that all power in heaven and earth is committed unto him, and of course that he is our Lord. This confession, therefore, includes in it an acknowledgment of Christ's sovereignty, and a sincere recognition of his authority over us. To confess Christ as Lord, is to acknowledge him as the Messiah, recognized as such of God, and invested with all the power and prerogatives of the Mediatorial throne. This acknowledgment is consequently often put for a recognition of Christ in all his offices (Charles Hodge, *A Commentary on the Epistle to the Romans*, p. 341). (Compare 1 Cor. 12:13; Phil. 2:11; Rom. 14:9; Acts 11:20; Matt. 10:32; Luke 12:8; 1 John 4:15.)

Besides confession, faith is required by the gospel: "and shalt believe in thine heart that God hath raised him from the dead." We are not merely to have faith in Christ as a person, nor even merely in Him as crucified for our sins, but specifically, we are to have faith that God has raised Him from the dead. Faith in His bodily resurrection really includes all the rest. It involves believing that He was and is all that He claims to be, all that He is represented in the Scriptures as being. By raising Him from the dead, God the Father has placed His seal of endorsement and approval on the whole finished work of Christ. The person who does not believe in Christ's resurrection cannot really believe on Him as Savior.

At the present day some religious leaders and teachers very perversely set up an antithesis between "faith in a person" and "faith in a doctrine." They claim that "faith in a person" (that is, in Christ as a person) is much better and more important than faith in a doctrine (such as Christ's atonement or His resurrection). This perverse teaching has a pious sound on the surface of it, and many are deceived by such smooth language. As a matter of fact, this distinction is just a subtle way of denying or evading doctrines such as the atonement and resurrection of Christ. The man who says, "Faith in Christ as a person is more important than belief of doctrines about Christ" really means, "The doctrines are not true and cannot be accepted, but we intend to keep on calling ourselves Christians, and claiming to have the person without the doctrines." This manner of denial or evasion is just one of the sophistical subtleties of present-day unbelief.

Actually, it is not possible to have faith in Christ as a person apart from faith in doctrine about Christ. Jesus Christ is separated from us by more than nineteen centuries of time. We cannot come into direct contact with Him in the way His contemporaries did by meeting Him on the roads of Galilee or Judea and seeing Him face to face. That is impossible for us. How, then, can we come in contact with Christ? Only by the truth concerning Him that is given to us in the Bible. Truth about Christ is our means of contact with Christ. No one can really believe in Christ without believing certain definite statements (truths or doctrines) about Christ, including especially the statement "that God hath raised him from the dead." Christianity is not a form of vague, hazy mysticism; it involves contact with the Christ of history through belief of the scriptural doctrines concerning Him.

Faith in Christ, to be real, must not only involve acceptance of the true doctrines concerning Him, but also must be in the heart. Not only in the mind, or intellect, but in the heart. The term "heart" here means not merely the affections or emotions, but the whole inner man. Real faith in Christ is much more than a mere mental assent to doctrines. Even the devils have that kind of faith (Jas. 2:19). Saving faith involves two elements. Both of these elements must be present or it is not true saving faith. The first element is knowledge, that is, *knowledge of the truth.* This is absolutely necessary, but it is not enough of itself. The second element is *trust*, that is, personal trust or commitment to Christ for salvation and eternal life. Trust cannot exist without some knowledge; we cannot trust Christ unless we know Him to be trustworthy. The person who really believes in his heart will have not merely true knowledge, but also personal trust in Christ as Savior.

How different this concept of faith is from the cheap, diluted "believism" of the present day! Many raise their hands in an evangelistic meeting, or sign a "decision card" stating that they accept Jesus Christ as their Savior, who show not the slightest evidence of real heart faith in Him, and who certainly do not in any adequate way confess Him as Lord before the world. Thousands feel sure of their eternal salvation because they have "accepted Christ" in some meeting, who have not the slightest desire or intention of really acknowledging Christ as the Lord of their lives. They have no intention whatever of separating from their sinful lusts and habits or of taking up the cross and suffering the reproach of Christ before the world. They just claim they are saved because they have accepted Christ. What the apostle

Romans 10:1–10

Paul places before us in Romans 10 is very different. It is very simple, indeed. It involves no gigantic tasks, no impossible achievements, but it calls for a confession of the total lordship of Christ over the universe and over my own life, and a heart faith that involves a personal commitment of my all to Him. Anything short of this is not genuine.

Verse 10 again stresses the importance of both heart faith and public confession. A public confession (profession) is the proper evidence of faith. If, because of fear, embarrassment, shame, or any other reason a person refrains from confessing Christ publicly before men, he is not a Christian, though he may secretly be a believer. If his faith is real, he will overcome his reluctance and will confess Christ before men, as commanded in Scripture.

Questions:

1. What does the person who really wants salvation find in the gospel?
2. What did Naaman the Syrian finally learn?
3. What two requirements are involved in the gospel way of salvation?
4. What is involved in confessing Jesus Christ as Lord?
5. Why is faith in Christ's resurrection required for salvation?
6. Why do some teachers set up an antithesis between "faith in a person" and "faith in a doctrine"?
7. What do those who make this distinction really mean?
8. Why is it not possible to have faith in Christ as a person apart from doctrines about Him?
9. What is meant by the word "heart" in 10:9–10?
10. What is meant by believing in the heart?
11. What two elements are involved in true saving faith?
12. Why can we not trust in Christ apart from knowledge about Christ?
13. What is wrong with the "believism" of the present day?
14. What is the relation between confession and faith?
15. What should we think of a person who claims to be a Christian but is unwilling to confess Christ publicly before men?

Romans 10:1–10

The Gospel Is Suited to the Needs of All Men, and to Be Preached to All. 10:11–21

Lesson 46

"For the Scripture saith, whosoever believeth on him shall not be ashamed" (10:11, quoted from Isa. 28:16). Paul confirms what he has been saying by this quotation from Isaiah, which sets forth two truths. First, the gospel way of salvation is suited to all mankind: "whosoever." It is therefore not limited to the nation of Israel, but adapted equally to both Jews and Gentiles. It is universal. It is suited to the needs of sinners regardless or race, nationality, or other distinctions.

In the second place, the verse from Isaiah teaches that faith is the means by which salvation is secured: "Whosoever believeth." Moreover it is not mere general faith by which salvation is secured, but specifically faith in Christ: "Whosoever believeth *on Him*"—on the precious cornerstone and sure foundation laid by God in Zion. Many people talk about faith today in a very vague and general way. It is not faith as a psychological attitude nor religious faith in general ("faith in religion," as some people say) that saves us, but specifically faith in Jesus Christ. The Bible never regards faith as a psychological attitude, and it never regards faith as a force. Many people today speak of faith as a force, and say such foolish things as "Faith has more power than dynamite." Actually, faith has no power whatsoever. Faith is not a power. It is not a force. It is a channel of connection. Christ has the power, and faith is our channel or link of connection with Christ. The modern notion of faith as a psychological attitude that has value or power of its own is destructive of Christianity. Faith is not our Savior; Christ is our Savior.

Saving faith terminates and rests upon Christ as its object: "Believeth *on Him*." These two words, "on him," indicate that faith involves the element of personal trust or commitment. This means receiving and resting upon Christ alone for salvation, as He is offered to us in the gospel.

"For there is no difference between the Jew and the Greek: for the same Lord over all is rich unto all that call upon him" (10:12). This verse explains the meaning of the "whosoever" of verse 11: there is no difference, in the matter of salvation, between Jews and Gentiles. There were indeed many differences between Jews and Gentiles, but as to their being sinners needing salvation, and as to the way by which they could be saved, there were no differences—all were upon the same footing, guilty and needy before God; all could receive salvation in exactly the same way, by the free grace of Him who is Lord over all.

It is difficult, and perhaps impossible, to decide whether the word "Lord" in verse 12 refers to God or to Christ. Arguments can be given on both sides. However, this is not really a question of any great importance. "Doctrinally, it matters little which view be preferred. Faith in God is faith in Christ, for Christ is God. This is the great truth to be acknowledged. The condition of salvation, under the gospel, is the invocation of Christ as God" (Charles Hodge, *A Commentary on the Epistle to the Romans*, p. 345).

To "call upon" the Lord is an expression frequently found in the Bible (Gen. 4:26; 12:8; Isa. 64:7; Acts 2:21; 9:14; 22:16; 1 Cor. 1:2; 2 Tim. 2:22). To call upon the Lord, in the religious sense, implies a true faith in Him. "Whosoever believes" and "Whosoever shall call upon the name of the Lord" are really just two ways of saying the same thing.

"For whosoever shall call upon the name of the Lord shall be saved" (10:13, quoted from Joel 2:32). This quotation from the prophet Joel is really identical in meaning with the verse quoted from Isaiah in Romans 10:11. Joel's prophecy, which is here cited, deals with the coming of the Messiah and the period of blessing that He would bring. In that period, whosoever calls upon the name of the Lord shall be saved—whether Jewish or Gentile, irrespective of all national or racial distinctions. Note that this same text of Joel was quoted by Peter on the day of Pentecost in Acts 2:21. The apostle has thus shown that the salvation of all believers in Christ, regardless of whether they be Jew or Gentile, was not only his own doctrine, but also that of the Old Testament, as evidenced by the words of the prophets Isaiah and Joel.

Though this truth was so plainly taught in the Old Testament, the Jews of Paul's day were blind to it. Even the apostle Peter learned it with difficulty (Acts 10; Gal. 2:11–16).

The notion of the special position of Israel had become so deeply impressed upon the Jews that they failed to realize that this special

position as the people of God was not an end in itself, but a means *10*
to an end—that through Abraham's seed all the families of the earth
should be blessed. They failed to realize that the special position of
Israel was not intended by God to be permanent, but only temporary, *11*
during the preparatory stage of redemption until the coming of the
Messiah. So, by thinking of their special position as permanent and
as an end in itself, they were blind to the Old Testament prophecies
of the salvation of the Gentiles. They failed to take account of these
prophecies and to take them seriously. *12*

Questions:

1. What two truths are taught by Isaiah 28:16 that Paul quotes in 10:11?
2. What is the difference between faith in Jesus Christ and faith as a mere psychological attitude?
3. Why is it wrong to speak of faith as a force?
4. What is the object of saving faith?
5. What truth is indicated by the words "on Him" in 10:11?
6. In what respect was there no difference between Jews and Gentiles?
7. What is implied by calling upon the name of the Lord?
8. What text from the prophet Joel does Paul quote?
9. What is the meaning of Joel's prophecy?
10. How can we explain the fact that the Jews of Paul's day were blind to the Old Testament prophecies of the salvation of the Gentiles?
11. What error did the Jews hold concerning the purpose of their special position as the people of God?
12. What error did the Jews hold concerning the God-intended duration of their special position as the people of God?

Lesson 47

Paul has shown that the gospel way of salvation is suited to the needs of all men, both Jews and Gentiles. He has shown that the Old Testament prophesied the calling and salvation of the Gentiles. These truths imply that the gospel must be made known to all mankind. Accordingly, the apostle next proceeds to discuss the propagation of the gospel by the method of preaching.

Romans 10:11–21

"How then shall they call on him in whom they have not believed? and how shall they believe in him of whom they have not heard? and how shall they hear without a preacher? and how shall they preach, except they be sent? As it is written, How beautiful are the feet of them that preach the gospel of peace, and bring glad tidings of good things!" (10:14–15). This is an argument to prove the necessity and obligation of missionary work, of sending the gospel message forth to all mankind.

It is a recognized biblical truth that when God wills an end, He also wills the means thereto. When He willed that Noah and his family should be saved from perishing in the flood, He also willed that Noah should build the ark and that he and his family should enter into it (Gen. 6–9). When He willed that Jonah should be saved from perishing in the sea, He also prepared a great fish to swallow the prophet (Jonah 1:17). When He willed that Cornelius and his family should be saved, He also willed that Peter should go and preach the gospel to them (Acts 10). This principle holds true, regardless of whether we are speaking of God's will in the sense of His decree or foreordination or in the sense of His commands addressed to men. Except in the special case of miracles, God's way of attaining the end is through the use of appropriate means.

This is eminently true in the case of the salvation of the Gentiles. Since God has from of old planned and predicted their calling and salvation, as we have seen by the statements from Isaiah and Joel, then it must also be God's intention that the *means* of their calling and salvation shall exist. As Paul points out, to call upon the name of the Lord implies faith in the Lord (Jesus Christ); to have faith in the Lord implies possession of knowledge about the Lord; to have knowledge about the Lord implies someone who can impart this knowledge, a preacher; to go as a preacher (missionary) implies being sent as one. The proper inference from this is that it is the God-given task and duty of the Church to send out missionaries to preach the gospel to all mankind.

Many Christians of the present day are comparatively indifferent to the missionary obligation. What they contribute toward this task is small indeed compared to what they spend upon themselves and upon the ordinances of religion at home. Some have the curious idea that missionary work is a form of charity or philanthropy comparable to the work of the Red Cross, to which they are willing to give a nominal contribution from time to time. Such is not a proper idea of the missionary task. It is a God-given commission, binding upon the Church 10 by divine authority, which it is the business of every Christian to be concerned about and to support liberally. When we support true missionary work we are not giving money to charity; we are rather paying an obligation. We are debtors, as Paul said he was, "both to the Greeks, and to the barbarians, both to the wise, and to the unwise"—that is, to all the world (1:14).

Much that is called missionary work today is not truly the preaching of the gospel in the sense of the apostle Paul. In the large, "liberal" denominations much "missionary work" is carried on that is in reality merely a form of humanitarianism or social service, rather than a real 11 preaching of Christ crucified to sinners. What God has laid upon His Church is the obligation to carry on and liberally to support real missionary work that carries the saving truth of the gospel of Christ to 12 sinners at home and abroad. Needless to say, no person who is not a believing, saved Christian can be a real missionary to others.

The last two or three years, much attention has been called in the secular and religious press to Dr. Albert Schweitzer of Africa. (*Editor's Note:* Dr. Albert Schweitzer lived from 1875–1965. He received the Nobel Peace Prize in 1952 for his philosophy of "Reverence for Life," and sought a universal ethical philosophy.) He has not only been called "a great missionary," but by some he has even been called "the greatest Christian in the world." That Dr. Schweitzer is a great man no one can deny. He is truly a many-sided genius, with outstanding achievements in the fields of theology, medicine, and music. But Dr. Schweitzer is not a Christian at all according to the Bible and the orthodox Christian faith. The enthusiastic articles about him fail to call any attention to his theological views, which are well-known in theological circles from his voluminous writings. For example, his famous book, *The Quest of the Historical Jesus*, sets forth the theory that Jesus expected to return to this earth on the clouds of heaven within the lifetime of His disciples, but that He was mistaken and the victim of a delusion. Needless to say, such a Jesus cannot be the Savior of the world and such a Jesus is not the Christ presented in the Scriptures, nor is He the Christ whom Paul preached. The present writer has heard real Christians speak in the highest and most enthusiastic terms about Dr. Schweitzer. They should know better, but they have been misled by articles in the secular and liberal religious press. Dr. Schweitzer's work, remarkable as it is, is in reality humanitarian service rather than a preaching of the biblical *13* gospel to the people of Africa. The same statement may be made with truth concerning the work of the great Japanese author and social worker Dr. Toyohiko Kagawa. (*Editor's note:* Dr. Toyohiko Kagawa lived from 1888–1960). He is a great man, but what he promotes is not the gospel of God's Word.

Romans 10:15 is a quotation from Isaiah 52:7. This verse gives us the real meaning of the word "gospel": it means "glad tidings," "good news." *14* What is this "good news"? According to the Bible, it is the message of Jesus Christ and Him crucified as the Savior of sinners. "How beautiful are the feet" means, of course, what a wonderful, delightful, attractive errand it is that the missionary goes on. This is a joyful, beneficent task, to bring the light of the gospel to those sitting in darkness and the shadow of death. How willingly, how eagerly, we should support it. How sinful it must be to be grudging, reluctant, and stingy in our *15* support of the Church's missionary task. The church that neglects or refuses to carry on missionary work will tend to wither and die of its own self-centeredness. In this matter as in others, it is more blessed to give than to receive.

Questions:

1. What is Paul trying to prove in 10:14–15?
2. When God wills an end, what does He also will?
3. Give some examples from the Bible to show that when God wills an end He also wills the appropriate means thereto.
4. What is the bearing of this truth (that God wills the means as well as the end) on the subject of the salvation of the Gentiles?
5. What is implied in calling upon the name of the Lord?

Romans 10:11–21

6. What is implied in believing in the Lord?

7. What is implied in having knowledge about the Lord?

8. What is implied in going out as a missionary?

9. What is the proper inference to be drawn from Paul's argument in 10:14–15?

10. Why is it not correct to regard missionary work as a form of charity?

11. What is the real character of much so-called missionary work in some of the large denominations at the present day?

12. Why cannot a person who is himself not a saved, believing Christian be a true missionary of Christ?

13. Why is it not correct to speak of Dr. Albert Schweitzer as "a great missionary" and "the greatest Christian in the world"?

14. What is the true meaning of the word "gospel"?

15. Of what great sin are Christian people sometimes guilty in connection with the support of missionary work?

Lesson 48

"But they have not all obeyed the gospel. For Esaias saith, Lord, who hath believed our report?" (10:16). It is no argument against the duty of preaching the gospel to all mankind to say that many who hear the gospel do not accept it. God has commanded that the gospel be preached to all mankind, but He has not elected all human beings to eternal life, nor is it to be expected that all who hear the gospel will accept it and be saved. This rejection of the gospel by many is not merely a fact of present-day experience; it is also stated and predicted in the Bible. Paul quotes from the prophet Isaiah to show that it was predicted by him (Isa. 53:1). Isaiah's statement concerns the general rejection of the gospel. This is taught also elsewhere in the Bible. Jesus Christ came unto His own, and His own received Him not (John 1:11). Jesus carefully instructed His disciples as to how they were to conduct themselves in the face of a refusal to hear and receive their message (Matt. 10:14; Mark 6:11; Luke 9:5). Later, Paul and Barnabas carried out this instruction at Antioch of Pisidia (Acts 13:50–51).

It is sometimes urged as an objection against missionary work today that the work is not successful. Those who urge this objection mean "not successful" if measured by worldly standards such as might be applicable to a business enterprise—an oil company or an automobile factory, for example. The unconscious assumption behind this objection is that missionary work is expected to bring about the immediate or early conversion to Christianity of all or most of those who are reached with the gospel. But this assumption is unwarranted. The command to preach the gospel to all mankind is not based upon the expected results of the work. It proceeds from the will and command of God. The work will be successful, if faithfully performed, in the sense that it will have the result that God intends it to have, namely the salvation of those persons throughout the world whom He has foreordained unto eternal life. That multitudes of people show no interest whatever in the gospel and even willfully reject it is no more than what the Bible has predicted. It does not constitute a valid objection to the missionary obligation that rests upon the Church.

"So then faith cometh by hearing, and hearing by the word of God" (10:17). In this verse the word "hearing" is used in reference to the word "report" in verse 16 (Isa. 53:1). The Greek word used for "report" means literally the act of hearing, and so it is used to designate that which is heard. Isaiah's question, "Lord, who hath believed our report?" implies that believing depends upon a report, that is, on something heard, on hearing. Before men can believe the gospel, they must first hear it, they must first come in contact with it. Faith consists in accepting the heard message as true and in putting one's trust in the one of whom the message speaks. "So then faith cometh by hearing."

The apostle adds, "and hearing by the Word of God" (10:17). The expression "the Word of God" in this verse, of course, does not mean simply the Bible or written Word of God. It means the word or command of God that is the real basis of the missionary task. The missionary enterprise is no mere voluntary effort of Christian people; it is a divinely appointed task. It brings an authoritative message, and it proceeds from the word or command of God.

Two truths that Paul has already stated, are confirmed in this verse, namely: (1) that knowledge is necessary to faith, and (2) that it is God's purpose that this knowledge shall be sent to the Gentiles.

"But I say, Have they not heard? Yes verily, their sound went into all the earth, and their words unto the ends of the world" (10:18). Here Paul's argument is rather condensed and abrupt, making it difficult to understand. Just what is the apostle speaking about in this verse? Some scholars hold that he has the Jews in mind. But this would not be in harmony with the subject under discussion, which is not now the rejection of the Jews, but rather the calling of the Gentiles. If verse 16 refers to the Gentiles, the presumption is that verse 18 must still be speaking of the Gentiles, for there is no indication of a change of subject. Moreover in verse 19 where Paul certainly intends to speak of Israel he uses the name.

Taking verse 18 as referring to the Gentiles, then, what is Paul's purpose in this verse? Paul's language is taken from Psalm 19:4, but in the Psalm the subject dealt with is God's revelation in the realm of nature, whereas Paul is speaking of the gospel of Christ. The apostle is merely using language borrowed from the Psalm to express a different idea. It is true, of course, that the universal revelation of God in nature was, in a sense, a providential prediction of the universal proclamation of the gospel; both were intended by God to be universal. Paul's meaning, however, is that the gospel had already, in his time, broken out from the narrow channel of the ancient covenant nation of Israel and had become a universal message sent to all the world. This of course must not be pressed to mean that in Paul's day the gospel had already reached every continent and nation and tribe, for this was manifestly not the case. It was true, however, that the gospel had been widely preached through the then-known world.

Questions:

1. Is it an argument against missionary work to say that many who hear the gospel do not accept it?
2. What text from Isaiah does Paul quote to show that the rejection of the gospel by many was foreseen and predicted in the Old Testament?
3. What do many people mean when they assert that missionary work is not successful?

Romans 10:11–21

4. What assumption is behind the charge that missionary work is not successful?
5. In what sense is Christian missionary work truly successful?
6. What is the literal meaning of the word "report" in 10:16?
7. What is meant by the statement, "faith cometh by hearing"?
8. What does the apostle mean by saying that hearing comes by the Word of God?
9. What two truths are confirmed by 10:17?
10. In 10:18, is Paul speaking of the Jews or of the Gentiles?
11. From what place in the Old Testament is the language of 10:18 derived?
12. What is the meaning of that statement in the Old Testament?
13. What is Paul's meaning in the words quoted in 10:18?
14. In what sense were the words of 10:18 true in Paul's time?

Lesson 49

"But I say, Did not Israel know? First Moses saith, I will provoke you to jealousy by them that are no people, and by a foolish nation I will anger you" (10:19). Here again Paul's extreme brevity and condensation of his argument raises problems of interpretation. He says, "Did not Israel know?" But what was it that Israel knew or did not know? One answer is that it was the gospel. Another view holds that it was the truth of their own rejection and God's purpose to call and save the Gentiles. Of these two possible interpretations, the second is probably the correct one, for two reasons: (1) Paul has been discussing the rejection of the Jews and calling of the Gentiles; and (2) the quotations from the Old Testament in verses 19–21 fit the second view best.

We may take the meaning, then, to be: "Did not Israel know the announced purpose of God to reject them and to save the Gentiles?" Paul next quotes Moses (Deut. 32:21). He says "first Moses" because he intends to quote from Isaiah immediately afterwards. The passage in Deuteronomy deals with the great mercies of God received by Israel, and the people's stubborn rebellion and lack of thankfulness to God. In Deuteronomy 32:21, Moses warns the children of Israel that as they had provoked God to jealousy by that which is not God (that is, by

idolatry), God would provoke them to jealousy by those that are not a 5
people. The meaning clearly is that God would eventually reject Israel
and choose, in their stead, Gentiles who formerly were not His people. 6
Certainly this statement of Moses is very plain, and if the Jews of Paul's
day had not been entirely blind to this truth, they would have known
it from Moses.

"But Esaias is very bold, and saith, I was found of them that sought
me not; I was made manifest unto them that asked not after me. But
to Israel he saith, All day long I have stretched forth my hands unto a
disobedient and gainsaying people" (10:20–21). The statement of Moses
in Deuteronomy 32:21 was plain enough, but here is one from Isaiah
that is even plainer, one that is unmistakable and cannot be evaded, a
"very bold" statement. The words are quoted from Isaiah 65:1–2. It will 7
be noted that the wording in Romans 10:20–21 differs somewhat from
that found in the Authorized Version of Isaiah 65:1–2. The reason for
this is that Paul is here following not the Hebrew but the Septuagint, 8
and he transposes the clauses. The King James or Authorized Version
of the Old Testament was of course made directly from the original
Hebrew. Paul often quotes from the Septuagint, which was natural
inasmuch as he was writing his epistle in the Greek language and to
Greek-speaking readers. The sense of the original Hebrew is accurately
given by Paul's quotation; the differences are merely in form. "I was
found of them that sought me not; I was made manifest unto them that
asked not after me." This statement of course describes the Gentiles. 9
They were not God's covenant people, they did not know God, and
they were not specially interested in or concerned about the true God.
Each nation had its own religion, its own philosophers, its own myths,
legends, customs, laws, ethical standards, and so forth. All were turned
aside to their own way in spiritual darkness. They were not looking for
the true God, but they found Him through the gospel of Jesus Christ. 10
Isaiah, then, predicted the inclusion of the Gentiles in the kingdom
of God. This, of course, implies that the day would come when Israel
would no longer be exclusively and uniquely the people of God, a time 12
would come when Jews and Gentiles would be in the kingdom on the
same terms and on an equal footing.

Romans 10:11–21

"But to Israel he saith, All day long I have stretched forth my hands unto a disobedient and gainsaying people" (10:21). To stretch forth the hands, in the Bible, signifies invitation or entreaty. In this verse we see the tender love of the Father for His erring and rebellious children. How often this was true of them through their long history! How many times they rebelled against God and turned to their own stubborn, sinful way! And yet the Father's heart yearned for their return to Himself. "All day long" means continuously. The rejection of Israel was not caused by any unwillingness of God to love and save them. It was caused by their own stubborn, stiff-necked unbelief, sinking finally into complete apostasy. It was their own fault.

Questions:

1. What is the meaning of Paul's question in 10:19, "Did not Israel know?"
2. Why does Paul say "first Moses" in 10:19?
3. What passage from Moses' writings does Paul quote in 10:19?
4. What subject is dealt with in the passage quoted from Moses?
5. What sin is described by the expression "provoking God to jealousy by that which is not God"?
6. What is meant by the statement "I will provoke you to jealousy by them that are not people"?
7. Why does Paul say that Isaiah was "very bold"?
8. How can we explain the fact that Paul's quotation from Isaiah 65:1–2 differs from the form found in the book of Isaiah in the Authorized Version?
9. What people are described in the statement "I was found of them that sought me not"?
10. How did it come to pass that God was found of them that sought Him not?
11. What is implied by Isaiah 65:1–2 concerning the position of Israel?
12. What is signified, in the Bible, by stretching forth the hands?
13. What attitude of God toward Israel is revealed by the statement that all day long He had stretched forth His hands to them?
14. Whose fault was it that Israel was finally rejected by God?

Romans 10:11–21

God's Rejection of the Jews Was Not Total, for a Remnant Shall Be Saved. 11:1–10

Lesson 50

Paul has plainly proved that the Old Testament predicted both the calling of the Gentiles and the rejection of the Jews. In the first 10 verses of chapter 11, he proceeds to teach that although God has rejected the Jews as a nation, this rejection is not total, for a remnant of the nation shall receive salvation.

"I say then, hath God cast away his people? God forbid. For I also am an Israelite, of the seed of Abraham, of the tribe of Benjamin" (11:1). The question asked here, "Hath God cast away his people?" is obviously raised because many might infer from chapters 9 and 10 that God *has* cast off His people; that is, that God has been unfaithful to His own declared purposes and promises. Paul says, in effect, "Does the argument I have presented in chapters 9 and 10 mean that God has cast off His people, thus going back on His own word and promises?" This question, he answers in his habitual way of making a strong negative assertion: "God forbid"—meaning, "Far from it; certainly not."

He then cites himself as an example to prove that God has not cast off His people. Paul himself was an Israelite, of the seed of Abraham, of the tribe of Benjamin, but he had not been cast off. Although an Israelite, he had been saved by the grace of God and was now a member of the true people of God, the Christian Church. And if Paul the Israelite was not cast off, certainly there were many others like himself, Jews who had become Christians. They were not cast off, but wonderfully saved. The rejection of Israel, therefore, could not be a total rejection. There would be some Israelites, at least, that would receive salvation and would be true children of God, true citizens of God's kingdom.

"God hath not cast away his people which he foreknew" (11:2a). In interpreting this sentence, much depends upon where the emphasis is placed. If the emphasis is placed upon "his people," the sentence means one thing; if it is placed upon "which he foreknew," it means something else. In the first case, if we place the emphasis on "his

people," then "his people" would mean the nation of Israel, and the
meaning of the sentence would be: "God has not cast off the nation
of Israel; He would not cast off those whom He foreknew." But if
the emphasis is placed upon "which he foreknew," then "his people"
means, not the nation of Israel, but the elect within the nation of
Israel, the true Israelites, the spiritual Israel, the Israel within Israel,
that part of Israel that God had foreknown.

The second of these two possible interpretations is to be chosen in preference to the first. On the first interpretation, verse 2a is
merely a repetition of the implication of verse 1. But on the second
interpretation, verse 2 has a definite meaning of its own. Moreover,
in Romans 9:6–8, Paul has already laid down the distinction between
the external nation of Israel and the inner spiritual core of true Israelites, so that this is not a new idea in this epistle. Also, the second
interpretation best fits what follows in chapter 11, where Paul speaks
of "a remnant according to the election of grace" (11:5). For these
reasons, the second interpretation of this verse is definitely the better one. According to this interpretation, then, 11:2a means: "God
has not cast away His elect people, those members of the nation of
Israel whom He specially foreknew." This is not only in harmony with
the context in Romans, but also in harmony with the doctrine of the
whole Bible, which teaches that an external, visible society and its
members may be cast off and perish in sin, but the elect of God can
never be cast off nor perish.

The word "foreknew" is used in the Bible in more than one
sense. As used in 11:2a, it certainly means more than mere "knowing
beforehand." In the sense of "knowing beforehand" or "knowing
from eternity," God's foreknowledge includes all creatures and all
events without distinction. In this sense, therefore, He "foreknew"
the Gentiles equally with the Jews; consequently it would involve no
uniqueness or distinction for the Jews to say that God "foreknew"
them, if "foreknew" in 11:2a meant nothing more than "knew beforehand." But it is obvious that in the expression "his people, which he
foreknew," the word "foreknew" is intended to set Israel apart as the
recipients of some special attention or favor of God, in distinction

from the other peoples of the world. Accordingly, we take "foreknew" in this verse as meaning "regarded as objects of God's special favor from eternity." Those whom God foreknew as His own can never be cast off; they shall live in communion with Him to all eternity. *10*

Questions:

1. What is the subject dealt with in 11:1–10?
2. Why does Paul mention the fact that he himself was an Israelite?
3. In the statement of 11:2a, on which phrase should the emphasis be placed?
4. What is the meaning of the expression "His people" in 11:2a?
5. How can it be shown that "His people" in 11:2a does not mean the nation of Israel as such?
6. In what two senses is the word "foreknow" used in the Bible?
7. What is included in God's foreknowledge, in the sense of knowing beforehand?
8. Why does "foreknew" in 11:2a not mean merely "knew beforehand"?
9. What is the meaning of "foreknew" in 11:2a?
10. What can never happen to those whom God has foreknown in the special sense of "known from eternity as His own"?

Lesson 51

"Know ye not what the Scripture saith of Elias? how he maketh intercession to God against Israel, saying, Lord, they have killed thy prophets, and digged down thine altars; and I am left alone, and they seek my life" (11:2–3). Paul now seeks to bring out the truth that a remnant of Israel shall be saved, and in order to do this, he speaks of the situation in the time of the prophet Elijah. The reference is to 1 Kings 19:10. It was under the reign of the wicked king Ahab, when the great majority of the nation had followed their rulers in turning from Jehovah to the worship of Baal. In Elijah's day, as in Paul's, it seemed *1* that the apostasy of Israel was complete. But in each case it was only partial. For in Elijah's day there remained a faithful minority: there was Obadiah, the hundred prophets he had concealed in caves, and the seven thousand whom God had reserved unto Himself, who had

not bowed the knee to Baal nor kissed his image. Doubtless, the faith- 2
ful in Elijah's day were but a small fraction of the total population of
the nation, a "remnant," yet they constituted the real Israel, the Israel
within Israel, God's people whom He foreknew. Similarly in Paul's day,
the rejection of Israel was not total. God still had His remnant whom
He had reserved for Himself, who were true believers. "Even so then
at this present time also there is a remnant according to the election
of grace" (11:5).

"According to the election of grace." What is meant by this expression? "Grace" means more than merely "kindness" or "favor"; it means
God's favor bestowed on the undeserving. Thus, the reason why a Par- 4
ticular person receives grace is not anything in that person himself, but
merely the sovereign love and mercy of God, the sheer good pleasure 5
of God, for which creatures cannot assign any reason other than that
"it pleased God" to act as He did. Therefore "remnant according to
the election of grace" means "remnant according to God's sovereign,
unmerited choice" (compare 9:11 and 11:21–24).

In the days of Elijah, the number of the faithful was much greater
than Elijah supposed. He thought that he alone was left to serve God, 3
but God informed him that there were seven thousand others. Similarly 6
in the time of the apostles, the number must have been much greater
than was outwardly apparent to a casual observer. James in Acts 21:20
speaks of "many thousands (Greek, 'many myriads') of Jews who believe," that is, of course, which believe on Jesus Christ. So it was not
as if all or nearly all of the Jews had been rejected.

"And if by grace, then it is no more of works: otherwise grace is no
more grace. But if it be of works, then it is no more grace: otherwise
work is no more work" (11:6). This is Paul's explanation of the meaning
of the word "grace" in verse 5. He points out that the two principles,
grace and works, are incompatible. Their election cannot be based
on both grace and works, for the two ideas are mutually exclusive. To 7
speak of election being both of grace and also of works is like speaking of an honest thief or a truthful liar; it is a contradiction in terms.
Election is either of grace or it is of works—one or the other, but not
both. Grace would not be grace if it were of works. The very idea of

grace is means "not of works." It is clear, too, that foreseen works are excluded from the ground of election, just as much as any other kind of works. The common Arminian view of election is that it is based on foreseen works; that is, that God has elected those whom He foresaw or foreknew (from eternity) would repent and believe on Christ. If this Arminian theology is correct, then election is not of grace but of works, for Arminianism represents God as electing men to salvation because He knows beforehand that they will repent and believe. Repentance and faith, in this system, are the works on which election is based. Such an election is not an election of grace.

It is apparent that Paul considered it of very great importance to exclude rigidly every element of personal works or merit from the doctrine of election. He stops in the middle of his argument about the Jews and Gentiles to make this emphatic statement about grace and works in 11:6. Many today claim to believe in the doctrine of election as taught in the Bible, yet pay very little attention to this truth. They seldom mention it, and perhaps are a little embarrassed by it. They try to avoid speaking about it or they speak of it apologetically, trying to tone it down a little bit, as if it were something to be just a little ashamed of. Evidently, Paul did not feel that way about the doctrine of God's sovereign election. He considered it a main point of the gospel and he taught it both consistently and insistently. We should go and do likewise. If it is a doctrine of God's Word, then it is nothing to be afraid of, ashamed of, or embarrassed about.

Questions:

1. Why does Paul mention the prophet Elijah and his type?
2. What was the religious situation of Israel in Elijah's day?
3. What mistaken idea did Elijah himself have about the religious situation?
4. What is the meaning of the word "grace"?
5. What is the reason why a particular person receives God's grace?
6. How many Jews were believers in Christ in the time of the apostles?
7. Why can election not be both of grace and of works?

Romans 11:1–10

8. What is the common Arminian view of the ground of election?
9. Why can foreseen repentance and faith not be the ground of election?
10. What was Paul's attitude toward the doctrine of sovereign election?
11. Why should we not be ashamed of or embarrassed about the doctrine of election?

Lesson 52

"What then? Israel hath not obtained that which he seeketh for; but the election hath obtained it, and the rest were blinded (according as it is written, God hath given them the spirit of slumber, eyes that they should not see, and ears that they should not hear) unto this day" (11:7–8).

The word here translated "seeketh" means an earnest, intense, persistent search. The Jews sought earnestly for righteousness, but they failed to obtain it, because they sought it not by faith but by works. This verse is a summary of Paul's argument to this point. Israel as a nation—the majority of the people—did not obtain righteousness, but those whom God had foreknown and elected obtained it. Since the rejection of Israel is not total, but only partial, the promises of God made to Israel in the Old Testament have not been abrogated or canceled. The believing, saved remnant are the real Israel, the real continuation of the Israel of old, the real inheritors of the promises. This truth may be illustrated as follows. Suppose that at some future time all of the United States except the states west of the Rocky Mountains were to sink beneath the waters of the sea. Although the greater part of the land area and population of the nation would be lost by such a calamity, the part of the country remaining would still constitute the nation. It would still be the United States of America and would be recognized as the legitimate continuation of our national life throughout the world. Similarly, the remnant of Israel that receives salvation through Christ is the real Israel. It (along with all Gentile Christians) is the true inheritor of the Old Testament promises. The promises have not been broken or canceled. They are fulfilled to whom they were really made by the election of grace.

Romans 11:1–10

"And the rest were blinded" (11:7b). The Greek word here translated "blinded" means basically, "to harden." Therefore Paul's statement could be translated: "And the rest were hardened." It is a recognized principle in Scripture that God may and often does punish sin by hardening the sinner, that is, by abandoning him to his sinful tendencies, so that as a result he becomes worse and worse. "They were hardened by God, i.e., abandoned by him to the hardness of their own hearts" (Charles Hodge, *A Commentary on the Epistle to the Romans*, p. 357).

Verse 8 is taken from several places in the Old Testament (as Isa. 6:9–10; Deut. 29:4; Isa. 29:10). These Old Testament passages apply partly to conditions in the times when they were first written, and partly they predict what would be in the future. They are thus properly applicable to the Jews of Paul's time (Compare Matt. 13:14). Many such prophecies have successive fulfillments—being first fulfilled on a smaller scale and later fulfilled on a larger scale, or in a more complete manner. What had occurred time and again in the Old Testament period, namely, people having eyes that could not (spiritually) see and ears that could not (spiritually) hear, happened much more completely among the Jews of apostolic times. In their blindness they could not see Jesus as the Messiah, and so they went on in their unbelief until dire disaster and destruction overtook them at the time of the destruction of Jerusalem in 70 A.D.

"This blindness and hardness were not mere calamities, nor were they simply the natural effects of the sins of the people. They were punitive inflictions. They are so denounced. God says, 'I will give you eyes that see not.' It is a dreadful thing to fall into the hands of the living God. The strokes of his justice blind, bewilder, and harden the soul" (Charles Hodge, *A Commentary on the Epistle to the Romans*, p. 358). Since this is true, how important it is that we beware of offending God, of presuming upon His mercy! "Our God is a consuming fire" (Heb. 12:29).

Verses 9 and 10 are quoted from Psalm 69:22–23, a prophecy of Christ's sufferings and of the judgments that shall be visited upon His enemies. We should note that this is one of the so-called imprecatory psalms that some people say is savage, vengeful, and unfit for Christian

Romans 11:1–10

devotional use. Yet it is plainly a prophecy of Jesus Christ and is referred | 3
to as such in the New Testament. Note Psalm 69:9, "The zeal of thine
house hath eaten me up" (compare John 2:13–17), and Psalm 69:21, "They
gave me vinegar to drink" (compare John 19:28–30).

Paul cites Psalm 69:22–23 as an Old Testament statement of the
divine judgments that would surely fall on the unbelieving, apostate
nation of the Jews.

"The Judgments here denounced are expressed in figurative language. The sense is, their blessings shall become a curse; blindness and
weakness, hardness of heart and misery shall come upon them. This last
idea is forcibly expressed by a reference to the dimness of vision, and
decrepitude of old age; as the vigor and activity of youth are the common figure for expressing the results of God's favor" (Charles Hodge,
A Commentary on the Epistle to the Romans, p. 358).

What Psalm 69 prays for actually happened to the Jews in Paul's
day and since his day. Thus what Paul has been stating about God's
rejection of the Jews is nothing new, for it was already predicted in the
Old Testament.

Questions:

1. What is the meaning of the word "seeketh" in 11:7?
2. What did Israel seek but fail to obtain?
3. What is implied, concerning the promises of God, by the truth
   that the rejection of the Jews is not total but only partial?
4. Who are the real inheritors of the Old Testament promises?
5. What is the basic meaning of the word translated "blinded" in 11:7?
6. In what way does God sometimes harden sinners?
7. What did their blindness prevent the Jews of Paul's day from seeing?
8. What was the result of the Jews' unbelief?
9. Why should all people beware of offending God by presumptuous
   sinning against Him?
10. From what Psalm is Romans 11:9–10 quoted?
11. What is the character of this Psalm?
12. What objections do some people raise against the so-called
    imprecatory Psalms?

Romans 11:1–10

13. How can these objections be answered?

14. What is the meaning of the statements of 11:9–10?

15. What is the relevance of 11:9–10 to the apostle's argument?

God's Rejection of the Jews Was Not Final, for there Is to Be a Conversion of Many of Them to Christ. 11:11–36

Lesson 53

We now come to a very difficult problem in the interpretation of the Epistle to the Romans, namely, does 11:11–36 predict a future conversion of the Jews (many, most, or all of them) to Christ? On a superficial reading of the chapter, this may seem an easy question to answer with yes, but the matter is not so simple as that. Some of the most careful, learned, and devoted Bible scholars have come to divergent conclusions concerning this question. We shall consider this problem further in the following lessons. At the outset, we should realize that we are entering a portion of the epistle concerning which Bible scholars differ, so that we must recognize the debatable character of the matter, and proceed very cautiously, avoiding positive assertions except where they can plainly be supported by valid proof.

For those who wish to undertake a more thorough study of the questions involved, here are some publications that are well worth careful reading:

"And So All Israel Shall Be Saved," by William Hendriksen, a professor of Calvin Seminary, Grand Rapids. This 36-page booklet was published in 1945 by Baker Book House, but is now out of print. It is a painstaking exegesis of Romans 11:26a. Professor Hendrikson comes to the conclusion that the words "And so all Israel shall be saved" refer to "the full number of elect Jews whom it pleases God to bring into the kingdom through the ages until the very day when also the *pleroma* (fullness) of the Gentiles shall have been brought in"; and he adds that "all Israel" is identical with the "remnant according to the election of grace" mentioned in 11:5. For Professor Hendriksen's arguments that lead to these conclusions, the student is referred to the booklet as a whole.

Romans 11:11–36

A Commentary on the Epistle to the Romans, by Charles Hodge. A reprinting of this classic was issued by Wm. B. Eerdmans Publishing Company, Grand Rapids, Michigan, in 1950; pp. 458. (*Editor's Note:* At the time of the printing of this book, Eerdmans still has Hodge's commentary in print.) Hodge concludes that "There is to be a future and general conversion of the Jews to Christ, and thus all Israel shall be saved" (p. 11–12, 360–382).

Prophecy and the Church, by Oswald T. Allis. This 339-page book is published by the Presbyterian and Reformed Publishing Company, 525 Locust St., Philadelphia, Pa. The subtitle is: "An examination of the claim of Dispensationalists that the Christian Church is a mystery parenthesis which interrupts the fulfillment to Israel of the kingdom prophecies of the Old Testament." This book contains a discussion of Paul's figure of the olive tree in Romans 11:16–24 (pp. 108–110). Though primarily a critique of dispensationalism, this book is very much worth reading in connection with the study of Romans 11:11–36. See review in *Blue Banner Faith and Life*, 1947, pp. 5457.

The Seed of Abraham, by Albertus Pieters. This book of 161 pages was published in 1950 by Wm. B. Eerdmans Publishing Company, Grand Rapids, Michigan. Its subtitle is "A Biblical Study of Israel, the Church, and the Jew." See review in *Blue Banner Faith and Life*, 1951, pp. 156–157. On the problem of Romans 11:11–36, Dr. Pieters says:

> St. Paul knows of no territorial restoration of his people in time to come, and takes no interest in it. He does speak, in the eleventh chapter of the Epistle to the Romans, of a spiritual restoration; but it is not clear in what form he expects it, whether after the Gentiles have been gathered in or parallel to it. He says that "All Israel shall be saved," from which it is not unnaturally concluded by some that eventually there will be a conversion, not of scattered individuals only, but of the group as a whole, so that there will no longer be in the world a body of Jews, standing in opposition to the gospel, as there is now and has been ever since his day. This may be the true interpretation, but a doubt is cast upon it by the frequent insistence of St. Paul on the "remnant" idea, according to which the promises of God are fulfilled to only a portion of the people, and yet therein are truly and

adequately fulfilled. If this conception must apply here, "all Israel" will mean the elect among Israel, and this agrees with his assurance that God did not cast off his people "whom he foreknew" (p. 147).

The Bible and Things to Come, by David Freeman. This 139-page book was published in 1939 by Zondervan Publishing House, Grand Rapids, and is now out of print. (*Editor's note:* This book was reprinted in 2010 by Kessinger Publishing, LLC.) A chapter entitled "The Jews, their Conversion and their Land" (pp. 58–77) is very helpful and illuminating. Mr. Freeman says: "There is unmistakable teaching to the effect that God will again visit them [the Jews] with His grace in their racial capacity" (p. 67), and "The Jews as a nation will be saved but only in the way in which they are converted now. Some day they, with others from all nations and kindreds, shall acknowledge with true faith their Messiah and Savior" (p. 77). In the judgment of the present writer, Mr. Freeman presents some arguments that have not been fully answered by those who hold the contrary view.

Among those Bible scholars who have held that Romans 11:11–36 predicts a future conversion to Christ of the Jews collectively are Henry Alford, Charles Hodge, W. G. T. Shedd, and Geerhardus Vos. Among those who have held the contrary view are Philip Mauro, Theodore Graebaer, and William Hendriksen. Enough has been said to indicate that Romans 11:11–36 is a very difficult passage. Those who claim that it is simple and its meaning is obvious only betray their own ignorance of the problems involved and the literature that has been written on the subject.

The present series of lessons will adhere to the view that a future collective conversion of the Jews to Christ is predicted in Romans 11:11–36. It must always be borne in mind, however, that the subject is debatable and that the last word on it has not yet been written.

Questions:

1. What difficult question is involved in the interpretation of 11:11–36?
2. How might this question be answered on the basis of a superficial reading of the passage?
3. Why is caution necessary in the interpretation of this passage?

Romans 11:11–36

4. What does Professor William Hendriksen hold concerning the conversion of the Jews to Christ?

5. What is the view of Charles Hodge on the conversion of the Jews?

6. What does Dr. Albertus Pieters say is "not clear" in Romans 11:11–36?

7. What view of the conversion of the Jews is maintained by Mr. David Freeman?

8. Name some Bible scholars that have held the view that Scripture predicts a future collective conversion of the Jews to Christ.

9. Name some Bible scholars that have held the contrary view.

Lesson 54

"I say then, have they stumbled that they should fall? God forbid: but rather through their fall salvation is come unto the Gentiles, for to provoke them to jealousy" (11:11). We should note that chapter 11 opens with the same form of expression: "I say then...God forbid." In verses 1–10, Paul has raised and answered the question, "Hast God cast away his people?" He has answered it by explaining that the rejection of the Jews is not total, because there is "a remnant according to the election of grace" that shall be saved. Having disposed of this question, he proceeds to another question, "Have they stumbled that they should fall?" which he answers in the verses that follow.

The gist of Paul's answer to this second question is that God's rejection of the Jews, as it was not total, is also not final. There is a contrast or comparison between the words "stumble" and "fall." They have stumbled, yes, but was this in order that they might fall? Was it in order that they might be permanently and irrevocably rejected? Clearly the word "stumble" implies a temporary disaster, while "fall" implies a permanent one. So the apostle teaches that the rejection of the Jews was not permanent and irrevocable, for he immediately answers his own question with an emphatic negative: "God forbid." God's intention in permitting the apostasy of the Jews was not that their rejection should be permanent and final, but rather (1) in order to bring about the salvation of the Gentiles, and thus (2) to provoke the Jews finally to jealousy.

We might wonder just how the unbelief of the Jews could facilitate the salvation of the Gentiles. That it did have that effect is the

teaching of Scripture (Acts 13:46; 28:28 compared with Isa. 49:46). 7
The Jews, even those who were professors of Christianity, were, in the
first place, very slow to allow the gospel to be preached to the Gentiles; 8
and in the second, they appear almost uniformly to have desired to 9
clog the gospel with the ceremonial observances of the law. This was
one of the greatest hindrances to the progress of the cause of Christ
during the apostolic age, and would, in all human probability, have 10
been a thousand-fold greater, had the Jews, as a nation, embraced the
Christian faith. On both these accounts, the rejection of the Jews was
incidentally a means of facilitating the progress of the gospel. Besides
this, the punishment which befell them on account of their unbelief,
involving the destruction of their nation and power, of course prevented
their being able to forbid the general preaching of the gospel, which
they earnestly desired to do (Charles Hodge, *A Commentary on the Epistle
to the Romans,* p. 361).

"By this stumble of the Jews out of their national place in God's favor,
and the admission of the Gentiles into it, the very people thus excluded
are to be stirred up to set themselves in the end effectually to regain, as
a nation, that preeminence from which they are now degraded" (Henry
Alford, *The New Testament for English Readers,* p. 939).

"For to provoke them to jealousy" (11:11). This means, of course, that
the salvation of the Gentiles is intended to provoke the unbelieving Jews 11
to jealousy. God's rejection of the Jews was not intended as a permanent
and final casting away, but to bring about the more rapid evangelization
of the Gentiles, and then ultimately, by the reaction of this upon the Jews,
to lead to the conversion of the latter to their Messiah. The expression
"to provoke them to jealousy" of course does not mean a sinful kind of
jealousy. The apostle only means that the salvation of the Gentiles was
intended to stir the Jews up to seek salvation for themselves through
the gospel.

"Now if the fall of them be the riches of the world, and the diminishing of them the riches of the Gentiles; how much more their fullness?"
(11:12). If the rejection of the Jews has brought so much benefit to the
world, then certainly even more benefit can be expected from their

conversion to Christ. The word "fullness" (Greek, *pleroma*) here is in 12
contrast to the "diminishing" in the first part of the verse. This word
pleroma is used with various meanings in the New Testament. It may
mean "fullness" (John 1:16; Eph. 1:2–33; or it may mean a supplementary
portion that is needed to make something complete (Matt. 9:16, where 13
pleroma is translated "that which is put in to fill it up"). Here, in Romans
11:12, we take it in the common sense of "fullness," as meaning the "full
restoration" or "blessedness" (Charles Hodge, *A Commentary on the Epistle*   14
to the Romans, p. 364), or "re-exaltation" (Henry Alford, *The New Testament
for English Readers*, p. 940) of the Jews.

Questions:

1. How does 11:11 resemble 11:1?
2. What is the meaning of the expression "God forbid"?
3. What question is raised by Paul in 11:11?
4. What is the gist of the apostle's answer to this question?
5. What two purposes did God have in permitting the apostasy of the Jews?
6. What is the difference in meaning between "stumble" and "fall" in verse 11?
7. Give some Bible references which show that the unbelief of the Jews facilitated the salvation of the Gentiles.
8. What was the attitude of many early Jewish Christians toward the preaching of the gospel to the Gentiles?
9. What hindrance did many Jewish Christians tend to place upon Gentile converts?
10. If the Jews as a nation had accepted Christianity during the apostolic age, what would have been the probable effect upon the Gentile world?
11. What is the meaning of the phrase "For to provoke them to jealousy"?
12. What meanings does the Greek word *pleroma* have in the New Testament?
13. What is the meaning of this Greek word?
14. What is Paul's argument in 11:12?

Romans 11:11–36

Lesson 55

"For I speak to you Gentiles, inasmuch as I am the apostle of the Gentiles, I magnify mine office: if by any means I may provoke to emulation them which are my flesh, and might save some of them" (11:13–14). These two verses are of the nature of a parenthesis in the apostle's argument. He pauses in his argument about the fall and restoration of the Jews to say a word about his own sentiments and conduct with reference to this great subject. Paul was the apostle of the Gentiles. Yet we know from his history as recorded in Acts that it was his fixed practice to preach the gospel first to the Jews in the places he visited. Here he speaks to the Gentiles, in the hope that his references to them may stir up some of his Jewish kinsmen to seek salvation and find it in Christ. It is clear that the salvation of the Gentiles and that of the Jews were closely interrelated. Every Christian should be deeply concerned about both. There was no real ground for ill-feeling on the part of either Jew or Gentile. Paul longed for the salvation of the Gentiles, not only for their own sake but also because this would prepare the way for the conversion of the Jews to Christ.

"And might save some of them" (11:14). This does not imply, of course, that Paul or any other preacher of the gospel could actually save sinners. The salvation of sinners is wholly a work of God, though it is a work in which God at some points makes use of human instruments. In our own day some preachers and evangelists speak very unguardedly about how many people they have saved or converted. The impression is easily given that the evangelist's efforts were sufficient to accomplish the salvation of his hearers. As Paul wrote, there was no such implication. The clear meaning is simple: "That I might be the instrument in God's hand toward the salvation of some of them."

"For if the casting away of them be the reconciling of the world, what shall the receiving of them be, but life from the dead?" (11:15). This verse is in part parallel to verse 12. The first part of the verse presents no special difficulty. "The casting away" plainly means God's rejection of the Jews; "the reconciling of the world" means the salvation of the Gentiles; "the receiving of them" means the future conversion of the Jews to Christ. But the last phrase presents a real difficulty. What does Paul

Romans 11:11–36

mean by the expression "life from the dead"? There are two opinions as
to the meaning of this expression in 11:15.

One view is that the expression "life from the dead" is a figure of
speech meaning "the transition from a state of depression and misery
to one of prosperity." This is the view held by Charles Hodge (*A Commentary on the Epistle to the Romans*, p. 365). According to this view, the
conversion of the Jews to Christ will be such a great joy and blessing
that it can figuratively be spoken of as "life from the dead." The Jews in
their unbelief, without Christ, are spiritually dead. When converted to
Christ, they will be spiritually alive.

The other view of this expression, "life from the dead," is that
the bodily resurrection of the dead at Christ's second coming is referred to. According to this view, the idea is that the Jews are to be
converted to Christ shortly before His second coming. Soon after
their conversion, therefore, the resurrection of the dead will follow.
Therefore their conversion can be spoken of as "life from the dead."
This view is taken by David Freeman in his book *The Bible and Things
to Come*. He says:

> What is meant by "life from the dead" here? Does Paul mean that the
> conversion of the Jews will bring with it the resurrection of the dead?
> If so, Israel's acceptance of the Messiah will bring the coming of Christ
> from heaven. This is exactly what the apostle means, because he relates
> the "life from the dead" to the "reconciling of the world." The former
> is the climax of the latter. "Life from the dead" must be something
> far higher and greater than the "reconciling of the world." What is
> that which can be greater than the reconciliation now experienced by
> the world, but the resurrection of life? Paul, in one sweep, views the
> blessedness of the redemption purchased by Christ from its beginning
> to its glorious consummation (pp. 67–68).

In a footnote Freeman adds:

> The phrase, *zoe ek nekron*, "life from the dead," cannot be toned down to
> a metaphorical meaning, implying a mere spiritual revival. The context
> will not permit this interpretation. The opposite of casting away
> requires a condition that is more glorious than "the receiving of

them." The beginning of the closing act of God's dealing with man only can be meant (p. 68).

In favor of the view held by Hodge is the consideration that nowhere else in the New Testament is the resurrection referred to as "life from the dead" (*zoe ek nekron*). Elsewhere the term for the resurrection is "the rising of the dead" (*he anastasis ton nekron*). Still we must admit that Paul could use the phrase "life from the dead' as a description of the event commonly referred to as "the rising of the dead." In the judgment of the writer, the interpretation given by Freeman is correct, and Romans 11:15 means that the conversion of the Jews to Christ will bring the return of Christ from heaven and the resurrection of the dead.

Questions:

1. What is the place of 11:13–14 in Paul's argument?
2. To whom did Paul regularly preach the gospel first when he entered a new field of work?
3. What was Paul's motive in speaking to the Gentiles in 11:13–14?
4. Does Paul's statement "If by any means I...might save some of them" imply that salvation is a work of man?
5. To what previous verse is 11:15 partly parallel?
6. What phrase in 11:15 is difficult to interpret?
7. What is the view held by Charles Hodge as to the meaning of the phrase "life from the dead"?
8. What other view is held as to the meaning of "life from the dead"?
9. What argument can be given to show that "life from the dead" must mean something more than a spiritual revival?
10. What difficulty is involved in understanding the phrase "life from the dead" as referring to the bodily resurrection of the dead?
11. If "life from the dead" means the resurrection, what great event will follow the conversion of the Jews to Christ?

Lesson 56
"For if the first-fruit be holy, the lump is also holy: and if the root

Romans 11:11–36

be holy, so are the branches" (11:16). We have here two striking figures of speech, both of which teach the same truth. The "firstfruit" is that portion of the kneaded dough that was offered as a heave-offering to the Lord (As Numbers 15:21 says, "Of the first of your dough ye shall give unto the Lord a heave offering in your generations"). This offering of the first of the dough sanctified the rest, which was used by the people for food. The "root" is that portion of a tree from which the growth and life springs up. The root nourishes and sustains the branches. First there must be a root before there can be any branches. We may therefore take "root" here as meaning "origin or "original portion." Obviously "root" is parallel and equivalent to "firstfruit." The argument is that the whole lump partakes of the character of the firstfruit, and the branches partake of the character of the root.

We must now consider what is meant by the "firstfruit" and "root." Some have held that the "firstfruit" and "root" mean the first Jews converted to Christianity (at Pentecost and soon after) who became the root of the Christian Church. A much more plausible view is that the "firstfruit" and "root" are Abraham, or perhaps the patriarchs Abraham, Isaac, and Jacob. It is clear that this view fits the context much better than the other one. Paul is arguing that the Jews shall be converted to Christ. He proves that they are in a certain sense "holy" because of their relation to their ancestor, Abraham, who was holy.

Next we must consider what is meant by the "lump" and the "branches." The only meaning that is consistent with the apostle's argument in this passage is that the lump and branches mean the Jews collectively, the Jews as a people. Paul's argument is, then, that as the patriarch Abraham was holy, so the Jews collectively are holy. The lump partakes of the holy character of the firstfruit, the branches partake of the holy character of the root.

We must take care to avoid a wrong understanding of the term "holy" in this connection. This is not the holiness of personal character produced by sanctification, but a technical holiness of position or standing. The terms "holy" and "holiness" are used in the Bible in more than one sense. There is the personal holiness of sanctification ("Follow... holiness, without which no man shall see the Lord," Heb. 12:14). There

Romans 11:11-36

is also the external holiness of position or relationship; for example, 5
Jerusalem is called "the holy city" (Matt. 4:5); "every pot in Jerusalem
and in Judah shall be holiness unto the Lord of hosts" (Zech. 14:21).
Note also Matthew 7:6, 24:15, 27:53; 1 Corinthians 7:14; Luke 2:23. These
passages, or at least some of them, use the terms "holy" and "holiness"
in the technical sense of "consecrated to the service of God," "set aside
for the service of God," "singled out as specially belonging to God." Paul
says in 1 Corinthians 7:14, "For the unbelieving husband is sanctified by
the wife"; clearly this cannot be the sanctification or holiness of heart
and life that follows the new birth, for it is an unbeliever that is said to
be sanctified. It must be a technical holiness of position or relationship.

Similarly in Romans 11:16, when Paul says that the lump and
branches are holy, he does not mean that the Jews collectively possessed
that holiness of heart and life that is produced by the Holy Spirit's
sanctifying work in believers. Clearly, the Jews collectively considered 8
are unbelievers, and therefore they are not sanctified or holy in that
sense. Yet there is a true sense in which they can be called holy. They
can be called holy in the technical sense by reason of their connection 6
with their root and firstfruit, the holy Abraham. Abraham was called
away from his home and country that he might be in a special relation
to God. That was a kind of holiness. The Jews of Paul's day and of our
own are the branches of which Abraham was the root. Therefore they
are, in a certain technical sense, holy.

When God called Abraham and separated him from the world that
he should be in a special relation to God, this did not concern Abraham
alone. God also had Abraham's posterity in mind.

> God, in selecting the Hebrew patriarchs, and setting them apart
> for his service, had reference to their descendants, as well as to
> themselves; and designed that the Jews, as a people, should, to the latest
> generations, be specially devoted to himself. They stand now, therefore
> and ever have stood, in a relation to God which no other nation ever
> has sustained: and, in consequence of this relation, their restoration 10
> to the divine favor is an event in itself probable, and one, which Paul
> afterwards teaches (vs. 25), God has determined to accomplish (Charles
> Hodge, *A Commentary on the Epistle to the Romans*, p. 367).

Romans 11:11–36

Questions:

1. What two figures are used in 11:16 to teach the same truth?
2. What Old Testament ordinance does the term "firstfruit" refer to?
3. What is meant by the "firstfruit" and "root"?
4. What is meant by the "lump" and "branches"?
5. What two kinds of holiness are spoken of in the Bible?
6. What kind of holiness is referred to in 11:16?
7. What does Paul's argument prove concerning the Jews as a body of people?
8. Why can the word "holy" in 11:16 not mean the holiness of heart produced by the sanctifying work of the Holy Spirit?
9. Does Paul's calling the Jews of his day holy imply that they were saved from sin unto eternal life? *no*
10. What great future event is probable by reason of the holy position of the Jewish people?

Lesson 57

We come now to Paul's figure of the olive tree, which is one of the most important passages in the whole Bible for testing the system of Bible interpretation called dispensationalism, which has been popularized by the writings of John Nelson Darby, by the Scofield Reference Bible, and by the Pilgrim Edition of the Holy Bible. In the course of the study of this passage, we shall note its bearing on the teachings of dispensationalism.

"And if some of the branches be broken off, and thou, being a wild olive tree, wert graffed in among them, and with them partakest of the root and fatness of the olive tree; boast not against the branches. But if thou boast, thou bearest not the root, but the root thee" (11:17–18).

Here Paul seeks to guard against the Gentile Christians harboring a wrong attitude toward the Jews. In view of the teachings of the apostle up to this point, it would be easy for his Gentile Christian readers to harbor a self-important, triumphant feeling over against the Jews. God has rejected the Jews and called the Gentiles to salvation! But this is no ground for any spiritual pride or carnal glorying; on the contrary, this affords reason for humility, thankfulness to God, and spiritual watchfulness. The apostle's

Romans 11:11–36

statements beginning with verse 17 are intended to guard against Gentile Christians feeling boastful over the Jews.

Paul is speaking of a good or cultivated olive tree. Some of the branches were broken off, and branches from a worthless wild olive tree were put in their place. (The King James Version uses the old form of the verb, "graffed," but in this lesson we shall use the modern form, "grafted," except when quoting from the Bible.) Thus there is a good olive tree with its original branches and a wild olive tree with its branches. Some branches are cut off from the good olive tree and cast aside; some branches are cut from the wild olive tree and grafted into the good olive tree.

We must consider, first of all, what is meant by the good olive tree. It cannot represent the Jewish nation as such, because the apostle teaches that by unbelief some branches were broken off from the tree (11:20) and that by faith some (Gentile) branches were grafted in. Obviously those Jews who refused to accept Jesus as the Messiah were not broken off from the Jewish nation as such, nor were Gentiles who accepted Christ incorporated into the Jewish nation as such. What, then, is the good olive tree? It must represent the true Israel, the body of people truly in covenant with God, to whom the gracious promises of God were addressed and to whom those promises really belonged—in a word, the Israel that really had a right to the name Israel.

There is only one good olive tree. Branches may be broken off and others grafted in, but the one good olive tree lives on. There is just one covenant people of God on earth, and it is continuous through both the Old Testament and the New Testament. This covenant people of God, represented by the one good olive tree, is the Old Testament Israel and it is the New Testament Church. The figure of the good olive tree proves the essential unity and continuity of the New Testament Church with the Old Testament Israel. Modern dispensationalism draws a sharp distinction between Israel and the Church, insisting that "Israel is Israel and the Church is the Church"—that is, denying the essential unity and continuity of the New Testament Church with the Old Testament Israel—but dispensationalism cannot do justice to Paul's figure of the olive tree. As a matter of fact, this passage has

Romans 11:11–36

proved rather embarrassing to dispensationalist interpreters.

Dispensationalism teaches that the promises of the Old Testament to Israel, Zion, Jerusalem, Judah, etc., do not belong to the New Testament Church, but strictly to the Jews and must be literally fulfilled to the Jews in a period still future. To apply these promises to the Christian Church is called "robbing Israel" by some writers. But in the light of Paul's figure of the olive tree, we must hold that the genuine Israel, to whom the promises were really addressed, is the covenanted body represented by the good olive tree that is one and the same in both dispensations. The Christian Church is therefore the true Israel to which the gracious promises of God in the Old Testament are addressed.

Remember that the good olive tree cannot be the Jewish people as such, for those Jews who rejected Jesus Christ are represented as broken off from the tree, but they certainly were not broken off from the Jewish people as such. The Jews who persecuted the apostle Paul and tried to kill him were still Jews. They were members of the Jewish people, but they were no longer branches in the good olive tree. They had been broken off by unbelief. So the good olive tree must mean the believing, covenant-keeping people of God, not the Jewish people as such. Into this tree some wild olive branches—Gentile Christians— were grafted. They did not become members of the Jewish people, but they became members of the genuine Israel, for they were incorporated into the organism of the olive tree and nourished by its life-giving sap.

The Gentiles are represented by wild olive branches. The wild olive is a worthless tree in itself. This impresses on our minds the spiritually destitute condition of the Gentile world, both of Paul's day and of our own day. The Gentiles were far from God, sunk in sin, deeply depraved, "without hope and without God in the world." But they were incorporated into the good olive tree and became new creatures in Christ Jesus.

Surely, then, there was no ground for boasting on the part of any Gentile Christians. They must remember that they did not bear the root, but the root bore them. They had been aliens, wild olive branches, but were incorporated into the good olive tree. All spiritual

Romans 11:11-36

good that they might possess came to them through the good olive) \
tree. They were only recipients, not contributors, of spiritual good.
Human pride and vanity might lead them to boast themselves over
the Jews, but Paul warns against this spirit: "Boast not against the
branches"—that is, against the Jewish branches that were broken off.

Questions:

1. What is the special importance of Paul's figure of the olive tree
    at the present day?
2. What two editions of the Bible have specially promoted the
    teachings of modern dispensationalism?
3. What is Paul's purpose in setting forth the figure of the olive tree?
4. What is signified by the good olive tree?
5. Why can the good olive tree not signify the Jewish nation as such?
6. What truth is taught by the fact that there is only one good olive
    tree in Paul's figure?
7. What truths concerning the relation between Israel and the
    Church are denied by dispensationalism?
8. To what practice do some interpreters apply the term "robbing
    Israel"?
9. What was the relation of the Jews who tried to kill Paul to the
    good olive tree? To the Jewish nation as such?
10. What truth about the Gentiles is brought out by Paul's represent-
    ing them as wild olive branches?
11. What was the source of all spiritual good possessed by Gentile
    Christians?

Lesson 58

"Thou wilt say then, The branches were broken off, that I might
be graffed in. Well; because of unbelief they were broken off, and thou
standest by faith. Be not high-minded, but fear: For if God spared not
the natural branches, take heed lest he also spare not thee" (11:19–21).

Here Paul guards against another possible kind of boasting on
the part of Gentile Christians. Even though the Gentile Christians
might have to admit that all their spiritual good had come to them

Romans 11:11–36

through their connection with the good olive tree, yet they might be inclined to boast that God had cut off Jewish branches in order that the Gentile branches might be grafted in. They might get the idea that it was because of some goodness or worthiness of their own that God made room for them in the olive tree. 1

The truth was that the Jewish branches were broken off because of their unbelief, not because of any fine qualities of the Gentiles. They 2 rejected Jesus Christ as their Messiah, so they were broken off. The Gentile Christians, by the grace of God, had come to believe in Jesus Christ as their Savior, and so they stood by faith where the Jews fell by unbelief. Here Paul teaches that the only way that anyone can retain a covenant relation to God is by faith. Those who have saving faith are 3 in the good olive tree; those who lack saving faith are out of the good 4 olive tree, or cut off from that tree.

The Gentile Christians, of course, might have ventured to assert that their faith was an act or work of their own, which they could claim credit for. While admitting that they did not have perfect righteousness of their own, they could conceivably claim to have faith and could claim credit for a decision of their own free will to accept Christ when others rejected Him. But apparently the Gentile Christians of Paul's day did not make this claim, for the apostle does not undertake to answer it. The fact is that the errors of Pelagianism and Arminianism were invented at a later date; they did not exist in Christian circles in the time of the apostles. Apparently it never occurred to the Gentile Christians of Paul's day to claim any credit for their faith. Of course, when Paul represents standing by faith as the opposite of a ground of boasting, he has the biblical idea of saving faith as pure receptivity of 5 God's free mercy.

Paul earnestly warns the Gentile Christians as a class—and by implication all Christians of every time and place—to "be not high-minded, but fear" (11:20). "The Gentiles will not be secure, because Gentiles, any more than the Jews were safe, because Jews" (Charles Hodge, *A Commentary on the Epistle to the Romans,* p. 369). Paul's statement in verse 21, "If God spared not the natural branches, take heed lest he also spare not thee," must not be taken as contrary to the doctrine of

Romans 11:11–36

the final perseverance of the saints (eternal security of believers). It does not imply that a true believer can fall away from grace and perish. We must bear in mind that Paul is not here speaking primarily of individual 6 believers and their salvation, but of Gentile Christians as a class, over the Jews. His words are an earnest warning against complacency, against a merely formal religious faith, against a presumptuous taking advantage of the goodness of God. The Gentile Christians must not suppose that their connection with the church and its privileges was forever safe just because they themselves, of that particular generation, had been grafted into the good olive tree. We see the pertinence of the apostle's warning throughout the history of the Church. North Africa was once dotted with Christian churches, where today the religion of Islam is almost universal.

"Behold therefore the goodness and severity of God: on them which fell, severity; but toward thee, goodness, if thou continue in his goodness: otherwise thou also shalt be cut off" (11:22). Here Paul mentions two aspects of God's character: His goodness and His severity. In our day, religion has suffered a great deal from a one-sided emphasis 79 upon the love of God. While the Bible says that "God is love," modern religion has held that God is love and nothing but love. The wrath of God has been objected to as an old-fashioned and harsh doctrine. But in the Bible, both the love and the wrath of God are insisted on, and 8 neither is emphasized to the exclusion of the other. In God's relation to men we see both displayed, His goodness and His severity.

> There is nothing in this language inconsistent with the doctrine of the final perseverance of believers, even supposing the passage to refer to individuals; for it is very common to speak thus hypothetically, and say that an event will not come to pass, unless the requisite means are employed, when the occurrence of the event had been rendered 10 certain by the previous purpose and promise of God; see Acts 27:31. The foundation of all such statements is the simple truth, that He who purposes the end, purposes also the means; and he brings about the end by securing the use of the means...Paul is not speaking of the connection of individual believers with Christ, which he had abundantly taught in chap. 8 and elsewhere, to be indissoluble, but of

the relation of communities to the church and its various privileges. There is no promise or covenant on the part of God, securing to the Gentiles the enjoyment of these blessings through all generations, any more than there was any such promise to protect the Jews from the consequences of their unbelief. The continuance of these favors depends on the conduct of each successive generation. Paul therefore says to the Gentile, that he must continue in the divine favor, "otherwise thou also shalt be cut off" (Charles Hodge, *A Commentary on the Epistle to the Romans*, p. 370).

Questions:

1. What kind of Gentile boasting is Paul warning against in 11:19–21?
2. Why were the Jewish branches broken off from the good olive tree?
3. What is the only way that a covenant relation to God can be retained?
4. What is the biblical idea of saving faith?
5. Why can no person claim any credit for his faith?
6. How do we know that Paul's warning of 11:19–21 is not contrary to the doctrine of the final perseverance of the believer?
7. What is the relevance of 11:19–21 at the present day?
8. What two aspects of the character of God are mentioned in 11:22?
9. From what wrong tendency has present day religion suffered?
10. How does Acts 27:22–24, 31, 34 help to show that warnings against apostasy are not inconsistent with the doctrine of the final perseverance of the saints?

Lesson 59

"And they also, if they abide not still in unbelief, shall be graffed in: for God is able to graff them in again" (11:23). Just as the continued standing of the Gentiles in the Church and its privileges depends on their faith, *so the Jews are excluded by nothing but by their unbelief.* Ceasing 1 to have faith would exclude the Gentiles, and ceasing to be unbelievers would admit the Jews again. "For God is able to graff them in again." God's power is not limited or frustrated. The obstacle is in the Jews themselves, and if that obstacle, in the course of God's mysterious providence, is removed at a future time, there is nothing to prevent the Jews from being grafted into the good olive tree again.

"For if thou wert cut out of the olive tree which is wild by nature, and wert graffed contrary to nature into a good olive tree; how much more shall these, which be the natural branches, be graffed into their own olive tree?" (11:24). There is a contrast here between the natural growth of branches in the tree that produced them, and the artificial ("contrary to nature") practice of grafting alien branches into the tree.

The Jews were the natural growth produced by the tree. The Gentiles were the alien branches grafted "contrary to nature" into the good tree. As a matter of fact, God had grafted the Gentile branches into the tree, though this, as "contrary to nature," might have been regarded as improbable. If the grafting in of the Gentiles actually took place, then surely it is probable that the Jews, who are "the natural branches," shall be grafted in again. The unnatural and therefore improbable has already taken place; it is therefore highly probable that something that would be according to nature will at a future time take place, namely, that the natural branches, the Jews, shall be again incorporated into the true Israel, the covenant people of God, the good olive tree. Paul calls it "their own olive tree." They were separate from it by their unbelief, but still the olive tree was where they belonged. Not that they in their unbelief had any claim to such a standing, but that in God's arrangement of things that was where they belonged.

"For I would not, brethren, that ye should be ignorant of this mystery, lest ye should be wise in your own conceits, that blindness in part is happened to Israel, until the fulness of the Gentiles be come in" (11:25). The great question concerning this verse is, does it predict a future conversion of the Jews collectively to Christ? Charles Hodge states that while there have been many interpretations of the verse, all of them can be reduced to two main views of the passage. One interpretation holds that this verse does not predict a future general conversion of the Jews, but only teaches that their blindness is not total, so that some of them will continue to be converted as long as Gentiles are still being saved. The second view holds that Paul here teaches that there is to be a general conversion of the Jews to Christ, which shall not take place until the fullness of the Gentiles shall have been brought in (*A Commentary on the Epistle to the Romans*, p. 371).

Hodge states that the first of these two views was prevalent at the time of the Protestant Reformation, and that scholars who sought to answer the extreme views of the Millennarian teachers of that day reacted to the opposite extreme and almost entirely explained away the prophetic character of the verse. He cites a statement attributed to Martin Luther, who declared that the hearts of the Jews are so extremely hard that their conversion is impossible, and added that "some invent such a madness from the Epistle to the Romans" (*A Commentary on the Epistle to the Romans*, p. 371).

Hodge declares that the second view of the passage has been the one generally accepted during all periods of the Church's history except the period of the Protestant Reformation, and that in his judgment it is the correct view. In support of this, Hodge states that this view best fits the whole trend of the context; that it is clear that the Jews are to be restored in the same sense that they were rejected, that is, as a body or community, which cannot be fulfilled by the small number of Jews converted along with the Gentiles through the history of the Church; and that it is plain that Paul is speaking of a great event, as shown by his manner of introducing the statement, "I would not, brethren, that ye should be ignorant of this mystery." If Paul was not introducing something new or specially important, why should he use such a form of words? "The gradual conversion of a few Jews is no *mystery* in the Scriptural sense of the word" (*A Commentary on the Epistle to the Romans*, p. 372). He adds that the word "mystery" in the New Testament is not generally used in the modern sense of "mystery," that is, something that baffles our understanding, but that it means something "hidden, or unknown; whether because it is an unrevealed purpose of God; or because it is future; or because it is covered up in parables or symbols...; or because it lies beyond the reach of the human mind" (*A Commentary on the Epistle to the Romans*, p. 372). This last sense, of course, corresponds to the modern usage of "mystery." Paul speaks of the blindness of the Jews until the fullness of the Gentiles be come in as a mystery, because this truth can be known only by special divine revelation. Thus Paul's use of the term "mystery" in verse 25 implies that he is speaking of something greater than that conversion of individual Jews to Christ which was already taking place in his own day.

"Lest ye should be wise in your own conceits." This is Paul's reason for the statement that he is about to make. He warns the Gentile Christians that they should not proudly assume that God has rejected the Jews forever, for this is not the case.

"Blindness in part is happened to Israel." This statement is true in two respects. Israel's blindness is not a total but a partial blindness, for all through the centuries of the history of the Church there has been a steady conversion of some Jews to Christ, so that the blindness has not been total at any one time. Also, it is not total with respect to their future history as a whole, for it shall not continue permanently; there shall come a time when not only scattered individuals but also the Jews as a community shall be brought to Christ. Paul is not referring to the degree of blindness. Those that were blind were completely blind. He is referring to the fact that at no time are all Jews blind to the truth, and that the blindness of the Jews collectively shall have an end.

"Until the fullness of the Gentiles be come in." This clause is differently interpreted, according to the two types of interpretation already mentioned. Some hold that it merely means that as long as Gentiles are still coming in, the Jews will continue to be partially blind, so that only a minority of them will be converted to Christ; but that nothing is implied as to any conversion of the Jews after the fullness of the Gentiles be come in. According to this view, the verse simply means that the status quo that existed in Paul's day will continue unchanged to the end of the world, after which (the fullness of the Gentiles having come in) there will follow Christ's second coming and the judgment day. This interpretation seems hardly to do justice to the way Paul introduces his statement as an important mystery.

The other interpretation of the clause is that Paul implies that after the fullness of the Gentiles come in, the Jews' blindness will be removed and they will be converted to Christ. The Greek words translated "until" in our English Bible are *achri hou,* followed by a verb in the aorist subjunctive. The correct translation is "until"; the usage of the Greek New Testament is against the idea of the meaning being merely "as long as the conversion of the Gentiles is continuing." The following instances of *achri* (until) may be cited: Revelation 15:8, "And no man was able to enter into the temple, till the seven plagues of the seven angels were fulfilled" (implying that after the seven plagues were fulfilled it was again possible to enter into the temple); and Revelation 17:17, "For God hath put in their hearts to fulfill his will, and to agree, and give their kingdom unto the beast, until the words of God shall be fulfilled" (implying that after the words of God have been fulfilled, the beast will no longer possess this dominion).

The second interpretation appears to be the correct one. The blindness of Israel will continue until the fullness of the Gentiles come in, after which, it is implied, their blindness will cease and they will be converted to Christ. This leaves the question of just what is meant by the fullness of the Gentiles coming in. The most probable meaning of "the fullness of the Gentiles" is the whole number of God's elect among the Gentiles. Some scholars hold that "the fullness of the Gentiles" means Gentiles converted to Christ from every nation of the world. In any case, when God's principal purpose concerning the salvation of Gentiles has been accomplished, the Jews' blindness will be removed and their conversion will follow.

It must be remembered that we are here dealing with unfulfilled prophecy, which is never completely clear until the time of fulfillment. Many questions will inevitably arise in our minds as to the exact time and manner of the fulfillment. These questions cannot be answered and need not be answered. It is possible, of course, that the Jews will be very suddenly and quickly converted to Christ. We must remember, too, that we cannot tell exactly when the fullness of the Gentiles have come in. These matters are part of God's secrets, which He has not revealed to us.

Questions:

1. Where did the obstacle lie that prevented the Jews from being grafted back into the good olive tree?

Romans 11:11–36

2. What is Paul's argument in 11:24 concerning the conversion of the Jews?

3. Why does Paul call the good olive tree "their own olive tree" in 11:24?

4. What unnatural and improbable event had already taken place in Paul's day?

5. What difficult question is involved in the interpretation of 11:25?

6. How many main types of interpretations of 11:25 are there?

7. What interpretation of 11:25 was common at the time of the Protestant Reformation?

8. What opinion concerning the conversion of the Jews was held by the Reformer Martin Luther?

9. What arguments can be given to prove that 11:25 predicts a future conversion of the Jews to Christ?

10. What is the importance of Paul's statement in 11:25, "I would not, brethren, that ye should be ignorant of this mystery"?

11. What is the biblical meaning of the term "mystery"?

12. In what respects is Israel's blindness partial?

13. What two views are held as to the meaning of the clause, "until the fullness of the Gentiles be come in"?

14. Give some New Testament references where the word "until" implies that after a certain event happens, a change will occur.

15. What is the probable meaning of "the fullness of the Gentiles"?

16. Why can we not fully answer the questions that may arise in our minds as to the fulfillment of 11:25?

Lesson 60

"And so all Israel shall be saved: as it is written, There shall come out of Sion the Deliverer, and shall turn away ungodliness from Jacob" (11:26). This is one of the most difficult verses in the Epistle to the Romans. The difficulty is in the first clause, "And so all Israel shall be saved." What is meant by the expression "all Israel"? Does this mean (1) the Jews collectively; or (2) the elect of God from both Jews and Gentiles; or (3) the elect of God among the Jews of all ages? Arguments have been put forth for each of these answers.

The first answer, that "all Israel" means the Jews collectively, is

Romans 11:11–36

the answer given by Charles Hodge, Henry Alford, W.G.T. Shedd, and
Geerhardus Vos. The second answer, that "all Israel" means the elect of
God from both Jews and Gentiles—that is, the Church—is the answer
given by Augustine, Calvin, and Philip Mauro. The third answer, that
"all Israel" means the elect of God among the Jews of all ages, is the
answer given by Herman Bavinck, William Hendriksen, O. Hallesby,
and Louis Berkhof. The arguments for and against each of these answers are summarized by Professor Hendriksen in his booklet *And So
All Israel Shall Be Saved.* For himself, he concludes that the "all Israel"
of verse 26 is identical with the "remnant according to the election of
grace" of verse 5.

One of the arguments against the view that "all Israel" means the
Jews as a people is the alleged silence of Jesus Christ on the subject of
a future conversion of the Jews. One verse that is sometimes cited as
evidence that Jesus foretold a conversion of the Jews is Matthew 19:28,
"And Jesus said unto them, Verily I say unto you, that ye which have
followed me, in the regeneration when the Son of man shall sit in the
throne of his glory, ye also shall sit upon twelve thrones, judging the
twelve tribes of Israel." This verse can be immediately dismissed as without relevance to the subject we are discussing. It speaks of something
that shall take place in the kingdom of glory after the second coming
of Christ. Therefore it has no bearing on the question of a conversion
of the Jews before His second coming.

Another verse that is sometimes cited in this connection is Luke
21:24, "Jerusalem shall be trodden down of the Gentiles, until the
times of the Gentiles be fulfilled." Against the idea that this speaks of
a future restoration or conversion of the Jews, it is held that this verse
only teaches that Jerusalem shall be trodden down of the Gentiles to
the very end of the times of the Gentiles, without implying that there
may or will be a change after that. This may be correct, but on the other
hand if the meaning is merely "Jerusalem shall be trodden down of the
Gentiles to the very end, until the end of the world," it seems a peculiar
way to express this idea by speaking of the times of the Gentiles being
"fulfilled." The natural reading of the verse would seem to imply that
Jerusalem shall no longer be trodden down of the Gentiles after the

times of the Gentiles have been fulfilled. (This is another instance of
the Greek *achri hou* with a subjunctive aorist verb). However, as this
verse speaks of the future of Jerusalem, and not of the conversion of
the Jews to Christ specifically, we will leave it to one side as of doubtful
bearing on our subject.

There is, however, one saying of Jesus that seems to have a definite
bearing on the subject, namely, Matthew 23:39, "For I say unto you, Ye
shall not see me henceforth, till ye shall say, Blessed is he that cometh
in the name of the Lord." Needless to say, Jesus is here speaking to
the unbelieving Jews, who despised and rejected Him and who soon
after this crucified Him. He tells them that they shall not see Him
again till they shall say "Blessed is he that cometh in the name of the
Lord." Can this refer to the scattered conversions of individual Jews
through the ages of Church history? The words certainly seem to imply
that a time will come when the Jews as a people shall accept Jesus as
their Messiah. This saying of Jesus, of course, does not make it clear
when and under what circumstances the Jews will say "Blessed he
that cometh in the name of the Lord." But as to the fact that at some
time they will say it, the text seems to be clear. It seems, therefore,
to prophesy a future conversion of the Jews to Christ.

Questions:

1. What three views have been held as to the meaning of "all Israel" in
    11:26?
2. Name some Bible scholars who have held that "all Israel" means the
    Jewish people.
3. Name some Bible scholars who have held that "all Israel" means the
    whole body of the elect of God from both Jews and Gentiles.
4. Name some Bible scholars who have held that "all Israel" means the
    elect of God among the Jews of all ages.
5. What argument concerning the meaning of "all Israel" in 11:26 is
    based upon the alleged silence of Jesus Christ concerning the future
    conversion of the Jews?
6. Why does Matthew 19:28 not have any bearing on the question of
    a future conversion of the Jews to Christ?

Romans 11:11–36

7.   What can be said about the bearing of Luke 21:24 on the question
     of a future conversion of the Jews?

8.   What saying of Jesus seems definitely to predict a future conversion
     of the Jews, and where is it found?

9.   What does this saying of Jesus fail to tell us about the future
     conversion of the Jews?

Lesson 61

"And so all Israel shall be saved: as it is written, There shall come
out of Sion the Deliverer, and shall turn away ungodliness from Jacob"
(11:26). In the last lesson we canvassed the various views that have been
held as to the meaning of "all Israel" in verse 26, and then we considered
the argument that "all Israel" cannot mean the Jewish people because
of the alleged silence of Jesus Christ upon the subject of a future
conversion of the Jews. We rejected one often cited text as irrelevant
to the subject, dismissed another as doubtful, and found that a third
(Matt. 23:39) seems definitely to prophesy a future conversion of the
Jews to Christ.

> Israel, here, from the context, must mean the Jewish people, and all
> Israel, the whole nation. The Jews, as a people, are now rejected; as a
> people, they are to be restored. As their rejection, although national,
> did not include the rejection of every individual; so their restoration,
> although in like manner national, need not be assumed to include the
> salvation of every individual Jew (Charles Hodge, *A Commentary on the
> Epistle to the Romans*, p. 379).

Hodge adds that "all Israel" in this verse therefore does not mean
(1) "all the true people of God," nor (2) "the remnant according to the
election of grace." The present writer believes that Hodge and those who
agree with his position are correct in this.

Those who reject the idea of a future conversion of the Jews make
much of the opening words of the verse: "And so." They point out that
Paul did not say "and then," but "and so," meaning (they say) that "all
Israel shall be saved" while the fullness of the Gentiles is being brought
in. We readily admit, of course, that there is a difference between "and

then" and "and so." But the phrase "and so" does not necessarily elimi- 3
nate the idea of a future conversion of the Jews to Christ. The Greek
can equally well be translated "and thus." Alford explains this as meaning "when this condition shall have been fulfilled" (*The New Testament
for English Readers*, p. 945), that is, when the condition described in the
last words of verse 25 shall have been fulfilled, namely when the fullness
of the Gentiles shall have come in. This seems a perfectly proper and
reasonable explanation of the force of the "and so."

In the second part of verse 26, Paul cites the Old Testament in
support of what he has just said. There is some difficulty in deciding Y
just what Old Testament passage or passages he is quoting. Isaiah 59:20
is the closest to the language used by Paul. Hodge suggests that Paul
may be giving a sort of summary of a number of passages, such as Isaiah
59:20–21; 27:9; Jeremiah 31:31–34; Psalms 14:7.

> The apostle teaches, that the deliverance promised of old, and
> to which the prophet Isaiah referred in the passage above cited,
> included much more than the conversion of the comparatively few
> Jews who believed in Christ at the advent. The full accomplishment
> of the promise, that he should turn away ungodliness from Jacob,
> contemplated the conversion of the whole nation, as such, to the
> Lord (Charles Hodge, *A Commentary on the Epistle to the Romans*, p.
> 374).

It will be observed that we have said nothing about the possibility
of a return of the Jews to Palestine. The reason is that the Apostle 5
Paul says nothing whatever about such a return. On this Alford says:
"I have not mixed with the consideration of this prophecy [Romans
11] the question of the restoration of the Jews to Palestine, as being
clearly irrelevant to it: the matter here treated being, their reception
into the Church of God" (*The New Testament for English Readers*, p. 946).

"For this is my covenant with them when I shall take away their
sins" (11:27). This verse is apparently quoted from Isaiah 59:21 and 27:9,
the latter in the form given in the Septuagint or Greek translation of
the Old Testament. It completes the proof from the Old Testament of
the truth that Paul has been setting forth.

Romans 11:11–36

All the apostle intended to prove, is proved by the language of the prophets. The covenant of God with his ancient people secured, after their apostasy and consequent banishment in Babylon, and their dispersion over the earth, and their rejection of Christ, the ultimate purging away of their sin, and their restoration, as a nation, to the Messiah's kingdom. This national conversion is also predicted in Zech. *6* 12:10, and in many other passages of the Old Testament (Charles Hodge, *A Commentary on the Epistle to the Romans*, p. 375).

In speaking of a future conversion of the Jews to Christ, we must, of course, realize that this does not imply that every individual Jew is to become a Christian.

Now, of course, the Apostle does not mean that all the Jews will be saved when Christ comes. If he meant this he would have to be understood as teaching that all the Gentiles are to be saved. Just as he does not mean by the "riches of the world" and the "riches of the Gentiles" the conversion of all Gentiles, so he does not mean by the "fullness" of the Jews the conversion of all the Jews. Any idea of a universal salvation is foreign to the teaching of the Bible (David *7* Freeman, *The Bible and Things to Come*, p. 69).

Questions:

1. What view was held by Charles Hodge as to the meaning of "all Israel" in 11:26?
2. What argument is based on the opening words of 11:26 by those who reject the idea of future conversion of the Jews to Christ?
3. How can this argument be answered?
4. What is Paul's purpose in quoting from the Old Testament in 11:26–27?
5. What can be said about the bearing of Romans 11 on a return of the Jews to Palestine?
6. What verse in Zechariah is understood to predict a future conversion of the Jews to Christ?
7. How can it be shown that the apostle Paul's statements do not imply that every individual Jew shall be converted to Christ?

Romans 11:11–36

Lesson 62

"As concerning the gospel, they are enemies for your sakes: but as touching the election, they are beloved for the fathers' sakes. For the gifts and calling of God are without repentance" (11:28–29). These two verses form a summary of what the Apostle Paul has taught about the rejection and future conversion of the Jews up to this point. "As in the whole context Paul is speaking, not of individuals, but of the rejection and restoration of the Jews as a body, it is evident that the calling and election which he here has in view, are such as pertain to the Jews as a nation, and not such as contemplate the salvation of individuals" (Charles Hodge, *A Commentary on the Epistle to the Romans*, p. 376). This consideration must be borne in mind or we will not be able to understand these two verses. If the calling, election, and salvation of individuals were under discussion, it would be quite impossible to say that the same people were both enemies as concerning the gospel and also beloved because the gifts and calling of God are without repentance. When we bear in mind that Paul is speaking of the rejection and future conversion of the Jews as a people, it all becomes clear.

"As concerning the gospel, they are enemies for your sakes" (11:28). The Jews were rejected for their unbelief. They were branches cut off from the good olive tree. By this rejection of them, salvation was brought to the Gentiles. In order to accomplish the salvation of the Gentiles, God regarded and treated the Jews as enemies. This implies, of course, that those who died in their unbelief were eternally lost. They had rejected the one and only way of salvation, Jesus the Messiah. From the book of Acts and from Paul's epistles we can see what bitter enemies the Jews were of the gospel of Christ. However the statement that, "they are enemies for your sakes" probably means that they are enemies of God, since it is of God that they are beloved for the fathers' sakes. Being enemies of God, they were of course also enemies of the gospel and of those faithful servants of God who proclaimed the gospel.

"But as touching the election, they are beloved for the fathers' sakes." Even while in the state of enmity against God and while being treated as enemies of God as concerning the gospel, they were in

Romans 11:11–36

another and very different sense beloved of God—they were beloved of God as touching the election, for the fathers' sakes. That is, these very Jews that were enemies of God as concerning the gospel were still being carefully watched over and kept by God against the day when the Jews as a people shall be converted to Jesus their Messiah. All in unbelief must perish in their sin, of course, but still they were beloved in one sense: as the stock whose descendants would one day be converted to the Messiah.

"For the gifts and calling of God are without repentance" (11:29). This verse as translated in the King James Version is not entirely clear. It is hardly necessary to mention the very crude misinterpretation that regards it as teaching that a sinner need not repent of his sins in order to be saved. "Repented" in this verse means a change of mind or purpose on God's part. The American Revised Version reads: "For the gifts and the calling of God are not repented of"; the Revised Standard Version, "For the gifts and the call of God are irrevocable"; and the Book of Books version, "For the gifts and the calling of God are such that He does not change His mind." God's gifts is a general, inclusive term for His favors; God's calling is the best and most important of His gifts. Paul states the principle that God's gracious purposes are not changeable, but irrevocable. The term "calling" is here equivalent to "election," as shown by the context, where they are used interchangeably. Those individuals whom God has elected to eternal life shall certainly be saved. If God has chosen a people to be His peculiar people, they shall remain His people, for His gracious purposes are unchangeable.

The choice of the Jews as a people of course implies nothing as to the personal salvation of particular individuals within that people. When God chose the Jews as His people, this did not imply that the majority of any one generation of Jews in Old Testament times should be personally saved unto eternal life. There exists today in some circles a very crude error that holds that, from Moses to Christ, each and every Israelite who complied with the external requirements of God's law was personally saved unto eternal life. This is of course entirely unfounded and untrue. God's choice of a people

as a people is one thing; His election and salvation of individuals is
another matter. In neither case does God "repent" of His purposes
or change His mind. We must not confuse the election of a people
to connections and privileges with the election of individuals to
personal salvation and eternal life.

Questions:
1. What is the place of 11:28–29 in Paul's argument?
2. Is Paul here speaking of God's choice of the Jews as a people, or
    of His election of individual Jews to eternal life?
3. Why did God regard and treat the Jews as enemies?
4. How can it be shown that in 11:28 "enemies" means "enemies of
    God"?
5. In what sense were the Jews beloved of God?
6. For what reason were they beloved of God?
7. What is meant by saying that "the gifts and calling of God are
    without repentance"?
8. What is the difference between God's "gifts" and His "calling"?
9. What other word does Paul in this context use as equivalent to
    "calling"?
10. What kind of "calling" is Paul speaking about here?

Lesson 63

"For as ye in times past have not believed God, yet have now
obtained mercy through their unbelief: even so have these also now
not believed, that through your mercy they also may obtain mercy"
(11:30–31). In these two verses Paul repeats and confirms what he has
already said, and he brings out the remarkable parallel between the cases
of the Jews and the Gentiles. The Gentiles were once unbelieving, but
obtained mercy through the unbelief of the Jews. The Jews are now
unbelieving, but shall obtain mercy through the salvation of the fullness of the Gentiles. This is not an exact parallel because the occasion
of obtaining mercy is different in the two cases. Yet the resemblance
is noteworthy.

"For as ye in times past have not believed God"—in the Greek "have

not believed" is literally "have disobeyed." This brings out the truth that
the Bible represents faith as an act of obedience to God, and unbelief as
disobedience to God. Men are not merely invited to believe on Christ;
they are commanded to believe on Christ, and those who do not believe
are disobedient to this command of God.

"For God hath concluded them all in unbelief, that he might have
mercy upon all" (11:32).

> Here the idea is, that God, in the dispensation of his providence and
> grace, has so ordered things, that all Gentiles and Jews, first the one,
> and then the other, should reveal their true character as sinners, and
> stand out in history confessed as unbelievers....Nor is mere permission
> all that is expressed. God's efficiency or control is directly asserted....
> The agency of God in giving men up to sin is punitive; it is consistent
> with their liberty and responsibility, and with his own holiness. He
> does not cause their sin, but he so orders his dispensations, that their
> sinfulness is revealed, and the mode of its manifestations determined.

> It seems also to enter into the design of the apostle to show that God
> had dealt alike with Gentile and Jew. They stood on the same ground.
> Both were dependent on sovereign mercy. Both had sunk into a state
> from which the grace of God alone could save them. As all were equally
> miserable and helpless, God determined to have mercy upon all, and
> to bring all, Jews as well as Gentiles, into the fold of Christ (Charles
> Hodge, *A Commentary on the Epistle to the Romans*, p. 377).

This brings us to the close of Paul's treatment of the plan of redemption. The next four verses (11:33–36) are a sublime expression of
the wisdom, knowledge, goodness, and grace of God. "Few passages,
even in the Scriptures are to be compared with this, in the force with
which it presents the idea that God is all and man is nothing" (Charles
Hodge, *A Commentary on the Epistle to the Romans*, p. 377). Henry Alford
says of these four verses that in them "the Apostle, overpowered with the
view of the divine Mercy and Wisdom, breaks forth into the sublimest
apostrophe existing even in the pages of Inspiration itself" (*The New
Testament for English Readers*, p. 498).

Romans 11:11–36

The question naturally arises, just what is the place of these four
verses in the Epistle to the Romans? Do they have a special relation
to the subject matter of chapters 9–11, namely, God's rejection of the
Jews and calling of the Gentiles? Or is the reference to the whole
doctrine of the epistle up to this point? Or is the reference limited
to the single matter of the future conversion of the Jews to Christ?
Charles Hodge observes that there is nothing to indicate any limitation to the immediate context, and so he concludes that the occasion
for this wonderful outburst of praise is the entire plan of salvation
revealed in the epistle up to this point (*A Commentary on the Epistle to
the Romans*, p. 377).

Three main ideas are presented in verses 33–36, namely, (1) in
Himself and in all His works, God is not only infinitely great and good,
but also incomprehensible to the human mind so that He transcends
human understanding; (2) God is entirely and absolutely independent
of man; (3) God is all-comprehensive, for He is the source, the means,
and the end of all that exists.

Questions:

1. What parallel is brought out in 11:30–31?
2. Why is this parallel not a perfect one?
3. What is the literal meaning of the phrase "have not believed God"
   in 11:30?
4. What is meant by the statement that God has concluded all in
   unbelief, that he might have mercy upon all?
5. Why does God's concluding men in unbelief not make God responsible for their sins?
6. What is the character of 11:33–36?
7. What question exists as to the relation of 11:33–36 to the rest of
   the epistle?
8. How is this question probably to be answered?
9. What three main ideas concerning God are taught in 11:33–36?

God Is Not Only Infinitely Great and Good, but also Incomprehensible to the Human Mind. 11:33

Lesson 64

"O the depth of the riches both of the wisdom and knowledge of God! How unsearchable are His judgments, and His ways past finding out!" (11:33). The first part of this verse may also be translated: "O the depth of the riches and wisdom and knowledge of God," making "riches" parallel to "wisdom" and "knowledge." If this translation is adopted, God's "riches" would mean His grace, His mercy to sinners. On the other hand, the translation given in the King James Version makes "riches" a description of God's wisdom and knowledge. As far as the grammar of the Greek is concerned, either translation is proper. Charles Hodge states that, inasmuch as the grace of God is a prominent subject in this epistle, the translation that regards "riches" as parallel to "wisdom" and "knowledge" is to be preferred (*A Commentary on the Epistle to the Romans*, p. 378). Henry Alford points out that in Philippians 4:19 the "riches" of God (same Greek word) is mentioned as a special attribute or quality of God. Alford also prefers to take "riches," "wisdom," and "knowledge" as parallel or coordinate attributes of God. He explains "riches" as meaning "the riches of the divine goodness" (*The New Testament for English Readers*, p. 498).

God is the Infinite Being. He is infinite in His being and in all His qualities or attributes. That is, there are no limits that can be applied to God. "God is a Spirit, infinite, eternal and unchangeable in His being, wisdom, power, holiness, justice, goodness, and truth" (*Shorter Catechism*, Q. 4). While modern religion tends to believe in a finite or limited God, the Bible teaches that God is infinite. Modern man has tried to make a god in his own image, a god who is really only a superman, a mere projection of the human mind. A prominent churchman of our own day has publicly said that the cry of humanity today is for a limited God, and that we can no longer respect any absolutes except those in the moral realm. Another prominent preacher holds that God can help us to love our fellow men but God cannot control the weather, so it is folly to pray for rain. This is just another instance of the modern notion of a finite God. Over the finite god of modern theology, the infinite God of the Bible

has one tremendous advantage: He is real, He really exists, and He is 6
the living and true God—not a mere figment of the human imagination.

People object to the idea of an infinite God today because this idea
cannot be analyzed by the human mind. It always baffles us. We cannot 7
draw a circle around it and say we understand it. Those who will worship no god except one whom they can fully understand and analyze
will not worship the God of the Bible. In reality they will worship only
their own human mind. They are idolaters just as truly as any heathen
that ever bowed down to wood and stone. The true God baffles the
human mind just because He is God. If we could understand Him, He
would not be God and we would not be creatures.

"We can only wonder and adore. We can never understand. And it is
well that it is so. What can be understood must be limited. What is fully
comprehended no longer exercises, excites, or enlarges. It is because
God is infinite in his being, and incomprehensible in his judgments
and in his ways, that he is an inexhaustible source of knowledge and
blessedness" (Charles Hodge, *A Commentary on the Epistle to the Romans*,
p. 378). We must realize that the Christian faith ends in mystery. Our
little knowledge that is possible by divine revelation soon carries us to 8
the borderland of mystery, where, as Hodge said, "we can only wonder
and adore," but never understand. Christianity has suffered terribly
from the inroads of 18th Century rationalism, which has continued to
have its baneful effects to the present day. The aim and ideal of 18th
Century rationalism was complete comprehension of all reality. This 9
required the rejection of everything in the Christian faith that could 10
not be completely understood or explained by the human mind. It
involved the rejection of the God of the Bible and the setting up of a
false god made in the image of the human mind. Over this false religion
of reason, we believe in the awful, mysterious, incomprehensible God
of the Bible—the living and true God.

There is a shade of distinction between God's "judgments" and
His "ways." God's "judgments" in this verse probably means His plans,
counsels, purposes, and decrees. These are declared to be "unsearchable," that is, not accessible to human study or investigation. They lie in 11
the realm of the secret things of God, which man cannot approach to

inquire into. God's "ways," on the other hand, would mean His methods
of procedure, the implementation of His eternal decrees in the works
of creation and providence. God's "ways," are said to be "past finding
out." The Greek literally means "untraceable"; it is an adjective formed
from the Greek word for "footprint." God executes His decrees in the
works of creation and providence, but it is beyond human ingenuity or
research to trace out these mysterious pathways; at most we can have
only a very limited, incomplete idea of God's "ways."

Questions:

1. What two opinions are there as to the meaning and purpose of
   the word "riches" in 11:33?
2. What verse in another of Paul's epistles shows that "riches" can
   be regarded as a distinct quality or attribute of God?
3. If "riches" is taken as a distinct quality of God, what is its meaning?
4. What is meant by saying that God is the Infinite Being?
5. What does much modern religion teach as to the being of God?
6. What great advantage does the God of the Bible possess over the
   god of modern theology?
7. Why do many people today object to the idea of an infinite God?
8. What is meant by saying that the Christian faith ends in mystery?
9. What is rationalism?
10. What harm has rationalism done to Christianity?
11. What is the difference between God's "judgments" and His "ways"?
12. Why are God's judgments unsearchable and His ways untraceable?

God Is Entirely and Absolutely Independent of Man.
11:34–35.

Lesson 65

"For who hath known the mind of the Lord? Or who hath been his
counsellor? Or who hath first given to him, and it shall be recompensed
unto him again?" (11:34–35). The first of these two verses teaches the
absolute independence of God in His plans and purposes. God's
counsel—His eternal decree—is not in any sense based on anything in
His creation. The questions "Who hath known the mind of the Lord?

Who hath been his counsellor?" of course imply the answer, "No one."
The teaching of the verse therefore is that God stands alone in His
plans and purposes and is not in respect of any of them limited by His
creatures.

This is the truth of the sovereignty of God. It is expressed many
times in the Bible by such phrases as "It pleased God," "It pleased the
Lord," "According to the good pleasure of His will." *The Westminster
Confession of Faith* and *Catechisms* also use similar expressions repeatedly to designate the sovereignty of God—His absolute supremacy and
independence in His plans and purposes.

This truth of the sovereignty and independence of God is greatly
spoken against at the present day. In the first place, it is denied by all
liberals and modernists who believe in a limited or finite God. Only
an infinite God can be truly independent in His plans. In the second
place, it is denied by all those who say that when God created mankind
He "limited Himself" so that after the creation of man He is no longer
supreme and independent. Such people confidently assert that God
is limited by the free will of His creatures. They do not even hesitate
to use such expressions as "God's hands are tied"; "God wants to save
you but He is helpless until you make your own decision"; "Give God a
chance" (or an "opportunity," which is evidently the same idea, namely
that God cannot act until the human will gives Him an "opportunity"
by acting first); "God has done all He can; now it is just up to you to
make your own decision," and many similar modes of speaking. All
of these flatter the natural man and his powers and detract from the
glory and honor of God by an implicit denial of His independence
and sovereignty.

There are those who assert that God has from all eternity foreordained what shall come to pass but that this foreordination is based
on His eternal foreknowledge of what would come to pass anyway.
In the matter of the salvation of sinners, this becomes the teaching
that God has from all eternity elected some to eternal life, but He has
elected those whom He foresaw would at some time of their life by
their own human free will decide to repent and accept Christ. This,
of course, is just an elaborate, roundabout way of saying that God's

eternal foreordination and election are not real and effective, but a mere *6*
verbal fiction. If God has foreordained the salvation of those whom
He foresaw would choose to be saved, then God's foreordination is a
fiction. This really amounts to God, in His eternal decree, deciding
to leave the eternal issues of life to the free will of sinful creatures. It
amounts to God leaving the whole matter to sinful man, and simply
ratifying the all-important decision made by human free will. This has
accurately been named the doctrine of "God elects those who elect
themselves." It regards man's choice as real and effective, whereas God's
choice is merely a formal ratification of man's choice.

These denials of God's sovereignty and independence do not arise
from careful exegesis of the text of Scripture. Talk with those who
advocate these views and in a few minutes it becomes evident that they
are basing them upon a kind of human reasoning. Because they cannot
harmonize God's sovereignty with man's freedom and responsibility, *7*
they try to escape from this paradox by virtually denying God's
sovereignty in the interests of man's freedom. The Reformed theology
for which our Church stands, on the other hand, reverently lets the
paradox stand unsolved, recognizing that this paradox (between God's
sovereignty and man's freedom) is deeply imbedded in the Scriptures,
and holds the two truths of God's sovereignty and man's freedom
without sacrificing one or the other.

A very crude misstatement of this subject is sometimes encoun-
tered. It is sometimes stated that Calvinism teaches God's sovereignty,
Arminianism teaches man's freedom and responsibility, and you have to
take both Calvinism and Arminianism to get the whole truth. If it were
not for the fact that this form of statement evidently appeals to some
people and has some popularity, it would hardly be worth answering. In
the first place, it is an absurdity to represent Calvinism and Arminianism as mutually complementary systems that have to be combined to
get the whole truth. Anyone who knows anything about the history of
this controversy knows that at the points of difference between them
Calvinism and Arminianism are mutually contradictory systems. In *9*
the early 1600s, the Arminians in Holland (then called Remonstrants)
issued a paper in which they called in question five articles of the creed

of the Reformed Church of Holland. This created controversy and a special synod was held—the Synod of Dort in 1618–1619—to settle the controversy. The Synod of Dort condemned the five points of the Arminians and adopted five articles of its own to set forth the truth. The five "Canons of Dort" are not complementary but contradictory to the five points of the Arminians. To say that Calvinism and Arminianism are just two sides of the same picture, as some say, is to talk through one's hat. It is like saying that the statement "Caesar crossed the Rubicon" and the statement "Caesar did not cross the Rubicon" are two sides of the same picture.

In the second place, the difference between Calvinism and Arminianism is not that Calvinism believes in God's sovereignty while Arminianism believes in man's freedom and responsibility. The real difference is that Calvinism believes fully in both God's sovereignty and man's freedom and responsibility without trying to solve the rational paradox that is involved, while Arminianism feels that the paradox must be solved and therefore denies the real sovereignty of God in the interests of holding on to man's freedom and responsibility. The real difference between the two systems, then, is a difference in their attitude to this paradox. Arminianism faces the paradox with a rationalistic attitude: the paradox must be solved at any cost. If this involves denying the real sovereignty of God, so be it; we must then say that God elected those whom He foreknew would of their own free will repent and believe. Calvinism, on the other hand, approaches this paradox with an attitude of reverence and godly fear: the paradox is one of the secret things that belong to the Lord our God. We need not solve it; we need only adhere to what the Scripture teaches concerning both of these truths that we cannot fully harmonize.

The Arminian view is prevalent today in American evangelical or fundamentalist circles. Some consider this only an academic question, of no practical importance. The truth is that nothing is more important than the truth about God and our relation to Him. The Arminian view implies that it is in the power of sinful man, without the effectual calling or irresistible grace of the Holy Spirit, to make a decision to repent and accept Christ. This in turn implies that the natural man cannot

be really totally depraved and dead in trespasses and sins. So it will be
seen that Arminianism involves very serious consequences.

Man cannot place God under any obligation, because God Himself
is the source, the cause and the end of all things.

> It is for the display of His character everything exists, and is directed,
> as the highest and noblest of all possible objects. Creatures are as
> nothing, less than vanity and nothing in comparison with God. Human
> knowledge, power, and virtue, are mere glimmering reflections from
> the brightness of the divine glory. That system of religion, therefore,
> is best in accordance with the character of God, the nature of man,
> and the end of the universe, in which all things are of, through, and
> to God; and which most effectually leads men to say, not unto us, but
> unto thy name be all the glory! (Charles Hodge, *A Commentary on the
> Epistle to the Romans*, p. 379).

This brings us to the conclusion of what is commonly called the
doctrinal part of the Epistle to the Romans. In these 11 chapters, God's
plan of salvation has been presented and defended more clearly and
completely than in any other part of the Bible. "The leading principle
of all is, that God is the source of all good; that in fallen man there is
neither merit nor ability; that salvation, consequently, is all of grace,
as well sanctification as pardon, as well election as eternal glory. For
of Him, and through Him, and to Him, are all things; to whom be
glory for ever. Amen" (Charles Hodge, *A Commentary on the Epistle to the
Romans*, p. 380).

Questions:

1. What great truth is taught in 11:34–35?
2. What expression is frequently used in the Bible and the Westminster
   Standards to designate the sovereignty of God?
3. What is the attitude of present day liberals and modernists to the
   sovereignty of God?
4. What are some of the statements made by those who say that God
   has "limited Himself" in His dealings with man?
5. What is wrong with the common saying, "Give God a chance"?

Romans 11:11–36

6. Why is it not correct to say that God has from eternity elected those whom He foresaw would of their own free will decide to repent and believe?

7. What paradox is deeply imbedded in the Scriptures?

8. Why is it not correct to say that Calvinism and Arminianism are both true and only two sides of the same picture?

9. What controversy was settled at the Synod of Dort? When and where was this synod held?

10. What is the real difference between Calvinism and Arminianism?

11. What is the right attitude toward the paradox between God's sovereignty and man's freedom?

12. Why is the difference between Calvinism and Arminianism an important matter?

13. Why cannot man place God under any obligation?

14. What is the leading principle of God's plan of salvation as revealed in the first 11 chapters of Romans?

Romans 11:11–36

Chapter 6

PRACTICAL DUTIES OF THE CHRISTIAN LIFE

The Duty of Cultivating Practical Personal Holiness.
12:1–21
Christian Devotion to God
Lesson 66

In this and the following chapters we have a message, not to the unsaved, but to Christian people. An unsaved person cannot even begin to live the kind of life here described. It is his duty to live that kind of life, but he cannot until he is saved and given the desire and the power to do so by divine grace. How wrong and foolish, then, is the type of contemporary evangelism that addresses the unsaved sinner with an invitation to adopt "the Christian way of life" or "Christ's way of life." Such "evangelism" contains no evangel—no gospel—but consists merely of good advice in the form of ethical teachings.

The apostle Paul here presents many practical duties of the Christian life. This chapter covers just about every kind of Christian duty. Yet these are not just a list of unrelated items. They are related as the features of Christian character and conduct.

Romans 12:1–21

These features of Christian character are all to be taken together, not singly or separately. We may not single out and stress some, while omitting or neglecting the rest. For example, 12:16a, "Be of the same mind one toward another" must not be allowed to eliminate 12:9b, "Abhor that which is evil, cleave to that which is good." These two obligations must be taken together and always kept in balance with each other.

Holiness is not adequate if it is lopsided. It is not adequate if it is not complete and well-balanced. Suppose someone is a wonderful church officer, but at home he is so mean that his family is always unhappy and miserable. That is not true Christian holiness. Or suppose some person is an ideal husband or wife or parent in the home, but is never willing to make any efforts or sacrifices for the work of the Church. Such is not true Christian holiness because it is one-sided; it is out of balance.

We know that an airplane propeller that rotates at tremendous speed must be carefully balanced. If not, it cannot function properly. A pilot once made a forced landing and one tip of his propeller hit the ground and several inches were broken off. What could he do? He cut the same amount off from the opposite tip, thus balancing the propeller again, and so was able to reach home safely. Even an ordinary four-blade electric fan will not work right if one blade is removed, leaving three. An ordinary flywheel is useless unless it is balanced. So it is with Christian character.

There are many one-sided Christians, whose character is incomplete and lacks balance. What should they do? Certainly they should not use the method adopted by the airplane pilot for emergency repairs. We must gain balance not by cutting down where we are long, but by building up where we are short.

Holiness, or Consecration to God. 12:1.

Holiness includes all the other features of character and life that are to follow. Holiness is not an abstraction in itself. It is not something that can be isolated. Holiness is not really coordinate with meekness, kindness, earnestness, etc. Rather, holiness includes all these, and they are the fruits of holiness in a Christian's life.

Romans 12:1–21

Holiness is consecration to God and His service. This, we are informed, is our "reasonable service." It is what God can reasonably expect of us.

We find holiness summarized in 12:21 in the words, "Be not overcome of evil, but overcome evil with good." Evil in this universe is no figment of the imagination. It is real; it is powerful; it must be faced and reckoned with. Either we will be overcome of evil, or we will overcome evil with good. We cannot be neutral or noncombatant in the conflict with evil. If we do not wage war against evil, evil will conquer us. But by God's grace we are enabled to wage war against evil and overcome evil with good.

Holiness is not an abstraction that we can have by itself. Holiness always takes the form of concrete Christian virtues, which we find taught in this chapter. Holiness in itself is complete consecration to God; holiness in its effects is overcoming evil with good; holiness in its manifestations is helpfulness, earnestness, meekness, kindness, and so forth. If we lack these specific Christian virtues, we do not have practical Christian holiness.

Questions:

1.   To what class of people is the message of Romans chapters 12–15 addressed?
2.   What is wrong with the type of "evangelism" that addresses the unsaved sinner with an invitation to "adopt Jesus' way of life"?
3.   What is meant by saying that the features of Christian character must be balanced?
4.   How is balance to be gained in cultivating Christian character?
5.   What is the relation between holiness and the various features of Christian character?
6.   What is the meaning of holiness?
7.   How is holiness summarized in 12:21?
8.   Why can we not be neutral in the conflict between good and evil?

The Secret of the Source of Holiness. 12:2
Lesson 67

Romans 12:2 tells us the secret of the source of holiness. First of all, we do not get it by copying the ways of this world: "Be not conformed to this world." As a matter of fact, the character of this world, and of worldly people—that is, people who are not saved Christians—is just the opposite of the Christian character described in this chapter. The worldly character is unholy, selfish, proud, unkind, and so forth.

What the Christian knows to be wrong and sinful, the world regards as legitimate. Take such a simple matter as Sabbath desecration, for example. We can easily think of many illustrations. What the Christian knows to be right and his duty, the world often regards with contempt and even ridicule. For example, to love our enemies is a Christian duty, yet the world regards it with contempt and ridicule. We cannot get holiness by copying the world or by acquiescing in the world's standards. If we accept the world's standards of right and wrong, we will sin against God and injure ourselves. In matters of conduct and conscience the world is seriously in error. If we follow the world, we run the risk of God's displeasure and righteous judgments. It is neither right nor safe to follow the will of the majority in matters of religion and morals.

Verse 2 goes on to tell how we do get holiness—not by being conformed to this world, but by being transformed by the renewing of our mind. But what does this mean? We might perhaps paraphrase it thus: "Do not let your life be a copy of the ways of the world, but have a changed character by receiving a new heart, so that it will be possible for you to live your life according to the will of God."

"The renewing of your mind"—getting a new mind—is the same thing as regeneration or being born again, except that we should understand that "the renewing of our mind" is not a once-for-all transaction, but something often repeated and indeed a continuous process in the Christian's life. This process begins with regeneration, or the new birth, and it continues throughout the Christian's life. It is the continuous working out of the new birth. Being born again is the beginning of the renewing of a person's mind. Sanctification is the continuation of the renewing of a person's mind. As in the case of the natural life, so in the Christian life: first there is birth and then there follows growth.

"Transformed by the renewing of your mind"—changed by receiving a new heart and a new way of thinking. The unsaved person thinks wrongly about everything connected with God, his soul, and his duty. But when a person is transformed by the renewing of his mind, God puts that person's mind on the right track, and he begins to think aright. He repents of his old sins. He begins to hate what he once loved. He begins to love and enjoy what he once hated. He is renewed in the spirit of his mind.

But how do we become transformed by the renewing of our mind? This is not something that we can do for ourselves. A railway locomotive can run when everything is all right, but if it is off the track, there is one thing it cannot do: it cannot get itself back on the track again by its own power or efforts. First it must be set back on the rails, and then after that it can run as it was designed to run. We cannot transform ourselves. We cannot renew our own heart or mind. We cannot, of ourselves, begin to love what we naturally hate, nor begin to hate what we naturally love. The Bible emphasizes this truth by the famous question: "Can the Ethiopian change his skin, or the leopard his spots? then may ye also do good, that are accustomed to do evil" (Jer. 13:23).

We cannot accomplish this for ourselves. But there is a way. This change comes into a person's life by the miraculous, almighty power of God. It is the work of God the Holy Spirit. It is mysterious; it cannot be analyzed or explained, "The wind bloweth where it listeth, and thou hearest the sound thereof, but canst not tell whence it cometh, and whither it goeth: so is every one that is born of the Spirit" (John 3:8). It is mysterious, yet it is real; it is powerful, and it brings obvious results. It changed Saul the persecutor into Paul the Christian. It changed the cannibals of the South Sea Islands into law-abiding, industrious Christian people who saved the lives and ministered to the needs of allied fliers who were forced to bail out over the jungles during World War II. It changed our own ancestors from furious, fierce, lawless, wild savages and barbarians, as they were two thousand years ago, to civilized Christian peoples—imperfect, it is true, often inconsistent, but still very different from what they were before Christianity reached them in the forests and wilderness of northern Europe and the British Isles. The renewing of the mind by the Holy Spirit is a reality. It brings results.

Romans 12:1–21

Since this change is the work of God the Holy Spirit, we should always seek this change from Him and always give Him the honor and glory of it. Do not dare to take any credit to yourself because you are different from the world. If you are not conformed to this world, but transformed by the renewing of your mind, remember that the credit for this does not belong to you. The Ethiopian cannot change his skin, nor the leopard his spots, and none of us can change his own character or heart. It is God who has made us to differ from the unsaved world. To God alone belongs the credit and the praise and the honor and the glory. We are His workmanship, created in Christ Jesus for good works, which God has before ordained that we should walk in them (Eph. 2:10).

Questions:
1. Why can we not gain holiness by being conformed to this world?
2. What is the difference between the Christian's standard of right and duty and the world's standard?
3. What is the meaning of the clause, "Be ye transformed by the renewing of your mind"?
4. What is the relation of regeneration to the renewing of our mind?
5. What is the relation of sanctification to the renewing of our mind?
6. Why can we not accomplish the renewing of our minds for ourselves?
7. Give some examples from Christian history of people who were transformed by the renewing of their minds.
8. Who is the source and agent of the change called "the renewing of our mind"?
9. Why are we not entitled to any credit for the renewing of our minds?

Helpfulness, or Practical Concern, for Our Fellow Christians. 12:4–8

Lesson 68

We shall omit discussion of verse 3 for the time being. This verse deals with humility or meekness, which we shall consider later in connection with some other verses of the chapter. Verses 4–8 deal with our relation to our fellow Christians. We cannot have real holiness without having helpfulness too. Centuries ago, many people had a very false idea of holiness. They thought that they could run away from the world and shut themselves up in a monastery or convent, or even all alone in a hermit's cell out in the forest somewhere, and there cultivate holiness by prayer and meditation, isolated from the society of their fellow men. There are people in the world who still think that way—not only the monks and nuns in Roman Catholic institutions, but there are also some Protestants who seem to have a somewhat similar idea of holiness. But biblical holiness is not like that. It is really a very practical matter. It expresses itself, not in running away from our fellow men, but in helpfulness to them. If we are truly holy, we will be concerned about the welfare and progress of our fellow Christians. We will realize that we cannot live the Christian life all alone. We will understand that we are all members of a body, and that our individual Christian life is connected with the lives of a great many other Christian people.

Each one of us has a part to perform as a member of that body, the Church, the body of Christ. We are one body in Christ, and everyone is a member with one another. Each and every one of us has a function to perform. Our functions are unique, and no one else can replace anyone else. God has called each Christian to a particular place and function in the body of Christ.

At this point we ought to guard against two common mistakes. First of all, in saying that each of us has a function to perform as a member of the body of Christian people, we do not mean that each person must have an official function to perform in the church as an organization. This portion of Scripture is dealing with something broader than merely official service in the organized church, such as the service of ministers, elders, deacons, teachers, and so forth. These official functions are only a part; they are not the whole matter, by any means. The service of Christian helpfulness that Paul is discussing is broader and more inclusive than official service in the church. For example, note verse 8, "He that giveth, let him do it with simplicity [or liberality]." This does not necessarily mean some official function of church officers, though that may be included, but the act of any Christian in giving something to the poor and needy or in contributing something to the support of the gospel. Again, "he that showeth mercy, with cheerfulness" (12:8). Clearly what is spoken of is something broader than official functions in the organized church. We can serve God faithfully and well and be a real help to our fellow Christians without holding office in the organized church. Every private Christian is a king and priest unto God.

It is important to emphasize this because there exists a tendency to think that every church member must have some sort of official function or duty in the church. This is not only an unbiblical idea, but it leads to great evils in practice. Not only are people assigned to positions or tasks for which they are not qualified, but they are thereby led to have a wrong idea of Christian service and to neglect, it may be, the real service that God would have them do. Moreover this tendency leads to the multiplication of offices, committees, and organizations for the mere purpose of providing functions for so many people. Church organization should be kept simple and workable. The tendency to multiply and complicate organization is a bad tendency. Ships are not built so that somebody can be captain of them; they are built because they are needed to transport people and goods. Organizations should not be set up just to keep more people busy about church work, but only to meet a real and definite need.

In the second place, we should not make the mistake of supposing that every Christian can be helpful in exactly the same way as other Christians. Many people make this mistake. They measure all pastors and their work by some one pastor whom they have admired, all elders by some one elder, and so on. But actually each Christian's capacity for service is special and unique. "Having then gifts differing according to the grace that is given to us" (12:6). Each of us has his own gift, bestowed on him by the Holy Spirit. We should not seek or desire, then, to be just like someone else; nor should we complain or be dissatisfied because our capacities are different from other people's. Rather, we should seek to discover what particular gift God has bestowed on us, and then use it for the glory of God and the benefit of our fellow Christians. That is the pathway to true helpfulness.

Romans 12:1–21

Questions:

1. What is the general subject of 12:4–8?
2. What false idea of holiness was common hundreds of years ago?
3. Why can we not live the Christian life all alone?
4. Why is it not correct to say that every Christian must have some official function to perform in the organized church?
5. What harm is done by multiplying organizations so that more people can be kept busy with church work?
6. What verse shows that it is a mistake to suppose that all Christians can be helpful in the same way?
7. What should be our attitude toward our own gift bestowed on us by the Holy Spirit?

Lesson 69

God is glorified not only by Christian ministers, but also by Christian farmers, Christian businessmen, and Christian school teachers. God is glorified by Christian people in every lawful occupation and walk of life—people who take their Christianity seriously and seek both holiness and helpfulness in their daily life.

In China, missionaries often had to discourage people from trying to become preachers. Many were converted so wonderfully that they immediately wanted to go to a school and learn to be a preacher. It was necessary to impress on such people's minds that their conversion to Christ did not imply that they were called to official service and that there were many other ways to serve God besides the official preaching function. God is glorified by Christian business men, Christian farmers, Christian soldiers, Christian policemen, Christian carpenters, Christian factory workers, and Christian mothers and housewives, just as truly as by Christian preachers.

Paul is stressing Christian helpfulness as an expression of Christian holiness. He mentions various Christian activities and duties: prophecy, ministry, exhorting, giving, ruling, and showing mercy. Prophecy here means what we would ordinarily call preaching today, the giving of a sermon or discourse in the assembly of the Church. Ministry refers to any kind of service or duty in the Church. Teaching and exhortation

Romans 12:1–21

are not necessarily distinct from prophecy; they may describe the same work from a different point of view.

What we should note here is that Paul commands us each to "wait on" his own particular work. The Christian who ministers is to "wait on" his ministering, the one who exhorts is to "wait on" his exhorting, the one who teaches is to "wait on" his teaching, etc. Note that in the English Bible the words "let us wait" are in italics, indicating that they are not found in the Greek text, but have been added in the English translation because the idiom of our language requires them to make the grammar and sense complete. In the Greek it is just, "Or ministry, on ministering," etc. That is to say, each of us is to concentrate on what God has committed to us to do. Each of us is to pay particular attention to his own particular task and his own special opportunity to be helpful to others.

There is hardly anything that glorifies God and helps the Church more than each person strictly minding his or her own business, as God has committed it to him or her. Remember the saying of Jesus to Peter when Peter asked about John, "Lord, and what shall this man do?" Jesus replied, "What is that to thee? Follow thou me" (John 21:21–22).

Nevermind if someone else makes a mistake sometimes, or if someone else fails in his task sometimes, or if someone else does not perform his task as well as we think we ourselves could perform it. Let each one of us concentrate on our own service to God in the sphere and circumstances in which God has placed us. If we have been called to special office in the church, let us concentrate on fulfilling the duties of our office faithfully. If we are private Christians, let us concentrate on helpfulness to our fellow Christians in the ways that God places before us.

Any amount of trouble can be caused in a church by a meddlesome spirit on the part of a few people. To be "a busybody in other men's matters" (Greek, literally, a supervisor of other people's affairs) is forbidden in God's Word, and is classified with such sins as murder and theft (1 Pet. 4:15). Yet this is hardly an uncommon sin, and it is a sin that has enabled the devil to do great harm to the Church. Sometimes one member of a church, or a little group, will carry on such a continuous fault-finding and criticism of the work of the pastor, the elders, or the deacons that their work is greatly undermined and the church as a whole greatly disheartened and discouraged. Yet the fault-finders and self-appointed critics may themselves be doing nothing or very little in the way of Christian service. Their meddling destroys the Church. If there are legitimate complaints or criticisms they should be presented, in a friendly and loving way, to the persons directly concerned, and if that fails, a complaint should be made in an orderly, lawful way to the courts of the Church. But continuous, undercover faultfinding and criticism of others, whom God has not placed under our jurisdiction, is very sinful.

We might think of any piece of machinery—an automobile, for example. Each and every part has its function to perform. A spark plug cannot do the work of a carburetor, nor can a gearshift take the place of a steering wheel. Each part has its specific function to perform, and when all are working harmoniously according to their proper functions, then true progress is possible. The maker of such an automobile will receive credit for having built an excellent machine, and the owner will derive satisfaction from the harmony and helpfulness of all the parts.

But sometimes it takes very little to stop an automobile entirely. A single broken wire will stop the most powerful car if it is the right wire. Two or three drops of water inside the distributor will bring a speeding machine to a stop. Think how much trouble two or three Christians can make if they cease to be helpful and become a stumblingblock to their fellow Christians. How important it is that we all live and work together in helpfulness and harmony.

Questions:

1. What other callings besides preaching can glorify God?
2. Why do not missionaries in foreign fields encourage every convert to try to become a preacher?
3. What is meant by "prophecy" in this chapter?
4. What is meant by "ministry"?
5. Why are the words "let us wait" in 12:7 printed in italics?
6. On what is every Christian to concentrate?

Romans 12:1–21

7. What does God's Word say about being a busybody in other people's matters?

8. What troubles are caused by meddling and fault-finding with the Christian service of others?

The Obligation of Christian Love. 12:9–10

Lesson 70

"Let love be without dissimulation" (12:9). Dissimulation means pretense, or hypocrisy. Presumably "love" in verse 9 means love to all men, since love for our fellow Christians is specially mentioned as "brotherly love" in verse 10. So in our love for our fellow men, we are to be sincere, without pretense or hypocrisy. There is a kind of love that consists merely in words without deeds. It is a mere pretense or sham. We may talk about how much we love our neighbor, yet shut our eyes to his need and pass by as did the priest and the Levite in the parable of the good Samaritan. There is no room in the Christian life for shams or deceits. Our love for our fellow men is to be sincere and genuine.

Abhor that which is evil; cleave to that which is good."

The words evil and good, in this passage, may be understood of moral good and evil, and the exhortation be considered as a general direction to hate the one and love the other. But the great majority of commentators, out of regard to the context, take the terms in a restricted sense, making the former mean injurious, and the latter kind. The sense of the whole verse would then be, 'Let love be sincere; strive to avoid what is injurious to others, and earnestly endeavor to do what is kind and useful.' As the words themselves admit of either of these interpretations, the choice between them depends upon the context. The latter is, on this ground, perhaps to be preferred (Charles Hodge, *A Commentary on the Epistle to the Romans*, p. 386).

"Be kindly affectioned one to another with brotherly love; in honour preferring one another." Here we have a command that specifically requires love for our fellow Christians. The Greek word here used for "kindly affectioned" is a word that is used to express the strong natural affection between parents and children. It may also be used of any

Romans 12:1–21

tender affection. "Here, no doubt, the idea is, that Christians should love each other with the same sincerity and tenderness as if they were the nearest relatives" (Charles Hodge, *A Commentary on the Epistle to Romans*, p. 396). But how far short we fall in the practice of this! Some churches might almost be described as hotbeds of hatred and enmity, with member set against member and group against group. Sometimes persons who might be considering becoming members get an inside view of such feuding and enmity and immediately decide against joining such a church.

"In honour preferring one another." This sentence, as translated in the King James Version, must be understood as an exhortation to humility. But the Greek word translated "preferring" means to lead, to go before, to set an example. And the Greek word translated "honor" may mean respect or kindness. The Revised Standard Version translates it: "outdo one another in showing honor." Charles Hodge gives the following as a possible paraphrase of the clause: "as to respect and kindness going before each other, or setting an example one to another." "It is not only an injunction of politeness, but that in all acts of respect and kindness we should take the lead. Instead of waiting for others to honor us, we should be beforehand with them in the manifestation of respect" (Charles Hodge, *A Commentary on the Epistle to the Romans*, p. 396).

The Obligation of Christian Earnestness. 12:11–13

"Not slothful in business; fervent in spirit; serving the Lord; rejoicing in hope; patient in tribulation; continuing instant in prayer; distributing to the necessity of saints; given to hospitality" (12:11–13). Here we have presented eight Christian duties, all of which may be summed up under the term "earnestness."

First of all, the Christian should be a busy person, not slothful in business. He should be active about his daily occupation of earning a living. This applies, of course, to everybody except those who by reason of youth, age, sickness, or infirmity are unable to work. A man may have a fortune in stocks and bonds, but if he is a Christian he will not spend his days in idleness nor will he squander them in selfish pleasures.

Rather, he will occupy himself with useful work, not because he has to work in order to eat, but because God requires a busy, active life from every Christian. Even those who do not have to work to earn a living must work to serve and please God. It is a sin not to work. "Six days shalt thou labor and do all thy work" is a divine commandment just as truly as "Remember the Sabbath day to keep it holy." The person who wastes his time during the week in idleness or foolishness is breaking the moral law of God just as truly as the person who does unnecessary work on the Sabbath day.

Next, the Christian is to be fervent in spirit, serving the Lord. We might paraphrase "fervent in spirit" as "enthusiastic." We are to be enthusiastic about our religion, enthusiastic in serving the Lord. Are we enthusiastic about our religion, or do we regard it as more or less of an unpleasant duty? Would we be willing to die for our faith as the martyrs did?

Communism has gained half the world and everyone knows that real communists are enthusiastic for their communist faith. We can call it fanaticism if we wish, but the fact remains that they are willing to make sacrifices and even to die for their faith. Is Christianity losing the battle because Christians do not take their faith as seriously as communists take theirs?

Someone has said that it is really much harder to live for one's religion than to die for it. No doubt there is much truth in this statement. Perhaps we in America are not likely to be called to suffer a martyr's death, though it is certainly possible. But, at any rate, we are called upon to live for our religion—to be fervent in spirit, serving the Lord. We are called to Christian earnestness. If we really have salvation, if the Spirit of God is really working in our hearts and lives, we will be dead earnest about our religion, and we will be dead earnest about life itself.

This earnestness will be manifested not only in our daily tasks, not only in our enthusiasm about our religion, but also, as we see in verse 12, by "rejoicing in hope," by being "patient in tribulation," and by "continuing instant in prayer." We will always have a deep happiness because of our Christian hope, the hope of eternal glory, of which God has told us that "eye hath not seen, nor ear heard, neither hath entered into the heart of man, the things which God has prepared for them that love Him" (1 Cor. 2:9). This happiness will be deeper than our frequent troubles. If we are called upon, in God's providence, to suffer tribulation, as all of us are at some time and in some way, we will not become sour or bitter by this experience. We will show our Christian earnestness by being patient in tribulation.

We will make prayer the habit and practice of our lives. We will not only pray in special emergencies—not just when we happen to find ourselves faced with death from starvation and thirst on a rubber raft out in the ocean somewhere—but we will pray daily, continuing instant in prayer. It sounds easy, of course, but it is perhaps the hardest of all Christian duties to perform. Satan has so many ways of diverting us from it and making us discouraged.

A story is told to the effect that Satan decided to go out of business and offered to sell his tools to the highest bidder. He was preparing to auction them off and had each tool marked with a price tag stating the lowest bid he would accept on that tool. Most had ordinary prices marked on them, but at one side there lay a wedge-shaped tool with an extremely high price marked on the tag. Someone asked Satan why he placed such a high price on what appeared to be a common wedge. He replied: "That is a special tool; it succeeds when all others fail. It is called Discouragement, and I can nearly always depend on it to destroy the happiness and usefulness of Christians whom I cannot influence by any of my ordinary methods or temptations."

The great enemy of prayer is discouragement. But by faith and Christian earnestness it can be overcome. Remember the story of Giant Despair in Bunyan's *Pilgrim's Progress*.

Questions:

1. What is the meaning of "dissimulation"?
2. What two interpretations of 12:9b ("Abhor that which is evil; cleave to that which is good") are possible, and which is probably the correct interpretation?
3. What is the meaning of the Greek word for "kindly affectioned" in 12:10?

Romans 12:1–21

4. What kind of love should we have toward our fellow Christians?
5. What is the true meaning and force of 12:10b ("in honor preferring one another")?
6. What Christian obligation is set forth in 12:11–13?
7. Why should every Christian lead a busy and industrious life?
8. What is the teaching of God's word on the subject of slothfulness?
9. What is said about the duty of working in the Ten Commandments?
10. Is it really harder to live for our religion than to die for it, and if so, why?
11. Do Christians equal communists in enthusiasm for their faith, and if not, what may be the reasons for this?
12. What is the effect of discouragement in the Christian life, and how may discouragement be overcome?

The Obligation of Christian Meekness. 12:3, 14–21
Lesson 71

There is a great deal about Christian meekness in this chapter. But, first of all, what do we mean by meekness? Verse 3 almost provides a definition of meekness: "not to think of himself more highly than he ought to think; but to think soberly, according as God hath dealt to every man the measure of faith." Meekness is also called humility, humbleness, and lowliness of mind. Also such terms as gentleness, forbearance, and condescension are closely related in meaning to meekness.

Meekness is really a kind of courage. We might think that meekness is the opposite of courage, but really meekness is the very highest and noblest kind of courage. Meekness is the calm courage that dares to face the realities of one's own life. Meekness is the courage that enables a person to admit a wrong; the courage that enables a person to say "I am sorry" and to ask for forgiveness. Meekness is the courage that enables a person to face suffering without panic. Meekness is the courage that enables a person to experience serious injustice without becoming cynical and bitter about it.

Meekness is the courage that dares to give up the ambition to be great and important, and is willing to take a lowly place and to do one's best for God in ordinary surroundings and circumstances. Meekness is the courage that dares to crucify human pride and vanity and selfishness, and dares to live a life of humble, unselfish helpfulness.

By nature we are all tremendous cowards. We are terribly afraid—afraid to take second place, afraid to crucify our worldly pride and ambition, afraid to confess that we have done wrong, afraid to ask for forgiveness, afraid to suffer pain, afraid to suffer injustice. We are moral cowards. But the Christian receives the grace of meekness. He receives the meek courage that enables him to face all these situations, to rise above them, and to conquer them by the power of God.

Now note the exhortation to meekness in Romans 12. First read verse 3. Ah, here is where we are all tempted to go astray! Think carefully, and we will realize that no one is immune to this subtle temptation, the temptation to have an exaggerated opinion of our own qualities, character, achievements, and importance. But if we grow in Christian meekness, the grace of God will enable us more and more to overcome this selfish pride.

Now note verse 14, which refers to conduct under persecution: "Bless them which persecute you: bless, and curse not." This text does not tell us to obey the wishes of the persecutors. It does not say that a Christian must agree with the demands or comply with the requirements of persecutors of Christianity. But it does say that, as to our personal attitude toward persecutors, we must not curse them, we must not hate them; we must "bless, and curse not." When they do us wrong, we must do them good, not wrong in return for wrong.

The great African bishop Cyprian, who was unjustly put to death by the Roman government in the year 258 after Christ, was arrested, tried by a Roman court, and ordered to offer sacrifice to the pagan gods of Rome. He refused. The judge advised him to consider his answer carefully, as his life was hanging in the balances. Cyprian replied. "Do your duty. This matter does not admit of consideration." Thereupon he was sentenced to be beheaded with the sword. His only answer as he heard the sentence of the court was to say, "Thanks be unto God." At the place of execution a great crowd had gathered, many of them friends and admirers of Cyprian. The executioner who was to wield the sword trembled at his task. Cyprian knelt and offered prayer, then expressed as his last wish that from his estate 25 gold pieces be given as a gift to the executioner who was to behead him. Thus Cyprian not only showed no bitterness or hatred, but also deeply impressed the public, both Christian and non-Christian, with the truth that for a Christian, "to die is gain." (*Editor's Note:* For more information on Cyprian, see the *Catholic Encyclopedia*.)

"Rejoice with them that do rejoice, and weep with them that weep" (12:15). Here Christian sympathy is enjoined upon us. The selfish Christian will be absorbed in his own affairs; he will not think of other people's joys and sorrows. But the meek, humble, and unselfish Christian will share in other people's joys and sorrows as well as his own.

"Be of the same mind one toward another" (12:16). This does not mean that unity and agreement are to be sought by the sacrifice of truth. If a member of the Church is teaching false doctrine, denying the truths of the Scriptures, we are not to agree with him for the sake of peace and harmony. Of course it would be wrong and sinful in God's sight to do that. There is a worship of outward peace and harmony in the churches today that is nothing but idolatry. It seeks external peace by the sacrifice of truth and righteousness. Some will not tolerate any serious discussion or debate on doctrinal or practical issues because they fear it will mar the "peace" of the Church. Objection is also raised against submitting matters in an orderly and lawful way to the courts of the Church, on the ground that this causes controversy and disturbs the "peace" of the Church. We should realize that there is no such ideal of peace at any price in the Bible. The Bible always puts truth and righteousness first, and it never commands us to seek peace at the cost of truth or righteousness. If we were as zealous for the glory of God as we are for the external peace and harmony of the Church, unexpected blessings might be poured out upon us.

But the text we are considering certainly does mean that we are to avoid a stubborn spirit that cannot brook opposition. We are not to become dissatisfied because we cannot have our own way about everything. In a magazine there appeared a letter seeking counsel. The writer of the letter said she wanted her own way all the time, and her husband wanted his own way all the time too, and they had a problem. How they could have a happy home, and what should she do? There is no way to have the blessings of happiness and harmony and at the same time insist on having our own way all the time.

We are not to sacrifice our real principles for the sake of peace, but on the other hand we must be careful to make sure that what we call principles are not really just plain stubbornness and a selfish desire to have our own way.

Questions:

1. What verse of chapter 12 approaches a definition of meekness?
2. What terms are synonymous with meekness or related to it?
3. Why is it true that meekness is the highest kind of courage?
4. What are some of the things that Christian meekness will enable a person to do?
5. To what subtle temptation are we all subject, as suggested in 12:3?
6. What does this chapter teach about conduct under persecution?
7. How did Cyprian exemplify Christian conduct in connection with his martyrdom?
8. What verse enjoins the duty of Christian sympathy?
9. How do we know that 12:16 does not mean that peace is to be sought at the cost of truth and righteousness?
10. Why is it wrong to have a stubborn spirit, and what harm will it do?

Lesson 72

"Mind not high things, but condescend to men of low estate" (12:16). It takes a truly great person to translate these words into life and character. Abraham Lincoln, although he was president of the United States, could talk with people from the humblest walks of life without the least arrogance because of his exalted position. It takes a truly great man to do that. Someone trying hard to maintain his own dignity could not do it. He would be too self-conscious.

As Christians we are to condescend to men of low estate. After all, in God's sight we are all men of low estate. There is no respect of persons with God. The Christian who receives the grace of meekness will not be trying to maintain his own dignity. He will not have a complex that will make him difficult for others to get along with.

"Be not wise in your own conceits" (12:16). "No species of pride is more insidious or more injurious than the pride of intellect, or a fancied superiority to those around us, which leads to a contempt of their opinions, and a confident reliance upon ourselves. The temper which the gospel requires is that of a little child, docile, diffident, and humble" (Charles Hodge, *A Commentary on the Epistle to the Romans*, p. 399).

"Recompense to no man evil for evils" (12:17). A missionary was once asked some questions about heaven by a man who had heard just a little of the gospel of Christ. One question asked was whether it will be possible for us in heaven to get even with those who treated us badly while we were on earth. The missionary replied by saying that those who have their heart set on revenge will not enter heaven at all.

The desire to get even with some person is a natural evil tendency of our sinful hearts. But we should realize that this desire is wicked, and we should crucify it with the rest of our sinful lusts.

"Provide things honest in the sight of all men" (12:17). Charles Hodge comments that the translation of this clause in the King James Version is unfortunate and gives a wrong idea of the meaning. "Paul does not mean to direct us to make provision for ourselves or our families in an honest manner, which is probably the sense commonly attached to the passage by the English reader, but to act in such a manner as to command the confidence and good opinion of men" (*A Commentary on the Epistle to the Romans*, p. 400). The clause may be an allusion to Proverbs 3:4, which in the Greek version of the Old Testament is similar in language to Romans 12:17.

"If it be possible, as much as lieth in you, live peaceably with all men" (12:18). This verse recognizes by implication, that there may be times when it is not possible to maintain peace. There are times when we must fight for the defense of our country; there are times when we must contend for the truth of God (Jude 3); there are times when it would be a base betrayal not to fight against evil. We cannot always maintain peace. Sometimes it is our duty to fight. But war is always an evil. It may sometimes be a necessary evil, it may be an unavoidable evil, but we must remember that it is an evil. We do not believe in war for its own sake, and we should not believe in controversy for its own sake.

The ideal is peace—not peace at any price, but peace "if it be possible." If it be possible, this means, without the sacrifice of something more precious and important than peace. Note well that the apostle speaks of living peaceably with all men—not just with our friends and neighbors, but with all men. This includes those who hate us, those who are attacking us and trying to work against us, and those who are not beneath taking a mean, unfair advantage of us. If it is possible, we are to live at peace with them.

This is meekness, the meek courage that dares to keep the peace even at the risk of being misunderstood or regarded as cowardly. The Christian should be known as a peaceful and peace-loving person. He will never glorify war for its own sake; he will hate war and will resort to it only because of grim necessity. In his personal relationships he will always seek for peace and goodwill when it is possible to do so without acting against conscience.

"Dearly beloved, avenge not yourselves, but rather give place unto wrath: for it is written, Vengeance is mine; I will repay, saith the Lord" (12:19). Here again we have a solemn admonition not to seek vengeance. The world talks continually about vengeance. As Christians we should not think in such terms. Even a nation at war should not seek vengeance. Revenge is far from the Christian ideal and spirit. Rather, we are commanded to give place unto wrath, and leave vengeance to the Lord.

God, who is absolutely just as well as merciful, will render retribution to evildoers. He will pay them according to absolute justice. No sin will be overlooked. God will render to all according to their deeds unless they repent and seek His mercy in Christ.

"Therefore if thine enemy hunger, feed him; if he thirst, give him drink: for in so doing thou shalt heap coals of fire on his head" (12:20). This verse is taken from Proverbs 25:21–22. It must not be misunderstood. This verse does not mean that war is not to be prosecuted against public enemies, foreign or domestic. But when the

Romans 12:1–21

conflict is over, we are to seek the real welfare of those whom it was
our duty to fight and oppose.

The early Christians lived out these precepts in their daily lives. In
a world in which meekness was all but unknown, they not only preached
meek courage, but also they lived it. In a world that had lost its conviction of the seriousness of life in a cynical pessimism and despair, the
early Christians lived a life of moral purity, deep earnestness, and coura-
geous meekness. They dared to be different. They dared to challenge
the world's ideas of nobility and greatness, and they amazed the world
with the character—Christian character—which they manifested. May
we, by God's grace, follow in their train.

Questions:

1. Why does it take a truly great man to condescend to men of low
   estate?
2. What kind of pride is especially insidious, and what harm does it do?
3. How should we treat the natural tendency of our hearts to desire to
   get even with those who have wronged us?
4. What is the correct meaning of "Provide things honest in the sight
   of all men"?
5. Why does Paul say "if it be possible" in 12:18?
6. Why it is not always our duty to maintain peace?
7. With what classes of people are we to try to live at peace?
8. Who reserves the right to take vengeance?
9. What is the true teaching of 12:20?
10. What traits of character did the early Christian exemplify?

The Christian's Civil Obligations. 13:1–7
Subjection unto the Higher Powers. 13:1–2
Lesson 73

Verses 1–2 are inadequately translated in the King James Version,
because of the use of the ambiguous word "powers" for the Greek
exousiai, which properly means authorities. Power and authority are not
identical. Recently, an American general was kidnapped by communist
prisoners of war on an island off the coast of Korea. (*Editor's Note:* The

author is probably referring to Gen. Francis Dodd, who was captured on May 7, 1952, at a prison camp on Koje.) While he was in the hands of the communists, the general possessed authority but no power. The communist prisoners who perpetrated this deed, on the other hand, had power but no authority. A bandit pointing a gun at a bank teller has power but no authority. The policeman who attempts to arrest the bandit has both power and authority. The Greek word *exousia* (plural, *esouaiai*), like the English word "authority," implies something more than mere power. These two words imply power that is in some sense or within some sphere of existence recognized or sanctioned.

It has sometimes been attempted to hold that "authority" (*exousia*) always means legitimate authority in the highest sense, that is, that which God approves of, that which is in accord with the moral law of God. This attempt breaks down, however, when we examine the usage of the word *exousia* in the New Testament. For we find that this word *exousia* is used time and again of Satan and Satan's kingdom. Some instances may be cited here. In each case the English word "power" is used to translate the Greek word *exousia* that properly means "authority."

Luke 22:53, "This is your hour, and the power of darkness."

Acts 26:18, "To turn them from darkness to light, and from the power of Satan unto God."

Ephesians 2:2, "The prince of the power of the air, the spirit that now worketh in the children of disobedience."

Ephesians 6:12, "For we wrestle...against powers...against spiritual wickedness in high places."

Colossians 1:13, "The power of darkness." Colossians 2:15, "Having spoiled principalities and powers."

Revelation 13:4, "The dragon which gave power unto the beast."

Revelation 13:5, "And there was given unto him a mouth speaking great things and blasphemies; and power was given unto him to continue forty and two months."

Revelation 13:7, "And it was given unto him to make war with the saints, and to overcome them: and power was given unto him over all kindreds, and tongues, and nations."

Revelation 13:12, "And he exerciseth all the power of the first beast before him."

It is clear, then, that the Greek word for authority is not limited to authority that is in accord with the moral law of God, but is also used of evil and satanic authority.

Romans 13:1 is translated thus in the Revised Standard Version: "Let every person be subject to the governing authorities. For there is no authority except from God, and those that exist have been instituted by God." Williams' Version translates as follows: "Everybody must obey the civil authorities that are over him, for no authority exists except by God's permission; the existing authorities have been established by him."

So much for the word "powers." The Christian is commanded to be subject to the higher powers. The apostle adds that "there is no power but of God" and that "the powers that be are ordained of God." We must now consider the meaning of these statements.

God is the ultimate source of all authority. Parents would have no authority over their children and magistrates would have no authority over citizens except for authority derived from God. This is true not only of moral and legitimate authority, but even of the authority of Satan. We learn from the book of Job that Satan cannot go a hair's breadth beyond what is permitted him by God. He has no power or authority whatsoever but what is derived from God. In a certain sense, God has given power or authority to Satan. We have already seen that the New Testament speaks of the authority of Satan and Satan's kingdom. Whatever authority Satan may have can come from no other source but God. This does not imply, of course, that what

Romans 13:1–7

Satan does is pleasing to God or in harmony with God's law.

After His resurrection Jesus said to His disciples, "All authority [*power* in KJV] is given unto me in heaven and in earth" (Matt. 28:8). This is legitimate authority in the highest moral sense; it is the authority that is pleasing to God, of which God approves, and that is in harmony with God's moral law. On the other hand, Revelation 13:3 speaks of authority given unto the wild beast from the sea. This authority, though coming ultimately from God, is wicked, immoral, and contrary to God's law.

Between the authority given to God's Son, the Lord Jesus Christ, and the authority given to the beast, there exists an intermediate zone of authority that proceeds from God and is "ordained of God" in a certain sense, yet is not legitimate or pleasing to God in the highest sense. This is the authority of civil governments that exist in the world but that do not recognize and obey the Lord Jesus Christ. The secular or non-Christian civil governments of the world are certainly not "ordained of God" in the highest sense; they are not pleasing to God in the highest sense, for they do not recognize and obey God's Son as they are commanded to do in Psalm 2:10–12. On the other hand, there is obviously a vast difference between, say, the United States government as it exists today, and the kingdom of the Beast as it is pictured in Revelation 13. The United States government fails to honor Jesus Christ, yet in general it fulfills the God-ordained functions of civil government, such as maintaining law and order. In so far as it fulfills the proper functions of civil government, it is "ordained of God" and it is our duty to obey its laws. In the providence of God, it is the government that exists over us.

Some have held that in Romans 13:17, Paul was not speaking of the non-Christian governments of world history, but of an ideal Christian state that would be realized at a future time. This interpretation, however, is untenable. Paul is talking about "the powers that be." In the Greek it is "the existing powers" (*hai ousai exoushi*). This phrase, "the existing powers" cannot possibly mean "the powers which do not exist now but will come into existence at a future time." The only interpretation that does not do violence to the Greek words is that Paul was writing of the powers that were in existence at the time he wrote the epistle. He uses the present tense throughout. He commands his readers

Romans 13:1–7

to obey the existing powers, to pay taxes to them, etc. The only powers they could obey or pay taxes to were those in existence in their time.

Questions:

1. Why is Romans 13:12 inadequately translated in the King James Version?
2. What is the difference between power and authority?
3. How can it be shown that in the New Testament the word "authority" is not limited to authority that is pleasing to God?
4. What is the ultimate source of all authority?
5. How can it be shown that the authority of Satan is derived from God?
6. What kind of authority is spoken of in Matthew 28:18?
7. What kind of authority is spoken of in Revelation 13:5?
8. What kind of authority exists that is intermediate between that of Matthew 28:18 and that of Revelation 13:5?
9. In what respect is the United States government of the present day displeasing to God?
10. What Scripture passage clearly commands civil magistrates to honor the Son of God?
11. In what sense is the present United States government ordained of God?
12. How do we know that Paul's expression, "the powers that be," means the governments of Paul's day and of our own day, not an ideal Christian state to be realized in the future?

Lesson 74

We have seen that the Apostle Paul in Romans 13:1 teaches that "the existing powers (authorities)" are ordained of God. That is, in a certain sense they exist in accordance with the will of God. They exist by His permission and providence. Even though they are displeasing to God by reason of their failure to honor and serve His Son, still He permits them to exist and to function in human society.

It is clear that this passage (vs. 1–2) is applicable to men living under every form of government, monarchical, aristocratical, or democratical, in all their various modifications. Those who are in authority are to be obeyed within their sphere, no matter how or by whom appointed. It is the *ousai exousiai*, the powers that be, the de facto government, that is to be regarded as, for the time being, ordained of God. It was to Paul a matter of little importance whether the Roman emperor was appointed by the senate, the army, or the people; whether the assumption of the imperial authority by Caesar was just or unjust, or whether his successors had a legitimate claim to the throne or not. It was his object to lay down the simple principle, that magistrates are to be obeyed. The extent of this obedience is to be determined from the nature of the case. They are to be obeyed as magistrates, in the exercise of their lawful authority. When Paul commands wives to obey their husbands, they are required to obey them as husbands, not as masters, nor as kings; children are to obey their parents as parents, not as sovereigns; and so in every other case. This passage, therefore, affords a very slight foundation for the doctrine of passive obedience.

We are to obey magistrates, because they derive their authority from God. Not only is human government a divine institution, but the form in which that government exists, and the persons by whom its functions are exercised, are determined by his providence. All magistrates of whatever grade are to be regarded as acting by divine appointment; not that God designates the individuals, but it being his will that there should be magistrates, every person, who is in point of fact clothed with authority, is to be regarded as having a claim to obedience, founded on the will of God...There is no limitation to the injunction in this verse, so far as the objects of obedience are concerned, although there is as to the extent of the obedience itself. That is, we are bound to obey all that is in actual authority over us, whether their authority to be legitimate or usurped, whether they are just or unjust. The actual reigning emperor was to be obeyed by the Roman Christians, whatever they might think as to his title to the scepter. But if he transcended his authority, and required of them to worship idols, they were to obey God rather than man. This is the limitation

Romans 13:1-7

to all human authority. Whenever obedience to man is inconsistent with obedience to God, then disobedience become a duty (Charles Hodge, *A Commentary on the Epistle to the Romans*, p. 406, 407).

"Whosoever therefore resisteth the power, resisteth the ordinance of God; and they that resist shall receive to themselves damnation" (13:2). The Revised Standard Version translates this: "Therefore he who resists the authorities resists what God has appointed, and those who resist will incur judgment." The Greek word *krima*, translated "damnation" in the King James Version, properly means simply "judgment." It does not necessarily mean eternal damnation. If obedience to magistrates is a duty, then disobedience to magistrates is a sin, and those who commit the sin will receive punishment for it. The reference of verse 2 is evidently not to a punishment that will be inflicted by the civil magistrates, but to a judgment of God. For he is discussing obedience as a duty required by God and disobedience as a sin against God.

We should clearly discern that what Paul is discussing here is not the right of magistrates to rule, but the duty of Christians to obey magistrates. Whether the magistrate has a right to rule is one question; whether Christian people ought to obey whatever magistrates exist in the providence of God is another question. What are the proper limits of Christian people's obedience to wicked magistrates, is still a third question. If these different questions are not clearly distinguished, only confusion and error can result. In Romans 13:1–7, Paul is not discussing the right of magistrates to rule, nor is he discussing the proper limits of obedience to wicked magistrates. He is teaching only the simple principle that it is the duty of Christian people to obey the existing magistrates. That the magistrates may be wicked men, and that it may be God's plan to overthrow the existing government and set up a better one in its place, is perfectly true. That there are well-defined limits to the obedience that Christian people ought to render to magistrates, is also perfectly true. But what the apostle is teaching is that it is the Christian's duty to obey the existing authorities as long as, in God's providence, they continue to exist as authorities.

Romans 13:1–7

Questions:

1. What principle is Paul laying down in 13:1-2?
2. How can it be shown that 13:1-7 does not teach the doctrine of "passive obedience," that the commands of magistrates are to be obeyed without any limits?
3. When is disobedience to magistrates a Christian duty?
4. What is the true meaning of the word translated "damnation" in 13:2?
5. What kind of judgment is referred to in 13:2?
6. What three questions must be clearly distinguished if we are to understand 13:1-2 correctly?

The Functions and Powers of Civil Government. 13:3-4

Lesson 75

"For rulers are not a terror to good works, but to the evil. Wilt thou then not be afraid of the power? do that which is good, and thou shalt have praise of the same: for he is the minister of God to thee for good. But if thou do that which is evil, be afraid; for he beareth not the sword in vain; for he is the minister of God, a revenger to execute wrath upon him that doeth evil" (13:3-4).

Here Paul states an additional reason for obedience to magistrates: not only is obedience our Christian duty, but magistrates are for the purpose of restraining evil and promoting good. In these verses we find the biblical teaching on the functions of civil government. Briefly stated, the function of the civil government as established by God is to administer justice in human society.

Civil government is necessary by reason of the existence of sin. Whether there would have been such an institution as the State in human society if the human race had never fallen into sin is a debated question. It may be granted that something analogous to the State would have existed, but it would have been very different from civil government as it exists in a sinful world. For in a sinless world the use of force would have been unnecessary, and there would have been no crime or injustice to punish. In a sinless world, the State would be merely an expression of the organic unity of the human race and would exist purely for cooperative purposes, not for the restraint of evil. But in the world of sinful, fallen humanity, the State exists to restrain evil. It is one of God's ways of restraining and limiting the effects of sin in human society.

The first clear revelation in the Bible of the institution of civil government is in Genesis 9:6, "Whoso sheddeth man's blood, by man shall his blood be shed: for in the image of God made he man." This divine command that murder shall be punished by the death penalty implies the existence of a constituted government of some kind that can execute the penalty.

Throughout the Bible, we find a great deal of teaching on the subject of civil government and its functions and duties. It is unmistakably clear that the primary function of civil government is the maintaining of justice in human society.

The State is, of course, only one of the divine institutions existing in human society. There are also the family and the Church. Each of these has its own proper sphere and its own proper functions to perform. None of them may trespass on the territory of another. For the United States government to enact a law specifying requirements for ordination to the office of the gospel ministry would be to trespass on the sphere of the Church. For the State to make a law forbidding parents to teach their children religion would be to trespass on the sphere of the family. According to the Bible, there are limits to the functions of the State. It may not take over the functions of the Church and the family.

In the totalitarian states of yesterday and of today we see the full development of the evil tendency of the State, or civil government, to take over everything. The totalitarian state crowds the family and the Church into narrower and narrower bounds, while the State assumes control of more and more areas of human life. It demands that all human organizations and activities be directed toward enhancing the greatness and glory of the State. Those which do not do this may be regarded as unnecessary and therefore forbidden. Parents are compelled more and more to surrender their children to the control of the State. The Church finds its very existence made contingent upon the will of the State. Human freedom vanishes as everything passes under the control of a totalitarian, unlimited State.

In democratic countries such as the United States of America the same tendency of the State to expand its areas of activity and control exists, though to a much smaller degree than in the totalitarian countries. In democratic nations this tendency is sometimes called "statism." It is seen in the civil government assuming control over more and more of the people's life and activities. Business, agriculture, education, and many other lines of activity are more and more brought under government regulation or control. There is also the tendency of the State to carry on business enterprises in competition with its own citizens.

State regulation and control of industry, business, etc., are not necessarily wrong. They are legitimate only to the extent that they are truly necessary for the maintaining of justice. And justice, of course, must not be taken in the narrow sense of mere punishment of individual lawbreakers. Justice in human society means equity between man and man, between group and group. The State is the arbiter between a man and his neighbor, between one group of people and another group of people, to see that justice is maintained. If justice requires that some particular line of activity, such as the postal service, be a government monopoly, then the State is warranted in acting accordingly.

But the tendency for the State to overstep all bounds and take over more and more of human life is certainly wrong and contrary to God's plan as revealed in the Bible. This is clear from the fact that the family and the church, as well as the individual, also have rights and functions that God has ordained, which the State may not take over. Certainly totalitarianism and statism are contrary to the Bible teaching of the functions and purpose of the State. God did not ordain civil government to be an all-inclusive provider for all the needs of human beings, nor is the chief end of man to enhance the greatness and power of the State. The State was instituted to restrain the consequences of sin by maintaining justice in human society—justice in the truest and broadest sense.

Romans 13:1–7

Questions:

1. What additional reason does Paul state why Christians should obey magistrates?
2. How may the divinely-intended function of civil government be briefly stated?
3. Why is civil government necessary in human society?
4. Would the State as we know it have existed in a sinless world?
5. Where in the Bible is the institution of civil government first revealed?
6. What three divine institutions exist in human society?
7. Why may no one of these institutions trespass on the territory of the others?
8. What tendency reaches its fullest development in totalitarian states?
9. What is the effect of totalitarianism on the family and on the Church?
10. What becomes of human freedom under a totalitarian government?
11. What is meant by statism?
12. To what extent is government regulation or control of business, industry, etc., legitimate?
13. What is the meaning of justice in human society?
14. What does the Bible imply concerning the tendency of the State to take over more and more of human life?

Lesson 76

In Romans 13:3–4, Paul teaches that the state is to praise them that do good and to punish them that do evil. "Do that which is good, and thou shalt have praise of the same" (12:3b). Some have wondered how Paul could make such a statement about the civil government when the Roman Empire persecuted Christians unto death. The explanation is simple. Paul is speaking of the ordinary course of government, not of exceptional circumstances and conditions. The Roman Empire did not always persecute Christians. We easily tend to forget the time element that was involved. In the early period of the Christian Church, as pictured in the book of Acts, it was the Jews who persecuted Christianity while the Roman government protected

Romans 13:1–7

the Christians. There were occasional outrages on the part of Gentiles against Christians, as at Ephesus (Acts 19). But it should be noted that this riot at Ephesus was not instigated by government officials but by private parties. It was subdued and order was restored by the town clerk, a local official subordinate to the Roman Empire. He reminded the rioters that they might be held responsible by higher authorities (of the Roman Empire) for their disorderly conduct on that day. Thus we see the Roman Empire maintaining justice, law, and order in the face of an angry mob stirred up by the silversmiths of Ephesus. Paul's Roman citizenship protected him time and again from the violence of the Jews. At this early period, the Roman Empire with all its faults, maintained justice, law, and order.

Later, of course, there was a change. The Jews passed out of the picture with the destruction of Jerusalem in A.D. 70, and Rome embarked on a program of bitter persecution of Christians. When Paul wrote "Do that which is good, and thou shalt have praise of the same," he did not of course mean that no government would ever persecute Christians. Paul himself did good, yet he was beheaded by the Roman Empire. But persecution is after all the exception. As a general principle it is true that those who are orderly and law-abiding, who do good, are praised and protected by the state.

Paul teaches also, that the civil magistrate is authorized to use force for the restraint of evil and the punishment of evildoers. "He beareth not the sword in vain: for he is the minister of God, a revenger to execute wrath upon him that doeth evil" (13:4b). The use of the sword implies the death penalty. This in turn implies the power of lesser penalties in the administration of justice. If the state has the God-given authority to punish murder with death, it also has the God-given authority to punish theft, arson, or perjury with fine or imprisonment.

There is a great deal of sentiment arrayed against the death penalty today. Many oppose it, strange to say, on religious grounds. Yet it must be insisted that the death penalty for murder has the sanction of both the Old Testament and the New. Scripture not only authorizes the punishment of death for murder, but Scripture requires it. No human government is at liberty to change this requirement of God's Word. Those who oppose the death penalty on religious grounds invariably have a sentimental view of religion that does not take account of the awful reality of sin nor of the holiness and righteousness of God.

The passage of Scripture we are studying also has a bearing on the question of pacifism. Those who say that the use of force is always wrong in dealings between nations do not take account of the whole teaching of Scripture on this subject. If the civil magistrate "beareth not the sword in vain," he is empowered to use force against evil when necessary. But there is no difference in principle between the use of force to restrain evil within a nation and the use of force to restrain evil between nations. If it is right for a policeman to shoot a murderer or robber who is resisting arrest, it is also right for a nation to use armed force to protect itself or others against an aggressor nation. Those who hold that all international evil can be dealt with adequately without force do not understand the real wickedness of the human heart nor the nature of evil as it is revealed in the Bible.

Questions:

1. How could Paul say that those who do good will be praised by civil rulers, when the Roman government persecuted Christians unto death?

2. Who were the chief persecutors of Christianity in the early period of the Church, as pictured in the book of Acts?

3. What was the nature of the riot of Ephesus, and what was the connection of the Roman government with it?

4. What change in the persecution of Christianity came with the destruction of Jerusalem in A.D. 70?

5. What does Romans 13 teach about the use of force to restrain evildoers?

6. What is the teaching of Scripture on the penalty for the crime of murder? Where is this taught in the Bible?

7. What is the bearing of 13:3–4 on the question of pacifism?

8. What truths of the Bible do pacifists fail to grasp?

Romans 13:1–7

The Christian's Proper Attitude toward the Civil Government. 13:5–7

Lesson 77

"Wherefore ye must needs be subject, not only for wrath, but also for conscience sake. For for this cause pay ye tribute also: for they are God's ministers, attending continually upon this very thing" (13:5–6). The apostle here teaches that obedience to magistrates is not only a civil duty that will be enforced by the state, but that it is a religious duty, a part of our conscientious obedience to God. We are to obey the lawful commands of magistrates, not only because we have to, but also because we ought to. We are not to obey merely because of "wrath," that is, not merely because of the fear of suffering penalties, but also as a matter of conscientious devotion to God. This implies that we are to be law-abiding citizens, not only when there is some probability or danger of our being caught and punished for transgression, but also when there is no probability or danger of our being caught or punished. We are to obey the law even when we could easily break it without fear of consequences. This is the high ideal of Christian duty toward civil government that is taught in the Word of God. Where this is taken seriously, Christians will be models of law-abiding conduct. For example, a Christian should be scrupulously exact and honest in making out his income tax return, not only because the law provides penalties for dishonesty, but much more because to cheat on one's income tax is to sin against God.

God's Word requires of us that we obey not merely those laws of the state that we believe to be fair and just, but also those laws that we may believe to be unfair and unjust, as long as they are the law of the state. The individual Christian is not empowered to pick and choose among the laws of his country and decide which he should obey and which he may disobey. The Christian is to obey all the laws, even those that he regards as unfair to him. Unfortunately in the United States there have been some laws that were obviously designed to benefit one class of the population at the expense of another class; for instance the discriminatory laws of a few years ago that placed a heavy tax on the sale of oleo margarine. These laws were not designed to benefit all the people, but to protect the interests of some against others. Many Christian people objected to these laws and felt that they were unjust and unfair. But no one had a right to disregard or disobey them on that account. Those who objected had a right to work for the repeal of the laws, but as long as they were on the statute books, they had to be obeyed as a matter of Christian duty.

There is really only one exception to the principle that a Christian must always obey the laws of the state and that is that when obedience to the laws of the state would involve disobedience to the law of God, it is the Christian's duty to obey God rather than men. For example, a law (such as has existed in some countries) requiring a government license or permit to preach the gospel is null and void in the sight of God, and should be disregarded by Christian people. To comply with such a law by applying for a license to preach the gospel is to render the things of God to Caesar. We are commanded by Jesus Christ to preach the gospel, and we have no right to make His command contingent upon the permission of the state. Similarly, a law requiring people to engage in idolatrous worship should be disobeyed, as was done by Daniel's three friends. Again, a law forbidding people to change their religion is contrary to the commands of God and should be disobeyed. God commands every person in the world to become a Christian, and no civil law forbidding this can be regarded as valid.

Questions:
1.   What does the Apostle Paul teach in 13:5?
2.   What does Paul mean by the phrase "not only for wrath"?
3.   When must the Christian obey the laws of his country?
4.   How should a Christian make out his income tax return?
5.   Why should a Christian obey even those laws which he considers unjust?
6.   Under what circumstances is it our Christian duty to break the laws of the state?
7.   Give some examples of possible laws that a Christian ought not to obey.

Romans 13:1–7

8. Show from the history of Moses' parents, of Moses, of Daniel, and of the apostles, that it may be our duty to break human laws.

Lesson 78

"For they are God's ministers, attending continually upon this very thing" (13:6b). The state and its officials are properly regarded as God's servants. They serve God in fulfilling the proper functions of civil government faithfully. The country does not exist for the government, but the government for the country, and both for God. In some totalitarian countries, officials have become extremely proud and arrogant, so that even petty officials have a haughty and overbearing attitude, as if they were doing the common people a great favor just to let them exist. In totalitarian states, officials easily come to think that the country exists for them. Instead of trying to serve the public, they think the public exists to support and serve them. This is, of course, a completely upside-down view of the relation between officials and people. The government and its officials exist for the benefit of the people. They are God's servants to men for good. This is not only true in a democracy such as the United States, but it is true under any form of government, rightly considered. The Roman Empire at the time of Paul's writing this epistle was certainly not a free democracy. Yet even at that time, Paul wrote that civil rulers are God's servants for people's benefit.

Even though the civil rulers may be ungodly men who have no idea of serving God, still in God's reckoning of things they serve as His servants to accomplish some of His purposes in human society. Even in dealing with non-Christian officials in a non-Christian government, the Christian is to look at matters from God's viewpoint. He is to remember that civil government exists in human society for the restraint of evil and that even these non-Christian officials, in spite of their infidelity, are used by God for the accomplishment of this purpose. The Christian is to regard the government not merely as the government regards itself, but as the Bible regards human government, from the standpoint of God's purpose in human society.

"Render therefore to all their dues: tribute to whom tribute is due; custom to whom custom; fear to whom fear; honour to whom honour"

Romans 13:1–7

(13:7). Since civil government is an institution of God for the benefit of human society, it follows that we must do our duty toward it. This involves not merely obeying its laws, but also positive support both financial and by our influence. Here "tribute" means ordinary taxes, as on land or property; "custom" means duty levied on merchandise. "Fear" (*phobos*) and "honor" (*time*) are essentially the same, differing only in degree. "Fear" means proper respect for superiors; "honor" means a proper esteem for our equals in human society.

Questions:

1. What is the place of the state and its officials in relation to God?
2. Does the country exist for the government or the government for the country?
3. For whom do both the country and the government exist?
4. What attitude on the part of public officials is common in totalitarian countries?
5. Why should the Christian regard even non-Christian rulers as servants of God?
6. Besides obeying the laws, what duties do we owe to the government?
7. What is meant by "tribute" and "custom"?
8. What is the difference between "fear" and "honor"?

Lesson 79

Before leaving the discussion of Romans 13:1–7, the bearing of this passage on the Covenanter principle of political dissent should be considered. That principle is set forth in the Covenant of 1871 in the following sentence:

> We will pray and labor for the peace and welfare of our country, and for its reformation by a constitutional recognition of God as the source of all power, of Jesus Christ as the Ruler of Nations, of the Holy Scriptures as the supreme rule, and of the true Christian religion; and we will continue to refuse to incorporate by any act, with the political body, until this blessed reformation has been secured (Sec. 3).

Romans 13:1–7

In compliance with this pledge of the Covenant of 1871, members of the Reformed Presbyterian Church of North America consider themselves bound to refrain from such political acts as voting and holding office, where an unqualified oath to support and defend the Constitution of the United States is involved. (For the use of the "Explanatory Declaration," see *Minutes of Synod*, 1939, p. 105, and subsequent years; 1951, pp. 138–9; 1952, pp. 139–44).

This Covenanter position of political dissent, which we believe to be scriptural, came to be held as a matter of church principle as a result of the experiences and conflicts of the Covenanters of Scotland in the 17th Century. The student is referred to the *Scottish Covenanters*.

This principle is based on the Mediatorial Kingship of Jesus Christ over the nations. By this we mean that Christ is not only king of our own personal lives and head of the Church, but also Lord of heaven and earth, and that everything, including the government of every country in the world, ought to be in obedience to Christ. The nations of the world should recognize and honor Him as King of kings and Lord of lords (Matt. 28:18; Eph. 1:20–21; Phil. 2:9–11).

The United States of America ought to recognize Christ, but as a matter of fact it does not recognize Him. The highest source of authority recognized by the United States Constitution is "the people." This amounts to putting the people in the place of God as the source of political authority by representing the people as the highest power. As the Constitution recognizes no authority higher than "the people," it ignores both God and His Son Jesus Christ.

We cannot conscientiously swear an oath to "support and defend" the Constitution in its present form, because we cannot conscientiously swear to support and defend what we believe to be wrong. We hold that it is a sin for the Constitution to ignore the Lord Jesus Christ. If we were to swear to support and defend the Constitution, we would then become guilty of complicity in that sin. The only way we can keep clear of the guilt of this sin is to dissent from the Constitution as it stands today. (A modified form of oath may properly be used.)

We believe that Christians should not hold political office under the present Constitution of the United States, because the person

Romans 13:1–7

who takes the oath of office must swear to support and defend the Constitution in its existing form, which leaves God and Christ out.

We also believe that Christians should not vote in political elections under the Constitution in its present form, because everyone who votes accepts the Constitution under which the election is held. The men who are elected must also take the oath of office, pledging themselves to support the Constitution as the voter's representatives. It is not right to ask another person to do something that we will not do ourselves because we believe it to be wrong.

This principle of political dissent makes the Reformed Presbyterian Church very unpopular, but our aim is not to seek popularity. We are only seeking to serve God and follow Christ faithfully and consistently. We want our Savior to say to us, "Well done, good and faithful servant." If we are reproached and called unpatriotic because we do not vote or hold political office, we should reply that we are seeking our country's true welfare, and also that our religious duty to God cannot be subordinated to patriotic loyalty to our country (Acts 5:29).[1]

Coming now to the bearing of Romans 13:1–7 on this subject of political dissent, two errors must be avoided. In the first place, there are some who say that Romans 13:1–7 contradicts our position of political dissent and requires us to vote and hold office if elected, under the present Constitution of the United States. Since we are commanded to be subject to the powers that be, it is argued it must be our duty to vote and to hold office if elected.

This argument sounds plausible, but it is not valid, for it is based on confused thinking. It confuses the duty of citizens with the functions of rulers. To obey the laws, to pay taxes, to "be subject unto the higher powers"—these are the duty of citizens. These matters pertain to the civil realm. They are civil matters.

To hold office or to vote for others to hold office on the other hand, is not a civil matter. It is a political matter. The man who holds office is not being "subject unto the higher powers"—he himself is one of the higher powers. The man who votes for another to hold political office is not being "subject unto the higher powers"—he himself is one of the higher powers. The voter and officeholder are not subject to the government—they *are* the government. In a democracy, such as the United States of America, every person who votes is a ruler; every voter is part of the government. It is the voters who determine the character, policies, and actions of the government. Voting is a political function—a function of rulers.

God's Word commands that "every soul be subject unto the higher powers," but this by no means implies that it is the duty of the Christian to become one of the higher powers by voting or holding office. If there are substantial reasons why the Christians should not vote or hold office, then it is the Christian's duty to refrain from these political acts.

The second error that must be avoided, in considering the bearing of Romans 13:1–7 on the Covenanter position of political dissent, is the view that this passage of Scripture does not apply to Christians of the present day, but only to those living under an ideal Christian state to be realized at some future time. The argument of those holding this view is that Paul could not command Christians to be subject to an immoral government that fails to give due recognition to God and His Christ. Since Romans 13:1–7 clearly commands subjection to government, it is held that the apostle's meaning must be that Christians are to be subject to such Christian governments as may come to exist. We have already noted the impossibility of this interpretation (see Lesson 74). Paul is speaking of the existing powers (*hai ousai exousiai*, present participle), which can only mean the powers in existence at the time he wrote the epistle. We may repeat part of the last paragraph of Lesson 74 here: Paul is not discussing the right of magistrates to rule, nor is he discussing the proper limits of obedience to wicked magistrates. He is teaching only the simple principle that it is the duty of Christian people to obey the existing magistrates. That the magistrates may be wicked men, and that it may be God's plan to overthrow the existing government and set up a better one in its place, is perfectly true. That there are well-defined limits to the obedience that Christian people ought to render to magistrates, is also perfectly true. But what the apostle is teaching is that it is the Christian's duty to obey the existing authorities as long as, in God's providence, they continue to exist as authorities.

For a further study of this subject, the reader is referred to a booklet entitled *The Responsibility of the Christian in Government,* by Professor John Murray, of Westminster Theological Seminary. This booklet can be obtained on request to The Christian Amendment Movement. (*Editor's Note:* In 2012, this booklet was not available.)

Questions:

1. What principle is set forth in Section 3 of the Reformed Presbyterian Covenant of 1871?
2. How did this position come to be held as a matter of church principle?
3. On what truth of the Bible is the principle of political dissent based?
4. What duty do the nations of the world owe to Jesus Christ?
5. What is the highest source of authority recognized by the Constitution of the United States?
6. Why can we not conscientiously swear an oath to support and defend the Constitution in its present form?
7. Why can we not conscientiously vote or hold office under the Constitution in its present form?
8. What should we reply when we are charged with lack of patriotism because of our position of political dissent?
9. How can we answer those who claim that Romans 13:1–7 implies that it is our duty to vote and to hold office if elected?
10. Explain the distinction between civil matters and political matters.
11. Why are voting and holding office not civil duties?
12. Who are the real "higher powers" in a democracy?
13. What is the literal meaning of the phrase "the powers that be"?
14. How can it be shown that Paul in 13:1–7 is not referring to subjection to a future ideal Christian state, but to the government existing when he wrote the epistle?
15. What booklet published by the Christian Amendment Movement provides a further study of this subject?

Romans 13:1–7

The Christian's Social Obligations

Obligations in Human Society to Be Discharged. 13:8

Lesson 80

"Owe no man any thing, but to love one another: for he that loveth another hath fulfilled the law" (13:8). The apostle here teaches that it is the Christian's duty to discharge all his social obligations with the exception of love, a debt that can never be paid off.

Some have regarded this verse as forbidding the Christian to incur debts or borrow anything. This idea, however, is not contained in the text. It only commands that debts must be duly paid; we must not continue to owe them. It is true, of course, that this implies that we are not to incur debts when we have no certain prospect of repaying them. But the ordinary use of credit in business or personal affairs is not here forbidden, and it is sanctioned in other parts of the Bible. "The command, however, is 'Acquit yourselves of all obligations, tribute, custom, fear, honor, or whatever else you may owe, but remember that the debt of love is still unpaid, and must remain so'" (Charles Hodge, *A Commentary on the Epistle to the Romans*, p. 409). Even when all debts of money and service have been discharged, there remains a continuing debt of love to our neighbor.

The Obligation of Love to Our Neighbor. 13:9

"For this, Thou shalt not commit adultery, Thou shalt not kill, Thou shalt not steal, Thou shalt not bear false witness, Thou shalt not covet; and if there be any other commandment, it is briefly comprehended in this saying, namely, Thou shalt love thy neighbor as thyself" (13:9). This verse confirms the truth stated in verse 8, and at the same time reminds us that love for our neighbor is not to be a mere emotion or feeling of goodwill toward him, but is to be expressed in our actual conduct toward our neighbor. Of course these commandments are not to be understood only in the negative sense of "thou shalt not." Rightly understood, they also imply a divine command to practice the contrary virtues. We are not only to refrain from doing harm to our neighbor; we are to do him positive good.

"Love worketh no ill to his neighbor: therefore love is the fulfilling of the law" (13:10).

Romans 13:8–10

That is, as love delights in the happiness of its object, it effectually
prevents us from injuring those we love, and, consequently, leads us
to fulfill all the law requires, because the law requires nothing which
is not conducive to the best interests of our fellowmen. He, therefore, who loves his neighbor with the same sincerity that he loves
himself, and consequently treats him as he would wish, under similar
circumstances, to be treated by him, will fulfill all that the law enjoins;
hence the whole law is comprehended in this one command, Thou
shalt love thy neighbor as thyself (Charles Hodge, *A Commentary on
the Epistle to the Romans,* p. 410).

The whole law, that is, in so far as it concerns our duty to our
neighbor, which is the subject under discussion here. There is also the
first table of the law, concerning our duty directly to God, but that is
not the subject here being discussed.

The Christian Duty to Live a Holy Life. 13:11–14

"And that, knowing the time, that now it is high time to awake
out of sleep: for now is our salvation nearer than when we believed.
The night is far spent, the day is at hand" (13:11–12a). We are here
taught that it is high time to awake out of sleep. Here "sleep" is a
figure for a condition of spiritual indifference or sluggishness. Those
who are absorbed in worldly pleasures and business and have little or
no concern about God, their souls and eternity are living in a state of
spiritual sleep. Even true Christians may often, for a period of time,
fall into such a condition of spiritual slumber, so that they are not
active and alert concerning the things of God.

The person who is spiritually asleep should wake up. Paul says
that it is high time to wake up. As a reason, he adds that now our
salvation is nearer than when we first became Christians. Here "salvation" may be taken as meaning our complete deliverance from sin at
the time of our death, or it may be taken as referring to our complete
deliverance from sin and all its consequences at the resurrection day.
Or it may include both of these ideas under the general meaning of
"complete deliverance from sin." Whether we think of the day of our

own going to be with the Lord or of the day of His coming to earth again, it is true that the great deliverance is nearer to each of us than it was when we first believed on Jesus Christ. We have already covered some ground, we have already passed some time, once for all, and are that much nearer to our complete deliverance from sin. This thought should be an encouragement to every Christian to keep wide awake in the Christian life.

There are in the churches today many members who are spiritually asleep in the sense spoken of by Paul in this passage. Whether these members have been born again of the Spirit, only God knows with certainty. But church members who cannot find a reference in the Bible, who cannot pray except to repeat a formal little prayer from memory, who attend divine worship only occasionally and sit daydreaming and gazing around the room when they do attend, and who cannot tell whether David lived before or after John the Baptist—such church members are spiritually asleep, and it is high time for them to wake up. Probably many such nominal church members are not saved; some may be born again, but in a state of long-arrested spiritual development. It is high time for them to awake out of their sleep. The existence of such members is one of the causes of the present powerlessness and ineffectiveness of the churches.

Questions:

1. What is meant by the command to "owe no man anything"?
2. How do we know that this verse does not forbid the ordinary use of credit in business or personal affairs?
3. What kind of debts should a Christian not incur?
4. What debt of the Christians can never be fully discharged?
5. How can our duty to our neighbor be summarized?
6. Why is love the fulfilling of the law concerning our neighbor?
7. Besides our duty to our neighbor, what duty do we have?
8. What is meant by "sleep" in 13:11?
9. Why is it high time to awake out of sleep?
10. What is meant by "salvation" in 13:11?
11. What is the effect of sleeping members on the churches today?

Romans 13:11–14

Lesson 81

"The night is far spent, the day is at hand" (13:12a). Here we must consider what is meant by "the night" and "the day." One suggested meaning is that "the night" means the period of time when it was possible for the Jews to persecute Christianity, while "the day" means the new era that would dawn after the destruction of Jerusalem in A.D. 70. But this is too narrow a meaning to suit the context. Moreover, the cessation of Jewish persecution did not bring real relief to the early Christians; rather, it was followed by the much longer and more severe persecution by the Roman Empire. Another suggested meaning is that "the night" means the present life of every Christian, while "the day" means the life eternal that will soon dawn upon each one. This interpretation is more plausible and may be the correct one, or it may be part of the correct one. The third possible meaning is that "the night" means the history of this world since man's fall into sin, while "the day" means the new world of eternity that will be absolutely free from sin. In view of the usage of the terms "the day," "the day of the Lord," "that day," in Paul's epistles and elsewhere in the Bible, this third interpretation would seem to be the correct one. The statement, "The night is far spent, the day is at hand," would then mean: "The age-long history of this sinful world is nearing its conclusion, and the new age of eternity is about to dawn." This, of course, does not imply anything concerning the actual time of the Lord's second coming. Of that day and hour no man knows; Paul did not know it any more than we do today; it has not been revealed to men. What is meant is not the "nearness" of the second coming in terms of calendar time, but its "nearness" in terms of the biblical philosophy of history.

According to the biblical view of history, when Jesus Christ was crucified and rose from the dead, the end of the world began. Everything before that was preparatory for Calvary; everything after that is part of the final winding up and conclusion of this world's affairs in preparation for eternity. Compare 1 Peter 1:19–20; Hebrews 1:1–2; Hebrews 9:26; 1 Corinthians 10:11. All these texts teach that the apostles and early Christians were living in the last days as God counts the days. In our common life of today, we go by calendar time. But if we understand

Romans 13:11–14

the Scriptures, we must try to grasp their philosophy of history and see how God reckons time. According to the Bible's view of history, "the end of all things is at hand" (1 Pet. 4:7), the second coming of Christ is "near," and He is coming "quickly," because His coming is the next great redemptive event in God's program. Moreover, it is the final redemptive event in God's program of the ages. It looms above and ahead of every one of us as the tremendous miracle that God will surely bring to pass, which will bring the history of this world to a sudden stop.

It is the evening of history. The long, weary at-hand day of the world's sin, suffering, and struggle is almost over. We do not know how many years, whether many or few, remain before the Lord shall come on the clouds of heaven, nor does it matter. The world will not continue indefinitely on its present course; it is hastening on to its consummation. Time will issue into eternity, labor into rest, faith into sight, and struggle into victory. But it is even later than the evening of history; the evening and the long night have almost passed and a new day is about to break—the morning of eternity. This world and its concerns are "passing away" (1 Cor. 7:31; 1 John 2:17); the world of eternity, in which all things shall be made new, is "at hand." The serious Christian should live daily in the sobering consciousness of this truth. He should live as one who knows that "the day is at hand."

Our reluctance to think of the dawn of eternity as "at hand" is one sign of our failure to grasp the Bible's philosophy of history. Many Christians, instead of eagerly anticipating the Lord's second coming, rather tend to hope that it will be deferred until some of their own plans and programs can be carried to completion. We hope that the end of human history will not come now, when we have important undertakings in process. Such an attitude is really contrary to the biblical view of history. God's thoughts are higher than our thoughts, and His ways than our ways. When we let our plans, projects and programs—even those that concern the kingdom of God—steal the spotlight of our hope away from God's great redemptive event, the "dawn of the day," we no longer have a truly religious attitude, and we are no longer truly walking by faith. God's next great redemptive act should take precedence over

Romans 13:11–14

all our activities. We must always do all our planning and working in the light of eternity. Eternity is absolutely important; time is only relatively important. When we regard time as more important than eternity we are no longer on biblical ground.

Questions:

1. What possible meanings have been suggested for "the night" and "the day" in 13:12?
2. How do we know that "the night" does not mean the period of Jewish persecution of Christianity?
3. What meaning of "the night" and "the day" is the most probable one and why?
4. Does the statement, "The day is at hand," imply that the second coming of Christ is near in terms of calendar years?
5. According to the Bible, when did the end of the world begin?
6. Why is it true that "the end of all things is at hand"?
7. What do 1 Corinthians 7:31 and 1 John 2:17 teach concerning the present world?
8. What should be daily in the mind of every Christian?
9. Is it right to hope that the second coming of Christ will be deferred until our own plans and activities can be completed?
10. What can be said about the importance of time and the importance of eternity?
11. Where should our ultimate Christian hope be fixed?
12. How should we always do our planning and working?

Lesson 82

"Let us therefore cast off the works of darkness, and let us put on the armor of light" (13:12). The Christian's belief that the dawn of eternity is at hand is not merely a theoretical matter. It is to be a practical matter. If "the night is far spent" and, "the day is at hand," think what a godly, earnest, sober life every one of us ought to live! Think what a desperately serious matter life is! If we really believe that "the day is at hand," how can we drift through life with our main thinking and attention riveted to our own ambitions and pleasures?

Romans 13:11–14

Paul here urges the truth that "the day is at hand" as a strong reason why the Christian should live a serious, earnest, and holy life. "Night" and "darkness" are associated with sin and sorrow; "day" and "light" with righteousness and joy. The evils of this present life will soon be past, and the morning of eternal joy will soon dawn. Since this is true, we should cast off the works of darkness and put on the armor of light. We should renounce everything we need to be ashamed of, everything that has to be concealed and kept secret. At the same time, we should clothe ourselves with what is suitable to the light of day. The idea of taking off and putting on clothing is suggested by the Greek words used. "We are to cast off one set of garments and put on another. The clothes which belong to the night are to be cast aside, and we are to array ourselves in those suited to the day" (Charles Hodge, *A Commentary on the Epistle to the Romans,* p. 412).

"Let us walk honestly, as in the day; not in rioting and drunkenness, not in chambering and wantonness, not in strife and envying" (13:13). This continues the thought of the preceding verse, specifying what kinds of works are to be put off by the Christian, as the next verse states what is to be put on in place thereof. The word here translated "honestly" does not mean exactly what we mean today by "honestly"; in modern English the word "honest" has come to mean "truthful" or "upright in dealings concerning property." But as used here the word "honestly" means "becomingly," "properly," "legitimately."

Next, Paul specifies three kinds of sins to be cast aside, and he uses two words for each kind: (1) rioting and drunkenness; (2) chambering and wantonness; (3) strife and envying. The first of these classes is sins of intemperance; the second, sins of impurity; and the third, sins of discord. It will be observed what a wide range of sins is spoken of here. Some people's sins are of one kind and some of another. Some who would never be involved in rioting and drunkenness may be guilty of sins of impurity that the apostle calls "chambering and wantonness."

Others, who would not commit sins of either of these classes, may be keeping the Church of God in constant problems and troubles by their sins of discord—their sins of strife and envying. What is the real profit, in God's sight, of being clear of sins of intemperance and impurity, if we are constantly provoking God and disheartening His people by our endless sins of discord?

"But put ye on the Lord Jesus Christ, and make not provision for the flesh, to fulfill the lusts thereof" (13:14). Here we come to the positive side of the matter. The Christian is not merely to put off the works of darkness; he must also put on the armor of light. He is not only to cast off intemperance, impurity and discord; he is also to put on, in their place, the Lord Jesus Christ.

To "put on the Lord Jesus Christ" means to have such an intimate union with Christ that people will see Christ living in us. It means to be so filled with His Spirit and so controlled by His will that our lives will manifest Him to the world around us.

"And make not provision for the flesh, to fulfill the lusts thereof." In this sentence, some have understood "the flesh" to mean "the body." But it is unlikely that that is true meaning. This expression, "the flesh," must include not only the sins of intemperance and impurity that the apostle has just mentioned, but also those of strife and envying. But strife and envying are sins of the mind, not of the body. Elsewhere in Paul's epistles he uses the term "the flesh" to mean everything that is corrupt in the human personality, that is, to mean our sinful nature. See Galatians 5:19-21, where Paul lists seventeen "works of the flesh," of which ten are sins of the mind rather than of the body: idolatry, witchcraft, hatred, variance, emulations, wrath, strife, seditions, heresies, envyings. If these sins of the mind are included in "the works of the flesh," then "the flesh," as Paul uses the term, cannot mean simply the human body; it must mean our whole corrupt or sinful nature. The true meaning of Paul's admonition, then, is "'Do not indulge the desires of your corrupt nature'" (Charles Hodge, *A Commentary on the Epistle to the Romans*, p. 413). The Christian has these desires; he has not yet been wholly freed of them; they constitute a burden and a temptation to him; but he is not to yield to them; he is not to allow them to dictate the course of his life. They are to be subdued, kept under control, crucified.

Romans 13:11-14

Questions:

1. What practical lessons are to be drawn from the truth that "the day is at hand"?
2. What are associated with "night" and "darkness," and what with "day" and "light"?
3. What idea is suggested by the words "cast off" and "put on"?
4. What is the meaning of "honestly" in 13:13, and how does this differ from the common meaning of the word today?
5. What three classes of sins are we commanded to cast off?
6. Which of these classes of sins constitutes the greatest temptation to Christian people at the present day?
7. What does it mean to "put on the Lord Jesus Christ"?
8. What is meant by "the flesh" in 13:14?
9. How can it be shown that "the flesh" does not mean simply the human body?
10. How is the Christian to deal with his sinful desires?

The Christian's Duty toward Weak Brethren. 14:1–13
Lesson 83

In this section of the epistle, Paul sets forth the treatment to be accorded weak brethren, who have doubts and scruples about various matters that are not really, in themselves, moral questions at all. We cannot tell with certainty just who the weak brethren were whom Paul discusses in this chapter. Various theories have been proposed, but it seems very probable that some of these weak brethren, at least, were Jewish Christians who not only continued to observe the precepts of the ceremonial law about foods, but who even went far beyond the requirements of the law in their effort to avoid possible violations of that law. Many of the early Christians had a Jewish background. Even after becoming Christians, some of them continued to feel that they ought to obey various precepts of the Old Testament ceremonial law, such as the regulations about clean and unclean foods and the ordinances about special festival days. This apparently created a problem in the churches, and specifically in the church at Rome. If this problem were not carefully handled, serious consequences might result.

Romans 14:1–13

In order to understand this section of the epistle, we must realize that those who felt they must obey the precepts of the ceremonial law were wrong. Paul does not treat this as a matter about which both sides were right nor even as a matter about which both sides were partly right. He treats it as a matter about which one side was right and the other side was wrong, and he is concerned that those who were right should be considerate in their treatment of those who were wrong.

The Apostolic Council in Acts chapter 15 settled for all time the question of whether the ceremonial law is binding on Christians by decreeing that it is not. Paul in Romans 14, regards those who felt they ought to obey the ceremonial regulations as the exception in the Church. He is concerned that these weak brethren be treated with love, sympathy, and forbearance. At the same time, he makes it clear that these brethren's special ideas are wrong. They are the result of being "weak in the faith." Since the weak brother's ideas are wrong, they must not be made into a creed or rule to be imposed upon the church as a whole.

"Him that is weak in the faith receive ye, but not to doubtful disputations" (14:1). This verse is not very clear in the King James Version. The American Revision (1901) is clearer: "But him that is weak in faith receive ye, yet not for decision of scruples." The Revised Standard Version (1948) reads: "As for the man who is weak in faith, welcome him, but not for disputes over opinions." Williams' translation reads: "Make it your practice to receive into full Christian fellowship people who are overscrupulous, but not to criticize their views." Here Paul states that weak and scrupulous brethren are to be received into Christian fellowship in spite of their weak faith.

> Faith here means, persuasion of the truth; a man may have a strong persuasion as to certain truths, and a very weak one as to others. Some of the early Christians were, no doubt, fully convinced that Jesus was the Messiah, and yet felt great doubts whether the distinction between clean and unclean meats was entirely done away. This was certainly a great defect of Christian character, and rose from the want of an intelligent and firm conviction of the gratuitous nature

of justification, and of the spirituality of the gospel. Since, however, this weakness was not inconsistent with sincere devotion to Christ, such persons were to be received (Charles Hodge, *A Commentary on the Epistle to the Romans*, p. 412).

"But not to doubtful disputations" ("not for decision of scruples," ARV). Two Greek words are involved here. The first, *diakrisels*, means the faculty of discrimination, judgment, or decision. The other Greek word, *dialogismoi*, means scruples, worries or doubts in a person's thinking. In view of the context (14:2), Hodge gives the meaning of verse 1 as, "Him that is weak in faith, take to yourselves as a Christian brother, treat him kindly, not presuming to sit in judgment on the opinions of your brethren" (*A Commentary on the Epistle to the Romans*, p. 417).

"For one believeth that he may eat all things: another, who is weak, eateth herbs" (14:2). One man has confidence, as far as religious principle is concerned, to eat anything; another man, who is weak in his faith limits himself to a vegetarian diet. This does not mean, of course, that all foods are equally wholesome, nor that the normal Christian eats just anything, regardless of considerations of health and hygiene. Paul is not discussing the wholesomeness or harmfulness of foods; he is only discussing the matter of religious scruples about foods. As far as religious principle is concerned, the normal Christian is convinced that he may eat anything; no kind of food is to be refused on religious grounds as religiously defiling or unclean.

The Old Testament ceremonial law did not require a vegetarian diet. It did not forbid the eating of all kinds of flesh. Certain kinds were permitted, while other kinds were forbidden. But the scrupulous Jews, especially when living in a pagan environment, sometimes became afraid to eat any kind of flesh, or indeed any prepared food, lest they defile themselves by eating something forbidden in the law. They would eat only that which they could personally trace from its natural condition to its entrance into their own mouth, and so restricted themselves to a diet of herbs, that is, to a vegetarian diet. To make sure of avoiding all unclean meats and all foods that might have been offered to idols, they limited themselves to vegetables.

Romans 14:1–13

Questions:

1. What new subject does Paul take up in this section of the epistle?
2. What was the religious background of many of the early Christians?
3. How did many Jewish Christians feel about the precepts of the ceremonial law?
4. Were these Jewish Christians right or wrong in their attitude toward the precepts of the ceremonial law?
5. What great question was settled for all time at the Apostolic Council in Acts chapter 15?
6. How does Paul in Romans 14 regard those who felt that they should obey the ceremonial law?
7. Why are the weak brother's ideas not to be made into a creed or rule to be imposed on the church as a whole?
8. How is 14:1 translated in the American Revised Version?
9. What duty is taught in 14:1?
10. What is the meaning of the second part of verse 1?
11. Does 14:2 mean that a Christian can eat anything he feels like eating regardless of considerations of health?
12. What is the true meaning of the statement, "One believeth that he may eat all things"?
13. What is meant by "eateth herbs" in 14:2?
14. Did the Old Testament ceremonial law require a vegetarian diet?
15. Why did some scrupulous Jews limit themselves to a vegetarian diet?

Lesson 84

"Let not him that eateth despise him that eateth not; and let not him which eateth not judge him that eateth: for God hath received him" (14:3). "There is mutual forbearance to be exercised in relation to this subject. The strong are not to despise the weak as superstitious and imbecile; nor the weak to condemn those who disregard their scruples. Points of indifference are not to be allowed to disturb the harmony of Christian fellowship" (Charles Hodge, *A Commentary on the Epistle to the Romans*, p. 418). There were these two classes of people in the churches: One was strong and correct in faith, the other was weak and erroneous in faith. Yet both classes existed, and Paul commands mutual forbearance. "For

Romans 14:1–13

God hath received him"—that is, God has received the weak brother to His kingdom—in spite of the weak brother's errors. The exhortation to forbearance applies to both classes, the strong and the weak. "The Jewish converts were perhaps quite as much disposed to condemn the Gentile Christians, as the latter were to despise the Christian Jews; Paul therefore frames his admonition so as to reach both classes. It appears, however, from the first verse, and from the whole context, that the Gentiles were principally intended" (Charles Hodge, *A Commentary on the Epistle to the Romans*, p. 419).

While the particular question of eating meats, which Paul is discussing, is not an important issue in most Christian circles today, still the principle that the apostle enunciates remains valid for all time. Divergent views about things that are indifferent in themselves—things that are not required nor forbidden by scripture—are not to be allowed to disrupt Christian fellowship. It is easy to think of modern examples. The use of communion tokens is indifferent in itself. So is the question of whether the Sabbath morning service is to be held at 11 o'clock or at some other hour. So is the particular method or system of Bible reading to be used in the practice of family worship. So, also, is the frequency of observance of the Lord's supper and the number and time and place of the preparatory services. We could easily think of many more examples. Matters of this kind, which do not involve a clear-cut issue of right and wrong, are not to be allowed to destroy Christian unity and fellowship. The strong are not to despise the weak and scrupulous, nor are the weak and scrupulous to sit in judgment on the strong and condemn them.

"Who art thou that judgest another man's servant? to his own master he standeth or falleth" (14:4a). God has not appointed the strong Christian, who is correct in his faith, to pronounce judgment on the weak Christian, who is erroneous and overscrupulous in his faith. After all, the weak brother is a Christian; therefore he belongs to Christ. He is Christ's servant, so Christ is the one who has the right to pronounce judgment on him.

As in Paul's day, so at the present day, there are many self-appointed judges in the churches who do not hesitate to pronounce a condemning judgment on some of the opinions, scruples, or practices of their

Christian brethren. In our day, we have not only the strong judging the weak, but also the opposite situation, where the weak pronounce judgment on the strong. Those who have scruples about some particular matter often are not satisfied with having their scruples sympathetically tolerated by the majority. They demand that the whole church conform to their scruples and constantly disturb the peace of the church by carrying on a propaganda along that line. All such, whether strong or weak, should pay heed to the apostle's question: "Who art thou that judgest another man's servant?"

"To his own master he standeth or falleth" (14:4b). It is the Lord Jesus Christ who has jurisdiction over him, not some self-appointed critic in the church. "Yea, he shall be holden up: for God is able to make him stand" (14:4c). God is able to save the weak Christian to the uttermost, in spite of his weak and erroneous faith. Here is an added reason for forbearance toward our Christian brethren. No matter how weak a man may be in his Christian faith, still if he is a Christian, we may not disregard this and treat him as if he were a non-Christian, an outsider. "The brethren are not responsible to each other, or the church, or their scruples. God is the Lord of the conscience. To him they must answer. Before him they stand or fall" (Charles Hodge, *A Commentary on the Epistle to the Romans*, p. 420).

Questions:

1. What is meant by "mutual forbearance"?
2. What wrong attitude toward the weak Christian must the strong Christian avoid?
3. What wrong attitude or action toward the strong Christian must the weak Christian avoid?
4. On what ground does Paul command mutual forbearance in 14:3?
5. Is the question of eating meat an important question in most Christian circles today?
6. What permanent principle can be discerned in 14:3?
7. What is meant by "things which are indifferent in themselves"?
8. Give some present-day examples of practices that are indifferent in themselves.
9. Whose servant is the weak Christian?

Romans 14:1–13

10. Who has the right to pronounce judgment on Christian people?
11. Is the warning of 14:4 still necessary at the present day?
12. How do weak Christians sometimes pronounce judgment on strong Christians?
13. Why may we never treat a Christian as a non-Christian or outsider?
14. Who is the Lord of the conscience?
15. What is the meaning of the statement, "God is able to make him stand"?

Lesson 85

"One man esteemeth one day above another: another esteemeth every day alike. Let every man be fully persuaded in his own mind" (14:5). The reference here is apparently to the various festival days of the Old Testament ceremonial law. Just as that law distinguished between clean and unclean meats, so it distinguished between days. Evidently, some Jewish Christians felt that they should continue to observe these days in a special manner. This belief was wrong; it was a weakness. But as it was not a vital matter, it was not to be allowed to disrupt the unity of the church.

This verse has been used by some people as a proof that the observance of the Sabbath day is not a Christian duty, but an optional matter to be left to every individual's preference. This is, however, a very strained interpretation of the verse.

> It is obvious from the context and from such parallel passages as Gal. 4:10....and Col. 2:16....that Paul has reference to the Jewish festivals, and therefore his language cannot properly be applied to the Christian Sabbath. The sentiment of the passage is this: "One man observes the Jewish festivals, another man does not." Such we know was the fact in the apostolic church, even among those who agreed in the observance of the first day of the week (Charles Hodge, *A Commentary on the Epistle to the Romans*, p. 420).

"Let every man be fully persuaded in his own mind" (14:5b). Here Paul states the principle that one man's conscience cannot control another man's actions. Each one must act according to his own conscience and avoid doing what he believes to be wrong. It is strange but true, that even at the present day there are people in the churches who seem to think that God has made their conscientious convictions the standard for other people's conduct. By their attitude, if not in spoken words, they say, "You must do this because I believe it is your duty," or "You must abstain from this practice because I feel it is wrong." It is evident that this same spirit existed in the church at Rome in Paul's day, and that to oppose this wrong tendency, the apostle wrote, "Let every man be fully persuaded in his own mind." Of course, a person's conscience may err and need correction. But it is to be corrected by the Word of God, not by the conscience of some fellow Christian. We cannot solve our moral problems by making some other person's convictions our guide; we must be convinced in our own conscience of what God requires of us. This idea that some church members have, that God has somehow appointed them as keeper of their brethren's conscience, is a great evil, and also (if they could only realize it!) a great presumption and sign of egotism.

"He that regardeth the day, regardeth it unto the Lord; and he that regardeth not the day, to the Lord he doth not regard it. He that eateth, eateth to the Lord, for he giveth God thanks; and he that eateth not, to the Lord he eateth not, and giveth God thanks" (14:6). This does not mean that the person who observes the Jewish festival days and the person who does not observe them are equally right, nor that the person who eats flesh and the person who eats only vegetables are equally right. On the contrary, the one class is right and the other wrong; the one class is "strong" and the other "weak." In this verse, Paul merely states that both classes of Christians are acting conscientiously from motives of devotion to God. It is not a case of the one class faithfully serving God, while the other class wantonly commits sin. Both classes are acting as they conscientiously believe they ought to act, from motives of devotion and thankfulness to God. The strong Christian, who disregards the observance of the Jewish festival days and who eats common food without religious scruples, shows by the fact that he gives God thanks that he is acting conscientiously. Clearly, a person could not give God thanks for something that he believed to be sinful or forbidden to use. In the same way, the brother who observes days and abstains from meat, weak and mistaken though he be, still believes that he is acting according to the will of God, for he, too, gives God thanks.

"For none of us liveth to himself, and no man dieth to himself" (14:7). That is, no real Christian will regard himself as his own master nor hold that he is free to do as he pleases. He will realize that both in his life and death, his chief end is to glorify God. He will acknowledge that he is not his own, but has been bought with a price, even the precious blood of Christ. Therefore he is Christ's servant, to live according to the will of God and for God's glory. Paul clearly means to imply that all who accept this principle are to be treated as true Christians, whatever errors or weaknesses they may have about interpretation of the will of God concerning particular matters. Those who recognize and admit that they belong wholly to Christ, having no authority over their own life or death, are to be received as our Christian brethren.

Questions:

1. What kind of "days" does Paul mean in 14:5?
2. What was the attitude of some Jewish Christians toward these special days?
3. Why were differences about observance of days not to be allowed to disrupt Christian fellowship?
4. How can it be shown that 14:5 does not refer to the Christian Sabbath?
5. What principle is involved in Paul's statement: "Let every man be fully persuaded in his own mind"?
6. How is this principle violated by some people today?
7. How is an erring conscience to be corrected?
8. Has God appointed some people as keepers of other people's conscience?
9. How do we know that 14:6 does not mean that both the classes mentioned were equally right?
10. What is the real meaning of 14:6?
11. In 14:6, what is shown by the fact that both classes of Christians give God thanks?

Romans 14:1–13

12. What truth is taught by 14:7?

13. Why is a Christian not free to do as he pleases?

14. Who are to be received as our Christian brethren?

Lesson 86

"For whether we live, we live unto the Lord; and whether we die, we die unto the Lord: whether we live therefore, or die, we are the Lord's" (14:8). This verse repeats the thought of verse 7 in a more explicit form. The word "Lord" in this verse clearly means Jesus Christ, as is evident from the context of verse 9.

The devotion specified in verse 8 is that which the creature owes to the Creator, and since this devotion is to be rendered to the Lord (Jesus Christ), it proves the deity of Christ—it proves that Christ is God. Note how the terms "God" and "Lord" are used interchangeably in verses 6–9. This forms a strong evidence for the deity of Jesus Christ.

"For to this end Christ both died, and rose, and revived, that he might be Lord both of the dead and living" (14:9). In this verse, the word "revived" is a poor translation of the Greek, because in our common English speech the word "revive" is used of the recovery of someone who was only in danger of death, but not actually dead. The Greek verb here translated "revived" really means simply "lived"; the word "again" that is added in some versions is not found in the Greek text.

By His death, Christ purchased His people for His own. By His resurrection, He attained to His present glory as King and Lord of all. His present exaltation and glory and dominion are represented in the Bible as the reward of His sufferings and death. (Compare Phil. 2:8–9.) Here in Romans 14:9, Paul teaches that Christ's authority as Savior and King is not limited to this present world. It extends to the life after death, for He is the Lord both of the dead and the living.

We should realize how different this idea of Christ is from the common view of Jesus in liberal Protestant circles today. The common liberal view denies that Jesus is truly God, but holds that He was a great and good man. He is regarded as a teacher and example rather than as Redeemer and Lord. But the Christ that Paul believed in was and is Lord both of the dead and the living. He is truly God.

Romans 14:1–13

"But why dost thou judge thy brother? or why dost thou set at nought thy brother? for we shall all stand before the judgment seat of Christ" (14:10). (In this verse, the most reliable Greek manuscripts read "the judgment seat of God" instead of "the judgment seat of Christ," and for this reason the American Standard Version (1901), the Revised Standard Version (1946), and most other modern versions read "God" instead of "Christ." As Christ is God, and Paul has been using the terms "God" and "Lord" (Christ) interchangeably in this chapter, this difference in the Greek manuscripts is not important.)

> If a man is our brother, if God has received him, if he acts from a sincere desire to do the divine will, he should not be condemned, though he may think certain things right, which we think wrong; nor should he be despised if he trammels his conscience with unnecessary scruples. The former of these clauses relates to scrupulous Jewish Christians; the latter to the Gentile converts. The last member of the verse applies to both classes. As we are all to stand before the judgment seat of Christ, as he is our sole and final judge, we should not usurp his prerogative, or presume to condemn those whom he has received (Charles Hodge, *A Commentary on the Epistle to the Romans*, p. 422).

"For it is written. As I live, saith the Lord, every knee shall bow to me, and every tongue shall confess to God" (14:11). This is a quotation from Isaiah 45:23. It will be noted that Paul does not quote the exact words of Isaiah; he varies them somewhat while giving the same sense. This is to be explained by the fact that the Holy Spirit is the real author of both Isaiah and Romans. When an author is quoting from his own writings, he is at liberty to make any changes he may see fit, which would not be proper in quoting the writings of another. Romans 14:11 is just as truly inspired as Isaiah 45:23, the Holy Spirit being the real source of both. "As I live" gives the correct meaning of the phrase "I have sworn by myself," which occurs in Isaiah 45:23. "The apostle evidently considers the recognition of the authority of Christ as being tantamount to submission to God, and he applies without hesitation the declaration of the Old Testament in relation to the universal dominion of Jehovah, in proof of the Redeemer's sovereignty. In Paul's estimation, therefore, Jesus Christ was God" (Charles Hodge, *A Commentary on the Epistle to the Romans*, p. 422).

Verse eleven confirms the truth stated in the last part of verse ten: "We shall all stand before the judgment seat of Christ." The Old Testament prediction, "To me every knee shall bow," confirms this. Here, as so often in his epistles, Paul takes pains to show the harmony of his doctrine with that of the Old Testament Scriptures. What the apostle was teaching was not some strange novelty, but truth fully in harmony with and revealed in the Old Testament.

"So then every one of us shall give account of himself to God" (14:12). This verse summarizes the truth of individual personal responsibility to God that Paul has been teaching. Every one of us shall give account of himself to God. We are not to give account of our brother, but of ourselves. As each Christian is to render his own account to God, we can see how presumptuous and improper it is for some to undertake to pass judgment on others.

"Let us not therefore judge one another any more: but judge this rather, that no man put a stumblingblock or an occasions to fall in his brother's way" (14:13). "Let us not judge one another any more," is an admonition that Christian people of the present day, as of Paul's day, would do well to heed. Almost every church has some people who are living in constant violation of this divine precept. They may be the strictest of the strict about many other matters, but about this precept of Romans 14:13 they are completely neglectful. With sharp tongues they pass censorious judgment on other Christians whom God has not placed under their jurisdiction. This is one of the great sins that mar the peace, holiness, and edification of the Church.

Questions:

1. Who is meant by the word "Lord" in 14:8?
2. What kind of devotion is specified in 14:8?
3. What does 14:8 show concerning Jesus Christ?
4. What inference can be drawn from Paul's interchangeable usage of the terms "God" and "Lord" in 14:6–9?
5. Why is the word "revived" in 14:9 a poor translation?

Romans 14:1–13

6. What is the literal meaning of the word translated "revived" in 14:9?
7. What is the relation between Christ's sufferings and His exaltation?
8. Besides this present world, what does Christ's authority include according to 14:9?
9. How does the Christ of Paul differ from the Jesus of liberal Protestantism?
10. What variation exists among Greek manuscripts in the wording of 14:10?
11. From what Old Testament book is 14:11 quoted?
12. How can we explain the fact that Paul did not quote the exact words of the Old Testament?
13. What is shown by Paul's frequent quoting of the Old Testament?
14. Of what shall every Christian give account to God?
15. Why is the admonition of 14:13, "Let us not judge one another any more," suited to the churches of the present day?

How the Strong in Faith Should Use Their Christian Liberty. 14:13–23

Lesson 87

"But judge this rather, that no man put a stumblingblock or an occasion to fall in his brother's way" (14:13b). The apostle now proceeds to a new topic, though it is one related to that which he has just been discussing. This new topic is how the strong in faith ought to use their Christian liberty. It is not enough that a Christian be "fully persuaded in his own mind" that certain conduct is right. Something more needs to be considered, namely, the effect of one's conduct on others. A Christian must not only be fully persuaded that what he proposes to do is right, but he must also take care that he does not injure some brother by what he does. So Paul now takes up the question of Christian liberty and how it is to be exercised.

We take verse 13b as addressed to the strong Christian, who is admonished not to put a "stumblingblock" in the way of the weak Christian. We must therefore consider, what is the "stumblingblock" to which Paul refers. "Stumblingblock" and "occasion to fall" clearly mean practically the same thing: some object or obstacle in one's path that occasions stumbling and falling. But to what in the Christian's conduct do these terms refer?

In order to understand Paul's meaning, we must realize what kind of weakness it was that characterized the weak brethren about whom he is speaking in this chapter. This particular point has often been missed in discussions of this chapter and applications of it to modern problems. It has often been alleged that the weakness of the weak brethren was a readiness to indulge in sinful practices, such as intemperance. According to this idea, the weak brethren were weak because they were ready victims of temptation and found it very difficult to let certain things alone. In other words, their weakness was a weakness of indulgence or excess.

But this idea will not fit Paul's statements in this chapter at all. The weak brethren he is describing were not people who were ready at the slightest suggestion to fall into intemperance. They were not guilty of any intemperance whatever. On the contrary, they were total abstainers from certain things. They would not eat flesh at all, but confined themselves to a diet of vegetables. The weakness of the weak brethren, therefore, was not the weakness of a tendency to indulgence or intemperance; on the contrary, it was the weakness of religious scruples about the use of certain things. It was their *not* eating flesh that was their weakness. Those who were strong were able to eat it without any scruples; the weak had scruples about it.

What, then, is the stumblingblock that the strong are not to place in the way of the weak? In view of what follows (verses 14–23) it is evident that the stumblingblock to which the apostle refers is some action on the part of the strong Christian that encourages or prompts the weak Christian to do what he, the weak Christian, believes to be wrong. The "falling" on the part of the weak Christian is not the sin of falling into intemperance of any kind; it is the sin of daring to do something about which he is not "fully persuaded in his own mind," something about which he still has doubts or scruples. (Note verse 23, "And he that doubt-eth is damned if he eat, because he eateth not of faith: for whatsoever is not of faith is sin." Here it is clear that the sin by which the weak brother falls is not the sin of eating, but the sin of eating in spite of his doubts, the sin of eating without faith that it was right for him to do so.)

Romans 14:13–23

We shall study verses 14–23 in more detail in the following lessons. We have only glanced at them to learn the true meaning of the "stumblingblock" and the "fall" mentioned in verse 13. It has been shown that the "fall" of the weak Christian was not a fall into intemperance or sinful indulgence of any kind, but a daring to do something about which he had doubts—something that was not wrong in itself and about which the strong Christian did not have any scruples. The "stumblingblock" was an action on the part of the strong Christian that would encourage the weak Christian to do something about which he had scruples.

Questions:

1. What new topic does Paul take up at this point in the epistle?
2. Why is it not enough that a Christian be "fully persuaded in his own mind" that something he intends to do is right?
3. Is the second part of 14:13 addressed to the strong Christian or to the weak Christian?
4. Was the weakness of the weak brethren in this chapter a tendency to intemperance?
5. What was the real nature of the weakness of the weak brethren? What verses in the chapter show this?
6. What is the "stumblingblock" to which Paul refers?
7. What was the "falling" that the weak brother was in danger of?
8. What does 14:13 show about the nature of the sin the weak brother was in danger of committing?
9. Why should Christians avoid putting stumblingblocks in the way of weak brethren?
10. Does the strong Christian have a right to act as he pleases regardless of spiritual danger to the weak brother?

Lesson 88

"I know, and am persuaded by the Lord Jesus, that there is nothing unclean of itself: but to him that esteemeth anything to be unclean, to him it is unclean" (14:14). "The distinction between clean and unclean meats is no longer valid. So far the Gentile converts are right. But they should remember that those who consider the law of the Old Testament on this subject as still binding, cannot, with a good conscience, disregard it. The strong should not, therefore, do anything which would be likely to lead such persons to violate their own sense of duty" (Charles Hodge, *A Commentary on the Epistle to the Romans*, p. 423).

"I know, and am persuaded by the Lord Jesus." This means that what Paul is about to say is not a conclusion which he has arrived at by his own reasonings, but something that he knows by divine revelation. There is a possible allusion here to the words of Christ in Mark 7:14–23. "There is nothing from without a man, that entering into him can defile him." Our Lord is speaking here, of course, of religious defilement. Paul, in Romans 14:14, is speaking of religious uncleanness. The old distinctions and prohibitions of unclean foods, in the ceremonial law of the Old Testament, have been abrogated; they are no longer binding. Nothing is therefore to be regarded as "unclean of itself." Compare Acts 10:9–15, where the same teaching is given. Although the truth is that nothing is "unclean of itself," still there were members in the Church of Rome in Paul's day who did not grasp this simple truth. In their thinking, there were many things that were "unclean of themselves." And so the apostle adds, "To him that esteemeth anything to be unclean, to him it is unclean" (14:14b). That is, the Christian who still believes that something is "unclean" cannot safely partake of it. To him it is still unclean, because in eating of it he would be doing something that he believes to be sinful; thus he would violate his own conscience. It is a sin to act against one's conscience, even when that conscience is ignorant and misguided. It is not a sin to eat "unclean" meats, but it is a sin to do anything that a person believes to be forbidden by God. The sin is not the sin of eating meats, but the sin of disregarding one's conscience.

"But if thy brother be grieved with thy meat, now walkest thou not charitably" (14:15a). The phrase "now walkest thou not charitably," is better translated "thou walkest no longer in love," as in the American Standard Version (1901). If the strong Christian insists on his freedom to eat any kind of meat under all circumstances and in any company, then he is in danger of having a bad effect on the weak brother. And to insist on one's own rights and freedom, while disregarding the spiritual condition of others, is contrary to the duty of Christian love. The strong Christian must therefore take care that he does not by his use of meat injure the weak brother, who is burdened by scruples about meat.

"Destroy not him with thy meat, for whom Christ died" (14:15b). Here we see the soul-destroying nature of any disregard of conscience. How could the strong Christian's eating of meat destroy the weak Christian? Meat itself is of course not harmful, nor is it religiously defiling. But the strong Christian must be on his guard lest by his eating of meat he destroys the weak Christian. Destroy is, clearly, a very strong word; it is much stronger than merely to injure, offend, or grieve the weak brother. The word "destroy" involves the destructive nature and tendency of sin, its tendency to destroy the soul and alienate it from God. Of course, it is perfectly true that God is able to make the weak Christian stand (14:4) and that those whom God has foreknown and predestinated shall certainly be glorified (8:30). These things are true, certainly, but Paul is not speaking of the keeping power of God; he is speaking of the destructive tendency of sin. When he uses the word "destroy" in Romans 14:15, he refers to what sin will do if it is not restrained or removed by the grace of God.

Sin, apart from God's grace, will certainly destroy the sinner eternally. The weak Christian commits a sin when he acts contrary to his own (misguided) conscience. The strong Christian should therefore stop and think; he should remember what a terribly dangerous, destructive thing sin is before he uses his own freedom in any way that might lead the weak Christian to commit a sin.

While the question of clean and unclean meats is no longer a debated question in most Christian circles, the principle that is embodied in verse 15 remains permanently valid. The strong Christian must never use his freedom in such a way as to destroy the weak Christian; he must never use his freedom in such a way as to lead the weak Christian to do something that the weak Christian believes to be wrong. There are many applications of this principle at the present day. Many people today, as in Paul's day, have conscientious scruples about various matters that are not really forbidden by God. For example, there are sincere Christians who believe that life insurance is sinful. The great majority of Christian people hold that life insurance is morally legitimate. They have a right to take out life insurance, but they must not try to persuade or encourage those who have scruples about it to do so, lest these "weak brethren" act against their conscience and so fall victim to the destructive power of sin.

Questions:

1. What does Paul mean by saying, "I know, and am persuaded by the Lord Jesus"?
2. What passage in the gospels may be alluded to in 14:14? What is the teaching of Christ in that gospel passage?
3. What kind of uncleanness was Christ speaking about in Mark 7?
4. What kind of uncleanness was Paul speaking of in 14:14?
5. What incident in the book of Acts teaches that nothing is unclean of itself? Where it is found?
6. What truth did some members of the church at Rome fail to grasp?
7. What is the meaning of the statement, "To him that esteemeth anything to be unclean, to him it is unclean"?
8. Why is it a sin to act against one's conscience, even when that conscience is misguided?
9. What is the true meaning of "not charitably" in 14:15?
10. Why may not the strong Christian insist on his freedom to eat any kind of meat at any time and place?
11. What is the effect of any disregard of conscience?
12. How could the strong Christian's eating of meats "destroy" the weak Christian?
13. Does 14:15 imply that a saved Christian can fall away from God and perish in his sins? If not, how can we explain the use of the word "destroy" in this verse?
14. What will sin certainly do apart from God's grace?
15. What should the strong Christian realize before exercising his own freedom?
16. What permanently valid principle is embodied in 14:15?
17. What applications does this principle have today?

Romans 14:13–23

Lesson 89

"Let not then your good be evil spoken of" (14:16). This is presumably addressed to the strong Christian, and the "good" is the strong Christian's freedom to eat meats. The meaning then is, "Do not use your liberty, which is good, in such a way that it will occasion evil, and bring censure upon you."

> "For the kingdom of God is not meat and drink; but righteousness, and peace, and joy in the Holy Ghost" (14:17). "This is a new reason for forbearance. No principle of duty is sacrificed; nothing essential to religion is disregarded, for religion does not consist in external observances, but in the inward graces of the Spirit.... There is no sin in abstaining from certain meats, and therefore, if the good of others requires this abstinence, we are bound to exercise it" (Charles Hodge, *A Commentary on the Epistle to the Romans*, p. 424).

While in the Old Testament under the ceremonial law there was an emphasis on external things, Christianity is different. The kingdom of God—the reign of God over His people—does not consist is such external matters as meat and drink, but in the spiritual things: righteousness, peace, and joy in the Holy Spirit.

> These words are to be taken in their Scriptural sense. Paul does not mean to say, that Christianity consists in morality; that the man who is just, peaceful and cheerful, is a true Christian. This would be to contradict the whole argument of this epistle. The righteousness, peace, and joy intended, are those of which the Holy Spirit is the author. Righteousness is that which enables us to stand before God, because it satisfies the demands of the law. It is the righteousness of faith, both objective and subjective; peace is the concord between God and the soul, between reason and conscience, between the heart and our fellow-men. And the joy is the joy of salvation; that joy which only those who are in the fellowship of the Holy Ghost can ever experience (Charles Hodge, *A Commentary on the Epistle to the Romans*, p. 425).

"For he that in these things serveth Christ is acceptable to God, and approved of men" (14:18). This verse confirms the preceding one.

Romans 14:13–23

By "these things," the apostle clearly means "righteousness, and peace, and joy in the Holy Ghost." Where these exist, differences about meat and drinks should not be permitted to disrupt the bonds of Christian fellowship. The person who has the genuine "righteousness, and peace, and joy in the Holy Ghost" is not only acceptable to God (who is the author and giver of these spiritual graces), but is also "approved of men." This does not mean that the faithful, spiritual Christian will always be "approved of men," nor that he will ever be approved of all men. Sometimes the faithful, spiritual Christian will find himself in a small and despised minority, while the majority applauds more popular and man-pleasing teachings. The faithful Christian will always find some people opposed to him and his principles. Moreover he will nearly always find some within the visible church who are opposed to him and his principles. But eventually the faithful Christian will be "approved of men." His testimony for truth and right may be ignored and it may be despised, but the day will come when God will bring forth his righteousness as the light and his judgment as the noonday. It has happened many a time in the history of the Christian Church that those who faithfully witnessed to the truth of God were reproached and persecuted for a long time, but eventually recognized as having stood for truth and righteousness.

"Let us therefore follow after the things which make for peace, and things wherewith one may edify another" (14:19). Here Paul places before the Christians at Rome the obligation to seek peace and mutual edification. Clearly this was much more important than the right of the strong Christians to exercise their liberty on any and all occasions. "Since Christian love, the example of Christ, the comparative insignificance of the matters in dispute, the honor of the truth, the nature of real religion, all conspire to urge us to mutual forbearance, let us endeavor to promote peace and mutual edification" (Charles Hodge, *A Commentary on the Epistle to the Romans*, p. 425).

Questions:
1. Is 14:16 addressed to the strong Christian or to the weak Christian?
2. What is the "good" mentioned in 14:16?

Romans 14:13–23

3. What is the meaning of 14:16?
4. What does Paul mean by saying, "The kingdom of God is not meat and drink"?
5. What kind of righteousness is meant in 14:17?
6. What kind of peace is meant in 14:17?
7. What kind of joy is meant in 14:17?
8. What does the apostle mean by "these things" in 14:18?
9. Why is the person who has genuine righteousness, peace, and joy in the Holy Spirit acceptable to God?
10. Will the faithful Christian always be "approved of men"?
11. Can the faithful Christian expect that all in the visible church will approve of him?
12. What experience have many in the history of the Church had?
13. What obligation is placed before Christians in 14:19?
14. Why should Christians seek for peace and mutual edification?
15. What is more important than the exercise of the strong Christian's liberty?

Lesson 90

"For meat destroy not the work of God" (14:20a). This clause is somewhat similar to Romans 14:15b. There is some question as to the precise meaning of the phrase "the work of God." Some take this as meaning "a Christian brother," or "the Christian status of a brother." But perhaps the most probable meaning is the edification mentioned at the close of the preceding verse. "Thus it will mean, thy fellow Christian, as a plant of God's planting, a building of God's raising" (Henry Alford, *The New Testament for English Readers*, p. 962). Obviously there is no comparison of importance between this "work of God" and the strong Christian's right to eat certain kinds of foods. The one so far transcends the other in importance that no truly spiritual Christian should have any hesitation whatever as to how to act when the weak brother's edification is at stake.

"All things indeed are pure; but it is evil for that man who eateth with offense" (14:20b). Here "all things" evidently means "all kinds of food," "all articles of diet." The Greek word for "pure" may also be translated "clean" (*kathara*). The statement that "all things are pure" means, of course, pure from the religious point of view, that is, not involving spiritual or religious contamination or defilement. We must remember that Paul is not discussing the wholesomeness of foods, but the matter of religious scruples about certain foods. Obviously not all kinds of food are pure from the hygienic standpoint. A loaf of bread may have arsenic in it and be not only injurious but lethal. Paul, however, is not discussing such matters. He is discussing how the strong Christian should exercise his Christian liberty, or refrain from exercising it, in view of the religious scruples of the weak Christian concerning the use of certain articles of diet. We are not interpreting the apostle correctly if we introduce into his statements modern hygienic considerations about the wholesomeness or harmfulness of particular kinds of food or drink.

"But it is evil for that man who eateth with offense" (14:20c). The Greek word here translated "evil" is *kskon*, which means not merely harmful or injurious, but sinful, that is, morally evil. The question about this clause is, does "that man who eateth with offense" mean the strong Christian who eats in such a way as to lead the weak brother to offend, or does it mean the weak brother who eats when his conscience does not approve? Both of these interpretations have been advocated, but the former is the one that has commonly been held and is probably the correct one. According to this view, the clause is a warning to the strong Christian to avoid eating in such a way as to cause his weak brother to offend, that is, to do what his conscience disapproves. In favor of this interpretation is the fact that the sentence stands between two others, both of which are addressed to the strong Christian who is in danger of offending the weak brother (Henry Alford, *The New Testament for English Readers*, p. 962).

"It is good neither to eat flesh, nor to drink wine, nor any thing whereby thy brother stumbleth, or is offended, or is made weak" (14:21).

That is, abstaining from flesh, wine, or anything else which is injurious to our brethren, is right, i.e., morally obligatory;...The words stumbleth, offended, made weak, do not, in this connection, differ much from each other. Calvin supposes they differ in force, the first being stronger than the second, and the second than the third. The sense then is, "We should abstain from every thing whereby our brother is cast down, or even offended, or in the slightest degree injured." This, however, is urging the terms beyond their natural import. It is very common with the apostle to use several nearly synonymous words for the sake of expressing one idea strongly (Charles Hodge, *A Commentary on the Epistle to the Romans*, p. 426).

It will be noted that in our English Bible, the words "any thing" in this verse are printed in italics, showing that they are not found in the Greek text, but have been added by the translators for the sake of making the meaning clear in English. The Greek text may be literally translated: "Good [it is] not to eat flesh nor to drink wine nor in which thy brother stumbleth, or is offended, or is made weak." (The most important Greek manuscripts omit the words "or is offended, or is made weak.") As will be seen from the above literal translation, something must be supplied to complete the meaning of this verse. Various suggestions have been made. Alford supplies the words "to do any thing," making the verse read: "It is good not to eat meats nor to drink wine, nor (to do any thing) in which thy brother stumbles, or is offended, or is weak" (*The New Testament for English Readers*, p. 962). Another suggested form is: "It is good neither to eat flesh nor to drink wine nor (to drink anything) in which thy brother stumbleth." Charles Hodge prefers the form suggested by Alford. So understood, the verse asserts that we should do nothing that injures others.

We have already noted that the weakness of the weak brethren in this chapter is not the weakness of a tendency to indulgence or intemperance, but the weakness of religious scruple that induced the weak brethren to refrain absolutely from the use of certain things that the strong Christians knew they were free to use. Inasmuch as 14:21 occurs in this context and is a part of this discussion of a specific subject (how the strong in faith should use their Christian liberty), this verse must be understood as dealing with matters concerning which the weak brethren had religious scruples. Out of consideration for the weak brethren, the strong ought to be willing to forgo the exercise of their liberty insofar

Romans 14:13–23

as the spiritual interests of the weak brethren require this. It is not of the essence of Christian liberty that it must be exercised in the sight of men. Scripture teaches, rather, that it is to be exercised in the sight of God and that God holds the Christian responsible for his use or abuse of this freedom.

Questions:

1. What is the probable meaning of the phrase "the work of God" in 14:20a?
2. What is the relative importance of "the work of God" and the Christian's right to eat certain foods?
3. What is meant by "all things" in 14:20b?
4. What does Paul mean by saying that, "all things are pure"?
5. In 14:20 is Paul speaking of the harmfulness or wholesomeness of foods from the hygienic standpoint?
6 What is the meaning of the word translated "evil" in 14:20?
7. What problem exists as to the interpretation of the phrase, "that man who eateth with offense" in 14:20?
8. What is the probable reference of the phrase "that man who eateth with offense"? What argument can be given to support this view?
9. Why are the words "any thing" printed in italics in 14:21?
10. What suggestions have been offered as to the words to be supplied to complete the grammar of 14:21?
11. What form probably sets forth most correctly the complete thought of verse 21?
12. What was Alford's opinion as to the meaning of the expression, "stumbleth, or is offended, or is made weak"?
13. What was Charles Hodge's opinion of the same matter?
14. What is the teaching of the verse according to Charles Hodge?
15. What personal sacrifice should strong Christians to be willing to make for the sake of the spiritual interests of their weaker brethren?
16. Who will hold the Christian responsible for his use or abuse of his freedom?

Romans 14:13–23

Lesson 91

"Hast thou faith? have it to thyself before God" (14:22).

Paul presents in this verse, more distinctly than he had before done, the idea that he required no concession of principle or renunciation of truth. He did not wish them to believe a thing to be sinful which was not sinful, or to trammel their own consciences with the scruples of their weaker brethren. He simply required them to use their liberty in a considerate and charitable manner. He, therefore, here says, 'Hast thou faith? (i.e., a firm persuasion, e.g., of the lawfulness of all kinds of meat) it is well, do not renounce it, but retain it and use it piously, as in the sight of God' (Charles Hodge, *A Commentary on the Epistle to the Romans*, p. 427).

"Have it to thyself" (14:22). This clause involves, first of all, an admonition to retain our faith, that is, our conviction of the lawfulness of those matters concerning which the weak brethren had scruples. The strong Christian is to "have" his faith—he is not to renounce it and accept in exchange the scruples of the weak. Secondly, this clause, "have it to thyself," teaches that the strong Christian is not to insist on exercising his conviction publicly; he is not to make an issue of it before weak brethren who cannot imitate his conduct without committing the sin of disregarding their own conscientious scruples. The strong Christian can "have" his faith, his convictions, as a matter of principle, without insisting on exercising them to the spiritual harm of the weak brethren.

"Before God" (14:22). This means "in God's presence" or "in God's sight." "As God sees and recognizes it, it need not be exhibited before men. It is to be cherished in our hearts, and used in a manner acceptable to God. Being right in itself, it is to be [used] piously, and not ostentatiously or injuriously paraded and employed" (Charles Hodge, *A Commentary on the Epistle to the Romans*, p. 427).

"Happy is he that condemneth not himself in that thing which he alloweth" (14:22b). A clear conscience is a great blessing, and the man who has a clear conscience is a happy man. The man who does not allow himself to do something of which he secretly disapproves will have a clear conscience. Since a clear conscience is a source of happiness, the "faith" spoken of in the first part of verse 22, to which the strong Christians at Rome had attained, was a valuable possession and not to be surrendered or renounced. "It is a blessed thing to have no scruples (the strong in faith is in a situation to be envied) about things in which we allow ourselves" (Henry Alford, *The New Testament for English Readers*, p. 963).

"And he that doubteth is damned if he eat, because he eateth not of faith: for whatsoever is not of faith is sin" (14:23).

> That is, however sure a man may be that what he does is right, he cannot expect others to act on his faith. If a man thinks a thing to be wrong, to him it is wrong. He, therefore, who is uncertain whether God has commanded him to abstain from certain meats, and who notwithstanding indulges in them, evidently sins; he brings himself under condemnation. Because whatsoever is not of faith is sin; i.e., whatever we do which we are not certain is right, to us is wrong (Charles Hodge, *A Commentary on the Epistle to the Romans*, p. 427).

Note the similarity of the teaching here with that of Romans 14:14.

The word "damned" should be translated "condemned" as in the American Standard Version (1901). It does not necessarily imply eternal damnation, but "convicted" or "found guilty of sin" in that particular matter. Obviously a weak Christian might eat meat concerning which he had scruples, thus committing the sin of violating his conscience, and still he might repent of this sin and be forgiven. Paul by no means implies that the person who, doubtingly, partakes of meat, is beyond the hope of salvation.

"For whatsoever is not of faith is sin" (14:23b). Henry Alford interprets this: "all that is not of (grounded in, and therefore consonant with) faith (the great element in which the Christian lives and moves and desires and hopes), is sin" (*The New Testament for English Readers*, p. 963). Whatever a Christian does that does not proceed from the principle of faith is sin.

Questions:

1.   What idea does the apostle present in the first part of verse 22?

Romans 14:13–23

2. What is meant by "faith" in 14:22?

3. What is included in the admonition, "Have it to thyself," verse 22?

4. What is involved in the phrase "before God," 14:22?

5. What is the meaning of the statement: "Happy is he that conde-meth not himself in the thing which he alloweth"?

6. What great source of happiness is referred to in 14:22?

7. What is meant by the statement: "He that doubteth is damned if he eat"?

8. How should the word "damned" be translated? What does it involve in this verse?

9. What is meant by the statement: "Whatsoever is not of faith is sin"?

10. How can a Christian be sure that what he is doing is right?

It Is the Duty of All Christians to Imitate the Unselfishness of Christ. 15:1–13

Lesson 92

In the first section of Chapter 15, the apostle enforces the doctrine taught in the preceding Chapter by appropriate arguments. In reality, Chapter 15 continues the thought of Chapter 14 without any break.

"We then that are strong ought to bear the infirmities of the weak, and not to please ourselves" (15:1). This verse forms a summary or conclusion drawn from the whole argument of Chapter 14. The strong Christian, who is not troubled by doubts or scruples about the lawfulness of various kinds of food, is right, whereas the weak Christian is wrong. This does not imply that the strong Christian can do as he pleases regardless of the effect of his actions on the weak brother. As far as the lawfulness of foods is concerned, the strong Christian has a right to eat anything (14:14), but for him to insist upon exercising this right regardless of the bad effect on the weak brother would be a selfish disregard of the obligation of Christian love. Something that is legitimate in itself may be improper under certain circumstances by reason of the effect on the weak brother.

The strong Christian, therefore, is to "bear the infirmities of the weak," rather than selfishly insisting on doing as he pleases. That is,

Christian self-denial may be called for, and if it is called for, it should be willingly and cheerfully accorded. What real profit is there in being right in questions about foods if a person is wrong in his attitude toward his Christian brethren? In comparison with the spiritual welfare of the weak brother, the liberty to eat specific foods fades into insignificance.

Yet it must be remembered here, as all through this section of the epistle, that the weak brother is mistaken and his ideas are wrong. They are weaknesses, they are infirmities; that is, they result from an incomplete grasp of the principles of Christianity. The tragedy is that the weak brethren so often regard their own weakness as their strength and not only retain it with conviction as a matter of religious principle, but also attempt to enforce their scruples upon the whole church, including the strong Christians whose conscience is not burdened by such scruples about things that are not really moral questions at all. We may repeat here a few sentences from Lesson 83 of this series: Paul in Romans 14 regards those who felt they ought to obey the ceremonial regulations as the exception in the Church. He is concerned that these weak brethren be treated with love, sympathy, and forbearance. But at the same time he makes it clear that these brethren's special ideas are wrong, they are the result of being "weak in the faith." Since the weak brother's ideas are wrong, they must not be made into a creed or rule to be imposed upon the church as a whole.

"Let every one of us please his neighbor for his good to edification" (15:2). Instead of insisting on pleasing ourselves, we should aim to please others. "We are not simply to ask what is right in itself, or what is agreeable, but also what is benevolent and pleasing to our brethren. The object which we should have in view in accommodating ourselves to others, however is their good" (Charles Hodge, *A Commentary on the Epistle to the Romans*, p. 432). "For his good to edification" means that we are to seek to act so that our brethren will be edified (built up as Christians) and so truly be benefited. We are not merely to try to please our brethren; what we are to seek is their true welfare, their religious or spiritual benefit.

There may be circumstances, of course, when the true edification of our brethren will be promoted by opposing their mistaken ideas rather than by yielding to their scruples. We find an example of this kind in Paul's own conduct with reference to his fellow apostle, Peter, as recorded in Galatians 2:11–16. It is interesting to note that it concerns a matter closely related to the question of clean and unclean foods discussed in Romans 14. Peter first ate freely with Gentile Christians; then later "he withdrew and separated himself, fearing them which were of the circumcision." Under these circumstances Paul did not say: "Peter is a weak brother on this question of eating with Gentiles; to avoid offending him, I will refrain from eating with Gentiles during this visit to Antioch; I will not even mention the embarrassing subject." Paul did not say anything like that. On the contrary, he tells us that he "withstood him [Peter] to the face, because he was to be blamed" (Gal. 2:11). But certainly we are to understand that Paul's conduct on this occasion was motivated not by selfishness but by Christian love and a sincere desire to be spiritually helpful to Peter and the others who were of the same opinion. In this particular case, not only the interests of truth but the spiritual welfare of Peter himself required open opposition and rebuke. In other cases, Paul was willing unselfishly to deny himself for the spiritual benefit of others.

Our action must always be unselfish, our motive must always be love, for our brother's edification, but the particular course of conduct to be used in seeking his edification must be decided according to circumstances.

Questions:

1. What is the general subject of 15:1–13?
2. Of what argument is 15:1 the conclusion?
3. What kind of conduct, on the part of the strong Christian, would amount to a selfish disregard of the obligation of Christian love?
4. What is the relative importance of the strong Christian's liberty to eat foods and the weak Christian's spiritual welfare?
5. What tragedy is often involved in the attitude of weak Christians toward the kind of problems Paul has been discussing?
6. Why may not the special ideas of the weak brethren be made into a creed or rule for the whole church?

Romans 15:1–13

7. What is the meaning of the word "edification"?

8. What is the difference between pleasing our neighbor and pleasing our neighbor for his good to edification?

9. Will the edification of weak brethren always be promoted by refraining from conduct concerning which they have scruples?

10. What lesson is taught by Paul's rebuking Peter as recorded in Galatians 2:11–16?

Lesson 93

"For even Christ pleased not himself; but, as it is written, The reproaches of them that reproached thee fell on me" (15:3). Jesus Christ is the perfect example of unselfishness, and "the example of Christ is constantly held up, not merely as a model, but a motive" (Charles Hodge, *A Commentary on the Epistle to the Romans*, p. 433). The point of the reference to Christ here is His unselfishness: He unselfishly surrendered His own will to the will of His heavenly Father. He underwent sufferings for the glory of His heavenly Father. He underwent sufferings for the glory of God. The "reproaches" that fell on Christ were really reproaches on God; it was because of His identification with the will and purpose of God that He suffered them.

In speaking of the unselfishness of Jesus Christ, Paul quotes from Psalm 69:9. This is one of the Messianic Psalms, that is, it is a prophecy of Jesus Christ the Messiah. As such it is cited several times in the New Testament (note John 2:17; 15:25; 19:28; Acts 1:20). This fact should be pondered by those who glibly tell us that there is nothing about Christ in the Psalms.

Just as Jesus Christ was supremely unselfish in surrendering Himself to the will of God, so the Christian should be unselfish in seeking the accomplishment of God's will and purpose in his Christian brethren. He should put the spiritual welfare of others and the edification of the Church above all merely personal considerations. If our Christian love is real, it will not be merely abstract; it will take a concrete form that will be manifested in our unselfish attitude toward others.

"For whatsoever things were written aforetime were written for our learning, that we through patience and comfort of the Scriptures might have hope" (15:4). By "whatsoever things were written aforetime" the apostle clearly means the Old Testament Scriptures, the Old Testament as a whole, as shown by the word "whatsoever." The Old Testament as a whole (and, of course, the New Testament likewise) is the infallible Word of God given by divine revelation for the salvation and spiritual benefit of men. From the Scriptures we learn patience, we receive consolation, and so we have hope.

We should note well what this implies concerning the Scriptures. First of all, it implies their historical truthfulness. We cannot receive patience, comfort, and hope from the Scriptures unless they are true. The record of God's mighty works and His dealings with His people of old cannot help us unless it is a true record. If a large part of the Old Testament is unreliable and even historically false, as the liberal critics claim, then its religious value is destroyed.

The "neoorthodox" theologians of the present day claim that Scripture can be historically false and at the same time religiously true. One of these men is quoted as saying that whether or not the serpent in the garden of Eden actually spoke is a matter of no importance; the important thing is not whether the serpent spoke, but what the serpent said. We reject this attitude toward the Scriptures as an absurd sophistry. The Scriptures are either historically true, or they are religiously worthless. We affirm, as the Bible itself affirms, that the Scriptures are true.

Secondly, this verse that we are considering implies the organic unity of the Scriptures. It implies that the Old Testament, no less than the New, is the word of God with a direct message for Christian people. Not part but all of the Scriptures were written for our learning: "whatsoever things were written aforetime were written for our learning." The extreme dispensationalism that isolates one part of Scripture from another part of Scripture, saying "This promise is for Israel; that promise is for the Church; this portion is for the Jews; that portion is for Christians"—this system is false. Every part of Scripture is for all of God's people. Every promise of God is for all who are in Christ. "For all the promises of God in him are yea, and in him Amen, unto the glory of God by us" (2 Cor. 1:20). If all the promises of God are "yea" in Christ, then all the promises of God must be for all those people who are in Christ.

Romans 15:1–13

In the third place, this text (15:4) implies that we ought to be earnest students of Scripture. If all Scripture was written for our learning, then we ought to be busy about learning it. The Bible is not a lazy man's book. We cannot expect to get much from it by reading it two minutes a day (or two minutes a week). If we expect to get something out of Bible study, we will have to put something in—some time, some effort, some eagerness, and some thinking. We should get over the worship of "inspiration" and go to work in earnest to get some information by learning what is in the Bible. We can never have real "inspiration" in a mental vacuum; we have to know the truth.

"Hope" in this verse means, of course, religious hope in the Christian sense. It does not mean a hope of gaining the object of worldly ambitions, such as wealth or business success; it means a sure confidence that ultimately we shall receive all the blessings that Christ has purchased for us and promised to us. Christian hope means a sure confidence that God's goodness and mercy shall follow us all the days of our life, and that we shall dwell in the house of the Lord forever. It means that we are assured of our complete, absolute redemption from sin and all its consequences—its guilt, its defilement, its enslaving power, the sufferings it causes, and its very presence in our environment. On the positive side, it means communion with Christ in glory to all eternity. This is the hope to which we may attain by patiently learning what is in the Scriptures of God.

Questions:

1. What psalm is quoted in 15:3?
2. What class of psalms does this psalm belong to?
3. What is the meaning of the statement quoted from the psalm, "The reproaches of them that reproached thee fell on me"?
4. Of what does Paul hold Christ up as an example?
5. How can the Christian follow Christ's example?
6. What does the apostle mean by the expression, "whatsoever things were written aforetime"?
7. What does Paul's statement imply concerning the character of the Scriptures?

Romans 15:1–13

8. What absurd claim do the neoorthodox theologians make concerning Scripture?

9. What does Paul's statement imply concerning the relation of the various parts of Scripture to each other?

10. What promises of God are for those who are in Christ?

11. What does Paul's statement in 15:4 imply concerning the Christian's habits of Bible study?

12. What is the meaning of "hope" in 15:4? What does it include?

Lesson 94

"Now the God of patience and consolation grant you to be likeminded one toward another according to Christ Jesus" (15:5). In this verse, the expression "to be likeminded one toward another" does not mean that there must be no differences of opinion among the members of the church, but rather that the members are to have a harmonious feeling and attitude toward each other. It is possible to differ in opinion about minor matters and still preserve a mutually harmonious attitude. "According to Christ Jesus"—that is, following the example of Christ and obeying His command. The strong and weak brethren might differ about the question of eating foods, but in spite of this difference of opinion they were to seek harmony and unity in their relation to each other.

This attitude of harmony and unity does not come by will power or human planning. It is a gift of God, God who is the source and author of patience and consolation. Hence the apostle prays that God may grant to the members of the church of Rome to have a right attitude toward each other. We should remember this when we try to heal divisions and envious party spirit in a church of the present day: real harmony and unity do not come by human planning. They are a spiritual gift granted by God, and to be sought from Him.

"That ye may with one mind and one mouth glorify God, even the Father of our Lord Jesus Christ" (15:6). "This harmony and fellowship among Christians is necessary, in order that they may glorify God aright. To honor God effectually and properly, there must be no unnecessary dissensions among his people" (Charles Hodge, *A Commentary on the Epistle to the Romans*, p. 434).

Romans 15:1–13

"Wherefore receive ye one another, as Christ also received us, to the glory of God" (15:7). Here the apostle exhorts the Roman Christians to mutual fellowship. The word "receive" here means, of course, receive to Christian fellowship; compare verse 1. The whole body of believers are to receive each other to Christian fellowship; there must be no individuals or groups within a church withholding fellowship from other individuals or groups within a church. It is perfectly plain that mutual fellowship is a simple Christian duty. Yet how often this obligation is disregarded at the present day! How often Christian fellowship is marred and broken by a selfish, stubborn spirit on the part of some in a church! Sometimes some members of a church will hardly speak to certain other members, and if they do speak, it may be in such a cold and formal tone that they might better have remained silent. All such conduct is a violation of the command to receive one another.

The apostle urges two reasons why Christians should receive one another. Firstly, Christ has received us. Our Savior in His great kindness and love, has received us sinners as His own. Shall we who are the recipients of this amazing grace presume to refuse to receive our brethren who like ourselves have been received by Christ? If Christ has received us, we also ought to receive one another.

Secondly, the glory of God demands that we receive one another. A church that is torn by internal faction and party strife cannot glorify God as it should. Some differences of opinion may be unavoidable for the time being, but if God is to be glorified there must at least be a kind and friendly feeling among the members toward each other. If there is bitterness and strife, God's Spirit is grieved, and God is not glorified but dishonored.

Questions:

1. Is it wrong for differences of opinion on minor matters to exist among the members of a church?
2. What is the real meaning of the expression "to be likeminded one toward another"?
3. In spite of their differences about questions of foods, what were

Romans 15:1–13

the strong and the weak brethren all to seek for?

4. How does an attitude of harmony and unity come to a church?
5. Why can real harmony not come by human planning or effort?
6. What is the meaning of the word "receive" in 15:7?
7. What conditions in a church are forbidden by 15:7?
8. What two reasons does Paul give why Christians should receive one another?
9. How is the fact that Christ has received us a motive for us to receive one another?
10. Why can a church torn by party strife not glorify God properly?

Lesson 95

"Now I say that Jesus Christ was a minister of the circumcision for the truth of God, to confirm the promises made unto the fathers" (15:8). "The apostle intends to show how it was that Christ had received those to whom he wrote. He had come to minister to the Jews, verse 8, and also to cause the Gentiles to glorify God, verse 9" (Charles Hodge, *A Commentary on the Epistle to the Romans*, p. 435). These two classes made up the membership of the church at Rome. Paul undertakes to show that Christ has received both.

The expression "a minister of the circumcision" means "a minister sent to the Jews." The, word "minister," of course, means "servant." "For the truth of God"—that is, to maintain God's truthfulness in fulfilling His promises, as the apostle presently explains.

> The truth of God is his veracity or fidelity. Christ had exhibited the greatest condescension and kindness in coming, not as a Lord or ruler, but as an humble minister to the Jews, to accomplish the gracious promises of God. As this kindness was not confined to them, but as the Gentiles also were received into His kingdom, and united with the Jews on equal terms, this example of Christ furnishes the strongest motives for the cultivation of mutual affection and unanimity (Charles Hodge, *A Commentary on the Epistle to the Romans*, p. 435).

"And that the Gentiles might glorify God for His mercy; as it is written, For this cause I will confess to Thee among the Gentiles, and

Romans 15:1–13

sing unto Thy name" (15:9). The mercy for which the Gentiles were to glorify God is, of course, the great mercy of salvation through Christ, with all the blessings that accompany and follow it; in a word, the mercy that changed the Gentiles from being strangers and foreigners and made them citizens of the kingdom of God. Christ by His work of redemption has accomplished two things: He has maintained God's truthfulness by fulfilling the promises made to the fathers, and He has brought the Gentiles into His kingdom so that they too may praise and glorify God for His mercy.

"As it is written, For this cause I will confess to Thee among the Gentiles, and sing unto Thy name" (15:9b). This is quoted from Psalm 18:49. It is one of a number of Old Testament passages that predicted that the knowledge and worship of the true God was at some future time to be extended to the Gentiles. "In Psalm 18:49, David is the speaker. It is he that says: 'I will praise Thee among the Gentiles.' He is contemplated as surrounded by Gentiles giving thanks unto God, which implies that they were the worshippers of God" (Charles Hodge, *A Commentary on the Epistle to the Romans*, p. 435).

"And again he saith, Rejoice, ye Gentiles, with His people" (15:10). This is a quotation from the Septuagint (Greek version) of Deuteronomy 32:43; a parallel, and nearly identical, passage is Psalm 67:3, 5.

"And again, Praise the Lord, all ye Gentiles; and laud Him, all ye people" (15:11). This verse is quoted from Psalm 117:1.

"And again, Esaias saith, There shall be a root of Jesse, and He that shall rise to reign over the Gentiles; in Him shall the Gentiles trust" (15:12). This verse is quoted from Isaiah 11:1, 10. This passage of Isaiah clearly and definitely predicts that the coming Messiah would reign, not only over the Jews, but also over the Gentiles. Paul's quotation is again taken from the Septuagint though the meaning is identical with that of the original Hebrew.

> The promise of the prophet is, that from the decayed and fallen house of David, one should arise, whose dominion should embrace all nations, and in whom Gentiles as well as Jews should trust. In the fulfillment of this prophecy Christ came, and preached salvation to those who were near and to those who were far off. As both classes had been thus kindly

received by the condescending Saviour, and united into one community, they should recognize and love each other as brethren, laying aside all censoriousness and contempt, neither judging nor despising one another (Charles Hodge, *A Commentary on the Epistle to the Romans*, p. 436).

By four different quotations from the Old Testament, Paul has shown that it was God's plan from of old to save and receive the Gentiles as well as the Jews. The fact that Christ has saved and received both should be a powerful motive toward mutual love and harmony in the Church, which is Christ's body.

"Now the God of hope fill you with all joy and peace in believing, that ye may abound in hope, through the power of the Holy Ghost" (15:13). Paul here prays for the Christians at Rome. He prays that they may be filled, not only with joy, but with "all joy"—that is, all possible joy, not only with peace, but "all peace"—the fullness of peace. Being filled with all joy and peace in believing, they were to abound in hope, by the power of the Holy Spirit. To believe, to abound in hope, etc., were the duty of the Roman Christians. Yet Paul prays that "the God of hope" may fill them with these graces. "Thus constantly and intimately are the ideas of accountableness and dependence connected in the sacred Scriptures. We are to work out our own salvation, because it is God that worketh in us both to will and to do, according to his good pleasure" (Charles Hodge, *A Commentary on the Epistle to the Romans*, p. 436).

"That ye may abound in hope." The fullness of joy and peace in Christian people causes them to "abound in hope." All these graces and attainments are "through the power of the Holy Ghost," who is the author of all good and the source of all blessings. Thus the apostle concludes this section of the epistle with a reminder that we are completely dependent upon the grace of the Holy Spirit.

Questions:

1. What two classes of Christians made up the membership of the church of Rome?
2. What is the meaning of the word "minister" in 15:8?

Romans 15:1–13

3. What was the purpose of Christ's coming as a "minister" to the Jews?

4. What is meant by the "truth" of God?

5. What is the mercy for which the Gentiles were to glorify God?

6. How many Old Testament passages does Paul quote in 15:9–12?

7. What is implied concerning the Gentiles in Psalm 18:49?

8. What is predicted concerning the Messiah in Isaiah 11:1, 10?

9. What Christian duty is emphasized by the fact that Christ has saved and received both Jews and Gentiles?

10. In 15:13, what does Paul pray that the Roman Christians may be filled with?

11. What is the connection between our duties and our dependence upon the Holy Spirit?

12. With what thought does the apostle bring this section of the epistle to a close?

---

1. The present *Testimony of the Reformed Presbyterian Church of North America* says: "It is sinful for a Christian to take an oath which compromises his supreme allegiance to Jesus Christ. It is also sinful to vote for officials who are required to take an oath which a Christian himself could not take in good conscience. Voting involves the voter in responsibility for any act required of the official as a condition of holding his office." Deut. 10:20, Isa. 45:22-23; 2 John 1:11; 1 Tim. 5:22 (Chap. 25: "Of the Civil Magistrate," para. 16)

Chapter 7

PAUL'S MISSIONARY WORK AND PLANS FOR FURTHER SERVICE

Paul's Work as Missionary to the Gentiles.
15:14-21
Lesson 96

As the apostle Paul approaches the end of his Epistle to the Romans, he assures them of his confidence in their Christian standing and character. He then goes on to say something about his own work as a missionary to the Gentiles, and then adds something about his plans and purposes concerning future work. We shall now take up this section.

"And I myself also am persuaded of you, my brethren, that ye also are full of goodness, filled with all knowledge, able also to admonish one another" (15:14). This statement means, of course, that the Roman Christians are full of goodness, etc., by the grace of God through Christ. It cannot mean that in themselves, apart from Christ, are full of goodness, for this would be a contradiction of the whole teaching of the first part of the epistle. Note that Paul addresses them as "brethren," that is, Christians. It is because they are Christians that they can be said to be full of goodness; the goodness spoken of is that produced by the Holy Spirit's work of sanctification in their lives.

"Nevertheless, brethren, I have written the more boldly unto you in some sort, as putting you in mind, because of the grace that is given to me of God" (15:15). Paul does not imply, in writing the truths of this epistle to the Roman Christians, that they are totally ignorant of these truths; rather, his aim is to call to their minds truths that they already know in an effort to emphasize, expound, and apply these truths. However well the Roman Christians might understand the truths of the Christian faith, their understanding would not equal that of the Apostle Paul, who was specially inspired by the Holy Spirit and who received direct revelations from God. So Paul's writing these truths to the Romans implied neither any presumption on his part nor any gross ignorance on their part. Every Christian has his place and function in the body of Christ, and Paul's place and function, as an apostle, was to be an inspired, authoritative teacher of truth. However well grounded in the truth the Roman Christians might be, they could still learn much from what Paul wrote to them.

"That I should be the minister of Jesus Christ to the Gentiles, ministering the gospel of God, that the offering up of the Gentiles might be acceptable, being sanctified by the Holy Ghost" (15:16). The word here translated "minister" (*leitourgos*) is a Greek word that means a public official or civil servant, but this same Greek word is frequently used in the Scriptures to describe the office of a priest (Deut. 10:8; Heb. 10:11). Paul, of course, was not a priest in the literal sense; his office was not that of a priest but of an apostle. Christian ministers are not priests except in the sense that every Christian is a priest (1 Pet. 2:9; Rev. 5:10). But the verse we are dealing with is figurative language. It represents Paul the apostle as a priest. Every priest, of course, must have a sacrifice that he offers up to God. In the text, the Gentile Christians are represented as Paul's sacrifice, which he as a priest offers to God. Literally, of course, the Gentiles were not a sacrifice, any more than Paul was literally a priest. But by speaking of the Gentiles as a sacrifice, a certain truth is brought out. The Gentiles who had been deeply involved in sin, were offered as a holy offering to God, "being sanctified by the Holy Ghost."

Romans 15:14–21

As the sacrifices were purified by water and other means, when pre-pared for the altar, so we are made fit for the service of God, rendered holy or acceptable, by the influences of the Holy Spirit. This is an idea which Paul never omits; when speaking of the success of his labors, or of the efficacy of the gospel, he is careful that this success should not be ascribed to the instruments, but to the real author. In this beautiful passage we see the nature of the only priesthood which belongs to the Christian ministry. It is not their office to make atonement for sin, or to offer a propitiatory sacrifice to God, but by the preaching of the gospel to bring men, by the influence of the Holy Spirit, to offer themselves as a living sacrifice, holy and acceptable to God (Charles Hodge, *A Commentary on the Epistle to the Romans*, p. 439).

It is improper to speak of a minister of the gospel as a "priest" in any other sense than the sense in which all Christians are priests. Scripture teaches the universal priesthood of believers, but among believers, there is no special class holding an office of priesthood. It is one of the corruptions of Roman Catholicism that in this system the Christian minister has become a priest, while the sacrament of the Lord's supper has become the sacrifice of the mass. Those Protestant denominations that tend to speak of the minister of the gospel as a "priest" should take care lest they think of the minister as a sacrificing priest and of the sacrament as a sacrifice.

Questions:

1. As Paul approaches the end of his epistle, of what fact does he assure the Roman Christians?
2. What is the source and nature of the goodness of which the Romans are said to be full in 15:14?
3. How do we know that this does not mean that they were in them-selves good by nature?
4. Did Paul's writing this epistle to the Roman Christians imply that they were ignorant of the truths taught in the epistle?
5. Why was it not presumptuous on Paul's part for him to write an Epistle to the Romans instructing them in the truth?

Romans 15:14–21

6. What is the common meaning of the word translated "minister" in 15:16?
7. What religious office does this word often describe in Scripture?
8. Why was Paul not a priest in the literal sense?
9. Name two New Testament passages that speak of all Christians as priests.
10. In the figurative language of 15:16, what sacrifice is offered up to God?
11. Why could the Gentile Christians appropriately be called a sacrifice offered to God?
12. How were the literal sacrifices of Old Testament times purified for offering upon the altar?
13. How were the Gentiles purified from their sin to make them a sacrifice suitable for offering to God?
14. When speaking of the success of his labors, or the efficacy of the gospel, what truth is Paul careful to guard?
15. What are the errors of Roman Catholicism concerning the office of the ministry and the sacrament of the Lord's Supper?

Lesson 97

"I have therefore whereof I may glory through Jesus Christ in those things which pertain to God" (15:17). As Paul was appointed by God to be an apostle and missionary to the Gentiles, and as God has also made his efforts for the conversion of the Gentiles successful, Paul has a God-given right to teach and exhort the Roman Christians with the authority and confidence that characterize the epistle. But this "glorying" was not a sinful human boasting, rising from human pride or conceit. On the contrary, it was only "through Jesus Christ" that Paul had any ground for glorying or boasting. The credit, after all, belonged to Christ; Paul was the servant of Christ. Paul's glorying is a glorying "in those things which pertain to God." Paul would not boast of himself, his worldly attainments, or his educational advantages, but only of "those things which pertain to God"—the preaching of the gospel and the work of the Holy Spirit which accompanied that preaching. Paul's was not a proud but a humble kind of glorying. It was a glorying that took no credit to self, but gave all the credit to the Lord.

"For I will not dare to speak of any of those things which Christ hath not wrought by me, to make the Gentiles obedient, by word and deed, through mighty signs and wonders, by the power of the Spirit of God; so that from Jerusalem, and round about unto Illyricum, I have fully preached the gospel of Christ" (15:18–19). In verse 18, Paul carefully explains that he had no intention of claiming any credit for himself; he would not even dare to speak of anything except what Christ had done through him.

> He would not glory in the flesh, or in anything pertaining to himself, but only in Christ, and in what he had accomplished. The conversion of the Gentiles was Christ's work, not Paul's; and therefore Paul could glory in it without self-exaltation. It is to be remarked that the apostle represents himself as a mere instrument in the hands of Christ for the conversion of men; the real efficiency he ascribes to the Redeemer. This passage, therefore, exhibits evidence that Paul regarded Christ as still exercising a controlling agency over the souls of men, and rendering effectual the labors of his faithful ministers. Such power the sacred writers never attribute to any being but God (Charles Hodge, *A Commentary on the Epistle to the Romans*, p. 440).

"To make the Gentiles obedient, by word and deed" (15:18b). To make the Gentiles obedient, of course, means to make them obedient to the requirements of the gospel of Christ. They were made obedient not merely "by word," but also "by deed." That is, not merely was the truth of the gospel preached to them, but this preaching was accompanied by the inward operation of the Holy Spirit that alone could make it truly effectual for their salvation. The outward preaching of the gospel, though necessary, is not of itself sufficient to bring men to salvation. There must be in addition the effective operation of the Holy Spirit. Compare Acts 16:14, where it is said of Lydia that the Lord opened her heart, so that she attended unto the things that were spoken by Paul. The fact that the outward preaching of the message is powerless by itself should remind us of our dependence upon the power of the Holy

Spirit for real results. Mere campaigns and programs of evangelism or missionary work will not bring a single soul to salvation unless the power of the Holy Spirit gives new life. Therefore we should always pray that this life-giving operation of the Spirit may accompany the preaching of the Word.

"Through mighty signs and wonders, by the power of the Spirit of God" (15:19a). The Greek words of this text may be literally translated: "In power of signs and of wonders, in power of the Holy Spirit." (The correct Greek text has "the Holy Spirit," not "the Spirit of God" as in the King James Version.) Thus two forms of power are mentioned as making Paul's preaching effective for the conversion of the Gentiles. Firstly, there was the power of miracles, here called "signs and wonders." Secondly, there was the power of the Holy Spirit's working in the hearts of the hearers.

Miracles are called "signs" because they are manifestations of the direct working of God in human history. A miracle is an instance of the creative, direct working of God, as distinguished from His ordinary mode of working through the laws of nature. To provide food for people through natural conditions of soil and climate, sunshine and rain, which permit planting and harvest, milling of grain into flour, and baking of it into bread, is truly a work of God, but it is not a miracle, for it is accomplished through natural means. It is a work of God's providence, but it is not a miracle. To feed five thousand people by the instantaneous multiplication of five loaves and two fishes, on the other hand, is a miracle. The laws and forces of nature cannot account for it; it proceeds from the direct operation of God. The miracles of the Bible are supernatural events. They are not products of the natural order, and cannot be explained by nature or science.

Miracles are called "wonders" because of the effect which they produce on the minds of those who witness them. They cause people to wonder, to stop and think, to recognize that here is the direct working of God. Miracles, therefore, serve as credentials of the gospel message. As only God could bring the miracle to pass, the message that the miracle accompanied must be of God. On the miracles performed through the Apostle Paul, see Acts 19:11–12.

Romans 15:14–21

Besides the power of miracles, Paul mentions the power of the Holy Spirit. In addition to the miracles (which themselves were works of the Holy Spirit), there was the powerful operation of the Holy Spirit in human hearts, by which the conversion of the elect was accomplished. Compare to 1 Corinthians 2:4, where Paul says, "And my speech and my preaching was not with enticing words of man's wisdom, but in demonstration of the Spirit and of power." Paul did not place any reliance in his own ability as an orator or preacher, but only in the power of the Holy Spirit which accompanied and followed the preached message.

Paul adds that "from Jerusalem, and round about unto Illyricum", he had fully preached the gospel of Christ (15:19b). Illyricum was the region across the Adriatic Sea from Italy. Today this territory is occupied by Yugoslavia and Albania. We should remember that at the time Paul wrote the Epistle to the Romans, he had never visited Rome. At this time Illyricum was the western limit of the territory he had reached with the gospel message. "In this wide circuit had the apostle preached, founding churches, and advancing the Redeemer's kingdom with such evidence of the divine cooperation, as to leave no ground of doubt that he was a divinely appointed minister of Christ" (Charles Hodge, *A Commentary on the Epistle to the Romans*, p. 441).

Questions:

1. What God-given right did Paul have as an apostle and missionary to the Gentiles?
2. Why was Paul's glorying not a sinful boasting?
3. What kind of things did Paul boast of?
4. Why did Paul not claim any credit for himself?
5. What truth concerning Jesus Christ is implied by Paul's words in 15:18?
6. To what were the Gentiles made obedient?
7. What did Paul mean by saying that the Gentiles were made obedient "by word and deed"?
8. Why is the outward preaching of the gospel not sufficient to bring men to salvation?
9. What truth concerning Lydia is taught in Acts 16:14?

Romans 15:14–21

10. Of what should we be reminded by the fact that the outward preaching of the gospel is powerless by itself?

11. What should we pray for to accompany the preaching of the Word?

12. How may the first part of 15:19 be literally translated?

13. What two forms of power made Paul's preaching effective?

14. Why are miracles called "signs" in the Bible?

15. What is the difference between a miracle and an event that is not a miracle?

16. Why can the miracles of the Bible not be explained by natural laws or science?

17. What does Acts 19:11–12 tell us of miracles performed through the Apostle Paul?

18. Besides the power of miracles, what other power made Paul's preaching effective?

19. Where is Illyricum, and what countries occupy the region today?

20. What were the eastern and western limits of Paul's preaching at the time he wrote this epistle?

Lesson 98

"Yea, so have I strived to preach the gospel, not where Christ was named, lest I should build upon another man's foundation" (15:20). The Greek word here translated "strived" means literally "to love honor"; hence it signifies "to do something as a matter of honor." Paul regarded it as a matter of honor to do pioneer missionary work. He made it his business to preach the gospel where Christ had previously been unknown. He had no ambition or desire to build upon another man's foundation. Others would follow him, and would build upon the foundation that Paul had laid; but it was Paul's special honor and privilege to do the pioneer missionary work.

For a preacher of the gospel to build upon another man's foundation is not necessarily wrong. As Wesley said, "God buries His workman but He carries on His work." In 1 Corinthians 3:10, Paul solemnly warns those who shall build upon the foundation laid by him, that they must take heed how they build thereupon.

Romans 15:14–21

Yet there is a kind of building on another man's foundation that is certainly wrong and contemptible, namely, when a minister or missionary comes in contact with people who are already Christians and attempts to persuade them to leave their own church and join that church, so that he can have the credit for gaining new members for his church. Unfortunately, this kind of "sheep stealing" is very common, and it is often the small and comparatively pure and faithful denominations that are the victims of the practice.

There can of course be no objection to Christian people changing their church membership on the basis of sincere conviction of truth. It is every Christian's duty to join the church that he believes to be closest to the scriptural pattern. If ministers who cultivate members of other churches would make their appeal upon this high plane of conviction of truth, no one could rightly complain. Such competition between churches would be ethical and honest. But it is to be feared that the attempt to proselyte members of other churches is seldom conducted on such a high plane at the present day. Lower and more worldly motives are appealed to, or bait of some sort is offered as an inducement to people to leave a strict and faithful church for one that is larger and of a more popular type. This is a form of building on another man's foundation that should be regarded with contempt by all right minded people. Small denominations that struggle hard to maintain biblical standards of faith and life are constantly up against this unethical competition.

"But as it is written, To whom he was not spoken of, they shall see: and they that have not heard shall understand" (15:21). The Old Testament reference here is Isaiah 52:15, where it is prophesied that the Christ shall be preached to the Gentiles. Thus Paul's missionary work among the Gentiles was a fulfillment of Old Testament prophecy. Here, as so often in Paul's epistles, having stated a point, he cites the Old Testament Scripture to show its harmony with his own teaching.

Paul's Hope to Visit Rome on the Way to Spain. 15:22–29

"For which cause also I have been much hindered from coming to you" (15:22). The meaning of this verse is that Paul's intention of visiting

Rome has been delayed by his desire to engage in pioneer missionary work, preaching the gospel where Christ had not been named. In Rome, of course, there was already a church; the gospel had been preached there. For Paul to preach in Rome could not be called pioneer missionary work, because the foundation there had already been laid by others.

"But now having no more place in these parts, and having a great desire these many years to come unto you" (15:23). What does Paul mean by "having no more place in these parts"? Some scholars understand the word "place" as opportunity, as in Hebrews 12:17 ("no place of repentance"). The meaning then would be that Paul no longer had any opportunity for preaching the gospel at Corinth, where he was at the time of writing Romans, or that he had no more opportunity for preaching in that region. The more probable meaning is, however, that he had already covered the ground, so that there remained no more unevangelized territory; "having no longer a place in these parts where Christ is not known" (Charles Hodge, *A Commentary on the Epistle to the Romans*, p. 442). This does not mean, of course, that Paul in his missionary work covered every town and village of a region. From the book of Acts we know that Paul selected the strategically important centers for his preaching—such cities as Ephesus, Thessalonica, Athens, and Corinth. In these cities he would be heard by people from the entire surrounding area, and the gospel of Christ would soon be known throughout the region. Paul did not stay on indefinitely in any one center. Having established a church with its officers and members, he then left it to carry on the local work, while he pressed on to new territory.

"A great desire" is a very strong expression in the Greek. It means a longing, a very earnest desire, a supreme desire. Paul tells the Roman Christians that for many years he had had this intense longing to visit them. We can see from this that the church at Rome had been in existence for several years already.

Questions:
1.   What is the literal meaning of the word "strive" in 15:20?
2.   What did Paul regard as a matter of honor?

Romans 15:22–29

3. What does Paul mean by building on another man's foundation?
4. Is it always wrong for a preacher of the gospel to build on another man's foundation?
5. What warning does Paul give in 1 Corinthians 3:10?
6. What form of building on another man's foundation is wrong and contemptible?
7. On what basis is it right for Christian people to change their church membership?
8. When is the attempt to proselyte members of other churches wrong?
9. What truth does Paul cite from Isaiah 52:15?
10. What had delayed Paul's intended visit to Rome?
11. What is the probable meaning of Paul's statement that he had "no more place in these parts"?
12. Does Paul's statement mean that in his missionary work he had covered every town and village of the region where he was?
13. What kind of centers did Paul select for his preaching?
14. How would the gospel message soon become known throughout the area?
15. What was Paul's practice with regard to staying in a place where he had founded a church?
16. What kind of desire did Paul have to visit the Roman church?
17. How long had Paul had this desire? What does this show as to the length of time there had been a church at Rome?

Lesson 99

"Whensoever I take my journey into Spain, I will come to you" (15:24a).

Whether Paul ever accomplished his purpose of visiting Spain, is a matter of doubt. There is no historical record of his having done so, either in the New Testament, or in the early ecclesiastical writers; though most of these writers seem to have taken it for granted. His whole plan was probably deranged by the occurrences at Jerusalem, which led to his long imprisonment at Caesarea, and his being sent in bonds to Rome (Charles Hodge, *A Commentary on the Epistle to the Romans*, p. 442).

Romans 15:22–29

Clement of Rome, who wrote from Italy around 96 A.D., states that Paul "reached the bounds of the west." Spain was the western limit of the Roman world. The "Tarshish" spoken of in the Old Testament was probably a part of southern Spain. Rome had held power in Spain since about 200 B.C., and in Paul's day the civilization and culture of the southern part of Spain was thoroughly Romanized and had been so for nearly a century.

The fact that Paul purposed to visit Spain, the western limit of the Roman world, shows how seriously he took his commission as the apostle of the Gentiles. He was not satisfied with the great accomplishments already achieved, but longed to press on to the regions beyond. Even so, the church of the present day should not be willing to settle down complacently in its existing limits, but should eagerly press on to the regions beyond, as God gives opportunity and ability to do so.

"For I trust to see you in my journey, and to be brought on my way thitherward by you, if first I be somewhat filled with your company" (15:24b). Paul's intention was, firstly, to visit the church at Rome, the capital of the empire, that he might enjoy mutual Christian fellowship with the members of the church; and secondly, to make final preparations for the journey to Spain at Rome, with the help of the Roman Christians. "To be brought on my way" is an expression that implies not only the courtesy of a send-off, but the making of some sort of provision for the journey. (See Acts 15:3; 1 Cor. 16:6; 2 Cor. 1:16.)

"But now I go unto Jerusalem to minister unto the saints" (15:25). To "minister" here means to provide for the needs of the saints. The Greek word can mean any kind of service. Paul's trip to Jerusalem was a part of his service to the Christians there.

"For it hath pleased them of Macedonia and Achaia to make a certain contribution for the poor saints which are at Jerusalem" (15:26). "Them of Macedonia and Achaia" means, of course, the Christians in those places. As compared with the condition of the Christians in Palestine, those in the Gentile world were well-off. The word here translated "contribution" is the Greek *koinonia*, elsewhere translated "communion" or "fellowship." The phrase "to make a certain contribution" may be literally translated "to bring about a certain communion" or "to bring about a certain participation." The Christians in Palestine were victims of persecution and consequent economic distress. The apostolic council at Jerusalem (Acts 15) had requested that Paul, in his missionary work among the Gentiles, would collect funds for the relief of the needy Christians in Palestine (see Gal. 2:9–10). This task Paul undertook and carried out faithfully. This financial relief was one way of promoting goodwill between the Jewish and Gentile elements in the early Church and of helping to eliminate the prejudice of the Jewish Christians against their Gentile brethren in Christ.

"It hath pleased them verily; and their debtors they are. For if the Gentiles have been made partakers of their spiritual things, their duty is also to minister unto them in carnal things" (15:27). Paul represents the gifts of the Gentile Christians for the relief of the needy Christians of Palestine as not merely a freewill offering ("it hath pleased them"), but also as a moral obligation ("their debtors they are"). Salvation came to the Gentiles through an Israelitish channel. The Christ on whom the Gentiles believed was, as to his human nature, a Jew. Such spiritual obligations must not be forgotten. The Gentile Christians must remember that they were wild olive branches grafted into the good olive tree. In recognition of this spiritual benefit, the Gentile Christians ought gladly to share their material possessions with the needy Jewish Christians of Palestine. Any gift of money could be at best only a small and inadequate recognition of their indebtedness. In short, in asking the Gentile Christians to contribute money for the relief of the Jewish Christians of Palestine, Paul was not begging for charity but was only asking the Gentile Christians to do what was right—he was only asking them to show their gratitude and Christian love in a practical way. From the references to this matter in Paul's various epistles it is evident that, for the most part, the Gentile Christians cooperated wholeheartedly in this enterprise.

Questions:

1. What do we know about whether Paul ever visited Spain?
2. What event may have interfered with his plan to visit Spain?

Romans 15:22–29

3. What statement of Clement of Rome may imply that Paul did reach Spain?

4. What name is given in the Old Testament to a part of Spain?

5. When did Rome begin to hold power in Spain?

6. What was the position of Spain in the Roman world?

7. What does Paul's intention to visit Spain show about his attitude toward his missionary task?

8. What should the church of the present day learn from Paul's attitude toward the missionary task?

9. What was Paul's two-fold purpose in his plan to visit Rome?

10. What is implied in the expression "to be brought on my way" in 15:24?

11. What is the meaning of the word "minister" in 15:25?

12. What is meant by "them of Macedonia and Achaia" in 15:26?

13. How may the expression "to make a certain contribution" be literally translated?

14. What was the condition of the Christians in Palestine at this time?

15. What request was made of Paul by the apostolic council of Acts 15?

16. How would goodwill between Jewish and Gentile elements in the Church be promoted, and prejudice eliminated?

17. Was the contribution to the needy Christians of Palestine merely a freewill offering?

18. Why were the Gentile Christians the "debtors" of the Jewish Christians of Palestine?

19. How did the Gentile Christians cooperate in contributing money for the saints in Palestine?

Lesson 100

"When therefore I have performed this, and have sealed to them this fruit, I will come by you into Spain" (15:28). Here Paul speaks of the money contributed by the Gentile Christians as "fruit." Ordinarily we would not speak of money as fruit. But in this case it really was fruit. The wild olive branches, having been grafted into the good olive tree, now bear fruit—the fruit of Christian love, unselfishness, and

Romans 15:22–29

good works. This money that Paul was taking back to Jerusalem was evidence of the real Christian faith and life of the Gentiles. It has been said that money is the acid test of a person's Christianity. If his purse/wallet has not been converted to Christ, there may be reason to doubt that a person's soul has been truly saved. Real salvation produces real fruits. The contributions Paul was carrying to Jersusalem would be more than merely a material help to the needy Christians there—they would be a testimony and tribute to the mighty work of God's Spirit among the Gentiles to whom Paul had preached.

Those professing Christians of the present day who are selfish and stingy about financial support of Christ's Church and kingdom should consider seriously whether they have really passed from death into life. Faithful and generous support of Christian work is one of the evidences of real spiritual life in a person. Those who grudgingly contribute as little as they feel they can decently can, are not evidencing the real work of the Spirit in their lives. Some, who think that one dollar is a liberal offering to put in the collection plate at church, do not hesitate to spend several times that amount on an unnecessary luxury or entertainment that they want. God, however, is not mocked.

Paul speaks of "sealing" the fruit (money) to the Christians at Jerusalem. To "seal" here means to deliver it safely to them. The handling and transmission of this money was a serious responsibility, and Paul took it very seriously. We may well believe that he felt relieved when the fund had been safely handed over to the proper officers of the church in Jerusalem. Paul not only took the preaching of the gospel seriously—he also took the handling of church funds seriously. Not only the spiritual, but the material things belonged to God and were to be so regarded. There is no room for carelessness or slipshod methods in the financial affairs and business transactions of a church. Church officers who handle church business or property in a slipshod manner are not performing their duty as God requires it to be performed. The faithful servant of God will conduct himself in an efficient and responsible manner, as Paul did. Paul, the great apostle and former pupil of Gamaliel, did not consider himself above attending to financial matters.

Romans 15:22–29

When this important business had been completed, Paul intended to visit Rome en route to Spain. "And I am sure that, when I come unto you, I shall come in the fulness of the blessing of the gospel of Christ" (15:29). At the beginning of this Epistle to the Romans (1:11–12) Paul had expressed his desire to see the Roman Christians, that he might impart to them some spiritual gift, and that they and he might be encouraged by their mutual faith in Christ. Now at the end of the epistle he states his confidence that when he does visit them, it will be with abundant blessing from Christ. Paul had experienced such rich blessings in other places where he had labored that he felt assured that the Lord would continue these blessings to him in the future. The gospel of Christ is the source of blessings, and as Paul's one purpose in visiting Rome would be the promotion of the gospel, he could confidently predict abundant blessings to accompany his visit.

Questions:

1. What word does Paul use, in 15:28, to describe the money contributed by the Gentile Christians?
2. Why could contributions of money be spoken of as "fruit"?
3. What is meant by saying that money is the acid test of a person's Christianity?
4. Of what was the money Paul was taking to Jerusalem an evidence?
5. If a professing Christian is selfish and stingy about contributing to Christ's Church and kingdom, what should he seriously consider?
6. What does Paul mean by the word "sealed" in 15:28?
7. How would Paul probably feel when the money was safely delivered to the proper officers of the church in Jerusalem?
8. Besides the preaching of the gospel, what matter did Paul take very seriously?
9. Why is there no room for careless or slipshod methods in the financial affairs and business transactions of the church?
10. What wish did Paul express at the beginning of this epistle?
11. What confidence does Paul express in 15:29?
12. On what ground did Paul's confidence rest?

Romans 15:22–29

Paul Asks for the Prayers of the Roman Christians. 15:30–33

Lesson 101

"Not I beseech you, brethren, for the Lord Jesus Christ's sake, and for the love of the Spirit, that ye strive together with me in your prayers to God for me" (15:30).

> Prayer (and even intercessory prayer) has a real and important efficacy, not merely in its influence on the mind of him who offers it, but also in securing the blessings for which we pray. Paul directed the Roman Christians to pray for the exercise of the divine providence in protecting him from danger, and for the Holy Spirit to influence the minds of the brethren in Jerusalem. This he would not have done, were such petitions of no avail (Charles Hodge, *A Commentary on the Epistle to the Romans*, p. 443).

The Apostle Paul realized his need of the prayers of his fellow Christians.

Paul urges two reasons why the Roman Christians should pray for him. Firstly, they should pray for him "for the Lord Jesus Christ's sake," that is, because of their devotion to Christ. If they loved Christ and really wished to see Christ's kingdom prosper, they would pray for Paul, who was Christ's servant. Secondly, they should pray for Paul because of "the love of the Spirit," that is, because of that Christian love of which the Holy Spirit is the author and source. "He appeals, therefore, not only to their love of Christ, but to their love for himself as a fellow Christian" (Charles Hodge, *A Commentary on the Epistle to the Romans*, p. 443). If we really love our fellow Christians, we will pray for them.

"That ye strive together with me in your prayers to God for me" (15:30b). The Greek word for "strive" in this verse is the word from which our English word "agonize" is derived. It implies a very earnest effort, a very deep concern. Our hasty, formal prayers could hardly be described by such a word. Only a deep spiritual earnestness could lead to such praying as Paul speaks of. Note the word "together": they were to strive together with Paul. As he went through hardships and dangers for the sake of the gospel, the Roman Christians were to participate in this conflict by their prayers.

"That I may be delivered from them that do not believe in Judaea" (15:31a). This is the first of three special objects that Paul asks the Roman Christians to pray for. They are asked to pray that the apostle will be delivered from the wrath and violence of the non-Christian Jews at Jerusalem. We should realize that the apostle was about to enter territory where Christianity was persecuted. It was at Jerusalem that Stephen was stoned and James beheaded a few years before. While the violent persecution had subsided, the bitter opposition remained beneath the surface, and might flare up again at any time. Paul knew well what he had to fear from his fellow Jews. All through his career as an apostle they persecuted him and tried to kill him.

"And that my service which I have for Jerusalem may be accepted of the saints" (15:31b). This is the second thing that Paul asks the Roman Christians to pray for—the successful completion of his business on his trip to Jerusalem. There was need to pray for this, too. For it was not only the non-Christian Jews that were opposed to Paul. There were also those among the Christian Jews who regarded him with suspicion and bitterness. The fact that he was engaged in preaching the gospel to the Gentiles would lead the more narrow-minded of the Jewish Christians to be prejudiced against him. "Paul desired that the work of love on which he was to go to Jerusalem might be favorably received by the Christians of that city. Paul labored for those whom he knew regarded him with little favor; he calls them saints, recognizes their Christian character, notwithstanding their unkindness, and urges his brethren to pray that they might be willing to accept of kindness at his hands" (Charles Hodge, *A Commentary on the Epistle to the Romans*, p. 444).

"That I may come unto you with joy by the will of God, and may with you be refreshed" (15:32). This is the third object for which Paul asks the Roman Christians to pray.

Paul seemed to look forward to his interview with the Christians at Rome, as a season of relief from conflict and labor. In Jerusalem he was beset by unbelieving Jews, and harassed by Judaizing Christians;

in most other places he was burdened with the care of the churches; but at Rome, which he looked upon as a restingplace, rather than a field of labor, he hoped to gather strength for the prosecution of his apostolic labors in still more distant lands" (Charles Hodge, *A Commentary on the Epistle to the Romans*, p. 444).

The work of the Apostle Paul would have been difficult even under favorable circumstances; it was rendered much more difficult by the conflicts and opposition that he constantly faced. Nothing is harder to bear than the opposition of those who ought to be one's friends and supporters in the work of the Lord. Paul knew from experience the bitter taste of opposition by not only the world, but many in the Church. No wonder he looked forward to his visit at Rome as a time of much-needed relief from conflict. So he urges the Roman Christians to pray that he may come to them with joy.

"Now the peace of God be with you all. Amen" (15:33). This is Paul's prayer for the Roman Christians—a brief prayer, but a very inclusive one. "The peace of God, that peace which God gives, includes all the mercies necessary for the perfect blessedness of the soul" (Charles Hodge, *A Commentary on the Epistle to the Romans*, p. 444). Christianity is the one and only religion that brings men the peace of God. It does this by first of all bringing men peace with God (Rom. 5:1). Through the blood and righteousness of Jesus Christ, the awful enmity between man and God is canceled and removed, and the sinner is reconciled to God. Thereupon the peace of God comes into the person's life. He is at war with sin—in bitter conflict with the world, the flesh, and the devil—but through it all he has the peace of God. The gospel does not promise us freedom from conflict, but it does promise us the peace of God in our lives.

Questions:

1. What is the efficacy of prayer, apart from its influence on the mind of the person who prays?

2. Why did Paul feel the need of the prayers of the Roman Christians?

3. What is the first reason that Paul urges the Roman Christians to pray for him?

4. What is the second reason that Paul urges the Roman Christians to pray for him?

5. What is meant by urging them to pray "for the love of the Spirit"?

6. What English word is related to the Greek word for "strive" in 15:30?

7. What truth is implied by the word "together" in 15:30?

8. What three things does Paul specially ask the Roman Christians to pray for?

9. Why would Paul need prayer that he be delivered from the unbelieving Jews in Jerusalem?

10. Why would Paul need prayer that his business at Jerusalem might be successfully completed?

11. How did Paul regard his anticipated visit to Rome?

12. What kind of opposition is the hardest to bear?

13. What is Paul's prayer for the Roman Christians?

14. What is meant by "the peace of God"?

15. How does the gospel bring the peace of God to men?

Romans 15:30–33

Chapter 8

CONCLUSION OF THE EPISTLE: PERSONAL GREETINGS

Paul Commends Phebe, a Servant of the Church at Cenchrea. 16:1-2

Lesson 102

I commend unto you Phebe our sister, which is a servant of the church which is at Cenchrea" (16:1). Cenchrea was one of the two harbors or seaports of Corinth in Greece, located about nine miles from the city of Corinth. We learn Paul had visited this place from Acts 18:18. Phebe was "a servant" of the Christian church in this town. The word "servant" may also be translated "deacon" or "deaconess." Whether Phebe was a deacon in the technical sense, that is, an ordained officer of the church, has been debated by New Testament scholars. Some have held that both men and women were ordained as deacons, while others consider it more probable that "deaconesses" such as Phebe held a different position; in other words, that a deaconess is not the same thing as "a woman deacon." Charles Hodge states: "It appears that in the apostolic church, elderly females were selected to attend upon the poor and sick of their own sex" (*A Commentary on the Epistle to the Romans*, p. 447). 1 Timothy 3:11 is a possible reference to women deacons (note that in this text the word "their" is in italics, not being in the Greek; and the word "wives" may equally well be translated "women").

At any rate, Phebe was a servant of the church at Cenchrea, whether or not servant be understood in the official sense as "deacon." Apparently Phebe was about to journey to Rome and would arrive there soon, before Paul himself could expect to be there. Hence he takes advantage of the opportunity afforded by writing the epistle to commend her to the church at Rome. The word translated "commend" means literally "to place together," hence it means "to introduce," implying, of course, to introduce someone with approval.

"That ye receive her in the Lord, as becometh saints, and that ye assist her in whatsoever business she hath need of you: for she hath been a succourer of many, and of myself also" (16:2). The Roman Christians are asked to receive Phebe "in the Lord," that is, as Christians welcoming a fellow Christian. This is to be done "as becometh saints." In other words, it was their Christian duty to welcome such a person as Phebe with proper friendliness and hospitality. Paul expresses his confidence in the Christian character of the members of the church at Rome when he asks them to welcome Phebe "as becometh saints."

We do not know the occasion of Phebe's visit to Rome, nor the nature of her business there. But there evidently was business, for Paul mentions it and asks that the Roman Christians assist her in it according to her need. It would be interesting if we could know what Phebe's business at Rome was, but the Bible does not satisfy our curiosity on this point. However, we may be sure that a foreigner arriving at Rome would need considerable assistance from someone before becoming able to find her way around in the capital and largest city of the Roman empire. Phebe may have been sent by the church on special business of some kind that would involve need for local assistance. Those who have served as foreign missionaries know how much a little timely help by local residents can mean.

Paul adds that Phebe had been a succorer, or helper, of many people. As Phebe lived at Cenchrea, one of the seaports of Corinth, it may be that she had made it her special business to help strangers disembarking there from ships. Possibly in this way she was able to bring people in contact with the preaching of the gospel in her church. Or possibly it was especially Christians embarking or disembarking at Cenchrea that were helped by Phebe. In the absence of information in the Bible, we can only guess at the exact nature of her work, but we can be sure that it was a worthy and helpful work.

"And of myself also." Again we can only wonder just how Phebe had helped Paul. But he gratefully acknowledges her help. People like Phebe smooth the path of missionaries today, as of old, and their good works are an honor to God's name. It was not only apostles like Paul and martyrs like Stephen that made Christianity successful in the ancient world, but also humble workers like Phebe, who made it their business to provide help where they found need. At the present day, it is not only the missionaries and ministers who advance the cause of Christ, but the rank and file of "lay" Christians who, when they see a need, set themselves to do something about it.

Questions:

1. Where was Cenchrea, and what was its importance?
2. How may the word "servant" in 16:1 also be translated?
3. What question exists as to the office and work of "deaconesses"?
4. What journey was Phebe apparently about to undertake?
5. What does the word "commend" in 16:1 mean?
6. How were the Roman Christians asked to receive Phebe?
7. Why would Phebe need help while at Rome?
8. What may possibly have been the special work of Phebe at Cenchrea?
9. Why can we not know definitely about the nature of her work?
10. What is needed besides ministers and missionaries to make Christianity successful?

Greetings to Many Christians at Rome. 16:3–16

Lesson 103

In verses 3–16, Paul sends greetings to no less than 26 persons whom he mentions by name plus others included in their households. From this we gain a view of the breadth of Paul's friendship. Though the apostle himself had never been in Rome, he nevertheless knows by name more than two dozen Christians then at Rome. Presumably, Paul was personally acquainted with these people, having met them elsewhere than at Rome. Or it is possible that in the case of some of these people he knew them indirectly, through others, or by correspondence. But it is more likely that he knew them personally, as he gives details about a number of them. If Paul knew this many people in the one city of Rome, how many Christian friends he must have had in various other parts of the empire! This warmth of personal friendship shows how false is that idea of Paul held by some people, according to which he was a scholar who was interested only in academic arguments or "theological hairsplitting." "A man that hath friends must show himself friendly" (Prov. 18:24), and the large number of Paul's friends proves him to have been a very friendly person.

This was Christian friendship. These were Paul's friends in Christ. He recognizes them as friends, fellow workers, etc., in the Lord. Their relation to Christ was more important to Paul than any other social relation such as their race or their nationality. Like Paul, we today should cultivate and value the friendship of the saints. We should not choose worldly people, to whom Christ means nothing, to be our special friends. Rather, we should rejoice in the fellowship of the saints.

This passage of the epistle also shows us how much women helped in the cause of the gospel. "From the beginning females have taken an active and important part in the promotion of the gospel. They seem, more than others, to have contributed to Christ of their substance. They were His most faithful attendants, 'last at the cross, and first at the sepulcher'" (Charles Hodge, *A Commentary on the Epistle to the Romans*, p. 453). Besides Phebe, several women are mentioned in this list of Paul's friends: Priscilla, Mary, Junia, Tryphena, Tryphosa, Persis, the mother of Rufus, Julia, and the sister of Nereus. Of some of these Paul says that they "labored in the Lord," or "labored much in the Lord." Priscilla with her husband Aquila was one of Paul's "helpers in Christ Jesus." The present writer has heard Paul called a "woman hater" because of his instructions concerning women in connection with public ministry and ruling office in the church (1 Cor. 14:34–35; 1 Tim. 2:11–15). But Paul was far from being a "woman hater," and it is clear that he welcomed,

Romans 16:3–16

appreciated, and highly valued the services of women in the promotion of the gospel. As in Paul's day, so in the churches of the present day, there is a wide field for Christian service open to women apart from the offices of minister and ruling elder, which it is clearly not scriptural for women to hold. We may be sure that the Christian women mentioned in Romans 16 did not seek to hold those positions in the church that God has limited to men, but devoted themselves wholeheartedly to those forms of Christian service that were appropriate for women. There are indeed forms of Christian service in which women can far excel men and some forms of service that must be performed almost exclusively by women.

"Salute one another with a holy kiss. The churches of Christ salute you" (16:16). The principle underlying this precept is valid and binding today, but the precise form of application of the principle is not binding. We are to salute or greet one another, but we are not bound to do it by a kiss. Kissing was a common manner of expressing friendship in those days; it is different today. "The exercise and manifestation of the feeling, but not the mode of its expression, are obligatory on us" (Charles Hodge, *A Commentary on the Epistle to the Romans*, p. 453). A friendly handshake and cheerful word of greeting will satisfy the obligation of verse 16 very well. On the other hand, where some members of a church have a grudge against other members and will not speak to them, or if they do speak, speak in tones of icy formality, they are breaking the God-given precept of Romans 16:16 and committing a sin against God.

Questions:

1. To how many people does Paul send greetings by name?
2. What is shown by the fact that Paul, who had never himself been in Rome, knew by name more than two dozen Christians in that city?
3. How do we know that Paul was a friendly person?
4. What kind of friendship existed between Paul and the people mentioned in 16:3–16?
5. Why should we not choose worldly people as our special friends?
6. How many women are mentioned by name in 16:3–16?

Romans 16:3–16

7. What was Paul's attitude toward women as Christian workers?

8. Why is it unfair to Paul to speak of him as a "woman hater"?

9. In what respect is the precept of 16:6 binding on us today?

10. Why are we not required to greet our fellow Christians by actually kissing them today?

11. How can the obligation of 16:16 be fulfilled today?

12. How do church members sometimes violate the God-given precept of 16:16?

Warnings against Divisions and False Doctrines. 16:17–20

Lesson 104

"Now I beseech you, brethren, mark them which cause divisions and offenses contrary to the doctrine which ye have learned; and avoid them" (16:17).

> While he urges them to the kind reception of all faithful ministers and Christians, he enjoins upon them to have nothing to do with those who cause divisions and offenses. There were probably two evils in the apostle's mind when he wrote this passage: the divisions occasioned by erroneous doctrines, and the offenses or scandals occasioned by the evil conduct of false teachers. Almost all the forms of error which distracted the early church, were intimately connected with practical evils of a moral character (Charles Hodge, *A Commentary on the Epistle to the Romans*, p. 450).

We should note that false doctrine and teachers of false doctrine, are to be avoided. Today many people think that differences about doctrine are not important as long as there is no seriously wrong conduct in a person's life. But right living comes from truth, not from falsehood, and false doctrine will result in evil living in the end.

Teachers of false doctrine are, first, to be "marked," and thereupon they are to be "avoided." Christian love does not require a soft tolerance of false doctrine any more than Christian love requires us to allow a burglar to rob our home or attack our family. Really, Christian love—love for the Church and its members—requires that false doctrine be rejected.

If we are to mark those who promote false doctrine, we must first know what the true doctrine is. Many Christians of the present day cannot tell the difference between true doctrine and false. Many cannot tell accurately what the doctrinal difference between their own church and some other church is. To mark and avoid false doctrine, we must make sure that we have an adequate and accurate knowledge of the true doctrine set forth in God's Word.

"For they that are such serve not our Lord Jesus Christ, but their own belly; and by good words and fair speeches deceive the hearts of the simple" (16:18). The word "simple" here means "unwary," the person who is not alert to questions of truth and error in religion. According to God's Word, "The simple believeth every word" (Prov. 14:15). Hence "the simple," the doctrinally unwary person, is constantly liable to be deceived. The false teachers of the present day, as of Paul's day, are selfish, crafty, and deceptive. The serious Christian will be on guard against them.

"For your obedience is come abroad unto all men. I am glad therefore on your behalf: but yet I would have you wise unto that which is good, and simple concerning evil" (Gen. 16:19). The Roman Christians must be not only good, but prudent. They "must not only avoid doing evil," but also be careful that they do not suffer evil (Charles Hodge, *A Commentary on the Epistle to the Romans*, p. 451). They should be "too good to deceive, too wise to be deceived" (Grotius, as quoted in Hodge, p. 451). As Augustine prayed, "Let the Scriptures be my pure delights; let me not be deceived in them, nor deceive others out of them" (*Confessions*, p. 253). "Paul would have them wise to know how to take care of themselves; and yet harmless" (Charles Hodge, *A Commentary on the Epistle to the Romans*, p. 451).

"And the God of peace shall bruise Satan under your feet shortly. The grace of our Lord Jesus Christ be with you. Amen" (16:20). Every true Christian and every true church gains the victory over Satan by the grace and power of God through Christ. This victory is promised to the Roman Christians. Satan is always working against the kingdom of Christ. Satan would soon become furiously active in stirring up persecution against Christians at Rome. Yet the promise would hold true,

Romans 16:17–20

and did hold true, that the God of peace would bruise Satan under their feet shortly. For by grace they gained the victory over Satan.

Greetings of Paul's Companions to the Christians at Rome. 16:21–23.

Several of Paul's companions and fellow workers are mentioned here. Among them is Brastus, the "chamberlain," that is, the treasurer, of the city of Corinth, an important official who had become a Christian. Tertius, mentioned in verse 22, is the one who wrote the epistle from Paul's dictation. These various people were associated with Paul in the work of Christ, presumably at Corinth.

Concluding Doxology. 16:24–27

Verses 25–27 form a long and complicated sentence in the Greek. The teaching, however, is clear. It is the power of God that establishes the Christian, and this power of God is exerted according to (through) the gospel of Jesus Christ. The gospel is referred to as "the mystery, which was kept secret since the world began, but now is made manifest" (16:25–26). Thus the gospel "is not a system of human philosophy, or the result of human investigation, but it is a revelation of the purpose of God. Paul often presents the idea that the plan of redemption was formed from eternity, and is such as no eye could discover, and no heart conceive" (Charles Hodge, *A Commentary on the Epistle to the Romans*, p. 452). From eternity the gospel was in the mind of God, until finally it was revealed to men, partly in the Old Testament, and fully in the New.

This gospel, which from eternity had been in the mind of God, was finally "by the Scriptures of the prophets, according to the commandment of the everlasting God, made known to all nations for the obedience of faith" (16:26). Here we note the harmony and essential unity of Paul's gospel with the teaching of the Old Testament prophets. The gospel is not something new and different from what is in the Old Testament; it is the same truth come to a fuller stage of realization in the world. For in Paul's day and our own, unlike the days of the Old Testament prophets, the gospel is indeed "made known to all nations for the obedience of faith."

"To God only wise, be glory through Jesus Christ for ever. Amen" (16:27). In this epistle, which ascribes the entire salvation of man wholly to God and His grace, it is fitting that the closing sentence be an ascription of glory to God through Christ. God is here described as "God only wise," for He is the being whose infinite, perfect wisdom is displayed in all His works, and particularly in the gospel concerning His Son.

Questions:

1. What does Paul warn the Roman Christians against in 16:17?
2. What is the relation between true doctrine and right living?
3. What is to be done about teachers of false doctrine?
4. Why is it wrong to say that Christian love requires us to tolerate false doctrines?
5. What must we know if we are to "mark" those who promote false doctrine?
6. What is the meaning of the word "simple" in 16:18?
7. Why is the simple person liable to be deceived in matters of religion?
8. What does Proverbs 14:15 say about the simple person?
9. What was the character of the false teachers of Paul's day, as described in 16:18?
10. Concerning what did Paul wish the Romans to be wise, and concerning what did he wish them to be simple?
11. What victory does every true Christian and every true Christian church gain?
12. By what power is this victory gained?
13. What position did Erastus hold in the city of Corinth?
14. What is the meaning of "chamberlain" in 16:23?
15. What is the meaning of the statement that Tertius wrote the epistle (16:22)?
16. What does Paul mean by saying that the gospel was a mystery kept secret since the world began?
17. What is the connection of the Old Testament Scriptures with the gospel, according to 16:26?
18. Why is God called "God only wise" in 16:27?
19. To whom is the entire work of salvation ascribed in this epistle?
20. In what work of God is His infinite wisdom particularly displayed?

Romans 16:24–27

The body text for Romans is set in 10.5 Hoefler Text set on 15. Chapter titles are set in Trajan Pro. The pillar image is from istockphoto.com.

Romans was typeset and designed on an Apple Macintosh operating system using Adobe InDesign CS6 and Adobe Photoshop CS6.

Cover design by Ariana Davenport Stitzer.